A FREE AND REGULATED PRESS

This thought-provoking monograph provides a systematic, philosophically-grounded reconceptualisation of press freedom and press regulation. In a major departure from orthodox norms, the book argues that press freedom and coercive independent press regulation are not mutually exclusive; that newspapers could be made to compensate their victims, through regulation, without jeopardising their free speech rights; that their perceived public watchdog status docs not exempt them; and, ultimately, that mandatory press regulation is not unconstitutional. In doing so, the book questions our most deeply-held, intuitive beliefs about the press and its role in society.

Why do we say the printed press has a duty to act as a public watchdog when there is no legally enforceable apparatus by which to ensure it does? Why does government constantly recommend that the press regulate itself when history shows this model always fails? Why do victims of press malfeasance continue to suffer needlessly?

By deconstructing the accepted view of press freedom and mandatory regulation, this book shows that both are deeply misunderstood. The prevailing notion that the press must serve the public is an empty relic of Victorian ideology that is both philosophically incoherent and legally unjustifiable. The press is obliged to make good, not do good.

A Free and Regulated Press

Defending Coercive Independent Press Regulation

Paul Wragg

·HART·

OXFORD · LONDON · NEW YORK · NEW DELHI · SYDNEY

HART PUBLISHING

Bloomsbury Publishing Plc

Kemp House, Chawley Park, Cumnor Hill, Oxford, OX2 9PH, UK

1385 Broadway, New York, NY 10018, USA

HART PUBLISHING, the Hart/Stag logo, BLOOMSBURY and the Diana logo are
trademarks of Bloomsbury Publishing Plc

First published in Great Britain 2020

A catalogue record for this book is available from the British Library.

Library of Congress Cataloging-in-Publication data

Names: Wragg, Paul, author.

Title: A free and regulated press : defending coercive independent press regulation / Paul Wragg.

Description: Oxford ; New York : Hart, 2020. | Includes bibliographical references and index.

Identifiers: LCCN 2020005187 (print) | LCCN 2020005188 (ebook) |
ISBN 9781509927234 (hardcover) | ISBN 9781509927258 (Epub)

Subjects: LCSH: Freedom of the press—Philosophy.

Classification: LCC K3255 .W73 2020 (print) | LCC K3255 (ebook) | DDC 342.08/53—dc23

LC record available at https://lccn.loc.gov/2020005187

LC ebook record available at https://lccn.loc.gov/2020005188

ISBN: HB: 978-1-50992-723-4
        ePDF: 978-1-50992-724-1
        ePub: 978-1-50992-725-8

Typeset by Compuscript Ltd, Shannon
Printed and bound in Great Britain by CPI Group (UK) Ltd, Croydon CR0 4YY

To find out more about our authors and books visit www.hartpublishing.co.uk.
Here you will find extracts, author information, details of forthcoming events
and the option to sign up for our newsletters.

For Bill Stark (1926–2013)

PREFACE

Orthodox press freedom theory, concerning the printed press, has nothing of any interest to say about victims of press malfeasance and, therefore, nothing to offer to regulatory design to tackle errant press behaviour. This simple truth, though, is unrecognised in the established academic literature and popular debate. Yet, it ought to be clear to anyone who has read Lord Justice Leveson's report on the culture, practices, and ethics of the press. By relying upon the established understanding of press freedom as a burdensome duty to act as a public watchdog and enable democratic participation, he succumbed to a way of thinking entirely focused on what the press does, and can do, for its readers and society at large. Victims do not figure in this analysis. In fact, it's worse than that – victims are not only ignored, there are something of a nuisance. For, regrettably, on this account, victims are reduced to something like a necessary sacrifice to pacify the press machine, and keep it running, or else an unfortunate case of collateral damage. Yet, neither Leveson nor those on whom he relied to articulate the meaning of press freedom were sufficiently cognisant of this problem. Even those that agitate for greater regulation of the press, including those ostensibly sympathetic to victims, seem unaware of the difficult implications raised by their own position. For, in arguing that the press ought to be more socially responsible, they rely upon a notion of press exceptionalism that would be jeopardised by the sort of state intervention that mandatory regulation necessitates. Inescapably, the superintendence of quality in press speech, demanded by their theory, generates serious problems in the realisation of *any* meaningful form of press regulation.

Consequently, in the debate on enhanced press regulation, to the limited extent that there is any meaningful debate, the two prominent, opposing sides find themselves deadlocked. Although the left-leaning social responsibility theorists and right-leaning libertarians are united in their belief that the printed press has a function that it must serve – to educate, monitor, and enable – they cannot agree on how this end is to be realised, let alone find an acceptable compromise that would permit the state to implement the scheme to facilitate it. This book aims to break this deadlock by providing a novel, alternative method of examining these issues and, consequently, the means of realising a meaningful scheme of effective, efficient press regulation that preserves press freedom. It does so by jettisoning the orthodox, teleological conception of the right and replacing it with a new conception. It is also the first major work to provide a rigorous, philosophically-coherent conception of press regulation itself. Consequently, it represents a major paradigm shift in our thinking on the press and its role in society.

A comprehensive overview of its arguments can be found in the preamble.

Paul Wragg
Leeds
November 2019

A NOTE ON LIBERTARIANISM
AND LIBERALISM

I use the term 'libertarianism' throughout this book and since the term is ambiguous, I ought to define it. We find the term used by Fred Siebert in *Four Theories of the Press*[1] to describe an alternative model of press freedom to social responsibility theory (or 'SRT' as I call it in the book). This conception, though, is not without its difficulties. Since much of it is an exegesis of Locke, Milton, and John Stuart Mill, it is easy to reach the conclusion that by libertarianism, Siebert means no more than classic liberalism. Although less commonly used, the term can also refer to socialist libertarianism, ie, the abolition of capitalism and the withering of the state to night-watchman status, which we find in the works of Pierre-Joseph Proudhon, William Godwin and Ferdinand Lassalle. This leads in the direction of anarchism, Marxism, and revolutionary socialism.

In this book, the term 'libertarianism' refers to neither of these conceptions – either classic liberalism or socialist libertarianism – but instead that particular brand of liberalism that recognises the market, not the state, as the only means of realising the ends of press freedom. In this sense, libertarianism – the sort I have in mind – is right-leaning. Its adherence to classic liberal principle is to further laissez-faire thinking. This finds particular expression in two passages from Siebert's account, where he emphasises the importance of the press's economic independence ('the problem of economic support of the mass media was never squarely faced by libertarian theorists. They were opposed to government support since it led to domination, and they trusted the capitalist system of private enterprise to find a way')[2] and the power of the market to regulate quality:

> let the public at large be subjected to a barrage of information and opinion, some of it possibly true, some of it possibly false, and some of it containing elements of both. Ultimately the public could be trusted to digest the whole, to discard that not in the public interest and to accept that which served the needs of the individual and of the society of which he is part. This was the well-known 'self-righting' process.[3]

And:

> In the place of state supervision, libertarian theory provides for a more informal type of control through the self-righting process and through the free competition in the

---

[1] FS Siebert, T Peterson, and W Schramm, *Four Theories of the Press* (Chicago, University of Illinois Press, 1956).
[2] Ibid, 52.
[3] Ibid, 51.

market place of information, opinions, and entertainment. The principal function of the state is to maintain a stable framework within which the free forces of individualism may interact.[4]

This could be understood as classic liberalism in which laissez-faire principles take centre stage, of which Adam Smith is the principal architect – and in an important sense, this is what I mean, but the term is avoided, for two reasons.

The first is etymological. Because the book, in presenting the differing views of how the goals of press freedom are to be realised, is, essentially, dissecting liberalism into its divergent strands, this calls for a clear demarcation between the different groups. This is problematic: not only are there many variations of liberalism, but also the term itself is subject to confusion. For example, Charles Murray has pointed out that, in the US, the term is socialist in outlook, ie, 'the politics of an expansive government and the welfare state'[5] whereas in Australia the Liberal Party is distinctly anti-socialist, being essentially conservative in nature, in the Burkean tradition. These etymological problems could be overcome by labelling the alternative positions 'classic liberalism' and 'social liberalism' instead. But this would generate confusion about the book's central thesis that we have lost sight of the goals of liberalism in the debate on press freedom. Since it is argued that these goals are best expressed in the work of John Stuart Mill, then the objection could be raised that *On Liberty*, being essentially a synthesis of British liberal thought from the Enlightenment (ie, Locke, Smith, Hume) and continental liberalism, especially Wilhelm von Humboldt, is – and should be called – Classic Liberalism. Obviously, this would make the distinction between the two positions (that which I champion and that which I criticise) implausible or otherwise highly tenuous. But it also creates problems with the other comparison – to the left-leaning position – because if SRT is termed Social Liberalism, then the distinction collapses since clearly, in his political opinions, Mill *was* a social liberal (at least to the extent he anticipated men like LT Hobhouse and their 'New Liberalism') because he thought the state had an important role to play in improving the lives of citizens, etc.

The second reason to use the term libertarianism is analytical. It better captures the philosophical position of newspaper owners, editors, and journalists who adhere to a more extreme version of right-leaning thinking about the realisation of liberal goals. Capturing this view is important to the inquiry if we are to understand why the press industry complains that coercive independent regulation represents an end to '300 years of press freedom.'[6] But we are unlikely to understand this view through the academic literature alone since, as a group, academics

---

[4] Ibid, 53.

[5] Charles Murray, *What it Means to be a Libertarian* (New York, Broadway Books, 1997), xii; see also CB Macpherson, *The Life and Times of Liberal Democracy* (Oxford, Oxford University Press, 1977), 1–2.

[6] See, eg, 'Press freedom in Britain is under attack – again', *The Spectator*, 31 December 2016; 'Daily Mail Comment: After 300 years, the freedom of Britain's Press is in peril. YOU can save it', *Daily Mail*, 9 January 2017; G Rayner, 'Investigative journalism to be 'stopped dead in tracks' by 'menacing' laws after Leveson Inquiry', *The Independent*, 15 October 2015.

veer toward the political left in large numbers and so the philosophical ground-work for the industry view is not to be found there, at least not in an intellectually satisfying way. Nevertheless, reference will be made to the works of academics who are, in no way, libertarian in this sense, but whose thinking can help shed light on the rationale of this right-leaning position.

ACKNOWLEDGEMENTS

This book is the product of an obsession that began not with the publication of Lord Justice Leveson's report, but long before that. Like all such books, it is the product of self-induced solitude, of bursts of inspiration (often at the most inopportune moments), of writer's-block-induced despair, of prevarication, of agonising over word choice, of the interminable editing of footnotes, of that quiet desperation that no one will read the finished version, and the even greater fear that they just might.

But it is also the product of listening, to colleagues past and present, to champions of the press and of regulation, to campaigners, to victims, to journalists, to historians, to lawyers, to philosophers, and to economists. Consequently, it is built upon the generosity of others, who have given much of their time to comment on various drafts and offer constructive criticism. I am especially grateful to RonNell Andersen Jones, Pete Coe, Rebecca Moosavian, David Rolph, Jan Oster, Daithí Mac Síthigh, Jake Rowbottom, and Tom Bennett. What made their contributions so valuable was that they disagreed with me on so many points and yet still encouraged me nonetheless. This spirited debate has caused me to modify my thoughts, on several occasions, not least so as to recognise, more explicitly, the important contribution that journalism continues to make to those 'real people' that Leveson spoke of so powerfully (and, on this, I am especially grateful to Professor Andersen Jones).

There were others who were supportive and instrumental in the initial process of obtaining a publishing agreement, especially Alastair Mullis, Peter Whelan, Pınar Akman, and Roberta Bassi, my editor at Hart.

And then there were others still who contributed to my thinking on the subject, over many years (and who may have been entirely oblivious to their impact): David Acheson, Eric Barendt, Allan Beever, Helen Belcher, Jason Bosland, Achas Burin, Dave Campbell, David Capper, Jenny Carroll, Emanuela Ceva, Ian Christie, Morgan Cloud, Mark Cole, Martin Conboy, Ian Cram, Rowan Cruft, Maire Messenger Davies, James Devenney, Charlotte Elliott-Harvey, David Erdos, Bruce Elman, Helen Fenwick, Julie Firmstone, Carl Fox, Amy Gadja, Tom Gibbons, William Gillies, Evan Harris, Julian Harris, Jonathan Heawood, Martin Hickman, Emily Hudson, Emma Jones, Mariette Jones, Rob Kahn, Jennifer Kinsley, Andrew Kenyon, András Koltay, Päivi Korpisaari, Ron Krotoszynski, Judith Lichtenberg, Jairo Lugo-Ocando, David Mangan, Barbara McDonald, Walter Merricks, Jon Mills, Dario Milo, Dorota Mokrosinska, Jane Mulderrig, Gavin Phillipson, Megan Richardson, Lori Ringhand, Chris Roederer, Joe Saunders, Konstantinos Stylianou, Gavin Sutter, Nick Taylor, Hugh Tomlinson QC, Jude Townend, Sir Michael Tugendhat, Hillary Young, James Weinstein, Lorna Woods, Russ Weaver and Vincenzo Zeno Zencovich.

I am also grateful to the Law School at the University of Leeds, Alastair Mullis and Michael Thompson specifically, for the support I've received. In Alastair, I am fortunate to have found an exceptional Head of School. In researching and writing the book, I benefitted from a period of study leave as well as a grant from the AHRC (AH-R00644X-1) and research assistance, paid for by the School, from Rachel Abernathy, whose diligent and thoughtful research provided me with a better understanding of US cases relating to press freedom (of course, all errors are my own).

Finally, the most important thanks are owed to my family, who have endured the most in the production of this volume, but have been my inspiration and most vital source of encouragement throughout. They have mixed feelings about this book.

CONTENTS

Preamble

Purpose

There is a malaise afflicting press freedom theory. The discussion, such as there is, has taken on a distinctly dogmatic overtone. Rather than contest its essential meaning, by means of probing analysis, the literature treats the conceptual debate as if it is not only settled but beyond question. Consequently, whether commentators openly embrace or privately doubt this conclusion, the literature itself contains little more than the blithe repetition of the same archetypal phrases to describe the press that we find in the collective consciousness: that it is a 'public watchdog', a 'fourth estate', and a 'check on power'. These terms are used intuitively and uncritically. They have become so deeply-engrained within the literature as to be not only axiomatic but also sacrosanct. Accordingly, the press is taken to have an indisputable *telos* or purpose that it must serve. It is this that illuminates the concept of press freedom and distinguishes it from individual freedom of expression. Moreover, the press has become entirely depersonalised – it is not the product of autonomous, thinking minds, but a dead entity; an unliving 'thing'. We see this attitude clearly in Lord Justice Leveson's conclusion that John Stuart Mill's classic defence of free speech, grounded upon autonomy and self-fulfilment, 'has no direct relevance to press freedom because, put simply, press organisations are not human beings with a personal need to be able to self-express.'[1] This attitude is debilitating. It curtails the options for tackling press malfeasance effectively. Policy-makers, sensitive to unsubstantiated claims that mandatory regulation would severely impair the press's capacity to fulfil its public function, are left with little room to manoeuvre. Voluntary self-regulation is seen not as the *best* solution to the problem of press malfeasance but the *only* solution. Yet, as the UK's experience demonstrates emphatically, this model is hopelessly ineffective; the regulator is entirely dependent upon the good faith and willingness of the industry to humour it when rebuked. This is the paradigm that this book confronts.

Although the book makes general claims about the press that are applicable to its broadcast and online forms, it focuses exclusively on the printed press. There are several reasons for this. Unlike the broadcast press, newspapers are not subject to compulsory forms of regulation but are, instead, largely unregulated in

---

[1] Lord Justice Leveson, *An Inquiry into the Culture, Practices and Ethics of the Press: Report* (HC 780, 2012) 62, [3.3].

a meaningful sense. In the UK and mainland Europe, voluntary self-regulatory schemes dominate. Yet newspapers continue to inflict unwarranted, serious harm on individuals. Since the cost of legal action is a luxury that few can afford, many suffer without receiving adequate compensation. Leveson saw this problem clearly enough when he said that comprehensive regulatory reform was needed to end the 'real harm … [inflicted upon] real people.'[2] This, though, remains unrealised.

The book's primary aim is to show that this goal can be realised without compromising press freedom. It does so by reconceptualising press freedom and by providing a philosophically-informed conceptualisation of press regulation, which the literature presently lacks. Specifically, it argues that this teleological conception is fatally flawed. It shows that the underlying propositions are specious: they are philosophically unsound, legally unjustifiable, and their historical pedigree is misjudged. No purpose can be externally imposed upon the press against its will. This is not to deny that the press can be a force for good. It *does* serve the public when it acts as a public watchdog. It *does* aid both public and private decision-making. Yet these descriptions have no prescriptive power. It cannot be said that the press *must* do these things. It is not obliged to be a public watchdog or to act as a check on power. It has no obligations to society at large to perform a social function. Press freedom can only be conceptualised as a negative freedom. The press can publish what it likes so long as it respects the rights of others. This non-teleological interpretation allows for the realisation of mandatory press regulation. Since public interest expression is not regulatable, there is no prospect of function creep that would otherwise jeopardise press freedom. For it is only the realm beyond the zone of press freedom that the regulator may patrol. What happens inside that zone is not its concern. The model of press regulation advanced in the book is independent from both government and the press industry. It provides the regulator with coercive powers to investigate complaints and award victims with compensation. Under this model, membership would be mandatory; as with the Danish press regulation scheme, all entities satisfying the definition of 'press' would fall under the regulator's jurisdiction automatically.[3]

To some, this inquiry will be insightful and to others, inciteful. Nevertheless, it is overdue. The academic commentary has accepted the status quo for too long. Accordingly, the primary object of critical inquiry is the press freedom literature rather than the press itself. Two major schools of thought dominate the intellectual agenda in this field: social responsibility theory ('SRT') and libertarianism.[4]

---

[2] Ie, not just so-called 'celebrities' – or the upper echelons of society – but *every* level of society; anyone who happens to fall under press scrutiny from time-to-time. Leveson, ibid, 50, [2.2].

[3] S 1(1), Danish Media Liability Act 1991.

[4] Both schools of thought are discussed in FS Siebert, T Peterson, and W Schramm, *Four Theories of the Press* (Chicago, University of Illinois Press, 1956). It was Theodore Peterson that coined the phrase SRT (see *Four Theories of the Press*, 73–103). Fred Siebert discusses the libertarian position at pp 39–71.

Briefly, SRT claims that since the press has this teleological function to serve, some external intervention is justified to ensure that it fulfils this obligation. This is a politically left-leaning position. Although libertarians agree with the central teleological premise, they argue that since the state is disqualified from adjudicating on performance of this function (because of its vested interest in an impotent press), only the market can determine this issue. This is a politically right-leaning position. The disagreement between SRT and libertarianism is at a stalemate. Those on the left cannot advance their regulatory reform agenda due to the various obstacles set for them by those on the right, including the concern that mandatory regulation imperils serious investigative journalism. By challenging this dominance, and by arguing for an alternative, third way of thinking about the issues, this book aims to break the deadlock by demonstrating how these obstacles can be overcome.

It does so by deconstructing the orthodox interpretation of these concepts before scrutinising them through the lens of normative legal theory as well as moral and political philosophy. This inquiry, therefore, informs the alternative set of normative moral principles that the book provides. Primarily, the book addresses the problem as it arises in the UK through an examination of global principles. It draws upon American and European scholarship in philosophy, law, and communication studies and the European experience of press regulation in practice, by reference to the regulatory codes of conduct that exist in 11 European countries: Austria, Belgium, Denmark, Finland, Germany, Ireland, the Netherlands, Norway, Slovakia, Sweden, and Switzerland.[5] Nevertheless, despite this, the conclusions it reaches are potentially applicable in all democratic states, regardless of local constitutional structures, but I leave it to others to pursue that claim. It should be noted that, when discussing the UK regulatory position, the standards code used by IMPRESS[6] – the only press regulator recognised in the UK under the Royal Charter on Self-Regulation of the Press – is not examined. I was part of the Code Committee that drafted the code and, given my involvement, it would have been disingenuous to critique it.

Since this is, primarily, a philosophical enquiry into the compatibility of press freedom with mandatory press regulation, there will be little discussion of the positive law. Although an appraisal of all the various laws that affect the press would, clearly, tell us something important about the meaning of press freedom, it cannot answer the questions animating my inquiry. It can only tell us what press freedom *is* and not what it *ought to be*. Similarly, the legitimacy of coercive independent press regulation cannot be determined solely by reference to the experiences of those in other jurisdictions or in other contexts. For example, the fact of

---

[5] This research relates to, and forms part of, another project I am involved in, entitled 'Defining Freedom of the Press', with colleagues from the Media and Communications, Philosophy, Ethics, and Linguistics schools of the University of Leeds, the University of Sheffield and Durham University. It is funded by the AHRC (AH-R00644X-1), http://defining-freedom-of-the-press.info/.

[6] www.impress.press/.

mandatory regulation of the printed press in Denmark, or of the broadcast press in many other jurisdictions, including the UK, is not proof of its compatibility with press freedom. Whilst these examples provide useful practical illustrations, they are not conclusive. That something happens or exists without objection does not mean that it is justified.

Context: The Leveson Inquiry

The book takes its title from the seminal work of the self-styled Commission on Freedom of the Press (otherwise known as the Hutchins Commission) which, in 1947, published its general report on mass communication (newspapers, radio, motion pictures, magazines, and books) under the title: *A Free and Responsible Press*.[7] This report, and those by the various Royal Commissions on the Press in the UK, as well as the academic literature it has inspired, are central to the theme of this book. It is this body of work that informs SRT.[8] This is the genesis of the teleological conception, at least as it is understood presently. The ideas underpinning this theory have enjoyed something of a recent revival having featured heavily in Leveson's report. Just as the Hutchins Commission spoke of the press as a 'public trust' that 'has responsibilities to the general spread of information [analogous] to those of a … trustee',[9] so too Leveson referred to press freedom as an 'instrumental good, to be valued, promoted and protected to the extent that it …. serve[s] its important democratic functions.'[10]

This attitude is not peculiar to commentators on the political left. Indeed, as Chapter 1 makes clear, this view can be found amongst those on the political right. It can also be seen in the attitudes of press owners and editors themselves, certainly those of a bygone era. For example, CP Scott said, of his beloved *Manchester Guardian*, that it stood for 'honesty, cleanness, courage, fairness, [and] a sense of duty to the reader and the community.'[11] Similarly, Lord Thompson, former owner of *the Times* and *Sunday Times*, said 'no person or group can buy or influence editorial support' from any of his newspapers,[12] whilst Cecil King, former owner of the Daily Mirror Newspapers group, believed it 'the duty of a newspaper first of all to explain fairly and adequately what a Government is trying to do.'[13]

---

[7] Commission on Freedom of the Press, *A Free and Responsible Press* (Chicago, University of Chicago Press, 1947).

[8] Siebert, Peterson, and Schramm, *Four Theories of the Press*, (n 8), 73–103.

[9] WE Hocking, *Freedom of the Press: A Framework of Principle* (Chicago, University of Chicago Press, 1947), 150 & 225.

[10] Leveson, (n 1), 63, [3.7].

[11] CP Scott, 'A Hundred Years', *Manchester Guardian*, 5 May 1921.

[12] As reported in Harold Evans, *Good Times, Bad Times*, (London, Orion Books Ltd, 1994), 4.

[13] Cecil King, *The Future of the Press*, (London, MacGibbon & Kee, 1967), 93.

Nevertheless, despite this, even Leveson, who concluded that comprehensive reform of press regulation was necessary, did not recommend mandatory press regulation. Despite making all the right noises – that the regulator should have the power to issue sanctions for non-compliance, that 'everyone' should be involved, and that the government should institute what he called a 'backstop regulator' if the industry failed to do so – he stopped short of recommending it. We see this in his apologetic, defensive repetition of two sentiments: first, that the 'ideal' solution was for the industry to mobilise voluntarily to institute the sort of regulatory scheme he had in mind, and secondly, the pains with which he emphasised that the alternative – government intervention – was *not* one of his recommendations:

- 'It is worth repeating that the ideal outcome is a satisfactory independent regulatory body, established by the industry, that is able to secure the voluntary support and membership of the entire industry.'[14]

- 'I will say again, because it cannot be said too often, that the ideal outcome from my perspective is a satisfactory self-organised but independent regulatory body, established by the industry, that is able to secure the voluntary support and membership of the entire industry and thus able to command the support of the public.'[15]

- 'From the outset, I have encouraged the industry to come together to create an independent regulatory regime that satisfies the need to provide public confidence.'[16]

- 'I repeat the refrain that what I want is for the industry to come together to organise their own independent regulatory system.'[17]

- 'I have made it clear that I firmly believe it is in the best interest of the public and the industry that an independent self-organised regulatory body is set up.'[18]

- 'I repeat, as I have made very clear that, by a very long way, my preferred solution, and hence my recommendation, is that the industry should come together to construct a system of independent regulation.'[19]

- 'With some measure of regret, therefore, I am driven to conclude that the Government should be ready to consider the need for a statutory backstop regulator being established …'[20]

---

[14] Leveson, (n 1), 1769, [4.48].
[15] Ibid, 1771, [6.1].
[16] Ibid, 1781, [7.1].
[17] Ibid, 1782, [7.7].
[18] Ibid, 1782, [7.9].
[19] Ibid, 1794, [7.2].
[20] Ibid, 1758, [3.34].

- 'I repeat, again, that I do not, at the moment, recommend any statutory backstop and to assert that I do will be to distort this Report and the clear recommendations that I do make.'[21]

Whilst this preference for voluntary self-regulation is consistent with the style of regulation that dominates the European scene, it is not obvious why Leveson should think this the preferable outcome. As we shall see, and as he was fully aware, the UK and European experience clearly demonstrates that compliance with regulatory decision-making in this model is contingent upon the indulgent submission of the will. The regulator is always beholden to the good faith of the regulated. Since this model provides no assurances for tackling press malfeasance, Leveson's attitude is mysterious.

Admittedly, Leveson was sensitive to the threat, or rather the perceived threat, to press freedom that mandatory regulation might represent. Yet, as will be argued, in Chapter 9 especially, these concerns are misplaced. To appreciate this point, we should be clear on what press freedom means. Of course, this is a central aim of the book, for I hope to revitalise the term by challenging the orthodox view that it is teleological. Nevertheless, it is helpful, as a preliminary point, to emphasise what strikes me as an inconspicuous ambiguity, especially in the popular debate, in which two senses of the term 'press freedom' appear. To better illuminate this confusion, I will distinguish these two senses by referring to one as 'freedom of the press' and the other as 'press freedom'. The former aligns with what might be called the prosaic sense of 'press freedom' and the latter with the formal definition that the purist would employ. Consequently, in its prosaic sense, the term means all that the press is entitled to do without incurring liability. We can imagine this as a zone of activity (which includes both newspaper content and newsgathering conduct) that the press is 'free' to engage in. This 'freedom of the press' concept, then, describes what Hohfeld would call the liberty-no right construct,[22] which is to say the absence of a right belonging to A to prevent B (the press) doing something that A objects to. The purist though would reject this interpretation of press freedom. She would say that the term embodies the reasons why the state guarantees the press the right to speak freely and, so, is short-hand for this justification. We can think of this as a smaller zone of activity, which sits inside that larger zone occupied by the liberty-no right construct. This smaller zone is also Hohfeldian and describes the right-duty construct belonging to the press, ie, the press's right to speak as against the state's duty to uphold that right.

From this brief description, we can see something of the problem that arises when the popular press laments the *diminution* in press freedom in the UK over, certainly, the past fifteen or so years, coinciding with the introduction of the Human Rights Act 1998, and the increased protection of privacy which

---

[21] Ibid, 1758, [3.35].
[22] WN Hohfeld, *Fundamental Legal Conceptions* (New Haven, Yale University Press, 1919).

followed. For what it is really decrying is the loss of freedom of the press. For example, whereas in 1990 the *Sunday Sport* incurred no legal liability when a reporter and photojournalist burst in upon an incapacitated TV actor, in his hospital bed, and proceeded to conduct an interview with him,[23] the same fact pattern today would incur liability under the misuse of private information tort. Consequently, it cannot be denied that the freedom of the press *has* diminished over time. Yet, for the purist, there has been no diminution of press freedom, as a matter of justification, because they would say (and I agree) the state does not afford the press its speech rights so that it can publish privacy-invading expression at will.

This book's inquiry is about regulation that impacts on freedom of the press, not press freedom. This is important to emphasise because mandatory press regulation is bound to reduce that larger zone of liberty-no right (from a press perspective) and increase that of right-duty (from a victim perspective), and so better protect victims when their reputational and privacy rights as well as rights to a fair trial are undermined by the press. Of course, these rights are protected, in theory, by the positive law but are not always maximally enforced due to the inefficiencies of the legal system. These inefficiencies, though, would be significantly reduced in the model of mandatory press regulation advocated by this book, for rights holders would have greater access to justice by means of cheap, efficient regulatory measures. Nevertheless, these encroachments upon the freedom of the press are unproblematic, as a matter of principle, so long as they do not interfere with press freedom.

This differential treatment of the term press freedom helps explain why the book argues in favour of coercive, independent press regulation. Press freedom, in the purist's sense, is unconnected to press malfeasance because unjustified breaches of the rights of others are outside the boundaries of permissible press freedom. Consequently, the regulation of press malfeasance leaves press freedom untouched. Moreover, it is only through mandatory regulation that it becomes possible to achieve the regulatory goal that Leveson sets, of ensuring 'real people' are protected from, or else compensated for, 'real harm'. Sadly, for victims of press malfeasance, Leveson's recommendations amounted to more of the same: the continuation of a (modified) self-regulatory scheme. As we shall see, in Chapter 2, this has been the UK Government's consistent policy since the 1940s. It continues to be so even though Leveson had said 'I cannot, and will not, recommend another last chance saloon for the press' (and yet he did) and that, to be effective, the 'new' scheme of press regulation must include everyone (it does not). Although Leveson agreed that all members of the press should feel compelled to join the tougher regulatory scheme, his strategy for compulsion was feeble, relying, as it did, on a misplaced sense that the press would be induced by an odd mixture

---

[23] *Kaye v Robertson* [1991] FSR 62.

of shame[24] and (dubious) incentivisation[25] – neither of which has worked in practice. This concern for victims, though, has been lost in the aftermath of the Leveson inquiry. Although the incumbent press regulator in the UK, the Press Complaints Commission ('PCC'), has been replaced by the Independent Press Standards Organisation ('IPSO'), the scheme is still voluntary and the proximity between regulator and industry still uncomfortably close. The reforms that have occurred seem superficial; certainly, it cannot be said that meaningful safeguards against press malfeasance are now in place. Consequently, victims of press malfeasance continue to suffer serious harm. This is tragic given it was, after all, a concern about the treatment of these victims, and the adequacy of the pre-existing regulatory regime to provide them with sufficient redress, which caused the government to initiate the Leveson inquiry into press malfeasance in 2011. Yet, since the government's decision to cancel the planned second part of Leveson's inquiry into the press, which would have scrutinised the question of phone-hacking in more detail, the prospects for meaningful reform seem bleak.[26]

Perhaps a book such as this would have been rendered nugatory had the government kept its promise to implement Lord Justice Leveson's recommendations.[27] Perhaps the need for it would have been even greater had it done so. For the Leveson report is riddled with such problematic reasoning and notable omissions that faithful rendition of its recommendations would be philosophically unsound. This book, then, both champions and criticises the Leveson report. It advocates fulfilment of certain recommendations and cautions against the use of others. In this way, the book springs from a deep-rooted sense of frustration with the premises, and execution of, the inquiry. Chief amongst these is the report's conception of press freedom. As will become apparent in Part 2, Leveson endorsed a left-leaning construction of the term that imbues the press with a duty or responsibility to aid democratic participation and to monitor power. This interpretation has attracted little critical attention amongst academic commentators. Indeed, I think Eric Barendt speaks for most, if not all, when he says 'Leveson's treatment of press freedom is hardly novel, though that is not meant as a criticism.'[28] Here, I must disagree – it strikes me, that the conception

---

[24] 'Failure to [mobilise voluntarily] would be a sad indictment of the inability of the press to put commercial interest to one side' (Leveson, (n 1), 1779, [4.37]); 'Given the public appetite for some accountability of the press, I do not think that either the victims or the public would understand if the industry did not grasp this opportunity'; (ibid, 1782, [7.9]) and 'Neither would they understand if I were not to consider the consequences of the industry failing to deliver the independent regulation that is required' (ibid, 1782, [7.9]).

[25] 'I believe that the model that I set out has real and significant benefits ... for the press', ibid, 1757, [3.28].

[26] P Walker, 'Leveson inquiry: government confirms second stage axed' *The Guardian*, 1 March 2018.

[27] Hélène Mulholland, 'David Cameron tells hacking victims he still has an open mind over Leveson', *The Guardian*, 7 October 2012.

[28] E Barendt, 'Statutory Underpinning: a Threat to Press Freedom?' (2013) 5(2) *Journal of Media Law* 189, 191.

undermines the report's recommendations. For it actively works against the imposition of a tougher regulatory regime by affording no protection against the claims, emanating from the right, that such regulation threatens this special function of the press. Moreover, since all the intellectual energies of this conception are devoted to the production of societally-valuable materials, it has so little to say about victims that it left Leveson with nowhere to go to defend them against the necessary connotations of safeguarding the public watchdog beast. Indeed, one wonders if Leveson himself sensed this because, by the end of the report, his notion of press freedom played no substantive part, as if it had been quietly abandoned.

Relatedly, Leveson treated our interest in press regulation as, somehow, unitary or monolithic, and so failed to recognise that there are competing interests at stake. Accordingly, he did not see that the interests of society at large, victims, and readers are not the same and that each involves separate considerations. In Part 3, I examine these interests closely and individually to show that victims' interests provide the most compelling justification for regulation. Indeed, I argue that beyond this concern for victims of press malfeasance, society has no regulatable interest at stake. Even readers' interests are limited; there are few that could conceivably lend themselves to regulatory provisions. Leveson's teleological conception of press freedom becomes even more significant when seen in this light. For, by framing press freedom in societal terms, he failed to see that his conception had nothing to say about victims; it provided him with no grounds on which to justify the coercive scheme of press regulation he recommended. Furthermore, his reliance upon the colloquial but inaccurate notion of 'ethics' as a set of rules which govern the professions (doctors, solicitors, etc) and not the proper notion of ethics, in the Kantian sense, of individuals deciding, for themselves, what actions and responses constitute the good life,[29] rendered the discussion confused, and confusing, through the constant oscillation between questions of what a person *should* do (according to morality) and questions of what a person *must* do (according to law). This confusion further taints the recommendations as to the nature of regulation and the legitimacy of using coercive measures to enforce it.

In short, Leveson's scheme of press regulation neither utilised a philosophically-sound notion of press freedom nor offered, let alone relied upon, a philosophically-informed notion of press regulation. Consequently, he was backed into a corner in which, although he sought to dismiss them, he could not nullify complaints that a statutory scheme of press regulation would be unconstitutional.[30] He did not do enough to reject this view. His equivocation lent a credibility to it that it did not, and does not, deserve. An important aim of this book, then, is to counter this view by demonstrating the legitimacy of both statutory and

---

[29] I Kant, *The Metaphysics of Morals*, L Denis (ed), M Gregor, trans, 2nd edn (Cambridge, Cambridge University Press, 2017). See discussion below.
[30] Leveson, (n 1), 1782, [7.8].

mandatory press regulation. This includes tackling the view, expressed by several participants at the Leveson inquiry, that this use of statute would be a 'slippery slope' that would justify anti-press legislation in the future, even that which undermined press freedom. Chapter 9 demonstrates the implausibility of this claim: there can be no 'function creep' through mandatory press regulation, not least because we have the language to differentiate press freedom from press malfeasance and so ensure that only the latter is regulated.

This argument is important to establish since it is only through statute that Leveson's goals for meaningful regulatory reform can be realised. I use the term 'meaningful', throughout this book, in a specific way. Formally, we can say that the UK has had a scheme of press regulation in place since the creation of the General Council of the Press in 1953.[31] Yet, as numerous public inquiries and successive iterations of the self-regulatory model demonstrate, it cannot be said that these modifications have resulted in *meaningful* regulation since the press, even today, remains free to disregard regulatory rebukes and, even, leave the scheme whenever it wants, consequence-free. Accordingly, for the purposes of this book, *meaningful* press regulation is that which provides victims with redress for the wrongs done to them by press malfeasance.

Structure

Rationale

Chapter 1 examines the historical pedigree of the teleological conception and finds it wanting. This notion belongs to a specific period in time – which I set at 1855–1947 and call the 'ideological phase' – and coincides with the zenith of the Liberal Party movement, in which maximal enfranchisement and the compulsory education agenda was in its prime. Yet, the circumstances justifying the teleological conception were radically different to today, for the Liberal Party had its own press, which it could command to serve its Enlightenment ambitions. Once its liberal agenda had been realised, however, the Liberty Party's raison d'etre expired and its newspaper empire, such as it was, collapsed. The teleological conception, however, did not perish, as it should have, but, instead, assumed its modern form as an analytical framework by which to judge the performance of newspapers. This critical phase began in 1947 and is marked by the novelty of the state (eg, the Royal Commission on the Press) and non-state bodies (the Commission on the Freedom of the Press) using this conception as a tool for criticising perceived deficiencies in the modern press.

---

[31] The history of press regulation is discussed in T O'Malley and C Soley, *Regulating the Press* (London, Pluto Books, 2000), 51–96 and J Curran and J Seaton, *Power Without Responsibility* 8th edn (Oxford, Routledge, 2018), 1–192.

Nevertheless, despite the apparent uniformity in critical thought about the nature and meaning of press freedom, we find profound disagreement in the literature about the mechanics of realising these teleological ends. This gives rise to the riddle that commentators do not acknowledge, let alone solve: if the press has obligations to society at large to perform certain public functions, then why are commentators not united in promoting mandatory regulation to ensure these obligations are performed correctly? After all, in other social contexts, such regulation exists, and with little dissent, eg, in the professions, the construction industry, works affecting the environment, motoring, public liability insurance, health and safety, the installation and maintenance of utilities, etc. What makes the press special? Those subscribing to the orthodox view would say it is the press's public-serving role that makes it exceptional; that its function as a 'fourth estate' compromises the state's capacity to establish (let alone administer) such a scheme. According to libertarians, only the market can be trusted to ensure the press delivers on its promises. Understandably, libertarians fear that quality control of press speech, by means of formal regulation, will enfeeble the press; that even well-intentioned oversight will become intolerably bureaucratic. Since SRT provides no means of overcoming these concerns – for the emphasis on quality is inextricably woven into its core principles – the deadlock cannot be broken and meaningful press regulation remains unrealisable. This book breaks that deadlock by demonstrating the implausibility of the press exceptionalism argument: it shows that the barrier to mandatory regulation is contingent upon the teleological conception. If this is abandoned, as I argue it should be (because it is philosophically incoherent), then mandatory regulation can be established without compromising press freedom.

Right

Part 2 advances this overarching argument by demonstrating the philosophical failings in the teleological conception. Chapters 3 and 4 show why the orthodox view ought to be abandoned whilst Chapter 5 establishes the limits of the press freedom concept: the entitlement to benefit from the state's free speech guarantee cannot be made contingent upon some positive obligation to do good. Press freedom means, and can only mean, a negative obligation not to unduly harm others combined with a positive obligation to make good any such harm it causes. In this way, I say press freedom is an obligation to make good, not do good. This marks a radical departure from the established literature.

The orthodox view, then, as shown in Part 1, is that press freedom has burdensome qualities that individual freedom of expression does not. These burdens manifest in the public watchdog role, that the press is supposed to monitor the use of power and serve the public good. Chapters 3 and 4 consider alternative manifestations of this obligation and scrutinise them from both a normative perspective, through the lens of theory, and a descriptive one, through the lens of the positive law. Chapter 3 imagines this obligation as a duty which correlates to a right. It follows that if the press has a duty to act, then there must be a rights-holder entitled to demand performance of that duty. Accordingly, acts by the press that are incompatible with its duty would provide grounds for interference by the rights-holder.

When we scrutinise the basis of this claim, we find it derives its moral force from flawed philosophical claims. Since this conception has great resonance with Kant's moral philosophy (and since Kant is sometimes prayed in aid of this high-minded position), the claim, which is found in both case law and commentary, is deconstructed by means of Kant's political philosophy, as it appears chiefly in the *Rechtslehre*. It is argued, in short, that neither Kant's political nor ethical theory supports the imposition of this sort of onerous obligation. Essentially, Kant says that the categorical imperative driving inner legislation is unenforceable by external influences and has no claim on the outer world, which is governed by the Universal Principle of Right (*Allgemeines Princip des Rechts*), which is defined in the *Rechtslehre* as this: 'any action is right if it can coexist with everyone's freedom in accordance with a universal law or if on its maxim the freedom of choice of each can coexist with everyone's freedom in accordance with a universal law.'[32] Interferences with rights are properly subject to coercion: 'if a certain use of freedom is itself a hindrance to freedom in accordance with the universal laws (ie, wrong), coercion that is opposed to this (as a *hindering* of a *hindrance to freedom*) is consistent with freedom in accordance with universal laws, that is, it is right.'[33] Indeed, this description of juridical duties is reflected in the positive law's treatment of press freedom. As will be shown, although judges sometimes speak of press freedom 'duties' in terms that are reminiscent of SRT's position, these references are misleading: the positive law does not support this sort of duty-right construct.

Chapter 4 takes a different approach and so imagines the obligation in the teleological conception as a limitation upon the press freedom right. To avoid linguistic confusion, it uses the term 'responsibility' to describe this obligation. It explores the possibility that, even if there is no duty on the press, there is a responsibility to act consistently with democratic ideals. This alternative treatment of obligation finds expression in notions like 'responsible journalism', which is an ethically-loaded term, usually deployed, in the commentary, as proof positive of some differential standard between individual and press speech. Users of the term 'responsibility', then, say that press freedom must be used in a specific way (a responsible way) to attract legal protection. Yet, as will be shown, this is inaccurate, for the law does not say that journalists must be responsible, in a way that individuals are not (or need not be). Instead, it says that if a journalist is to ride roughshod over another's reputational interests to make

---

[32] Kant, (n 29), [6:231]
[33] Ibid.

a point of significance to the public at large, then the law will only protect it if the damage to reputation was, in some way, unavoidable.

Finally, Chapter 5, outlines what I call the 'accountability' model of press freedom, which I argue is the only defensible conception of it. Here, I reject the burdensome interpretation of press freedom. I also challenge the orthodox view that press freedom *must* have different normative grounds to individual freedom of expression because the press *cannot* self-express (with the result that liberal accounts of free speech cannot apply). I demonstrate that this claim is based upon an erroneous interpretation of John Stuart Mill's account in *On Liberty*.[34] The central premise of the accountability model is that interferences with press speech or conduct are justified only when it has engaged in wrongdoing which causes harm. If these three elements – wrongdoing, causation, and harm – are not satisfied, then no liability can be imposed. This emphasis on wrongdoing thus preserves the special treatment that public interest expression receives. In other words, since press malfeasance corresponds to the wrongdoing-causation-harm construct and press freedom does not (for it involves no wrongdoing), then it can be said that press malfeasance and press freedom operate in two separate realms, of which only the former is regulatable.

Regulation

Part 3 explores the practical consequences of the accountability model. It examines existing press regulatory codes as applied in the UK and across Europe[35] to determine the legitimacy of enforcing such provisions by coercive means. Since it is argued that the legitimacy of press regulation depends upon its conformity with press freedom, the range of conceivable codes of conduct (which regulatory members must comply with to avoid coercive outcomes) is limited to those which do not unduly interfere disproportionately with the press's right to speak. Accordingly, Part 3 determines the parameters of coercive independent press regulation. In this Part, I categorise existing code provisions according to the three competing interests in press regulation: those of society, victims, and readers.

Chapter 6 examines clauses aimed at protecting societal interests in press freedom. As it demonstrates, SRT's teleological claims find their greatest expression in the common regulatory provision that newspapers must publish accurate information. This obligation can take two forms. It can stand for the (uncontentious) proposition that newspapers should avoid injuring the reputation of others through the dissemination of falsehood. Alternatively, it can take

---

[34] JS Mill, 'On Liberty', in JM Robson (ed), *Collected Works of John Stuart Mill*, vol XVIII (Toronto, University of Toronto Press, 1977).

[35] Specifically, Austria, Belgium, Denmark, Finland, Germany, Ireland, the Netherlands, Norway, Slovakia, Sweden, and Switzerland.

a broader, more onerous form, which penalises inaccuracy for the (perceived) damage it does to public and private decision-making. This second form is usually premised on society's 'right to know' and so extends the obligation beyond that owed to the reader to include society as a whole, on the basis that inaccuracy taints public debate (which then misinforms non-readers) and corrupts democratic participation (by voters acting upon misinformation/disinformation), which has grave consequences for non-readers as well. Coercive enforcement of this provision, though, would be incompatible with the accountability model. For, even if it could be shown that the dissemination of inaccurate information constitutes 'wrongdoing' (which is not conceded), the causal link between act and deleterious effect cannot be established. No one is forced to read a newspaper, let alone act upon its findings without engaging their critical functions. Consequently, the decision to trust newspapers and to believe its contents, is always a choice; it is the product of autonomous decision-making. Accordingly, the responsibility for those consequences is that of the autonomous agent alone. This is a significant finding since much of the libertarian resistance to mandatory regulation stems from the (understandable) fear that regulatory exuberance in superintending the quality of press speech emanates from this provision.

Chapter 7 relates to victim interests in an accountable press. It is crucial to the overarching argument in favour of coercive independent press regulation. These provisions are not limited to those that mimic positive law rights, such as privacy, libel, and the right to a fair trial, but extends to those that are comparable and compatible with existing rights. The chapter is divided into a discussion of provisions relating to newspaper content and to conduct (as part of the newsgathering process). It argues for the enforceability of discrimination provisions, to the extent that these satisfy the wrongdoing-causation-harm construct. Accordingly, only discrimination that targets specific individuals or groups and causes demonstrable harm will be captured. The discussion about conduct is sub-divided. The first subsection tackles unwanted contact. It argues that provisions prohibiting intrusion are legitimate even if the positive law does not protect against this sort of wrong (eg, UK law does not recognise the US intrusion into seclusion tort). The second subsection tackles covert conduct. It argues that provisions prohibiting clandestine recordings and subterfuge are legitimate only to the extent that they satisfy the wrongdoing-causation-harm construct. Problematically, many pre-existing provisions penalise the fact of covert conduct even in the absence of harm.

Certain pre-existing code provisions recognise what is known as a public interest exception. This means there will be no breach of the code if there is a public interest at stake which necessitates interfering (proportionately) with the victim's rights. The final part of Chapter 7 discusses the nature of this exception and demonstrates its compatibility with the accountability model. Since the publication of public interest expression cannot count as 'wrongdoing', it is not regulatable. Accordingly, this represents an important contribution to the book's overarching claim that press freedom and press malfeasance operate in two separate realms.

Chapter 8 concludes this Part by examining the legitimacy of enforcing pre-existing provisions which protect readers' interests. Ostensibly, these provisions police the contract between reader and press, to ensure that readers receive what they are entitled to. Alternatively, they protect the reader from unwarranted harm. Both types, though, are deeply problematic. Contractual performance cannot be regulated, at least not in the manner that the pre-existing provisions envisage. Even if we could show that the supply of accurate information was a contractual term (which is doubtful), the remedy would be compensation (the contract price) rather than specific performance. Similarly, provisions that purport to protect readers from harm fail on causation grounds (to demonstrate this point, the chapter focuses on the common provisions relating to the depiction of suicide). The chapter concludes by examining the treatment of reader autonomy that such provisions project. Problematically, such provisions impose, or else seek to impose, liberal thinking upon readers. For example, the typical accuracy clause treats readers not as autonomous agents capable of exercising healthy scepticism when receiving information, but as automatons who are infected by inaccurate information at the point of contact. Indeed, the thinly-veiled problem for many SRT advocates is that the threat to epistemic advance represented by inaccurate information is that it promotes reactionary agendas antithetical to liberalism, especially in its intolerance of migrants, feminism, and Islam. This, though, fails to recognise the liberal paradox: whereas all broad-minded people embrace liberalism (at least, as it relates to tolerance and plurality), forcing it upon the recalcitrant is a contradiction of its essential premise. Accordingly, SRT's agenda – to ensure the enlightenment of society and guarantee a state of perpetual progress – is utterly incompatible with the sovereignty of individuality. It cannot be realised without sacrificing autonomy.

Realisation

Part 4 discusses the conceptual issues arising from the realisation of coercive independent press regulation. It has very little to say, though, about the practical issues inherent in this project – at least, not to the extent of examining the fine details of the arrangements. I do not provide a draft statute to establish the scheme, as O'Malley and Soley do,[36] I do not talk about the process of policy-making, and the opportunities for offering professional development and education, as Rowbottom does,[37] and neither do I specify the composition of the board or the code committee, nor describe the ideal corporate structure that the regulator should take, as Leveson does.[38] Likewise, I say nothing about the funding arrangements.[39]

---

[36] O'Malley and Soley, (n 31), 191–199.
[37] J Rowbottom, *Media Law* (Oxford, Hart Publishing, 2018), 264–265.
[38] Leveson, (n 1), 1758–1760, [4.1]–[4.10].
[39] Ibid, 1761–1762, [4.14]–[4,17].

These are important issues, of course, but there is nothing philosophically inter-esting about them – or, at least, not to my mind. Instead, in asking how Leveson's chief regulatory goal of protecting 'real people' from 'real harm' is to be achieved, Chapter 9 scrutinises the claim that mandatory press regulation would be unconstitutional. Chapter 10, meanwhile, concludes the book by reflecting upon the previous chapters to answer the question of why we should regulate.

Chapter 9, then, is concerned mainly with the issue of compulsion. How do we compel the recalcitrant press to join a scheme of regulation that the press has consistently refused even to entertain the possibility of? It seems to me that there is only one method available to us, and that is by means of statute. As we have seen, above, Leveson was unconvinced by claims that *any* use of stat-ute to underpin regulatory arrangements would undermine press freedom, but stopped short of denying that statutory regulation (by which he meant, chiefly, *mandatory* regulation) would be unconstitutional. Chapter 9 grapples with this issue. Amongst other things, it argues that the status quo – of using contract to govern the regulatory relationship – is fatally flawed. Since contracts are the ultimate expression of consensual dealings, they are hopeless tools by which to regulate. For one thing, contracts are always escapable – and as IPSO's predeces-sor (the PCC) and other European regulators have seen, publishers will leave the scheme if they feel badly treated. This ineffectiveness makes mandatory regula-tion all the more important. The opposition to it, though, is hard to pin down. There are too many unspoken assumptions and misperceptions. Chief amongst these misperceptions is the assumption that statutory press regulation amounts to censorship, which is simply wrong. Leveson was guilty of this. His report panders too much to the unsubstantiated claim that mandatory regulation represents the 'thin end of the wedge' and the 'slippery slope' – but this sort of function creep can only occur if we lack the language to articulate the boundaries of both press regu-lation and press freedom. This is *not* true of press freedom. There is no language shortfall that would enable duplicitous regimes to make inroads into press freedom unnoticed by means of press regulation. As the previous chapters demonstrate, press malfeasance and press freedom belong to different realms. Legitimate press regulation cannot creep from one to the other unobserved.

Chapter 9 also argues against the use of sanctions as a disciplinary tool, and instead argues for their use as a compensatory tool. Disciplinary measures send the wrong signal. Since victims are the priority, it should be victims who benefit from the imposition of sanctions. Consequently, I argue that the regula-tor should be empowered to award compensation in amounts that recognise the unwarranted harm that undue press attention causes. Of course, Leveson had in mind that disciplinary sanctions would be used to fund the regulator, but this provides an unfortunate incentive to fine because the failing financial health of the regulator demands it.

Chapter 10 concludes by asking the same question twice (why regulate the press?). The first part asks – why *regulate* the press? – and so responds to an antic-ipated criticism relating to the necessity of regulation. For it might be argued that since the book seeks to limit regulation to circumstances where normative legal theory allows for intervention, it is an argument for law reform rather than regulation. In which case, why *regulate* at all? This, to my mind, would be the libertarian's response to what I say, for it is really an argument in favour of private concerns dealing with what is a (major) public issue. This reliance upon the market, though, is deeply flawed. First, the last 70 years (at least) have demonstrated that such reliance upon the private market[40] to address press malfeasance is seriously ineffective. The press continues to inflict untold harm on victims – often on, as Leveson saw clearly, those who are not famous and who do not have the financial resources to secure their rights. Also, this reliance permits a sort of 'divide and conquer' mentality to flourish within the industry. By settling claims before court proceedings are concluded – or worse, using superior financial muscle and bullying tactics to harangue victims to surrender their legal rights without compensation – the press can conceal the true extent of wrongdoing from public scrutiny. Coercive independent press regulation addresses this significant inefficiency in the realisation of justice. By providing cheap means of redress, it cures the disproportionate costs of pursuing, and defending, legal action (for both parties) and so produces both a time and cost-effective mechanism for settling disputes. Moreover, since the regulator has the power to commence investigations on its own initiative, it can shield, or at least provide some protection for, the complainant against the bullying tactics of the press. This may go some way to address the antagonism that regular targets of press retaliation face when they complain (rightly) about press bullying. The press will be prevented from doing deals in the dark to silence them.

The second criticism I anticipate is: why regulate the *press*? In other words, why am I focusing exclusively on the traditional press and have nothing to say about broadcast or the internet? There are several reasons for this. First, there remains something important in Nick Davies's warning that the traditional press, especially the powerful incarnations, such as the *Daily Mail*, still dictates both the news agenda of these other sources of communication and, perhaps even more significantly, the political agenda through the great influence it wields in Parliament and upon the executive.[41] Second, we should recognise that, in our complicated relationship with the press, and our expectations of it, we have, as commentators, never really got it right. How else are to explain the fact that European press regulators – in Belgium, Denmark, Germany and Sweden, to name a few – attribute the basis of regulation to this mythical public's right to know and not the very real problem of protecting victim's rights? In *After Virtue*,[42] Alasdair MacIntyre complained that modern philosophers misused the language of ethics that the Greats had given them, because they had lost

---

[40] It is not a total reliance, of course, for the Attorney General has the power to initiate contempt proceedings when the right to a fair trial is unduly compromised.

[41] N Davies, *Flat Earth News* (London, Chatto & Windus, 2008), 365–369.

[42] A MacIntyre, *After Virtue* (first published, 1981) (London, Bloomsbury, 2011).

touch with the origins of that language, especially the civic and social culture from which it emerged. We see the same happening in our modern treatment of press freedom, when commentators say the press is 'obliged' to educate the populace or protect us from the evils of corrupt power.

If we can achieve a better, philosophically-sound notion of both press freedom and press regulation now, we can use this in the future if and when newspapers disappear and are replaced by something else (be that the internet or something not yet invented). The danger – in not tackling this issue – is that our flawed conceptions of press freedom and press regulation remain and those mistakes continue into the next realm of mass communication. We have already seen this in the broadcast context. There was no philosophically-sound design underpinning the introduction of broadcast regulation in the mid-twentieth century but, instead, a confluence of historical accidents, in which, in the UK and US, the intellectual snobbery of the established press met with state designs on controlling the dissemination of information and produced something which is not an exemplar of free speech. Now, though, commentators regularly champion broadcast regulation as the paradigm of left-thinking, quietly forgetting that the restrictions placed upon broadcasters are tolerable only because the traditional press (and the internet) remains as a powerful source of correction to the regime of political interference and inhibited free speech that broadcasting represents.

Significance

This book represents a major departure from the orthodox views on press freedom and press regulation. By denying that the grounds for press freedom are axiomatic, and by rejecting much of what the established literature takes for granted, it challenges the reader to take a fresh look at the notion of press freedom, and to think again about the perceived unconstitutionality of *forcing* the press to engage with regulation. This sort of profound re-evaluation of press freedom and press regulation, at a conceptual level, is vital. It is only by doing so that the present deadlock may be broken in realising meaningful press regulatory reform.

Moreover, the book addresses a shortfall in the literature, for the compatibility of press freedom and mandatory press regulation has not previously received the level of forensic, schematic, and philosophical analysis that it does here. By doing so, it provides the sort of robust justification, as a matter of normative legal theory, that the academic literature lacks to prove that the establishment of an independent regulator, with powers to compensate victims of press malfeasance, is compatible with the state's press freedom guarantee. It shows that press freedom and press malfeasance occupy two distinct realms that do not overlap. Accordingly, press regulation exists outside the realm of press freedom and, simultaneously, press freedom exists outside the realm of press regulation. In this way, the one is no threat to the other; we do not need to compromise one project to realise the other. Consequently, the book provides the intellectual foundations for what Leveson called the 'backstop regulator' which, according to him, the public is now 'entitled to demand … to ensure that the press is accountable.'[43]

Although the book is critical of the press, it is not an 'anti-press' book. Neither is it evangelical about the press. In arguing for press freedom, it rejects the sort of 'sacrificial lamb' defence that views victims as collateral damage in what is otherwise a 'just war' orchestrated by the press against the corrupt and the power-ful. Arguments of this kind confuse two separate issues: the noble cause of press freedom and the indefensible consequences of press malfeasance. In other words, the shape of the debate is not linear but binary. Consequently, the book throws into sharp relief the needlessness of victim suffering and the emptiness of claims that such suffering is the price of democracy.

---

[43] Leveson, (n 1), 1757, [3.51].

PART 1

Rationale

1

Unity in Press Freedom Theory

I. Introduction

Ostensibly, there are multiple, conflicting theories of press freedom in the established academic literature. Yet the image this creates, of a concept comprehensively formulated by a means of an elaborate, rigorous, contested process, misleads as to the nature and scope of the press freedom debate. For, in truth, that debate is happening only at the margins – and relates, as we shall see, to the level of protection that ought to be afforded to press freedom compared to an individual's right to free speech. At the core, there is no debate. There is no rigorous scrutiny or contested treatment of press freedom's normative make-up. There is only the prosaic assertion that the justification for press freedom is teleological and for individual free speech, non-teleological. This teleology is said to manifest in the specific functions the press is expected to fulfil – to act as a 'public watchdog', as a check on power (ie, the fourth estate), and to provide political education to the masses (and so enable informed democratic participation). Consequently, this teleology is taken to create 'duties' and 'responsibilities' – that is, obligations imposed upon the press to realise its purpose – which the commentary uses to delineate the parameters of the press's right to free speech. This arrangement is taken to be so obvious and unremarkable as to be axiomatic.[1] Certainly, we find little resistance to it in the established literature.

The origins of this view can be found in press freedom's history (from the late eighteenth century onwards). But, as will be shown, in section three, the modern view is a corruption of that tradition, for when scrutinised we see not one but three distinct understandings of it in this period, arising from three phases in its history. These three traditional views are only loosely connected. In the first period, the romantic phase, the teleological view is merely foreshadowed: press freedom is

---

[1] See, eg, K Martin, *The Press The Public Wants* (London: Hogarth Press, 1947); C King, *The Future of the Press* (London: MacGibbon & Kee, 1967), 87–94; V Blasi, 'The Checking Value in First Amendment Theory' (1977) *American Bar Foundation Research Journal* 521, 538; M Gurevitch and JG Blumler, 'Political communication systems and democratic values' in J Lichtenberg (ed), *Democracy and the Mass Media* (Cambridge University Press, 1990), 270; D McQuail, *Media Performance*, (London: SAGE Publications, 1992), 35–36; OM Fiss, *Liberalism Divided* (Colorado: Westview Press, 1996), 149–150; T O'Malley and C Soley, *Regulating the Press* (Pluto Press, 2000), 1–4, 177–197; N Chomsky, *Media Control*, (n 20); R Bejesky, 'Press Clause Aspirations and the Iraq War', (2011–2012) 48 *Willamette Law Review*. 343, 393.

not an end but a means by which the electorate may monitor government and so protect its property interests. In this way, press freedom is valued for the benefits it affords its audience. In the second period, the ideological phase, the teleological view emerges: the ruling Liberal party sees the press as the means by which to provide the newly enfranchised masses with a political education and so enable democratic participation. In the third period, the critical phase, the teleological view is realised by inversion of the arguments in favour of press freedom. What was once a benefit is now a burden. The plea, from press to state for protection because of the public good it does, becomes a demand, from state to press that protection is contingent on it doing public good. Thus, in this period, this teleology takes on added political significance, such that the state asserts its ability to investigate press standards by means of public inquiry. What we find, though, is that modern thinking has adopted these views from the ideological and critical phases, but uncritically: it has not recognised that the ideological understanding had been discredited in its own time nor that the critical phase has no viability as historical understanding. That these understandings have thrived despite their implausibility is remarkable. This does not make them illegitimate, of itself, but demonstrates the need for serious reconsideration.

II. The Modern View

A. Introduction

The uniformity in modern press freedom thinking is apparent from the nature of the debate. Commentators do not dispute what press freedom means – or stands for – but how its goals (*telos*) are to be secured. In Siebert, Peterson and Schramm's classic text *Four Theories of the Press*,[2] the division is along political lines, relating to the different political goals arising in authoritarian, Soviet communist, and democratic states. It is not disputed that the press, in each, serves political goals, only what these goals mean for newspaper content. Of specific interest, for our purposes, are the two competing models in the democratic context, which they label the 'libertarian' and 'Social Responsibility' theories. Contemporary commentators, though, rarely refer to these theories by name, but they do adhere to their central tenets. Instead, they tend to say that there are three theories of press freedom[3] (all of which we find in SRT and libertarianism): (i) the traditional view that press freedom requires no special free speech guarantee from the state,

---

[2] FS Siebert, T Peterson and W Schramm, *Four Theories of the Press* (Chicago, University of Illinois Press, 1956).

[3] See E Barendt, *Freedom of Speech* 2nd edn (Oxford, OUP, 2005), 419–424; H Fenwick and G Phillipson, *Media Freedom under the Human Rights Act*, (Oxford, OUP, 2006), 20–32; J Oster, *Media Freedom as a Fundamental Right* (Cambridge, CUP, 2015), 25–54.

because the constitutional apparatus that protects individual rights to free speech is sufficient to safeguard the press's public watchdog role; (ii) the institutional view that press freedom is different and requires a higher threshold for state interference because of the vital constitutional role that the press plays; and (iii) the instrumental view that press freedom requires special privileges and immunities only when the democratic values underpinning it are especially at stake.[4] The instrumental view thus mediates between the traditional and institutional view by agreeing with the former that special free speech rights are not always required for the press but, in agreement with the latter, that the press is more significant at times than the individual is in enabling democratic values to thrive. Helen Fenwick and Gavin Phillipson have introduced a fourth perspective, which is that special burdens (as well as benefits) may be imposed upon the press to ensure the best expressive environment for the audience.[5] In this way, the 'specialness' of press freedom cuts both ways.

Superficially, at least, the traditional view presents the greatest opportunity for departure from the teleological view of press freedom. Yet, closer inspection reveals that there is no dissent from the orthodox conception, for adherents do not say that individual freedom of speech and press freedom are the same: quite the opposite, they emphasise the differences. What they do say, though, is that differential treatment in law will not serve the press in its fulfilment of its function. Thus Willian Van Alstyne says that no good can come from the arrangement: 'To trade away that protection [equivalence] for some few bits of privilege, purchased at the price of fastening fiduciary burdens upon every newspaper in the country' represents a very bad bargain.[6] Similarly, David Lange does not argue against the purposive notion of press freedom; his concern is simply that individual freedom of speech will 'wither' if treated as a subordinate to press freedom.[7] Perhaps the greatest proponent of the equivalence model is Eugene Volokh who has argued, amongst other things, that the First Amendment's reference to the press distinguishes not speakers but modes of speech and so means no more than the right of all to use technologies to disseminate information and ideas.[8] In doing so, he does not deny the instrumental significance of the press, he only disputes that the Framers intended to provide an institutional guarantee; all they meant to do, he says, is to recognise the different modes of disseminating information and ideas (ie, by speaking and by publishing).

The following sketches out the uniformity in press freedom thinking which, as will be seen, can be found in both the political and legal commentary of the

---

[4] Barendt, *Freedom of Speech*, ibid, 419–424.

[5] Fenwick and Phillipson, *Media Freedom under the Human Rights Act*, (n 3), 27–32.

[6] WW Van Alstyne, 'The Hazards to the Press of Claiming a "Preferred Position"' (1977) (28) *The Hastings Law Journal* 761, 770.

[7] D Lange, 'The Speech and Press Clauses' (1975) 23 *UCLA Law Review* 77.

[8] E Volokh, 'Freedom for the Press as an Industry or for the Press as a Technology?' (2011–12) 160 *University of Pennsylvania Law Review* 459.

modern period. These views crystallised in the decade between the mid-1970s and 1980s. This was a period of intense academic debate which witnessed a resurgence in press freedom scholarship. The easiest explanation for this is the marked social consciousness of the 1960s and 1970s coupled with the increasing disbelief in the power of the market to resolve social problems.

B. Political Commentary

Despite their different philosophical bases, we can see in Habermas's discourse theory[9] and Rawls's political liberalism[10] the mature statement of the 1970's politically left-leaning ideology (albeit it was not until the mid-1990s that these positions were fully developed in *Between Facts and Norms* and *Political Liberalism*). In Habermas's system, the function of the press converges, to some extent, with the obligations of the individual (a duty of civic-mindedness to participate willingly, rationally, and emphatically in the deliberation and formation of public opinion), with both playing a combined role in deliberative politics.[11] Whilst political institutions themselves represent 'strong' forms of public debate and opinion-formation (because the public cannot 'solve problems *on its own*'),[12] civil society is an important, though weaker, source by which social problems are identified and publicised. In this way, we see in Habermas all that is good in Kant and German Idealism. The press plays such a critical role in this that, Habermas argues, certain limitations should be placed upon it. First, from an internal perspective, the press 'ought to understand themselves as the mandatary of an enlightened public whose willingness to learn and capacity for criticism they at once presuppose, demand, and reinforce.'[13] Consequently, from an external perspective, 'the power of the media should thus be neutralized and the tacit conversion of administrative or social power into political influence blocked.'[14]

Like Habermas, Rawls emphasises the importance of civic-mindedness in his account of democracy. There is a need for society to take their political education seriously so that they can weigh up the competing claims by candidates for election.[15] Whilst press freedom plays a less conspicuous role in his

---

[9] J Habermas, *The Theory of Communicative Action, Vol. 1: Reason and the Rationalization of Society*, T McCarthy, trans, (Cambridge: Polity Press, 1984); *The Theory of Communicative Action, Vol. 2: The Critique of Functionalist Reason*, T McCarthy, trans, (Cambridge, Polity Press, 1987); *Between Facts and Norms*, W Rehg, trans, (Cambridge, Polity Press, 1996).

[10] J Rawls, *Political Liberalism* (New York, Columbia University Press, 1996).

[11] See Habermas, *Between Facts and Norms*, (n 9), ch 8. See further J Habermas, 'Political Communication in Media Society: Does Democracy Still Enjoy an Epistemic Dimension? The Impact of Normative Theory on Empirical Research' (2006) 16 *Communication Theory* 411–426.

[12] Habermas, *Between Facts and Norms*, (n 9), 359.

[13] Ibid, 378.

[14] Ibid, 378–379.

[15] See, eg, J Rawls, *A Theory of Justice* revised edn (Oxford, Oxford University Press, 1999), 194 revised edn, 200.

account, nevertheless its contribution is significant to ensure citizens 'have the means to be informed about political issues.'[16] We can better understand Rawls's position, if we see it through Dworkin's interpretation of the First Amendment. Like Rawls, Dworkin says that since greater access to information enables better decision-making about the good life, the power afforded to the press needs careful handling. Yet, he also says that press freedom cannot be justified entirely by marginal gains in audience welfare alone since that would jeopardise other important social norms, like fair trials, confidentiality, and national security, and thus the craving for greater power and privileges by the press must be weighed against the decrease in democracy that would result in granting such powers.[17]

Latterly, Onora O'Neill, echoing Habermas, has argued that the public *needs* a press that provides 'adequate communication' to enable meaningful democratic participation.[18] Since society needs only those modes of communication that 'best enable and least obstruct' its shared goals for communication – to realise the best form of liberal democracy through deliberative politics – then the press must not 'assume bogus authority nor mislead' and must respect divergent audience interests.[19] Noam Chomsky and Robert Chesney have said much the same, albeit in more polemical terms. Chomsky continues to castigate the press for its failure, he says, to report the world as it is, and not the world as government would like it to be,[20] whilst McChesney has argued that the mass media advances the interests only of the wealthy few.[21] Consequently, both say, democracy is poorly served by the existing state of press freedom.

Beyond political philosophy, we see parallel developments in the communication studies literature of the 1970s, especially in the work of Raymond Williams, James Curran and Denis McQuail. All three provided profound insights into – and a great deal of frustration with – the institutional press as an underperforming vehicle for realising a more culturally and politically advanced society. Williams's pioneering work in *Communications*[22] concerns the centrality of communication – in all forms, but particularly the press – to learning and, consequently, the realisation of an effective democracy. He was adamant that 'we must avoid the false opposition between a free press and a responsible press.'[23] Curran showed that the contribution of the popular press to political enlightenment and scrutiny had

---

[16] Ibid, 198.

[17] See, eg, R Dworkin, 'Is the Press Losing the First Amendment?' in *A Matter of Principle* (Cambridge, Harvard University Press, 1985), 381397.

[18] O O'Neill, *A Question of Trust* (Cambridge: Cambridge University Press, 2002).

[19] O O'Neill, 'Practices of Toleration' in Lichtenberg, *Democracy and the Mass Media*, n 1, 155–185.

[20] N Chomsky, *Media Control* 2nd edn (New York, Seven Stories Press, 2002).

[21] RW McChesney, *Rich Media, Poor Democracy* (Chicago, University of Illinois Press, 1999); RW McChesney and J Nichols, *Our Media, Not Theirs* 2nd edn (New York, Seven Stories Press, 2002).

[22] R Williams, *Communications* revised edn (Penguin Books, 1968).

[23] R Williams, 'The Press We Don't Deserve' in J Curran (ed), *The British Press: a Manifesto* (London, MacMillan, 1978), 18.

been grossly misrepresented;[24] that, instead of working *for* the public, as their champion, it had set itself *against* their interests: 'much of the press chose to side with privilege, and in some cases to actively bully the vulnerable.'[25] In this way, he showed how concentrated ownership and the inviolability of laissez faire principles had worked against viewpoint diversity; that the absence of meaningful, coherent public policy on newspaper markets had caused the government to miss a golden opportunity to rectify the problem in 1977,[26] by its failure to introduce state subsidies that would have supported pluralism.[27] Finally, McQuail, in *Mass Communication Theory*[28] and *Media Performance*,[29] provided the grounds for this sort of policy through his comprehensive method of assessing mass media performance (which, of course, is not limited to the printed press). These accounts are guided by traditional notions of the press as political educator, protector of civic rights, and check on power.

C. Legal Commentary

Press freedom scholarship in the US legal commentary was reinvigorated by a provocative article, in 1974, by Justice Potter Stewart.[30] Stewart argued that the Founders intended the phrase 'the press' in the First Amendment to create not only an institutional but a *structural* constitutional guarantee, in which the press was installed formally as the 'fourth estate'. This, he said, was evident from both American and British constitutional history (noting John Carlyle's attribution of the term to Edmund Burke). Said Stewart: 'The British Crown knew that a free press was not just a neutral vehicle for the balanced discussion of diverse ideas. Instead, the free press meant organized, expert scrutiny of government. The press was a conspiracy of the intellect, with the courage of numbers.'[31]

This view elicited support from scholars like Melvin Nimmer, Floyd Abrams, and Randall Bezanson, in the first instance. Nimmer, agreeing with Stewart, argued that the term 'press' in the First Amendment would be a redundancy if it did not have some special meaning. This he saw in two features of freedom that individuals benefit from that the press cannot: first, speech is a means to individual self-fulfilment; secondly, it has psychological value as a 'safety valve', by

---

[24] J Curran, 'Press History' in J Curran and J Seaton, *Power Without Responsibility* 8th edn (Abingdon, Routledge, 2018), 1–192.

[25] Ibid, 4.

[26] Royal Commission on the Press, *Final Report*, Cmnd 6810, 1977.

[27] See J Curran, 'Introduction' in *The British Press: a Manifesto*, (n 23), 1–11.

[28] D McQuail, *Mass Communication Theory* first published 1983, 6th edn (London, SAGE Publications, 2010).

[29] D McQuail, *Media Performance*, (n 1).

[30] P Stewart, 'Or Of The Press?' (1974–1975) 26 *Hastings Law Journal* 631.

[31] Ibid, 634.

which tension is dissipated through words instead of violent actions.[32] Abrams, meanwhile, saw this distinctiveness in the press's 'unique' ability to act as a check on power[33] (it is not that it 'invariably serves as a vigilant protector of the public ... few newspaper readers would recognise that [claim] ... it is [that it] is the *only* institution that can serve [this function]')[34] – a function that Vincent Blasi had said earlier was the most convincing basis for its First Amendment protection.[35] Bezanson, expanding on these ideas, concluded that the press has a *duty* to enable informed democratic participation and keep (political) power in check.[36]

But Stewart's position also generated dissent. David Anderson, for example, could not understand why Stewart had concluded press freedom did *not* create a right to information about government activities, given its pre-eminence in the political machine.[37] Anthony Lewis – in common with David Lange (see above) – disagreed that the press's 'crucial function' to check on power applied to them alone: 'if the First Amendment is to have meaning in today's political society, it must guarantee a basic right to scrutinize government and hold it accountable' regardless of the form that speech takes or its source (press or individual).[38] Similarly, Robert D Sack argued that the First Amendment protects the role of the press, not the institution, and so applies to *anyone* whose speech is a vehicle of information, educates the public, offers criticism, and provides a forum for debate.[39]

These ideas led, eventually, to a broad range of interpretations, including Edwin Baker's claim that press freedom had to be understood as a duality in which political press speech, as a means to informed democratic participation, could claim benefits that the commercial press, as a business activity, could not.[40] Cass Sunstein went further, to say that press freedom was of such significance that the state was justified in interfering to realise those ends (a claim that is given greater attention in the next chapter).[41] Frederick Schauer, meanwhile, found nothing distinctive in press freedom other than as a special context demonstrating government incompetence to make the 'right choice'.[42] Finally, Robert Post produced,

---

[32] MB Nimmer, 'Is Freedom of the Press a Redundancy: What Does It Add to Freedom of Speech?' (1974–1975) 26 *Hastings LJ* 639. See also O'Neill, *A Question of Trust*, (n 18), 90–91.

[33] F Abrams, 'The Press is Different: Reflections on Justice Stewart and the Autonomous Press' 7 *Hofstra Law Review* 563, 585, 1979.

[34] Ibid, 592.

[35] Blasi, (n 1).

[36] See, eg, RP Bezanson, 'Whither Freedom of the Press?' (2012) 97 *Iowa Law Review* 1259, 1273; 'The New Free Press Guarantee' (1977) 63 *Virginia Law Review* 731. See also E Barendt, 'Statutory Underpinning: A Threat to Press Freedom?' (2013) 5(2) *Journal of Media Law* 189, 191.

[37] DA Anderson, 'The Origins of the Press Clause' (1983) 30 *UCLA Law Review* 456, 537.

[38] A Lewis, 'The Right to Scrutinize Government: Toward a First Amendment Theory of Accountability' (1980) 34 *University of Miami Law Review* 793, 806.

[39] RD Sack, 'Reflections on the Wrong Question: Special Constitutional Privilege for the Institutional Press' (1979) 7 *Hofstra Law Review* 629, 633.

[40] CE Baker, *Human Liberty and Freedom of Speech* (New York, Oxford University Press, 1989).

[41] CR Sunstein, *Democracy and the Problem of Free Speech* (New York, Free Press, 1995).

[42] F Schauer, *Free Speech: A Philosophical Inquiry* (Cambridge, Cambridge University Press, 1982).

from this, his deliberative democracy theory,[43] which is, essentially, an extension of Habermas. Newspapers, as the major source of public discourse, enable citizens to experience meaningful self-government. Consequently, though, the free speech guarantee applies only to the extent audience interests are served; the economic interests of the speaker are entirely secondary.

D. Conclusion

Despite the legal commentary being dominated by US interpretations of the First Amendment's meaning – which does include the term 'press', something the free speech guarantee under Article 10 of the European Convention on Human Rights does not – there is a commonality between UK and US thinking, in both the legal and political commentary, on the meaning of the term. Press freedom is teleological. Consequently, 'duties' and 'responsibilities' exist for the press that do not for the individual. On this view, the press freedom right is a bargain in which the cost of legal protection is the fulfilment of the public watchdog role.[44] We see this expressed in Habermas's view of a public-issued mandate[45] and in Edward Gerald's claim that 'the mass media of communications are social institutions that serve the society by gathering, writing, and distributing the news of the day'.[46] This depicts press freedom as a sort of fiduciary relationship between citizen and press or an obligation to maintain the public's 'trust and confidence' in its watchdog capabilities.[47] Indeed, the various press regulators across Europe, such as Belgium's Raad voor de Journalistiek, Denmark's Pressenævnets, Germany's Presserat, and Sweden's Allmänhetens Pressombudsman, often refer to obligations of this sort.[48]

These ideas are not new. We see them in the history of press freedom. As we have noticed, the literature derives, or seeks to, some legitimacy from historical interpretations of press freedom, whether it is Stewart's renewal, and Blasi's

---

[43] See, eg, R Post, 'Meiklejohn's Mistake: Individual Autonomy and the Reform of Public Discourse' (1993) 64 *University of Colorado Law Review* 1109; 'Reconciling Theory and Doctrine in First Amendment Jurisprudence' (2000) 88 *California Law Review* 2353; 'Participatory Democracy and Free Speech' (2011) 97 *Virginia Law Review* 477 2011.

[44] In addition to contributions discussed here, further examples can be found in Andrew Kenyon's survey of the literature, 'Assuming Free Speech' (2014) 77(3) *MLR* 379.

[45] Habermas, *Between Norms and Facts*, (n 9), 378.

[46] JE Gerald, *The Social Responsibility of the Press* (Minneapolis, University of Minnesota Press, 1963), 3.

[47] See discussion in, eg, NGE Harris, 'Codes of conduct for journalists' in A Belsey and R Chadwick (eds), *Ethical Issues in Journalism and the Media*, (London, Routledge, 1992), 66; O'Neill, *A Question of Trust*, (n 18), 90–91; RG Natelson, 'Does "The Freedom of the Press" Include a Right to Anonymity? The Original Meaning' 9 NYU JL & Liberty, 160, 187, 2015; T Gibbons, 'Building Trust in Press Regulation: Obstacles and Opportunities' (2013) 5(2) *Journal of Media Law* 202, 208–212.

[48] See discussion in Part III.

elaboration, of Carlyle's 'fourth estate' claim, or James Curran and Jean Seaton's use of Stanley Baldwin's rebuke (actually, it was his cousin's, Rudyard Kipling's) that the manipulation of government by press barons was 'power without responsibility – the prerogative of the harlot throughout the ages.'[49] Yet, when we scrutinise this history (in the next section), we see that, devoid of their original context and conditions, the modern expression of these ideas is a corruption and requires serious reconsideration.

III. The Teleological View in its Historical Context

A. Introduction

In the UK and US, there are three distinct periods in this history: the first, the romantic period, is a fight for freedom against undue state repression, in which the connection between press freedom and societal progress is made acute, and state tolerance of religious and political criticism becomes the norm. This is a sort of golden age for journalism, in which the arguments from truth and (proto-) democratic participation achieve their greatest descriptive power as justifications for press freedom. We see this clearly, in the US, in, for example, the *Federalist Papers* and in Jefferson's view that given a choice between government without newspapers and newspapers without government, he would choose the latter. Yet, as we shall see, we cannot transpose principles from this period to our own, because they are contingent upon the peculiar environment of that time. We see something of this problem in the (rarely mentioned) caveat Jefferson adds: 'But I should mean that every man should receive those papers & be capable of reading them.'[50] This contingency is typical of the age. We see in it a sort of elitism or, otherwise, if that is not what he meant, a requirement that the public is suitably engaged in civic participation, which in those times it was to a far greater degree than today. This signals an important feature of contemporary thought at that time.

The second period – the ideological phase – coincides with the rise of 'new journalism' (as the British and some Americans called it) which radically altered the format and style of newspapers to make them 'popular' and affordable to the masses. This period begins, in the US, in 1833 with the publication of the penny newspaper for 'the common man' (the *New York Sun*)[51] and, in the UK, post-1855, following the repeal of the Stamp Act, and the end of taxes on publications.

---

[49] This is the title of James Curran and Jean Seaton's classic work on press freedom and regulation, *Power without Responsibility*, first published in 1981, now in its 8th edn, (n 24).

[50] Letter to Edward Carrington (16 January 1787) published in PL Ford, ed, *The Works of Thomas Jefferson, vol 5 (Correspondence 1786–1789)* (New York, GP Putnam's Sons, 1904), 253.

[51] See, eg, E Emery, *The Press and America*, 3rd edn (New Jersey, Prentice-Hall Inc, 1972), 166–170.

But that period is more synonymous with the advent of 'yellow journalism' in which sensationalism replaced sober reporting as the preferred style, at least in the battle for increased circulation. We see this on the continent as well. For example, the historian, Eric Hobsbawm, describes *La Presse*, established in 1836, as the forerunner to the modern newspaper: 'political but cheap, aimed at the accumulation of advertising revenue, and made attractive to its readers by gossip, serial novels, and various other stunts.'[52] In this period, we see clearly, within politics and from the older press, the beginnings of the lament for the loss of the romantic period. For in this period, we find not one but two ideologies, battling for supremacy: the progressive view of newspapers as vehicles for educating the masses, and the proprietorial view of them as vehicles for wealth creation. And this period sees the victor emerge: the latter.

The third period – the critical phase – begins, in both the UK and US, shortly after World War II, in 1947, with the introduction of public inquiries (in the UK) into press freedom to address the serious misgivings of the public about the state of newspapers. These have occurred at regular intervals ever since, with the seventh, the Leveson Inquiry into the Culture, Practices, and Ethics of the Press, concluding in 2012. Its parallel in the US can be seen, albeit in much weaker form, in the work of the Commission on Freedom of the Press (or the Hutchins Commission as it is otherwise known), which had no government mandate. This Commission reported its findings in 1947, and these are discussed below. Even in this phase, there remains a sentiment within established journalism that the press has a purpose. In the US, we see this in the work of editors, journalists, and owners, like Arthur Ochs Sulzberger Sr,[53] Ben Bagdikian,[54] and Katherine Graham.[55]

The following concentrates on the UK's experience of these three phases, but it should be borne in mind that the parallel can be seen clearly in US press history.[56] Although the teleological view of press freedom is apparent in all three periods, its nature does not remain static. Thus, we see a more restrictive version in the third period to that arising in the first or second. Most noticeably, its perspective has reversed entirely by the third so that whereas in the first it is presented as something beneficial to publishers, it has become entirely burdensome by the last. Whereas the benefits of press freedom, in this first period, are righteous – the crusade of justice; the exposure of corruption; the good of helping others – they are positively iniquitous by the third, being no more than the pursuit of profit, such that the righteous objectives are now burdensome, to 'even out' the bargain.

---

[52] E Hobsbawm, *The Age of Revolution: 1789–1848* (first published 1962) (London, Abacus Books, 2013), 227.

[53] See discussion in F Abrams, *Speaking Freely* (New York, Penguin, 2006), 11–12, 25.

[54] BH Bagdikian, *The Media Monopoly* 5th edn (Boston, Mass, Beacon Press, 1997).

[55] K Graham, *Personal History* (London, Weidenfeld & Nicolson, 1997).

[56] See LW Levy, *Emergence of a Free Press* (New York, Oxford University Press, 1985) and Emery, (n 51).

B. The Romantic Period

A leader in *The Times*, in 1852, savaged both the tyrannical policies of Napoleon in France and the timorous fawning of the British Government to him, in ignorance of his terrible acts. Its outspokenness prompted a stinging rebuke from Parliament, which urged it to act more responsibly in its reporting. *The Times*'s response is a shining example of the romantic period:

> Are we to bow to the same censure as that which has destroyed the press of Paris, or are we merely to print these things and abstain from the comment which they invite? … This island is the last asylum … for the liberal and constitutional ideas of the rest of Europe. Here at least the truth may be told in safety. It has never been the practice of this country to hold her liberties on the sufferance or forbearance of foreign potentates. We are not a free nation by the will of France, but by our own, and we trust the maintenance of our freedom, not to forbearance of our neighbours, but to our own strength.[57]

And:

> We owe it to the cause of liberty, humanity, and social order to do our best to prevent the public opinion of this country from being dazzled by the spectacle of successful vice, or intimidated by the vicinity of lawless power. We owe it to the purity of our national character to prove that wickedness is never more odious to us than in prosperity; and we owe it to the rest of the world to keep this great lesson constantly before the eyes of the English people, destined to act so mighty a part in its instruction for good or for evil. We have endeavoured to fulfil this *mission*, and we cannot believe that the national spirit is sunk so low as to wish us to desist from it from a craven fear of the mighty criminal whom we have endeavoured to drag before the unerring tribunal of public justice.[58]

The spirit of press freedom that these passages embody is not only the commitment to truth and justice but also the temerity to say what others will not. The word 'mission' is instructive: it is a self-imposed sense of purpose: to defy convention, to ignore etiquette, and to be impolitic, if that is required to scrutinise government properly.

Yet, the self-imposed nature of this purpose deserves emphasis. This can be seen in the sequel to these events. When Lord Derby, in the House of Lords, complained that if the press wants to 'share the influence of statesmen, so also it must share in the responsibilities of statesmen' because of the 'power' it derives 'from the confidence of the public',[59] *The Times* used the opportunity to compare the supposed duties and responsibilities of the statesmen with those of the journalist. Whereas, it said, the statesman conceals information 'until diplomacy is beaten in the race with publicity', the press 'lives by disclosures':

> For us, with whom publicity and truth are the air and light of existence, there can be no greater disgrace than to recoil from the frank and accurate disclosure of facts as they are.

---

[57] *The Times*, February 4th, 1852.
[58] Ibid, emphasis added.
[59] *The Times*, February 6th, 1852.

> We are bound to tell the truth as we find it, without fear of consequences – to lend no convenient shelter to acts of injustice and oppression, but to consign them at once to the judgment of the world … Of all journals, and of all writers, those will obtain the largest measure of public support who have told the truth most constantly and most fearlessly.[60]

It concluded:

> … our duty is to point out danger, however remote, whether it consist in the uncertain policy of a neighbouring State, or in our own disarmed condition; and a far heavier weight of responsibility than we now bear might be laid to our charge if we had neglected to describe the late occurrences in France in their true colours, or if we had affected to acquiesce, from a shortsighted and mistaken policy, in a revolution which calls for the utmost vigilance on the part of this country and of the rest of Europe.[61]

This is the press asserting its independence as well as its right to criticise: 'the duty of one [the press] is to speak; of the other to be silent. The one expends itself in discussion; the other tends to action.'[62] It is the right to be fearless, to be noisy, but not to be 'responsible' as in diplomatic. Most importantly, the language of 'duty' and 'responsibility' is intended to empower, not constrain: it is not used by the press to fence itself in. On the contrary, it is liberating; it is said defiantly.

To understand this, we need look no further than the work of Hume, Bentham and James Mill. In Hume's time, he says, continental Europe was constantly surprised by the 'extreme' freedom of the British press to say, essentially, 'whatever [it] please[s]' and 'of openly censuring every measure entered into by the king or his ministers.'[63] But that liberty was necessary to ensure the delicate balance between monarchical and republican (Hume's terminology) government was preserved so that neither gained too much power, especially the former. Bentham thought similarly: press freedom 'operates as a check upon the conduct of the ruling few; and, in that character, constitutes a controuling [sic] power, indispensably necessary to the maintenance of good government.'[64] As might be expected, James Mill was of the same view: 'the end which is sought to be obtained, by allowing any thing to be said in censure of the government, is, to ensure the goodness of government.'[65]

The value of this robust, uncensored criticism is in its effects upon the audience. In this way, the press is a means to an end, which is an informed populace, capable of dissenting, or rebelling, when it learns of intolerable government

---

[60] Ibid.

[61] Ibid.

[62] Ibid.

[63] D Hume, *Essays Moral, Political and Literary* (first published 1741) (London, Grant Richards, 1903), 8.

[64] J Bentham, *The Collected Works of Jeremy Bentham: On the Liberty of the Press*, Catherine Pease-Watkin and Philip Schofield, eds, (first published, 1821) (Oxford, OUP, 2012), 12–13.

[65] James Mill, *Essays on Government, Jurisprudence, Liberty of the Press, and Law of Nations* (London, J Innes, 1825), 18.

practices. Thus, Hume argues, any rush for arbitrary power could be averted by the press 'conveying the alarm from one end of the kingdom to other.'[66] For, or at least according to James Mill, 'the discontent of the people is the only means of removing the defects of vicious governments' and press freedom is 'the main instrument of creating discontent.'[67] But it is not only criticism of government that is valuable, says Bentham: the public has 'security' against 'misgovernment' only when its rulers have the 'wisdom' to know how to achieve the end of happiness for the governed and this wisdom 'can never be so near to perfection without, as with, these all-comprehensive means of information, which nothing but the liberty here in question can give.'[68] In this way, the press acts as a conduit between the rulers and ruled by providing information to both.

Accordingly, when Hume, Bentham and James Mill make these observations, they are not making teleological claims about press freedom. Instead, the object of their claims is government and its perfection. In this way, press freedom is the means to that end, and not an end of itself. In short, their claim is that for any person to be ruled in a manner that the people find tolerable requires two conditions to be fulfilled: first, that their liberties should be preserved (so it is that Hume stresses, in the Lockean tradition, the need for a 'watchful *jealousy* over the magistrates, to remove all discretionary powers, and to secure every one's life and fortune by general and inflexible laws');[69] second, that the actions of government are open and contestable. This latter point is achieved not through Parliament alone, but through voter scrutiny of their representatives' actions. 'Nothing [is] so effectual' says Hume 'to this purpose as the liberty of the press.'[70] Or, as James Mill puts it 'that an accurate report of what is done by [politicians] is necessary to be laid before the people, to enable them to judge of his conduct, nobody, we presume, will deny.'[71] This is because, he says, when the evidence is presented, carefully and skilfully, 'there is a moral certainty ... that the greatest number will judge aright.'[72]

But is this not, ultimately, a teleological account of press freedom? That the end it must serve is constitutional (to say 'democratic' would be misleading)? The difficulty with this is that Hume, Bentham and James Mill are speaking of press freedom instrumentally, and only instrumentally. Their central premise about the Lockean social contract is that a tolerable existence through coercive government depends upon the ruled being able to *judge* the actions of the ruler. The term 'judgement' is therefore critical and, of itself, requires two conditions to be fulfilled: (i) that the ruled must have the means of knowing what is done in their name; and (ii) that they will act rationally when they acquire this knowledge. The press

---

[66] Hume, (n 63), 10–11.
[67] James Mill, (n 65), 18.
[68] Bentham, (n 64), 14.
[69] Hume, (n 63), 10.
[70] Ibid, 11.
[71] James Mill, (n 65), 20.
[72] Ibid, 22.

freedom debate of Hume, Bentham and Mill's time is framed around this latter condition – for example, in Bentham's defence he acknowledges the complaint that open criticism of government is 'dangerous' and 'may lead to insurrection, and thus to civil war.'[73] His response is that press freedom is far less dangerous than to allow the same concerns to be expressed through public discussion.[74] In this, he echoes Hume: 'A man reads a book or pamphlet alone and coolly. There is none present from whom he can catch the passion by contagion. He is not hurried away by the force and energy of action.'[75] Consequently, 'the liberty of the press, therefore, however abused, can scarce ever excite popular tumults or rebellion.'[76] More importantly, though, for all three, it is the *product* of reading that is most valuable. Says Hume: 'it is to be hoped that men, being every day more accustomed to the free discussion of public affairs, will improve in their judgment of [their rulers], and be with greater difficulty seduced by every idle rumour and popular clamour.'[77] It is this belief in the educational value of critical political commentary that animates their Miltonian belief in the power of truth over falsehood.[78]

Consequently, what emerges clearly from these accounts is Socrates's call for, as Lord Acton would later put it, the urgency of 'incessant inquiry' into the use of power. Citizens should 'not content themselves with the verdict of authorities, majorities, or custom' for 'authority is often wrong, and has no warrant to silence or to impose conviction.'[79] We see this clearly in James Mill's claim: 'If the people have not the means of knowing the actions of all public functionaries they have no security for the good conduct even of their representatives.'[80] Similarly, Hume saw in government a constant tension between liberty and despotism which meant citizens must always be vigilant.[81] This also explains Bentham's horror that a Spanish editor should be prosecuted for criticising the Madrid police system: 'I am astounded! What? Is it come to this?'[82] It is the power of inquiry that animates their arguments, not the press itself. They would be equally animated – indeed Bentham was[83] – if it was the power to spread this information through public meeting that was threatened. It is in this sense, that reference to the press is shorthand for the liberty to scrutinise government and contest officialdom, that we should see John Wilkes's claim: 'the liberty of the Press is the birthright of a Briton, and is justly esteemed *the firmest bulwark of the liberties of this country*' (emphasis added).

---

[73] Bentham, (n 64), 13.

[74] Ibid.

[75] Hume, (n 63), 11, fn 1.

[76] Ibid.

[77] Ibid.

[78] Hume, (n 63), 11–12, (n 1); James Mill, (n 65), 22–23; Bentham, (n 64), 15.

[79] 'Sir Erskine May's *Democracy in Europe*' (first published, 1878) in *Selected Writings of Lord Acton: Volume 1: Essays in the History of Liberty*, J Rufus Fears (ed), (Indianapolis, Liberty Fund, 1985), 62.

[80] James Mill, (n 65), 24.

[81] See 'Of the Liberty of the Press', 'Of the First Principles of Government', 'Of the Origin of Government' and 'Of the Independency of Parliament' in *Essays Moral, Political and Literary*, (n 63).

[82] Bentham, (n 64), 7.

[83] Ibid, 23–51.

Yet we must see these claims in their historical and political context. The period 1789 to 1850 was a time of intense social, political and economic change, in the UK, US and across Europe. Revolutions in the US and France radically altered the political landscape and created widespread fears of social unrest. Liberalism was brought to bear in France and wider Europe through the successful military campaigns of Napoleon. In the UK, industrial revolution changed both the physical and social landscape, creating both bourgeois and proletariat. This was pivotal to the later political ideology of the nineteenth and twentieth century. As Eric Hobsbawn notes,[84] these changes, combined, created three distinct political positions: moderate liberalism, favoured by the upper-middle and liberal upper classes, which advocated rule by a constitutional monarchy and property-qualified parliamentary system (ie, an oligarchy); radical liberalism, favoured by the intellectuals, lower-middle classes and disgruntled gentry, which championed democratic republicanism, welfarism, and antagonism toward the rich; and proto-socialism, favoured by the newly-emerged industrial working class (or working poor), which found expression in the Chartist and anti-Corn Law league movements. This period, then, is characterised not only by the violent changes to the political landscape of the continent, but the deep-rooted 'hysteria', especially in Britain, of insurrection at home ('never in European history, and rarely anywhere else, has revolutionism been so endemic, so general, so likely to spread by spontaneous contagion as well as by deliberate propaganda').[85] Accordingly, the act of extending the franchise was placatory rather than progressive: 'the Reform Act of 1832 corresponds to the July revolution of 1830 in France, and had indeed been powerfully stimulated by the news from Paris.'[86] Whilst it is tempting to think of newspapers as the vehicle for the great radical politics of Bentham and James Mill, the reality is very different. Newspapers, of this period, were not aligned to radical-liberalism, but moderate liberalism and were concerned, most, with the preservation of property rights in a time of great political uncertainty.

This, then, is the age of a proto-democracy, with a limited electorate animated, politically, by a desire to preserve both the sanctity of property and the class-divided society. Bentham and James Mill are *radical* thinkers – they want something like universal suffrage – but it is a qualified radicalism by modern standards. Theirs is a radical liberalism; their defence of an extended franchise, though, is premised upon the shared interest of this wider class in the sanctity of property and its apparent deference to 'betters' in the ways of political thinking.[87] It is the social contract of John Locke, not Jean-Jacques Rousseau, that is their priority. Moreover, we must recognise that a newspaper was a luxury item in this

---

[84] E Hobsbawn, *The Age of Revolution: 1789–1848* (first published, 1962, Abacus Books, 2012), 142–144.

[85] Ibid, 138.

[86] Ibid, 140.

[87] CB Macpherson, *The Life and Times of Liberal Democracy* (Oxford, OUP, 1977), 33; WH Burston, *James Mill on Philosophy and Education* (London, The Athlone Press, 1973).

period – the imposition of tax by the Stamp Act made it so. Admittedly, popular political campaigns – including the Chartist movement and the Anti-Corn Law League – made use of newspapers to champion their cause, but there were only a few at their disposal, of which *The Poor Man's Guardian*, Cobbett's *Twopenny Trash* and *Reynold's Newspaper* are notable. Thus, the most accurate depiction of press activity, at this time, is revealed by seeing it as a happy clique of newspaper reader, propertied electorate, and statesman. In this way, the small readership of the newspaper (*The Times*, of this period, had a circulation of about 30,000)[88] is proportionate to the size of electorate (the Reform Act of 1832 made only minimal changes to the size of voting public – it was not until the Representation of the People Act 1884 that the franchise starts to match the adult population). They were united by their interest in the sanctity of property. Accordingly, newspapers spoke, openly and unapologetically, to the elite. *The Times*, for example – the leading newspaper of the period – was so densely packed with information that the parliamentary section alone might run to 60,000 words.[89] It is unsurprising, then, that, in 1851, a leading Chartist should complain: 'there are many persons in the country who are utterly unable to understand a London paper.'[90]

This sense of intimacy – of a small group of journalists speaking to a small group of voters about the activities of a small group of politicians – is heightened by the technological limitations of the time. We should recall that it was not until after the invention of telegraphy and the establishment of the railway network (both domestically and internationally) that news could travel at speed in any sort of meaningful sense. This did not happen until the mid- to late-nineteenth century.[91] Even when the newspaper network did develop to a scale that extended to the regions, where titles like the *Leeds Mercury*, the *Manchester Guardian* and the *Manchester Times* thrived, the parochialism and narrow focus on the interests of the propertied continued. Here, it was the interests of the middle class – the newly emerged bourgeois businessmen – which dominated, and only sometimes coincided with the interests of the labouring poor, usually against the insularity of London-centric political action and thinking. As Hobsbawm notes, the battle-cry in Manchester was 'what Manchester thinks today London will think tomorrow!'[92]

If we use these historical insights as the lens by which to see press freedom of this age, we can better understand the indignation of *The Times* toward government's criticism of their 'irresponsible' discussion of French politics. 'Our duty is to point out danger, however remote, whether it consist in the uncertain policy of

---

[88] See M Engel, *Tickle the Public* (London, Victor Gollancz, 1996), 21.

[89] See discussion in Engel, *Tickle the Public*, 24.

[90] Quoted in AJ Lee, *The Origins of the Popular Press in England: 1855–1914* (London, Croom Helm Ltd, 1976), 73.

[91] See E Hobsbawm, *The Age of Capital: 1848–1875* (first published 1975) (London, Abacus Books, 2013), 76–78.

[92] Hobsbawm, (n 52), 227.

a neighbouring State, or in our own disarmed condition.'[93] We also see *The Times* proclaim its greater freedom compared to the statesman:

> he cautiously guards from the public eye the information by which his actions and opinions are regulated; he reserves his judgment on passing events till the latest moment, and then he records it in obscure or conventional language …[94]

This article, then, is significant for its introspective qualities. It is a microcosm of what the press thought of itself, and its contribution to society. It is a declaration of self-importance, of lauding its own significance in the proto-democracy of the late eighteenth and early nineteenth century. And yet, although this attitude foreshadows the press freedom theory of today, it is not the same. This is a responsibility-free contribution to democracy. It is a descriptive account that emphasises the societal benefits that freedom, unmolested by state interference, can produce.

The liberal use of the term 'duty' in this article does not contradict this analysis. It is an affectation, typical of the age, that signals only self-imposed obligations and not externally imposable ones. It is that sense of propriety that informs much of the Victorian attitude toward life, in which the sense of responsibility toward others looms large, and finds expression in the Victorian work ethic, the abolition of slavery, the virtue of charity, concern for the poor, religious and sexual propriety ("lie back and think of England"), etc. As MacIntyre observes, in this period the terms 'dutiful' and 'virtuous' became interchangeable.[95] It behoves us, then to recognise the sentiments expressed in *The Times* as a product of this Victorian morality. When they say 'we are *bound* to tell the truth as we find it, without fear of consequences – to lend no convenient shelter to acts of injustice and oppression, but to consign them at once to the judgment of the world',[96] they are not accepting limitations upon their freedom, but demonstrating a sort of high-minded sincerity. It is a sort of shackling, in a sense, but one in which the shackled is always in possession of the key to its escape.

C. The Ideological Period

There are two features of the ideological phase – which I set at 1855 to 1947[97] – that deserve emphasis. The first is sociological: the meeting of a resourceful business-minded press with an increasingly educated buying public. The second is political: the advantages that both sides of the political divide – which at this time was the Conservatives and the Liberals – saw in utilising the press for political gain.

---

[93] (N 61).

[94] Ibid.

[95] A MacIntyre, *After Virtue* (first published 1981; London, Bloomsbury Press, 2017), 271.

[96] (N 59).

[97] But I am not alone in doing so. Stephen Koss also sees this period as distinctive, see S Koss, *The Rise and Fall of the Political Press in Britain* (London, Hamish Hamilton Ltd, 1981), 20–21; Denis McQuail also refers to it as the 'age of ideology', *Media Performance*, (n 1), 7.

Most importantly, it is in this period that we see the emergence of competing ideologies: the progressive and the proprietorial view. This battle pitted the enterprising spirit of the new entrants to the market (spurred on by the abolition of the Stamp Act) against both the nostalgic sentimentality of the established press (which loathed the new style of journalism) and the sanguine statesman who saw the press as pivotal to the democratic reforms they championed.

That politics had a sanguinity (that is alien to modern eyes) was due to several important contemporary social changes, not least amongst these was the increased social awareness, brought about by that burgeoning Victorian ideal of duty and responsibility toward others, which resulted in real political change. Consequently, the Liberal party – that alliance of Whigs, Peelites and Radicals – enjoyed a period of marked success, which saw them in office between the late 1860s and mid-1890s and then again in the early 1900s. This party secured a greater role for the state in enabling social change and welfare reform (a policy that would eventually split the party)[98] – and would later espouse the social liberalism of TH Green, JA Hobson[99] and LT Hobhouse[100] at the beginning of the twentieth century. The press was especially important to this ambition and, in short, the Liberal party believed that, following the Education Act of 1870, and successive changes to the franchise, the press would play a pivotal role in providing much-need political education to the newly enfranchised voter. To realise this ambition, the Liberty party not only established party newspapers with the purpose of improving the new reader's understanding of the political climate, and the party's policies, but also actively developed relationships with journalists to achieve the same result.[101] The Conservatives were not oblivious to these changes, but they were slow to replicate them, and when they did, it was to further their own reactionary ends. So it was that Sidney Herbert MP would rail against the practice of anonymisation in journalism, in favour of attribution, which, in his view, would make newspapers 'much safer instructors of the public' since the words of an honourable, established journalist could be 'taken for gospel'.[102] Here, then, we see the beginning of that peculiar modern attitude which champions the abandonment of critical thinking in favour of the kind of passive receptivity that easily becomes gullibility.

These social changes also transformed the press industry though, as we shall see, with decidedly mixed results for both the Liberal and Conservative party's political ideals. The abolition of the Stamp Act in 1855 and later changes to advertising laws saw the newspaper industry grow exponentially. But this was not universally welcomed by the press and a certain intellectual snobbery

---

[98] See, eg, A Sykes, *The Rise and Fall of British Liberalism* (London, Longman, 1997).

[99] See J Allett, *New Liberalism: The Political Economy of JA Hobson* (Toronto, University of Toronto Press, 1981).

[100] LT Hobhouse, *Liberalism* (London, Oxford University Press, 1911).

[101] All of this is set out clearly in the important works of Alan J Lee, (n 90), and Stephen Koss, (n 97).

[102] *The Leader*, October 30, 1858.

pervaded whereby 'new journalism' was viewed with unabashed derision. They were 'greengrocers': 'small capitalists of all trades who know nothing of Press traditions',[103] unskilled in either the art of writing or even, often, basic grammar – a concern that brought the Institute of Journalism into existence.[104] Into this ideological melange would come Northcliffe and Rothermere, JL Garvin and JA Spender, Beaverbrook and CP Scott, fighting for supremacy. It was not the newly-emergent avaricious owner that most troubled the established press but the new style of journalist that came with it – the 'hack' who hid behind anonymity to write purely for financial gain: these people were not 'members of the noblest of all professions' nor 'public educators' but 'pleasant knaves ... without the slight-est care for any cause in particular.'[105] The internal view of established journalism was of a calling, not a trade; it was a career by which to further the liberal ideals that the journalist, a man of education, moral fibre, and standing, felt the duty to propagate. Journalism, to the old guard, was 'a liberal profession' which new journalism threatened by its admittance of 'men of obscure birth, imperfect education, blunt feelings and coarse manners.'[106] These insights give us both a greater understanding of journalistic 'responsibility' – which amounted, at the very least, to sincerity in the expression of political views (a duty of integrity) and of the sneering contempt toward both the new journalist and the reader who would enjoy it, for – according to one anonymous critic – 'The superior thinker ... who invariably thinks out and substantiates his opinions for himself' is excluded because 'the righteous need no repentance.'[107] Instead, it is the ill-educated that are to blame because the 'vices' of contemporary journalism – 'gross partisan unfairness, a tendency to misrepresentation, and a general weakness of logic' – only exists because of the market for it: 'In other words, the British press could not platitudinise, dogmatise, shuffle and snuffle in its various styles if there did not exist a British public which liked to have these sorts of thing done for it.'[108] The similarity to present-day criticisms is striking.

It is important to see, in this phase, the great disconnect between progres-sive ideals and grim reality (a disconnect that also remains in our time). Here, as the electorate became not only extended in significant numbers but also greatly intellectually improved, was an opportunity to realise an enlightened social and political state. Yet, despite the political apparatus being in place – that is, a state committed to extending the franchise and improving lives through political intervention, and a willing public educator in, especially, the party-owned press – the experiment failed. Alan Lee reports that this was brought home spectacularly to the Liberal party, on regaining power in 1906, when they made heavy gains in

---

[103] C Bainbridge, *One Hundred Years of Journalism* (London, MacMillan Press, 1984), 34.
[104] See Bainbridge, *One Hundred Years of Journalism*, ibid, 33 66.
[105] Anon, 'The Farce of Journalism', *Progress*, January 1883.
[106] Lee, (n 90), 105.
[107] 'The Farce of Journalism', (n 105).
[108] Ibid.

the provinces despite the ascendency of the conservative press there: 'What was left of the Liberal vision of an educated democracy when a Liberal government was elected with a huge majority by illiterate or politically apathetic voters?'[109] The reasons for this failure are not hard to see. First, politicians and 'old journalism' seem to have over-estimated the popular appetite for a challenging, if intellectually nourishing, diet of high-brow political education. Secondly, the reading public wanted to be entertained, and not only informed, and, consequently, the newspaper contributed greatly to their leisure life, especially sport.[110] Northcliffe succeeded because he had:

> an extraordinarily sympathetic understanding of what the public wanted ... The personal must always come before the general ... Crime, love, health, (especially diet), and clothes – these are what the public want to read about. Every day there must be a new surprise, something to make people talk ...[111]

As Kingsley Martin would later say: 'Man is far less politically minded than Bentham and his friends imagined, and his judgments about public affairs are far less reasonable ... most of us would prefer not to bother our heads much about a Great Society, in which we feel only helpless digits among millions equally helpless.'[112]

Thirdly, and perhaps most importantly, the arrival of a more competitive environment, vying for ever greater shares of the market, introduced an unsolvable, systematic paradox in the press's *telos*, for the desire to lead in political education had to be tempered by or else made compatible with the need to follow public opinion about political matters. This 'absurdity' was well-recognised by the sophisticated press, who saw in this 'the story of the Frenchman who, pointing after a charging mob, intimated to his friend, "I must follow them; I am their leader".'[113] This dilemma was exacerbated by increasing reliance upon advertising revenue to supplement sales revenue and support the costs of production. Curran has called this the 'new licensing system' for, as he says, advertisers pressurised publishers to change content to suit more affluent readers, which dampened down – then extinguished – the radical spirit that had powered the liberalisation of the press.[114] It is unsurprising, then, in an age of shifting cultural interests, dynamic political thinking, financial pressures, and untapped potentiality in the *form* of newspaper content, that the role of political educator should be unachievable.

Nevertheless, the view – both within and outside journalism – that the press has a *telos* remained – but after this point, we must see it as either aspirational or sentimental (that is, a hankering for a rose-tinted past). The ideology that succeeds in this period is the proprietorial view and although that ideology

[109] Lee, (n 90), 186.
[110] See, eg, Lee, (n 90), 196; Bainbridge, (n 103), 34–35.
[111] King, (n 1), 53.
[112] Martin, (n 1), 30.
[113] 'The Farce of Journalism', (n 105).
[114] Curran, *Power Without Responsibility*, (n 24), 33–37.

retains something of the progressive belief in the educative, public watchdog role, it is a much more contingent interest, and usually deployed cynically – ie, when that function aligns with its overriding commercial priorities. Yet, we should not conclude that the Victorians thought new journalism entirely devoid of merit. Cecil King has suggested that the 'hostility' to it was 'simply [because] it was entertaining': 'they believed that the purpose of the printed word was to effect spiritual and mental improvement rather than to relieve the drabness and tedium of life.'[115] This analysis, though, is misleading. It was not that the Victorians thought entertainment wrong: in Herbert Spencer's utilitarian ethics, we see high praise for a well-rounded cultural development that takes in more than simply dry subjects: 'to become a pleasure-yielding person is a social duty.'[116] The problem was the sort of *moral* education that new journalism provided, and its effect on the social liberal project. For Lord Acton, liberty, as the suppression of external forces on internal morality, could only be achieved through the self-discipline of education, knowledge and well-being, and he saw the obstacles as 'not only oppression, political and social, but poverty and ignorance.' According to him, since liberty is 'the condition of duty, the guardian of conscience', the liberty of the press is fundamental to this grand project because the liberty of the press *is* the liberty of conscience and although conscience is individual, it is nevertheless to be refined though training and enlightenment, of a political, spiritual and religious nature.[117] In this way, we better understand the contemporary concern that new journalism *debased* popular morality not by its fascination with the sensational and trivial (because there is always room for entertainment) but by undermining the conviction in compassion toward others. In this way, it was calamitous that new journalism 'tended to foment rather than mollify "jealousies of race, religion, and class"' and gave rise to 'a spectre of demagoguery and jingoism, of mob rule and unreason'[118] (and, of course, these traits characterise the popular press of today). For the liberal ideal, of course, it was this last effect that was most awful.

Despite this, the progressive ideology concerning press freedom remained remarkably resilient throughout the period of 1855 to 1947, buoyed on, no doubt, by the political successes that the Liberals enjoyed, and, in a sense, became re-energised by the fact of the international conflict that characterises this period. We see this, for example, in the attitude of CP Scott who, according to Hobhouse, was determined that his *Manchester Guardian* should take a clear moral stance on the Boer War, Ireland, and the necessity of both commencing war against Germany in 1914, and in finding a just peace (in 1917) – even if these views were

---

[115] King, (n 1), 51.

[116] H Spencer, *The Principles of Ethics: Volume 1* (first published 1892; Indianapolis, Liberty Fund, 1978), 552.

[117] J Rufus Fears, *Selected Writings of Lord Acton: Volume III: Essays in Religion, Politics, and Morality* (Indianapolis, Liberty Fund, 1988), 490, 491, 493, 499, and 502.

[118] Lee, (n 90), 196, citing a contemporary commentator.

unpopular socially and politically.[119] This commitment is evident in Scott's famous 1921 article, 'The *Manchester Guardian*'s First Hundred Years':

> A newspaper has two sides to it. It is a business, like any other, and has to pay in the material sense in order to live. But it is much more than a business; it is an institution; it reflects and influences the life of a whole community; it may affect even wider destinies. It is, in its way, an instrument of government. It plays on the minds and consciences of men. It may educate, stimulate, assist, or it may do the opposite ... It may make profit or power its first object, or it may conceive itself as fulfilling a higher and more exacting function.[120]

Indeed, Scott exemplifies the pioneering spirit of liberals in the later part of this period, who sought to unite the commercial realities reflected in the proprietorial view with the civic-mindedness of the progressive view, albeit with a greater emphasis on the latter. We see this in his description of the character of newspapers: 'fundamentally, it implies honesty, cleanness, courage, fairness, a sense of duty to the reader and the community ... One of the virtues, perhaps almost the chief virtue, of a newspaper is its independence. Whatever its position or character, at least it should have a soul of its own.'[121] Clearly, for Scott, journalism remained a calling in which the journalist should be committed to a political position and the newspaper should be the vehicle for political education and social progress. He would, in 1928, say so explicitly: 'a free and independent press ... [is] an indispensable instrument of popular education and of popular government.'[122]

Likewise, Wickham Steed, the celebrated journalist, saw the importance of a newspaper that stood up to public opinion, especially in the climate of appeasement toward Germany in 1930s Fleet Street. In his 1938 book, *The Press*, he wrote – in a passage strikingly reminiscent of that 1852 *Times* article – that:

> my ideal newspaper ... [would] never ... fall into the grievous error of thinking the avoidance of conflict the same thing as peace ... [It] would seek to link the nations not only against war but in defence of individual freedom and of human right ...; just as, in matters national and social, it would work to harness all classes of citizens to the task of constructive improvements in the edifice of society.[123]

Thus, despite saying his perfect newspaper would be 'liberal, not Liberal', we see the virtue of civic-mindedness preserved in the ideal.

This sentiment is given even greater emphasis by Wilson Harris, then editor of *The Spectator*, who wrote in 1943: 'the newspapers may properly be described as

---

[119] LT Hobhouse, 'Liberal and Humanist' in *CP Scott 1846–1932: The Making of the "Manchester Guardian"* (London, Frederick Muller Ltd, 1946).

[120] Ibid, 161.

[121] Ibid.

[122] CP Scott, 'An Independent Press', *Manchester Guardian*, April 5th, 1928, reproduced in *CP Scott 1846–1932*, ibid.

[123] W Steed, *The Press* (1938), 244–8, quoted in A Smith (ed), *The British Press Since the War* (Newton Abbott, David & Charles, 1974), 29.

the eyes and ears of every man and woman in the land' – 'it is on newspapers that they depend for knowledge of the whole of contemporary life.'[124] Consequently:

> a good Press is as essential to a country's well-being as a good government, and the one is often the best security for the other; for a people adequately and honestly instructed on political issues by papers which ... refuse to distort facts for party ends will vote intelligently for the men and measures that the public interest demands.[125]

To his mind, it was accurate to say 'there can be no newspaper proprietor or editor who would admit that he aimed at anything but the dissemination of truth'[126] although whether he would place the stress in the same place we might is a different matter.

D. The Critical Period

That the notion of both a press *telos* and 'duty' should survive the ideological period to modern times is remarkable, but not entirely unsurprising given the state of world politics in 1947. In the UK, the need to usher in a new era of government transparency was both a political expedient to differentiate peacetime from the necessary secrecy surrounding wartime political activity[127] and a political necessity as Clement Attlee's socialists sought to rebuild the country as quickly as possible. But we must return to the dilemma that Scott identifies – between the newspaper as business and as a calling. His fusion of the two, whilst successful (then) for *The Guardian*, was not universally embraced by the sector. In the 1940s, the tension between the progressive and the proprietorial view of press freedom became a political issue, as both the public and politicians feared press might abandon its interest in the noble calling and focus instead solely on profit-making. In 1946, in the House of Commons, Michael Foot MP decried the 'serious decline' in the quality of press speech over the past 30 years (is it coincidence that this time frame marks the end of the Liberal party paper?).[128] This debate led to the appointment of the Royal Commission of the Press. This act heralded a new phase in press freedom thinking, in which government scrutiny of the press industry became the norm. It is in this period that the teleological conception as an analytical device became entrenched.

In the UK, we see this in the background to – and findings of – the Royal Commission of the Press, which was established at the National Union of Journalists' urging, which feared that avaricious press ownership threatened both freedom of opinion and the accurate reporting of news. The Commission's report

---

[124] W Harris, *The Daily Press* (Cambridge, Cambridge University Press, 1943), 1.
[125] Ibid, 2.
[126] Ibid, 13.
[127] See, eg, F Williams, *Press, Parliament and People* (London, William Heinemann Ltd, 1946).
[128] HP Levy, *The Press Council* (London, Macmillan, 1967), 4.

called the press 'the chief agency for instructing the public on the main issues of the day.'[129] It found that 'democratic society ... needs a clear and truthful account of events', and, more significantly, that 'the *responsibility* for fulfilling these needs unavoidably rests in large measure upon the Press, that is on the newspapers and the periodicals, which are the main source from which information, discussion, and advocacy reach the public' (emphasis added) and that despite the then recent addition of radio, the press remained in a 'central position.'[130]

Yet, as remarkable as it was for the state to impose, unilaterally, public functions on private entities, or what Habermas would later call the 'mandate' to serve the public, the press did not disagree. Cecil King, chairman of Daily Mirror Newspapers, in 1967, maintained 'it is the duty of a newspaper first of all to explain fairly and adequately what a Government is trying to do' and 'their duty to oppose and criticize when they feel the evidence shows that the Government is behaving in a foolish, weak or inadequate manner.'[131] *The Times*, of 3 May 1966, declared 'newspapers serve society ... the prime purpose ... is to give the news' written with a 'sense of responsibility.'[132] Certainly, (Sir) Harold Evans, at the *Sunday Times*, had a keen sense of this duty.[133] Indeed, even *The Sun*, in its first leader, of 15 June 1964, claimed to be 'an independent paper designed to serve and inform';

> a newspaper with a social conscience ... [that] will set itself the highest journalistic standards. If inadvertently, though in good faith, we ever fall below the objectives of truth and accuracy we have set ourselves the facts will be corrected with frankness and without delay. We want to hear our readers saying, "You can believe it because it is in the Sun."[134]

There is no dissent here from the political view.

Whether the press, let alone the public, believed it must perform these obligations is a different matter. Privately, they may well have agreed with the contemporary view: 'If you are a millionaire, chief owner of a chain of newspapers ... you mean, by the freedom of the press, your right to do what you like with your own property.'[135] Nevertheless, the progressive ideology had passed into a new phase, in which the public value of press freedom had changed status from benefit to burden: from a charitable act to serve the public, to an onerous obligation. We see in Francis Williams's comment the weight of this expectation: 'the freedom of the press does not exist in order that newspaper owners should grow rich.'[136] According to him, the fight to achieve press freedom carried with it an eternal obligation on not only owners and editors to the public, but also – and most

---

[129] Royal Commission on the Press, 1947–49, *Report* (Cmnd. 7700), Ch XI, [361]–[363].
[130] Ibid.
[131] King, (n 1), 93.
[132] *The Times*, 3 May 1966.
[133] See H Evans, *Good Times, Bad Times* 3rd edn (London, Phoenix, 1994).
[134] *The Sun*, 15 June 1964.
[135] Martin, (n 1), 20.
[136] F Williams, *Dangerous Estate* (Cambridge, Patrick Stevens Ltd, 1957), 251.

importantly – journalists themselves. 'The press is as much a custodian of national freedom and the qualities of civilisation as Parliament or the courts', he said:

> Those who control or write for newspapers have no more right to claim immunity from the historical responsibilities of their office on the excuse that these responsibilities come between them and commercial advantage than have Members of Parliament or judges: the positions of all three in our society are analogous, just as the independence of the press was won in the same struggle as that for a free Parliament and an independent judiciary.[137]

The ultimate safeguard, though, against the owner exploiting this power, by 'misusing' his paper's influence for his own, is, according to Williams, the journalist: 'He is the legatee of a great tradition. He cannot abdicate. He has loyalties greater than his pay packet and they should be paramount.'[138] All very noble, all very salutary. But, by 1957, the journalist's heritage was distinctly binary – a tradition as much of new journalism as of old. Indeed, by then, the old journalism – the newspaper of the romantic age – was long dead, as was the Party paper. Newspaper content was not only much more accessible but also much more diverse.

Yet, despite the distance between the lived experience, in which the proprietorial view reigned, and the political ideal, in which the progressive view doggedly resisted commercial realities, the Royal Commission's conclusions coincided with those reached by the (self-styled) Commission into the Freedom of the Press (otherwise known as the Hutchins Commission), which published its report in 1947. As with the Royal Commission, this inquiry, commissioned by Henry Luce, publisher of *Time* and *Life*, was prompted by both public and political disquiet over the increasingly concentrated ownership of the press. Like Britain, the US had had a similar experience: during the romantic phase, newspapers had been owned or else financed largely by political candidates and their parties, and they had also witnessed the explosion in 'yellow journalism' at roughly the same time (the 1830s) and then a general shrinkage in both titles and owners after the Great Depression.[139] The Hutchins Commission was tasked with identifying the purpose of the press (including, importantly, radio, television, and cinema) in a modern democracy – and its findings led to an impressive and voluminous body of work,[140]

---

[137] Ibid, 251–252.

[138] Ibid, 269.

[139] See, eg, discussion in J Lichtenberg, 'Foundations and limits of freedom of the press' in J Lichtenberg (ed), *Democracy and the Mass Media* (Cambridge, Cambridge University Press, 1990), 124.

[140] The Commission on Freedom of the Press, *A Free and Responsible Press* (Chicago, University of Chicago Press, 1947); WE Hocking, *Freedom of the Press: A Framework of Principle* (Chicago, University of Chicago Press, 1947); Z Chafee Jr, *Government and Mass Communications*, Vols I-II, (Chicago, University of Chicago Press, 1947); L White and RD Leigh, *Peoples Speaking to Peoples* (Chicago, University of Chicago Press, 1946); RA Inglis, *Freedom of the Movies* (Chicago, University of Chicago Press, 1947) and Llewellyn White, *The American Radio* (Chicago, University of Chicago Press, 1947). Although this work appears to have lost currency for lawyers it has retained it for communication studies scholars, eg, McQuail, *Media Performance*, (n 1); JC. Merrill, *The Dialectic in Journalism: Toward a Responsible Use of Press Freedom* (Louisiana State University Press, 1989); CJ Bertrand, *Media Ethics and Accountability Systems* (Somerset, Transaction Publishers, 2000).

of which William Ernest Hocking's *Freedom of the Press: A Framework of Principle* and Zechariah Chafee Jr's two volumes of *Government and Mass Communication* are exemplary.

Its chief concern was with the impoverishment of the press's commitment to aid public participation in democratic decision-making:

> Our society needs an accurate, truthful account of the day's events. We need to know what goes on in our own locality, region, and nation … We need a market place for the exchange of comment and criticism regarding public affairs. We need to reproduce on a gigantic scale the open argument which characterized the village gathering two centuries ago … We need to clarify the aims and ideals of our community and every other … These needs are not being met. The news is twisted by the emphasis on firstness, on the novel and the sensational; by the personal interests of owners; and by pressure groups.[141]

Hocking attributed these failings to the insidious influence of paid publicity and the appeal to audience predilections, which had undermined the capacity to act as an impartial umpire of important events.[142] Consequently, the Commission concluded, the impaired quality of press speech failed society:

> Too much of the regular output of the press consists of a miscellaneous succession of stories and images which have no relation to the typical lives of real people anywhere. Too often the result is meaningless, flatness, distortion, and the perpetuation of misunderstanding among widely scattered groups whose only contact is through these media.[143]

The responsibility to meet society's needs, Hocking argued, arose because 'the fullness and unbent integrity of the news' is 'a profound social concern':

> With the rights of editors and publishers to express themselves there must be associated a right of the public to be served with a substantial and honest basis of fact for its judgments of public affairs … Inseparable from the right of the press to be free has been the right of the people to have a free press. But the public interest has advanced beyond that point; it is now the right of the people to have *an adequate press*.[144]

This intertwining of private and public rights provides the public with a right 'to demand … that the editor's selection be made in the interest of the … people and not solely [based on] personal crotchet, the protection of a pet cause, or even editorial policy.'[145]

---

[141] Commission on Freedom of the Press, (n 140), 67–68.

[142] Hocking, (n 140), 40–46

[143] The Commission on Freedom of the Press, (n 140), 68.

[144] Hocking, (n 140), 168–169 (emphasis in original).

[145] Ibid, 157. Hocking also claims there is a legal right according to the positive law, 170–174. This sort of claim has been reiterated in, for example, Lichtenberg, *Democracy and the Mass Media*, (n 1), and most recently by Kenyon, (n 44). Cf, JC Nerone (ed), *Last Rights: Revisiting Four Theories of the Press* (University of Illinois Press, 1995) which questions whether the Commission's and Hocking's work is too ambiguous to establish this as anything other than a moral right, 93–100.

These views inspired the next generation of press freedom thinkers, including Carl Becker,[146] Fred Siebert,[147] Theodore Peterson,[148] Edward Gerald,[149] and William L Rivers and Wilbur Schramm,[150] who were also convinced, more or less, of its central thesis that, using Peterson's phrase, the press as an institution had a 'social responsibility' to its readers which, in broad terms, was to 'turn out the highest-quality product it can'[151] to 'serve ... society by gathering, writing, and distributing the news of the day'[152] and to service the democratic needs of the populace.[153]

IV. Conclusion

The view of press freedom in political philosophy has transmogrified from a means to an end. Prior to 1855, it formed part – an important part – of the fledgling theory of democracy then taking shape, in which, first, unencumbered reporting of government action ensured the voting public had a means of monitoring its representatives in Parliament and, secondly, critical commentary provided an outlet by which both electorate and elected could reflect upon the prudence of those actions. As Hobsbawm says, it was 'a vehicle of instruction, invective, and political pressure.'[154] But, although this period foreshadowed the teleological view of press freedom, commentators did not think of press freedom in teleological terms. Since their focus concerned ideal forms of both government and electorate, their treatment of the press was not analytical but descriptive. Indeed, they made no demands of the press, for it was never the object of their inquiries. The press was only incidental to what were their chief targets of their agenda: the ideal government and the ideal electorate. Accordingly, the realisation of an optimally-informed electorate depended upon a more open government that allowed the press to report its proceedings freely. Likewise, it depended upon voters (ie, the propertied classes) actively engaging with the reports that the press prepared and acting on the intelligence they received.

It was not until the ideological phase that the notion of a teleological press emerged but, crucially, the onus was placed on the party-owned press to serve

---

[146] CL Becker, *Freedom and Responsibility in the American Way of Life*, (New York, Vintage Books, 1955).

[147] FS Siebert, 'The Libertarian Theory' in Siebert, Peterson and Schramm, *Four Theories of the Press*, (n 2).

[148] T Peterson, 'The Social Responsibility Theory' in Siebert, Peterson and Schramm, *Four Theories of the Press*, ibid.

[149] Gerald, (n 46).

[150] WL Rivers and W Schramm, *Responsibility in Mass Communication* (New York, Harper & Row, 1969).

[151] Rivers and Schramm, ibid, 238.

[152] Gerald, (n 46), 3.

[153] Peterson, (n 148), 74.

[154] Hobsbawm, (n 52), 226.

this function: to educate the newly enfranchised masses in the ways of political participation. Although in the later period of this phase, we see enterprising, civic-minded owners and editors assume this responsibility after the death of the party-owned press, it is not until the critical phase that this teleological understanding took root, as politicians and commentators insisted that these obligations must be met by the recalcitrant press. No one can deny the fact of a public 'want' that the press act as a conduit between electorate and elected, nor of a 'want' for public education. What seems to have gone unnoticed, in our own time, though, is that 'want' has become 'need' and 'need' has become 'right' without any accompanying critical analysis to demonstrate how this strange transformation is justified. Moreover, contemporary commentators forget, or otherwise conveniently ignore, the fact that the progenitor of this entitlement is not the commercial press but the party-backed press. For, regardless of the obligations that the commercial press chose to place upon itself, it was only the party-owned press for whom obligations to educate and inform could be externally-imposed by politicians and the wider public with some justification.

This selective, self-serving treatment of the traditional view is characteristic of modern scholarship on the subject. Snippets of principle are deployed without contextualisation: be that, Carlyle's 'fourth estate', Scott's neat distinction that 'comment is free, facts are sacred' or Kipling's caustic criticism that newspapers exercise 'power without responsibility – the prerogative of the harlot throughout the ages.' What should be asked, though, of the traditional view is: when we claim to observe it, *which* press tradition are we talking about? Is it the tradition of the propertied seeking security for their social contract bargain? (As exemplified in the romantic age). The tradition of the Liberals utilising the press to instruct the newly enfranchised voter in politics? (The ideological age). Or the tradition of inverting press freedom – from a benefit to a burden – by which to use press freedom as a political tool to constrain ownership and criticise quality? (The critical age).

Curiously, it is the second and third that modern commentators cling to, even though it is only the first tradition that was successful – and then only relatively. Nevertheless, this idea, in the romantic age, of the press as a necessary feature of working democracy, is not immutable. We do not find it in ancient Rome or Athens, nor is it apparent at other constitutional moments, such as the time of the Magna Carta. Accordingly, we can say that the idea of the press as fundamental to democracy is not only a modern idea but also an aspirational one at that. For, although this idea informs the burdensome treatment of press freedom in the second and, certainly, the third phase, its historical pedigree is a matter of pure invention. The only version of the press that has ever been susceptible to the imposition of externally-determined societal obligations was the party-press, and that died out in the early twentieth century. And yet the emptiness of the teleological conception is hardly recognised. The notion of a *public* duty imposed upon *private* entities as well as a *telos* that both *defines* and *confines* our understanding of press freedom is treated as axiomatic but, when scrutinised, no longer justifiable, certainly not in its original terms. Nevertheless, it is this second and third phase which animates the academic notion of press freedom in both the legal and political commentary.

The meaning that we attach to press freedom is important. If it is teleological and does impose duties and responsibilities upon the press, then, politically and legally, these obligations are the proper object of regulation. There can be no ideological objection to oversight which monitors realisation of that end. But, despite the commonality in viewpoint upon meaning, it is the means of securing the ends of press freedom that has most deeply divided the academic and political community. As we shall see, in the following chapter, the conceptual clarity inherent in the teleological view has generated tremendous friction in realising its goals for if, as the teleological view supposes, press freedom *is* vital to democratic participation, then any superintendence of quality, even if well-intentioned, risks damaging the delicate eco-system in which the audience and press interests interact to secure those goals. Consequently, the teleological view creates a paradox: the ends of press freedom cannot be guaranteed without jeopardising those ends.

2

Division in Press Regulatory Theory

I. Introduction

Press regulation is common across Europe, but not universal. France, for example, does not have a regulator. Instead, the National Union of Journalists (Syndicat National Des Journalistes) provides a 'charter' of professional ethics which, it claims, is 'binding' (engagent) on all journalists. This charter defines the essential qualities of journalism – 'the pillars of journalistic action' – as 'critical thinking, veracity, accuracy, integrity, fairness, impartiality' (l'esprit critique, la véracité, l'exactitude, l'intégrité, l'équité, l'impartialité). The French approach mirrors that of the US, where the Canons of Journalism of the American Society of Newspaper Editors similarly states that journalists must be responsible, independent, sincere, truthful, accurate, and impartial. Yet neither France nor the US has any system in place to enforce these so-called 'obligations'. This, though, is a problem even in those countries that *have* regulators, like the UK and mainland Europe. Whilst these regulators employ the language of the teleological conception to describe the press's 'obligations' to society at large, they lack the necessary enforcement mechanisms that would make compliance with the code 'obligatory' in the conventional sense of that word.

When we examine the literature in this area, we see the reason for this conflict in regulatory objectives. It reflects the deep schism at the level of theory and policy concerning realisation of the teleological ideology, as section III will show. Social responsibility ('SR') theorists, who are, politically, left-leaning, argue that state intervention is not only legitimate but also necessary to secure the teleological goals of press freedom. Libertarians, who are, politically, right-leaning, disagree. They argue that the market is the only means of securing these goals. Nevertheless, in an important sense, the existence of this deep-rooted conflict is perplexing: if the basis of press freedom is teleological then why is there not universal agreement that regulation to secure these ends is legitimate? Perhaps most perplexing of all, why are SR theorists not insistent on this point? Why are they, instead, so chary? The answer, as section III will also show, is that the insistence on teleology works *against* meaningful reform, not *for* it. Because press freedom is treated as indispensable to democratic self-governance both the state and the market are necessarily constrained in their actions to ensure reformatory measures succeed. Consequently, the insistence upon the teleological conception of press freedom has created obstacles that prove fatal to the realisation of effective, meaningful press reform. Thus, the teleological imperative is self-defeating. Certainly, coercive regulation is prohibited, according to this schema. And yet, rhetorically at least, Lord Justice Leveson, in his report on press culture and ethics,[1] was in favour of coercive independent press regulation: it is no exaggeration to say that he saw it as the only meaningful solution to the recurrent problem of press malfeasance. Nevertheless, even he succumbed to the libertarian neurosis, and the SRT malaise, that mandatory regulation might jeopardise the teleological ends of press freedom. In this way, he foreshadowed David Cameron's enigmatic evasion that such a scheme would 'cross the Rubicon',[2] which, in Cameron's hands, signified something unconstitutional.

These concerns become understandable (although not entirely justifiable) when we consider some of the more radical schemes that SRT promotes to secure press freedom's teleological ends. I discuss two of these in section IV, relating to plurality and impartiality. My aim is to illustrate some of the theoretical and practical difficulties with these schemes and, in doing so, anticipate the argument, made later in the book (especially Part 2), as to why these schemes are unjustifiable according to normative legal theory. In this way, I signal something of the departure from SRT that this book represents.

II. Press Regulation in Practice

A. The Divergence in Regulatory Design

Despite its common use in everyday language, the meaning of the term 'regulation', in its formal sense, is contested.[3] It can be understood in broad terms to refer to any circumstances in which a body directs the actions or behaviours of a group, as where governments employ policies to influence citizen behaviours to achieve certain social or economic outcomes. For example, the heavy tax levy on cigarettes and alcohol is a form of regulation intended to defray the public health costs of treating associated illness and disease, and to discourage consumption on paternalistic grounds. Yet, the more conventional meaning of the term refers to those circumstances where a body is established with the power to govern the actions of a specific industry to achieve specific outcomes (usually, social or economic),

---

[1] Lord Justice Leveson, *An Inquiry into the Culture, Practices and Ethics of the Press: Report*, HC 780, November 2012. For a general discussion of the Leveson inquiry, its findings, and its aftermath, see the Journal of Media Law Special Issue: 'Media Law After Leveson' (2013) 5(2) *Journal of Media Law* 167–296; P Wragg, 'Time to end the tyranny: Leveson and the failure of the fourth estate' (2013) 18(1) *Communications Law* 11; P Wragg, 'Leveson's Vision for Press Reform: One Year On' (2014) 19(1) *Communications Law* 6.

[2] HC Deb, vol 554, col 449 (29 November 2012).

[3] See discussion in AI Ogus, *Regulation* (Oxford, Oxford University Press, 1994), ch 1; R Baldwin, M Cave, and M Lodge, *Understanding Regulation* 2nd edn (Oxford, Oxford University Press, 2012), ch 1.

by means of a system of measures, which may be detrimental (such as taxes or fines) or beneficial (such as subsidies). These directions are usually injunctive but, as Baldwin, Cave, and Lodge discuss, can also be facilitative or enabling.[4] Typically, the regulating body is capable of reprimanding non-compliance. It may be a government agency, such as the Health and Safety Executive or Ofsted, or a body that is independent from government, but nevertheless approved by it, such as Ofcom. An alternative to this sort of state-run or state-backed model is self-regulation. This form operates across a range of industries, including, the professions and sports. Usually, the body constituting the regulator is comprised of members from that field, and operates a code of conduct of the board's devising, albeit the nature of those standards might be directed by an underlying statute. For example, section 28, Legal Services Act 2007, requires the approved regulator to deliver the regulatory objectives set out in section 1 of that Act.

When we look to the regulatory arrangements that exist for the press in the UK and across Europe,[5] we see the ascendancy of the self-regulatory model, albeit, it must be said, in diluted form. Although each regulator operates a code of conduct that newspapers are expected to adhere to, with one notable exception (Denmark), compliance is *voluntary*, and often, as with the UK, so too is membership. Ireland operates a slightly different sort of scheme whereby members are said to be 'incentivised' to join and cooperate (we shall examine this arrangement shortly). Interestingly, as we shall see, especially in Chapter 9, it is a feature of the press reform debate, certainly in the UK, that the term 'self-regulation' is taken to signify voluntary compliance, as if 'self-regulation' and 'voluntary' are interchangeable terms. Similarly, the terms 'mandatory regulation' and 'statutory regulation' are taken to be opposites, as well as also interchangeable. This is strikingly idiosyncratic; this assumption is not prevalent in other industries: the professions, in the UK, at least, operate on a self-regulatory basis, but there is no palpable sense that doctors, lawyers, accountants, etc, treat professional conduct rules as optional.

Oversight is achieved by the regulatory hearing complaints concerning alleged breaches of the code, or by investigating alleged breaches of its own volition, and delivering edicts, in meritorious cases, on the action required to resolve the dispute. One of the starkest areas of divergence, in press regulatory practices across the UK and Europe, concerns the regulatory objectives that the code provisions serve. As noted in the Preface to this book, one of the more maddening aspects of the Leveson report was the marked failure to clearly discern the different interest groups affected by press malfeasance. Seen through the lens of these divergent concerns, the various regulatory provisions that exist across jurisdictions can be divided into three. The first correlates to society's (including the reader's) interests in a duty-bound press, ie, one that must serve the public. Thus, these provisions speak to a duty to produce information and ideas that have value in the democratic

---

[4] Baldwin, Cave, and Lodge, ibid, 3.
[5] As noted in the Preface, the following European countries will be examined: Austria, Belgium, Finland, Germany, Ireland, the Netherlands, Norway, Sweden, and Switzerland.

process, either because of their educational value, as a means of providing a better understanding of politics, or for their contribution to democratic participation, as a means of providing a check on political power, or for their contribution to the moral, social, and economic wellbeing of society, by providing a check on all other forms of power, particularly corporate power. Although statements of this sort are typically found in the preamble to the regulatory codes, they often manifest in a general 'obligation' to provide accurate information (as opposed to a personal right not to be subjected to defamatory statements). For example, the Raad voor de Journalistiek's code (Belgium) says 'a journalist must report information accurately. This comes from the public's right to know the truth.'[6] The Pressenævnets's code (Denmark) says: 'Breach of sound press ethics also includes the withholding of rightful publication of information of essential importance to the public.'[7] The Presserat's code (Germany) says: 'Respect for the truth, preservation of human dignity and *accurate informing of the public* are the overriding principles of the Press' (emphasis added).[8] The Allmänhetens Pressombudsman's code (Sweden) says: 'The role played by the mass media in society and the trust of the public of these media call for accurate and objective news reporting.'[9] These clearly speak to the sort of teleological view we saw in Chapter 1.[10] The other two categories are non-teleological and speak to the harm-principle of the liberal tradition. The second relates to personal rights, typically, but not exclusively, relating to the impact of both newsgathering and reporting on reputation and private life.[11] These provisions reflect victim's interests in an accountable press. The third relates to readers' interests, and so speaks to perceived harms to readers, such as restrictions on suicide reporting to avoid emulation and restrictions on financial reporting to avoid consumers sustaining losses from bad advice.[12]

The divergence in regulatory objectives manifests in the balance within regulatory codes between these categories and the logistics of who can complain. Interestingly, the Scandinavian codes are geared toward victim and reader rights rather than societal rights. Despite high-minded statements in the preamble to the contrary, the Danish code has no provisions of a purely teleological nature. Similarly, the UK and Irish codes have very little that could be categorised as a societal right, beyond the general requirement that newspapers provide accurate information (albeit there is a strange statement in the Irish code that '*readers* are entitled to have news and comment presented with respect for the privacy and sensibilities of individuals' (emphasis added)). The restrictions that most

---

[6] Raad voor de Journalistiek. December 2016. Code of Practice.

[7] Pressenævnet. May 2013. The Press Ethical Rules.

[8] Deutscher Presserat. March 2017. German Press Code – Guidelines for journalistic work as recommended by the German Press Council.

[9] Pressens Opinionsnämnd. June 2018. Code of Ethics for Press, Radio and Television in Sweden.

[10] These are discussed further in ch 6.

[11] See discussion in ch 7.

[12] See discussion in ch 8.

European countries place on who can complain adds to this marginalising effect. Usually, it is only those personally affected by breaches of press standards that can complain (Finland, Switzerland, and Germany are exceptional by allowing anyone to complain). Consequently, the capacity to enforce societal rights, such as they are, is severely curtailed, such that what might appear as a category one (society-at-large) right is, in practice, really a category two (victims) or three (readers) right.

Denmark is particularly strict on this. Only those with a 'legal interest' can pursue a complaint. This usually means those who are mentioned by the story (directly or indirectly) although the Pressenævnets has found that, for example, the parent of a child is entitled to complain on the child's behalf.[13] Complainants can be individuals, companies, organisations, associations, and public authorities. Interestingly, complaints can be brought on behalf of the deceased. Ireland, Sweden, and the Netherlands also require complainants to demonstrate that the alleged breach has affected them personally. Norway is similar. Complainants must be either the subject of the story or have 'consent' from that person to bring the complaint.[14] The picture is slightly more complicated in Belgium and Austria although broadly the same. Belgium operates two regulatory schemes: the Flemish press is regulated by the Raad voor de Journalistiek and the French and German press is regulated by the Conseil de Déontologie Journalistique. The former stipulates that complainants must have a 'personal interest' in the complaint whereas the latter is more inclusive: complainants may be personally affected or else simply a concerned reader. Austria operates a dual system which its calls the selbständige Verfahren (the independent procedure) and the Beschwerdeverfahren (the complaints procedure). The former can be initiated by anyone, although it is for the Press Council (Presserat) to decide whether to pursue the complaint or not. If it does, the subject of the complaint is not obliged to print the Press Council's decision (although it may be invited to). Instead, interesting decisions (Interessante Entscheidungen) are published on the Presserat's website. The complaints procedure is available only where the complainant has been personally affected by the respondent's newspaper's activity *and* that newspaper is a regulated member of the Presserat. The complaints procedure is unusual. It takes the form of arbitration and, by submitting to it, both parties forsake the right to bring legal proceedings based upon the dispute (or the Presserat's decision). Consequently, the complainant waives the right to pursue damages through the courts. The merits of this for the complainant are extremely limited: the only positive outcome is a binding obligation on the respondent newspaper to publish the Presserat's decision.[15]

---

[13] Case number 14-70-00671, KEN no 9704 of 23/9/2014.
[14] Norsk Presseforbund. June 2015. Code of Ethics of the Norwegian Press. Slik klager du til PFU (Complaints procedure).
[15] S 15, Verfahrensordnung der Beschwerdesenate des Österreichischen Presserates, (Rules of Procedure for Appeals), 6 March 2018.

B. The Problem of Enforcement

The voluntary nature of regulation, though, is a serious design flaw that afflicts the realisation of regulatory goals across Europe. None of these schemes, not even Denmark's, can be properly called a scheme of coercive independent press regulation, for there is nothing really within these schemes to achieve compliance or otherwise penalise non-compliance in a meaningful sense. Although many schemes claim to provide citizens with 'rights' of reply and the power to order corrections and apologies, few have the formal means by which to achieve these promises. The ultimate sanction that these regulators have at their disposal is to issue an adverse adjudication, usually with the instruction that the offending newspaper publishes it but, with the exception of Denmark, no power to penalise the failure to do so. Thus, these self-regulatory models are linked by an apparent belief that better ethical behaviour can be achieved through public shaming alone, on the basis that 'nobody likes being criticized.'[16] As Leveson realised, this belief has proven to be sadly mistaken: 'while it may be embarrassing for editors to publish adjudications, this sanction is not enough to deter repeat offending.'[17] Neither did he find these critical adjudications 'had a long-term impact on the behaviour and actions of publications or journalists who were found to have transgressed.'[18]

Admittedly, this ineffectiveness is not universally true across Europe. The Finnish press regulator, Julkisen Sanan Neuvosto (Council for Mass Media), is remarkably effective in achieving compliance with its code and its rulings.[19] Editors are compliant, submissive, and reverential. Yet the reason for this seems to be entirely cultural: the Finnish press is genuinely troubled by this sort of public rebuke.[20] This seems to be generally true of the Scandinavian countries. The picture is slightly more mixed in other countries. For example, although there are high levels of compliance in Germany, not all publishers have agreed to abide by the Presserat's code of conduct.[21] As Lara Fielden reported in 2011, one major absentee is the Bauer Media Group.[22] Although non-participation compromises the reach of adverse adjudications, it does not undermine regulation entirely, for the Presserat can publish decisions on its own website.

---

[16] G Robertson, *People Against the Press* (London, Quartet Books Ltd, 1983), 63.
[17] Leveson, (n 1), 1553, [6.43].
[18] Ibid.
[19] W Gore, 'The Only Way is Ethics: Finland's press regulation is outstanding but it just wouldn't fit Britain's complex media', *Independent*, 15 June 2014.
[20] Ibid.
[21] Its website does not specify *which* publishers refused; it just says: 'The majority of German publishing houses are committed to a commitment to comply with the Press Code when reporting in their newspapers, magazines and online media.'
[22] L Fielden, 'Regulating the Press: A Comparative Study of International Press Councils', (Oxford, Reuters Institute for the Study of Journalism, 2012), 42.

Denmark and Ireland have different regulatory arrangements. Fielden terms them 'mandatory' and 'incentivised' systems[23] since the Danish press regulator, the Pressenævnets, has coercive powers to penalise non-compliance whilst the Irish press regulator, which has no such powers, is special nevertheless because the Irish courts can take regulatory non-compliance into account when deciding defamation cases (under section 26, Defamation Act 2009). Consequently, although the Irish system is 'voluntary' – in the same way as the rest of Europe bar Denmark – compliance minimises legal risk and so is not properly merely ethical (in the sense that ethical decision-making is deontological not consequentialist).

But some scrutiny of the labels that Fielden attaches to the Irish and Danish systems is called for. The 'incentive' for Irish publishers to participate in voluntary regulation should not be overstated. It is fairly weak. It impacts only on a narrow area of press operations: not only is it limited to defamation claims, but also to a specific defence in defamation. Thus, it is only when the defendant claims qualified privilege, on the basis that the defamatory statement is a 'fair and reasonable publication on a matter of public interest', that regulatory compliance is relevant. Even then the 'incentive' operates in a limited way: a good track record of compliance with regulatory standards is just one of ten factors that the court can consider when deciding the case. We must see then that although Fielden was optimistic about this 'incentivised' model in her report to Leveson – not least because of the high membership rate amongst Irish publishers – that optimism must be tempered by the reality of the incentive. Moreover, when Fielden was writing, this provision of the Irish Defamation Act was untested in court.[24] No assessment could be made, therefore, as to its actual effect. In fact, since then, its impact has been non-existent. There have been no decisions in which a publication's regulatory track record has influenced the outcome. This is unsurprising. Given that civil law can only compensate the claimant and cannot penalise the defendant, any consideration of the defendant's regulatory compliance, as part of an evaluation of the instant case, can only operate at the margins of judicial reasoning; it cannot be central to the case's resolution: the defendant's general approach to accuracy impacts on whether the report was 'fair and reasonable' in the circumstances only if it speaks to an attitude prevalent in the newsgathering exercise for the report itself.

We see similar difficulties when we scrutinise Denmark's 'mandatory' scheme. Danish newspapers fall under the Pressenævnets's jurisdiction automatically (they must be published twice yearly to count). Its authority is derived from the Media Liability Act 1991 which stipulates that it has the power to determine what counts as good press practice (god presseskik). Section 34 obliges the press to conform to these standards. It also has the power to hear complaints based on those rules, to order newspapers to publish its decisions (or a summary) in a suitable place (section 49), and to order that successful complainants are provided with a 'right

---

[23] Ibid, 10.
[24] Ibid, 92.

to reply' where the publication of inaccurate information causes significant harm (sections 36–40). Yet only the failure to comply with section 49 is punishable by a fine or imprisonment of up to four months. Moreover, the Pressenævnets has no power to order members to compensate complainants. This, then, is mandatory regulation in its thinnest sense. It cannot be said that the Danish press *must* comply with the rules since the only consequence of non-compliance is an obligation to publish a summary of the adverse adjudication. Moreover, it cannot even be said that the Danish press must admit to wrong-doing. Since it can publish the decision without comment, the whole process can be reduced to a sort of bureaucratic undertaking.

Given the distinct possibility of non-compliance with regulatory decision-making, it is not clear why European regulators should persist with this strategy, nor why it should be thought desirable. Even the Danish system – the most coercive of all – only works if there is something terrible about publishing summaries of adverse adjudications, but what would this be? Although high levels of voluntary compliance in Scandinavia suggests the Scandinavia press, at least, believes regulatory reprimands would damage its market position, the British experience does not bear this out. Whilst there is no culture, nor expectation, of UK newspapers publishing adverse adjudications, they have been reasonably prepared to publish corrections, either ad hoc or on a designated page (although not usually prominently) with no apparent ill-effects. But by far the most telling event, of both the British press culture and the attitudes of its readership, has been the aftermath of Leveson's scathing report on press malfeasance. Following the briefest moment of contrition, the British press has been bullish in its stubborn refusal to engage seriously with Leveson's recommendations. Apart from some cosmetic changes to their self-regulatory body (in which IPSO replaced the PCC), and some modest alterations to its governance structure, little of note has changed. As we shall see, in Chapter 9, although this new body claims to have coercive powers to discipline serious and systematic breaches of its code, it has never used them (and, for reasons I outline there, its incentives to do so are extremely weak).

The problem, in Britain, has not been a lack of a European style regulator, for it has had one since at least 1991, when the PCC was established, if not 1953 when its predecessor, the Press Council, was created. The problem has been its inability to compel its members to comply with the code. It was this that rendered it vulnerable to public criticism and ineffective against press malfeasance, at least when it counted. Leveson made this point clearly in his report. The absence of any real powers to either compel membership or to sanction serious breaches of the code meant that the PCC was incapable of causing any real change to the prevalent culture of industry-wide malfeasance: 'Negotiated apologies, published adjudications and letters to proprietors are not in themselves adequate to prevent reoffending.'[25] Owner antipathy to adverse regulatory decisions was apparent in

---

[25] Leveson, (n 1), 1578, [8.9].

the evidence Leveson received: as one participant put it: 'Tabloid editors often talk of the "shame" they feel at a PCC adjudication, but – and I won't pull any punches here – they're lying. They couldn't care less what the PCC thinks …'[26] A press regulator that is simply tolerated by its members submits to its will only because members choose to, not because they have to. This is, and ought to be treated as, an insufficient guarantee of an accountable press.

Interestingly, Leveson himself favoured a coercive scheme (albeit not a mandatory one). His recommendations describe a regulatory body, demonstrably independent of both government and industry control and influence, that has the power to fine its members for serious or systematic breaches of the code. This aspect of his recommendations is contained in the recognition criteria (Schedule 3) contained within the Royal Charter on the Self-Regulation of the Press.[27] This Charter – controversial of itself as an emanation of prerogative power – created the structure for realising Leveson's ambitious scheme (such that there now exists a body corporate called the Press Recognition Panel that has the power to create a regulator meeting its criteria) but has not yet realised its potential (albeit it has recognised IMPRESS as an official press regulator) through, it must be said, the government's failure to implement measures that would have forced the recalcitrant press to become members of an approved scheme. It was these measures, contained within section 40, Crime and Courts Act 2013, which attracted fierce criticism from the international community – the World Association of Newspapers and News Publishers, specifically[28] – and which have subsequently been repealed without ever coming into force.[29] The decision not to make membership of approved schemes mandatory has been the single greatest failure, of not only the government, but also of the Leveson report, itself, which did not entirely agree with, but could not entirely resist, industry complaints that compulsory regulation would be unconstitutional. As Chapter 9 argues, a mandatory scheme is not only legitimate, it is essential.

Nevertheless, we should not lose sight of the reasons why regulation remains important. These reasons are obscured by the teleological view. As the Leveson inquiry demonstrates, press malfeasance, in both newsgathering and expression, causes what Leveson calls 'real harm … to real people.'[30] By this expression, he meant that press abuses affect not simply a small minority, which Paul Dacre charmingly defined as 'the rich, the powerful and the pompous', but, instead, a much larger group, which includes ordinary people – people without the financial resources required to fund litigation, without public relations advisors to handle and spin negative stories, without access to alternative media outlets to

---

[26] https://webarchive.nationalarchives.gov.uk/20140122175653/http://www.levesoninquiry.org.uk/wp-content/uploads/2011/11/Witness-Statement-of-Richard-Peppiatt.pdf.
[27] Sch 3.
[28] WAN-IFRA, *Press Freedom in the United Kingdom*, 15 March 2014.
[29] See discussion in ch 9.
[30] Leveson, (n 1), 50, [2.2].

give voice to alternative narratives, without access to the sort of mental health support that unwanted press attention necessitates. Instead, these are people that the press becomes fascinated with, often briefly, and whose lives are destroyed or irrevocably damaged for reasons of titillation, curiosity, or prurience. These are usually people without public office who have suffered some trauma in their lives that the press finds interesting and wishes to report upon. Recognising the existence of these press victims cannot colour our impression of everyday journalism. But the fact that these victims exist, and apparently in great number, globally, is, of itself, reason enough to seek a satisfactory regulatory solution to the problem.

III. The Ideological Divide Over Press Regulation

The division in regulatory objectives in practice reflects the considerable ideological disagreement at a theoretical level. This disagreement manifests in the distance between the respective camps over the extent to which safeguarding societal rights to a quality press are legitimate regulatory goals as well as the broader question of whether independent coercive press regulation is justifiable.

Those in favour of utilising regulation to further the teleological ends of press freedom belong to the SRT camp (even if they do not readily identify themselves in these terms),[31] which, as we saw briefly in the last chapter, finds its greatest expression in the work of the Hutchins Commission,[32] and which influenced, albeit indirectly, Leveson's view of press freedom as a differential, teleologically justified right.[33] According to the Hutchins Commission, the press is like a private school, which can enjoy 'the advantages and risks of experimental initiative' but remains obliged to perform its 'necessary public function for which a measure of social accountability would be appropriate.'[34] This characterises the prominent view amongst SR theorists: greater press regulation is required to safeguard the teleological ends of press freedom, which are too important to be left solely to the market or the press itself.[35] We see this in the work of commentators like, for example, Owen Fiss, Cass Sunstein, and Onora O'Neill, who argue that without regulatory intervention, public debate is not 'uninhibited, robust, and wide-open';[36] that a 'well-functioning debilitative process increases the likelihood

---

[31] The chief architect of this view is Theodore Peterson, who coined the phrase 'social responsibility theory' in FS Siebert, T Peterson and W Schramm, *Four Theories of the Press* (Chicago, University of Illinois Press, 1956), 73–103.

[32] The Commission on the Freedom of the Press, *A Free and Responsible Press* (Chicago, University of Chicago Press, 1947, 130–131.

[33] Leveson, (n 1), 1848, [2.18]. See discussion in ch 3.

[34] (N 32), 126.

[35] D McQuail, *Media Performance: Mass Communication and the Public Interest* (London, SAGE Publications, 1992), 30.

[36] OM Fiss, 'Why the state?' in J Lichtenberg (ed), *Democracy and the Mass Media* (Cambridge, Cambridge University Press, 1990), 147.

that political outcomes will respond to people's desires and aspirations';[37] and that this requires epistemological standards to be set through the inculcation of a truth-seeking discipline that includes 'careful inquiry' and 'fact-checking'.[38] The 'obligation' to serve this function is, for these commentators, the 'price' of constitutional protection from undue state interference.[39]

Those against this position belong to the libertarian camp (again, even if they do not readily identify themselves in these terms). Admittedly, this narrow taxonomy leaves those who associate with the left-wing but are firmly against the idea of regulation with nowhere to go. Although they would loathe the description, I am sure, I align these commentators with the libertarian camp by reason of their shared, strong opposition to the SRT's overarching aims.

Central to this deep division is the role of government, as the ultimate source of coercive powers, to deploy or otherwise sanction the use of penalties (such as fines or compensation) for non-compliance with the regulatory codes of conduct. Undoubtedly, government derives an advantage from an inhibited press. It is this issue that divides commentators over the use of independent coercive regulation to realise these teleological ends. If the state grants press freedom so that newspapers may serve teleological ends, then, as SR theorists say, some form of regulation to ensure that end occurs seems legitimate, for the right is contingent. But, at the same time, those teleological ends are in the monitoring of power, of which the state is the ultimate source. So, if the state grants the right so that it can be the object of scrutiny, then it cannot also oversee performance without compromising the integrity of that scrutiny. It cannot be both patient and surgeon at the same time. If the state wishes to protect this teleological function, then it is constrained in what it can do. This policy of minimal state interference reflects the libertarian ideal that the realisation of press freedom's teleological aim – to inform and educate – requires 'freedom from government controls or domination.'[40] Libertarians solve this riddle by leaving oversight to the market – and, in doing so, it seems to me, forsake their claim that newspapers must serve a teleological end, for the market's capacity to realise this 'must' is doubtful.

This does not mean that government is prevented from regulating the press at all because, clearly, it must (and does) adjudicate when press freedom conflicts with individual liberties. But it does mean, according to this theory, that the state can play little or no role in securing the *telos* of the press through coercive means. The libertarian view is well-captured by Fred Siebert, who says, even if the state thought intervention necessary to prevent unsound opinions forming, 'it would inevitably tend to suppress that which was critical of the state or which

---

[37] CR Sunstein, *Democracy and the Problem of Free Speech* (New York, Free Press, 1995), 244.

[38] See O O'Neill, *A Question of Trust* (Cambridge, Cambridge University Press, 2002) and 'Ethics for Communication?' (2009) 17(2) *European Journal of Philosophy* 167, 172.

[39] See, eg, Robertson, (n 16), 158; J Barron, *Freedom of the Press for Whom?* (Bloomington, Indiana University Press, 1973), 340.

[40] FS Siebert, 'The Libertarian Theory of the Press' in *Four Theories of the Press*, (n 31), 51.

was contrary to the opinions of government officials.'[41] Or, as Thomas Emerson puts it, 'the fact that the government is by necessity so heavily involved in radio and television, with all the dangers implicit in that situation, makes it important for the balance of the total system of expression that the press remains relatively free of government controls.'[42] Although Lucas Powe Jr was perhaps too alarmist when he said 'Power, when loosened from restraint, destroys more readily than it creates',[43] there is certainly something in his point that deserves consideration. Even if we are convinced that the probity of mature democratic government makes this sort of malignancy implausible, we should have regard to what Frederick Schauer calls the 'argument from government incompetence':[44] that the heavy-handedness of government structures is such that the superintendence of quality is bound to be cumbersome in achieving social goals. It is, as Thomas Scanlon puts it 'notoriously partisan and unreliable.'[45]

Admittedly, it may be that these concerns are exaggerated, and are not the obstacle that libertarians perceive. If we think, with Schauer, that the government is incompetent to make the right regulatory decisions, then this concern must apply across the entire spectrum of government activity, so why do we trust government to regulate the marketplace of goods through coercive regulation but not the marketplace of ideas? The economists Aaron Director and Ronald Coase saw this logical fallacy clearly. The market place of ideas, said Director, is the 'only area where *laissez faire* is still respectable.'[46] Coase – who went further than Director – was more direct: newspaper owners are businessmen just like any other producer of goods: 'the fact that businessmen are mainly influenced by pecuniary consideration is no great discovery. What else would one expect from the money-grubbers of the newspaper world?'[47] Moreover, the prospect that a government-backed regulator would not tolerate criticism of government is significantly reduced by the practical realities of regulation. First, it is not elected representatives that conduct regulation, but civil servants (or a body like them) who can be insulated from political influence. Thus, there is something in what one commentator has noted about the US position (and the same applies to the UK): state regulation of broadcast media has not, in empirical terms, resulted in these fears of intrusive government interference with dissent being realised.[48]

---

[41] Ibid, 51.

[42] TI Emerson, *The System of Freedom of Expression* (New York, Vintage Books, 1970), 688.

[43] LA Powe Jr, *The Fourth Estate and the Constitution* (Berkeley, University of California Press, 1991), 298.

[44] F Schauer, *Free Speech: A Philosophical Inquiry* (Cambridge, Cambridge University Press, 1982), 86.

[45] TM Scanlon, 'Freedom of Expression and Categories of Expression' (1979) 40 *University of Pittsburgh Law Review* 519, 534.

[46] A Director, 'The Parity of the Economic Market Place' (1964) 7 *Journal of Law and Economics* 1, 5.

[47] RH Coase, 'Market for Goods and Market for Ideas' in Coase, *Essays on Economics and Economists* (Chicago, University of Chicago Press, 1994), 70.

[48] GP Magarian, 'Substantive Media Regulation in Three Dimensions' (2008) 76 *George Washington Law Review* 845.

Secondly, in a formal sense, we can easily overcome the problem by denying the regulator the power to suppress or penalise speech critical of government. Indeed, this principle is universally recognised in the codes of conduct that the UK and European regulators operate: public interest expression is protected.[49] Although commentators might say, with Emerson, that regulation, under 'the watchful eye of petty public officials', chills speech,[50] the criticism applies universally, for all industries might say that greater regulation unduly impacts on dynamic decision-making and threatens the efficiency of production and sales. What makes speech different?

Of course, one significant difference is the nature of regulation in other contexts, compared to speech. In the marketplace of goods, the chief advantage of tougher regulation is to ensure that goods are of satisfactory quality on, say, health and safety grounds. It is hard to translate this concern to the press context, for what harm is caused by the low-quality newspaper that the consumer would need protection from through independent oversight? There is no physical harm, for example. Newspapers do not explode, as malfunctioning toasters do. The problem with this sort of paternalistic intervention is the lack of an objective, causally-justified reason lurking behind it. Laws making it mandatory to wear a seat-belt whilst driving are a classic example. As Anthony Ogus says, although superficially paternalistic, there are objective social policy justifications behind these laws, eg, the cost to the tax-payer of attendance by the emergency services and/or NHS medical care resulting from the failure to wear the seat-belt.[51]

Nevertheless, although these arguments provide reason to doubt the libertarian objection, we must recognise the trap that SRT has set for itself. For, in its insistence that the teleological ends of press freedom are a categorical imperative, it has provided libertarianism, inadvertently, with the ammunition with which to attack it. Although SRT does not explicitly acknowledge this failing, the tepid responses it provides suggests some sort of recognition of its impotency. We see this clearly in the Hutchins Commission's own conclusion: that for all their talk of duty and responsibility, and the veiled threat that 'no democracy ... will indefinitely tolerate concentrations of private power ... eventually governmental power will be used to regulate [it]',[52] they are so guarded about government intervention to secure these ends as to virtually discount it as an option, for they concede, timorously: 'we do not believe that the fundamental problems of the press will be solved by more laws or by governmental action.'[53]

We see this disinclination toward a mandatory scheme of coercive independent press regulation in the wider SRT literature. Geoffrey Robertson, writing in the early 1980s, epitomises this disconnect between rhetoric and action.

---

[49] See ch 7.
[50] Emerson, (n 42), 671.
[51] Ogus, (n 3), 51–52.
[52] The Commission on the Freedom of the Press, (n 32), 80.
[53] Ibid.

His uncompromising conclusion that the Press Council was a total failure that had forsaken the rights of the people – that it had 'not adjudicated public complaints speedily or effectively, its principles on cheque-book journalism, privacy and the right to reply have been continually flouted …'[54] – was not matched, in tone or ambition, by his modest plans for solving the problem, for even his ideal regulator 'would remain a voluntary body, dependent upon persuasion rather than law to promote compliance with its codes.'[55] Similarly, O'Malley and Soley, whose book, *Regulating the Press*, provides a full schematic for enhanced press regulation, including the draft legislation to establish it, envisage a regulator without coercive powers because, they say, their use would 'put at risk the future publication of a paper.'[56] Indeed, although James Curran had argued in the fifth edition of *Power without Responsibility*, published in 1997, that 'if publishers will not agree to binding self-regulation …, then these powers will have to be underwritten by statute',[57] the claim was quietly dropped by the seventh edition in 2010.

It is not unusual to find those like Claude-Jean Bertrand who recommend the use of codes of conduct that generate merely 'aspirational' ethical standards, which the press would not be expected to achieve, but should simply aim to achieve.[58] Similarly, Marc Franklin, writing in the early 1960s, thought it meaningful to say that 'one alternative to government activity is reliance upon journalists themselves to use discretion and responsibility in deciding what to print.'[59] In his view, it was not 'idle to hope' that editors would be sufficiently worried by the sense of shame to avoid pejorative terms like labelling someone 'a hunchback' if it was immaterial to the story.[60] Hocking was similarly convinced that this sort of shaming – for the failure to meet ethical standards – was sufficiently powerful to effect meaningful change. In his view, the press is motivated to preserve its reputation 'against the cynicism growing in the public mind toward the reliability of the news.'[61] Sadly, both views look decidedly quaint, for the twenty-first century press shows no such remorse for not only decades of public distrust but also, moreover, the shame, in the strongest sense, arising from the litany of unethical – and illegal – practices that Leveson uncovered in his inquiry. Quite obviously, reliance solely upon self-directed, ethical decision-making is a poor means of improving press standards. Nevertheless, this strategy appeases the fear, in both SRT and libertarianism, that the use of law to realise meaningful reform will

---

[54] Ibid, 6–7.

[55] Ibid, 148.

[56] Ibid, 188.

[57] J Curran and J Seaton, *Power Without Responsibility* 5th edn (London, Routledge, 1997), 369.

[58] See, eg, Claude-Jean Bertrand, *Media Ethics and Accountability Systems* (Somerset, Transaction Publishers, 2000), 46.

[59] MA Franklin, 'A Constitutional Problem in Privacy Protection, Legal Inhibitions on Reporting of Fact' (1963) 16 *Stanford Law Review* 107, 146.

[60] Ibid, 147–8.

[61] WE Hocking, *Freedom of the Press: A Framework of Principle* (Chicago, University of Chicago Press, 1947), 187.

compromise press freedom. This dilemma is neatly captured by Lee Bollinger: 'We are thus ambivalent. We want both a powerful and independent press that is free to check the government, and we also want a responsible press that is subject to government regulation.'[62]

It is this failure within SRT, to overcome the obstacles that the teleological view generates, which leads inexorably to the conclusion that self-regulation is the only pragmatic solution to the problem – not because self-regulation is the most attractive, but because there is no other candidate. It is this problem that has consistently proven to be the stumbling block for the UK Government as well. Its consistent policy, from 1949, when the first Royal Commission on the Press presented its findings, until the present, in Leveson's recommendations, has been nothing more than a sort of abject pleading with the press to improve its standards of its own volition. So it was that the first government inquiry ended with the creation of the Press Council, whose primary function 'should be to safeguard the freedom of the Press; to encourage the growth of the sense of public responsibility and public service amongst all engaged in the profession of journalism …; and to further the efficiency of the profession and the well-being of those who practice in it.'[63] And we find the same sentiments in Leveson's ideal outcome: 'what is required is independent self-regulation. By far the best solution to press standards would be a body, established and organised by the industry, which would provide genuinely independent and effective regulation of its members and would be durable.'[64] It must be said that this sanguinity is not peculiar to either public inquiries (for we see Lord Chief Justice Igor Judge, speaking in 2012, endorse the idea that self-regulation is the 'only' means of ensuring independence from government)[65] nor to the British establishment, for the same quixotic sentiments emerge in the Hutchins Commission's report: 'the Commission hopes that the press itself will recognize its public responsibility and obviate governmental action to enforce it.'[66]

This strategy has proved disastrous, for no incarnation of press regulator has been able to command the gravitas required – as Geoffrey Robertson put it, 'respected, feared and obeyed'[67] – to achieve the regulatory aims set for it. Instead, regulatory intervention is perceived to be, as one irritable journalist put it, a bothersome annoyance;[68] an imposition that works only to the extent that journalists 'waste' their time responding to the nagging tendencies of the regulator's communications.[69] Yet, the optics of self-regulation are poor because a regulator composed of mainly industry figures, even if it is respected internally, lacks the credibility, so far as the outside world is concerned, that it will act independently. Moreover, to be feared,

---

[62] LC Bollinger, *Uninhibited, Robust, and Wide-Open* (Oxford, Oxford University Press, 2010), 62.
[63] Royal Commission on the Press, 1947–49, *Report* (Cmnd. 7700), Ch XI, [683]–[684].
[64] Leveson, (n 1), 1758, [4.1].
[65] Lord Judge, 13th Annual Justice Lecture, 'Press Regulation', 19 October 2011.
[66] Ibid, 91.
[67] See discussion in Robertson, (n 16), 62.
[68] J Delingpole, 'IPSO: a great new way for bullies to muzzle the press' *The Spectator*, 6 June 2015.
[69] Ibid.

it needs to have powers to impose sanctions for breaches, but without chilling speech (for fear of adverse financial penalties) since these threaten the future of the press. And it needs total press approval. Yet it has proven difficult to strategise, let alone effect, an efficient means of obtaining *universal* press acquiescence to greater regulation. Nevertheless, no real change can be expected unless and until this happens. Leveson was acutely sensitive to this point: 'a new system of regulation should not be considered sufficiently effective if it does not cover all significant news publishers.'[70] Compliance, he said 'should not be a matter of choice.'[71] This requires the regulator to have industry credibility without compromising its capacity to inspire change.

This has led to something like quiet desperation in central government, which knows that the ultimate threat of government action is always an empty one for, if nothing else, all political parties fear, rightly or wrongly, that their prospects of re-election depend upon amicable press relations. For how is total – or even substantial – membership to be achieved especially if, as has happened, the industry refuses to comply with the recommendations for reform? On this point, Leveson's position was weak. He realised that meaningful press reform could be realised only through vigorous commitment to tougher regulation,[72] but had no serious proposals on how to achieve this. Instead, he relied upon a sort of moral indignation:

> Given the public appetite for some accountability of the press, I do not think that either the victims or the public would understand if the industry did not grasp this opportunity. Neither would they understand if I were not to consider the consequences of the industry failing to deliver the independent regulation that is required.[73]

And, additionally, on a fairly empty, distant threat of state intervention: should the press refuse to reform then 'my view is that there would then be no alternative but to provide in legislation for a backstop regulator to apply and enforce a Code.'[74] Incredibly, he said he paid no attention to this prospective problem because a panel of experts had assured him that 'independent self-regulation is the best solution and that, if the industry considers it carefully, it too will agree.'[75] In other words, no alternative planning was necessary because the industry would comply. Yet it did not. And now an alternative plan *is* necessary.

Moreover, the prospects of the industry embracing these higher ethical obligations by means of collective initiative are also dampened by the notable sea-change in owner and editor ideological attitudes toward press freedom. For, when we compare the attitudes of owners and editors in the early to mid-twentieth

---

[70] Leveson, (n 1), 1806, [23].

[71] Ibid, 1751, [3.1].

[72] Ibid, 1619, [2.26]; 1659, [5.1]; 1757, [3.28]; 1761, [4.11]; 1769, [4.48]; 1771, [6.1]; 1781, [7.2]; 1781, [7.3].

[73] Ibid, 1782, [7.9].

[74] Ibid, 1782, [7.10].

[75] Ibid, 1758, fn 44.

century with those today, we see a preference for the fusion of the progressive and proprietorial view in the former (of which, as we saw in the last chapter, CP Scott was representative), and something much more firmly proprietorial in the latter. This is not to say that the press of the past would have craved coercive independent press regulation, but they might have been more receptive to the arguments, if only rhetorically. We see this, for example, in the discernible shift in attitude toward the market's 'self-righting' process (ie, that the market will rectify deficiencies in the quality of information and education provided by newspapers), for what men like CP Scott, Harold Evans, and Cecil King thought was a matter of pride and self-respect, has become, for those like Paul Dacre (Associated News), Tony Gallagher (Telegraph Media Group) and Lloyd Embley (Trinity Mirror) – who all gave evidence at the Leveson inquiry – simply a matter of economics. These two strategies, though, do not point in the same direction.

So it was that in 1967, Cecil King could espouse high-minded morals, and say that his newspapers, the *Mirror* and the *Sunday Mirror*, would be forever radical, never reactionary[76] ('all newspapers in this country ... have a good record in their advocacy of racial tolerance ... One hates to think what might have happened ... had one or two large newspapers exploited popular prejudice on this issue'[77]) and speak with some authority for his fellow owners. This is true even when compared to Lord Thompson, for although he disagreed with King's view that owners were 'duty bound ... to take a deep and sustained interest in public affairs,' preferring instead to trust his editor to make the right decisions, he agreed with the sentiment.[78] Yet Thompson could afford the luxury of this deep-rooted faith in editorial autonomy because, in Harold Evans, he had the perfect editor to pursue the sort of agenda that he approved of: to expose social injustice and wrongdoing, in his battles against the censorship of restrictive contempt of court laws (in the Thalidomide case) and government secrecy (in the Crossman Diaries affair).[79] In this way, both King and Evans could align themselves with – and were aligned with – CP Scott in articulating press freedom as something dutiful and purposive: its function, said Scott, is to print 'news': that which 'ministers to knowledge, to curiosity, to education; in a real sense it makes the whole world one';[80] or, as King put it, its 'duty ... first of all [is] to explain fairly and adequately what a Government is trying to do';[81] and to provide comment on that performance, honestly, and without favour, even if that meant chastising the readership's favoured party, or supporting the opposition, as Evans was prepared to do when, in 1974, he

---

[76] C King, *The Future of the Press* (London, MacGibbon & Kee, 1967), 92.

[77] Ibid, 90.

[78] Ibid, 92.

[79] See, H Evans, *Good Times, Bad Times* 3rd edn (London, Phoenix, 1994).

[80] CP Scott, 'The Function of the Press' (1931) reprinted in *CP Scott 1846–1932: The Making of the "Manchester Guardian"* (London, Frederick Muller Ltd, 1946), 165.

[81] King, (n 76), 93.

backed the Labour party – a first for the *Sunday Times*.[82] Here we see the fusion of progressive and proprietorial views in action.

This is nothing like the modern attitude toward newspaper content, which, it might be said, Murdoch ushered in when he bought the *News of the World* in 1968 and then *The Sun* in 1969, and which is something less than high-minded. Murdoch, of course, changed the style of newspapers to something much more titillating (in every sense of the word) and caused his newspaper's political allegiances to oscillate between the Conservatives and Labour, depending upon his mood.[83] Whilst the *Daily Mail*, *Telegraph*, and *Mirror* have stuck to their political roots, to become the nation's leading right-wing (*Daily Mail* and *Telegraph*) and left-wing papers (*Mirror*), they have followed Murdoch's lead stylistically, and profited for it. Indeed, the race for market share has become so important that it determines both content and editorial approach. We see this most clearly in the *Daily Mail*'s coverage under Paul Dacre. But Lloyd Embley, then editor of the *People* (a Sunday title), was also forthright about this in his evidence to Leveson: 'As editor, I want to produce exciting and engaging newspapers and I want them to sell well but I also have a responsibility for the overall financial performance of the title … [I want to] highlight issues that are important to our readers.'[84] Those readers, he said, typically live in the North and have an average age of 52.[85] Likewise, we see in Hugh Whitlow's evidence, then editor of the *Daily Express*, the same claim: 'My motivation is for the paper to be successful, viable, the best-selling and the best product for our readership.'[86] Tony Gallagher, then editor of the *Daily Telegraph* and *Sunday Telegraph* said similarly – 'I want to produce a paper that people want to read, and I want the Daily Telegraph to be leading the news and breaking stories'[87] – although this was tempered by the claim he was under no financial pressure, only, what he called a 'self-imposed' journalistic one, and his further claim that the purpose of a newspaper is 'to act as a watchdog of those in government or positions of power' (something he described as a 'duty').[88] This difference, then, between this approach and that of Scott, Evans, and King (and the like) is the prioritisation of the reader's interests: tellingly, Dacre says this: 'I am held to account by my readers every day … if I do not connect with my readers' values and reflect their interests and aspirations, or if I offend them or am unfair or prurient, they will stop buying our newspapers. If that happens in great numbers

---

[82] Evans, (n 79), 258.

[83] See discussion in Evans, (n 79).

[84] https://webarchive.nationalarchives.gov.uk/20140122185257/http://www.levesoninquiry.org.uk/wp-content/uploads/2012/01/Witness-Statement-of-Lloyd-Embley.pdf, [17] and [26].

[85] Ibid, [24].

[86] https://webarchive.nationalarchives.gov.uk/20140122164523/http://www.levesoninquiry.org.uk/wp-content/uploads/2012/01/Witness-Statement-of-Hugh-Whittow.pdf, [19].

[87] https://webarchive.nationalarchives.gov.uk/20140122164347/http://www.levesoninquiry.org.uk/wp-content/uploads/2012/01/Witness-Statement-of-Tony-Gallagher.pdf, [40].

[88] Ibid, [39].

I will lose my job.'[89] There is none of the nobility or civic-mindedness here that we see in Scott, Evans, and King. This is pure self-interest. For Nick Davies, in his book, *Flat Earth News*, this prioritisation manifests in pandering too heavily to the actual or perceived outlook of the reader: in providing them with news, as well as opinion, that suits their worldview – of showing them the picture of the world that they *expect* to see: liberals, immigrants, single mums and those on benefits are bad; old, white middle class people are good.[90]

Consequently, we should be clear about at least some of the more business-orientated reasons against coercive independent press regulation. For although the press is regulated, in a broad sense, by the positive law, it does so rather inefficiently. Since rights to reputation, privacy, and a fair trial require those personally affected to sue, the prospect is a calculatable risk for the press, who can take into account both the likelihood of that individual suing, based on their personal wealth, etc, and the prospects of settling out of court, quietly and for a lesser sum. As Tony Gallagher, editor of *Daily Telegraph* and *Sunday Telegraph* told the Leveson inquiry, legal actions are threatened only 'occasionally.'[91] An effective regulatory system is a scarier prospect, for victims may be compensated, or else the newspaper fined, regardless of the victim's financial capacity to pursue litigation. Moreover, current British and European press codes restrict speech in more general ways, especially as they seek to govern discrimination, accuracy, and conflicts of (usually financial) interest. These areas of reporting are not litigable, in the main, for they often lack a named 'victim' who would have sufficient standing to sue. On this point, the press has stronger principled grounds for objecting to enhanced regulation.

Nevertheless, scepticism is called for concerning the fear expressed by Lord Black, on behalf of the press, to Leveson that *any* 'statutory regulation of the written word would be an unacceptable impingement on press freedom.'[92] And to this, we could add the fear that Cecil King expressed about the prospect of coercive independent press regulation: 'The idea of control was abhorrent; after all, the struggle for liberty of speech in print had been fought over three centuries. You could not have a Council without punitive sanctions, people argued, and sanctions would be intolerable.'[93] For, we can say, with Eric Barendt, that Black's fears about statute are 'neurotic rather than philosophical',[94] since, as Leveson said, commenting on Black's concerns, press freedom *is* regulated by statute, from defamation to contempt of court.[95]

---

[89] https://webarchive.nationalarchives.gov.uk/20140122174741/http://www.levesoninquiry.org.uk/wp-content/uploads/2012/02/Witness-Statement-of-Paul-Dacre.pdf, [6].

[90] N Davies, *Flat Earth News* (London: Chatto & Windus, 2008), 372.

[91] https://webarchive.nationalarchives.gov.uk/20140122164347/http://www.levesoninquiry.org.uk/wp-content/uploads/2012/01/Witness-Statement-of-Tony-Gallagher.pdf, [26].

[92] https://webarchive.nationalarchives.gov.uk/20140122191155/http://www.levesoninquiry.org.uk/wp-content/uploads/2012/07/Submission-by-Lord-Black-of-Brentwood1.pdf, [10].

[93] King, (n 76), 107.

[94] E Barendt, 'Statutory Underpinning: A Threat to Press Freedom?' (2013) 5(2) *Journal of Media Law* 189, 201.

[95] Leveson, (n 1), 67, [5.12].

This does not mean that all of the press's concerns about regulatory reform are without justification. Leveson's endorsement of the teleological conception of press freedom combined with the open-textured language, within the Charter, of the code of conduct's provisions does not dispel the concern, voiced by Black and others, that it represents the 'thin end of the wedge', for the reasons expressed above about the superintendence of quality.

Whilst it will be argued that coercive independent press regulation is legitimate and necessary, this scheme regulates 'freedom of the press' not press freedom.[96] By demonstrating the illegitimacy of the teleological view, in Part 2, the road-block to meaningful reform is removed. The net effect of this means that the quality of press speech is not something that could be regulated. Prior to that, I want to signal the difference between the position advocated in this book and that found in SRT by highlighting some of the logical and practical flaws subsisting in SRT's key proposals around quality: those that relate to the regulation of plurality (under the auspices of regulating ownership) and those relating to obligations of greater accuracy.

IV. The Press Reform Debate and its Discontents

A. Plurality

For SR theorists, the concentration of press ownership – including cross-platform ownership – is problematic. Of course, regulation – of the sort that forms the subject of this book – does not, and cannot, address the underlying competition issues that concentrated ownership and the threat of monopoly implies. In the UK, media ownership rules are governed by statute and overseen, ultimately, by the Competition and Markets Authority.[97] Consequently, there will be no discussion about the sort of anti-competitive practices that this sort of regulation seeks to address. This omission is unsurprising given that the SRT debate on concentrated press ownership is not usually concerned with anti-competitive practices, such as extortionate prices, or scarcity of resources, or externalities, or any of the traditional issues that competition and anti-trust lawyers discuss. Instead, that debate concerns the perceived crisis in realising the plurality value that a reduction in newspapers, or else newspaper owners, will cause. SRT adherents fear that, in the race for an ever-greater share of the market, and the profits which that brings, diverse and minority viewpoints will be squeezed out.

---

[96] See discussion in Preface.

[97] See, further, J Rowbottom, *Media Law* (Oxford, Hart publishing, 2018), 292–295 and E Barendt, J Bosland, R Craufurd-Smith and Lesley Hitchens, *Media Law: Text, Cases and Materials* (Harlow: Pearson, 2014), 277–288.

That a plurality of voices is a good thing is something which that literature treats as axiomatic. There is some recognition of this in government policy, albeit that recognition is tempered by government's unshakeable belief in the sanctity of property, the inviolability of laissez faire principles to govern the economic survival of newspapers, and the principled view that governments should not interfere with newspaper content for fear that such action undermines the fourth estate role[98] (see above). Curran has previously called this a 'legitimacy crisis', for the notion that a free market breeds financial independence through competition which breeds diverse viewpoints has not been realised.[99] Nevertheless, since the 1940s, there has been a steady move toward greater regulation of mergers and acquisitions of media outlets (including the press) to ensure some respect for plurality.[100] Consequently, the debate on news market structures has not been aided by the unhelpful conflation of two separate issues: the competition concerns arising, in which, for example, the state has a legitimate goal in preventing monopolies, etc, and the pluralism agenda in which the concern for maximal viewpoint diversity is the object.

Rachael Craufurd Smith and Damian Tambini have spoken of the need to match regulatory strategies with public interest objectives.[101] According to them, not only is there 'a convincing body of evidence to suggest that particular corporate or political affiliations can lead to media bias or the suppression of information' but also the over-reliance by time-pressured readers on the media (ie, not only the press) exacerbates the problem and 'undermines the democratic process.'[102] That, as the authors acknowledge, not enough is known empirically about the dynamic interaction between the media and consumer[103] is problematic but beyond the scope of our inquiry. We need not be concerned about the way news affects individuals in our search to critique the teleological view of press freedom. That consumers are misled by newspapers and uncritically accept politically-biased reporting does not tell us why newspapers should be constrained to tell the truth or separate fact from opinion. This cannot be determined until the question of obligation is settled.

Nevertheless, the aim of this section is to show how the ostensible ambition to restructure the information market to achieve greater plurality – an ostensibly content-neutral goal – thinly disguises the real goal of improving the *quality* of press speech and, consequently, this debate becomes subsumed within the larger one about the regulation of press speech. By showing this, I also want to signal

---

[98] See FS McChesney, 'A Positive Regulatory Theory of the First Amendment' (1987–1988) 20 *Connecticut Law Review* 355; A Breton and R Wintrobe, 'Freedom of speech vs efficient regulation in markets for ideas' (1992) 17 *Journal of Economic Behavior and Organization* 217.

[99] J Curran, 'Press freedom as a property right: the crisis of press legitimacy' (1979) 1 *Media, Culture and Society* 59, 59–60.

[100] See discussion in Curran, ibid.

[101] R Craufurd Smith and D Tambini, 'Measuring Media Plurality in the United Kingdom: Policy Choices and Regulatory Challenges' (2012) 4(1) *Journal of Media Law* 35, 50.

[102] Ibid, 36–37.

[103] Ibid, 50–53.

problems with the liberal paradise, in which citizens will choose the right sort of policy (the liberal policy) from the rest, that this ambition promotes. For individual autonomy presupposes that individuals will make bad as well as good choices and that these choices, if valid (ie, if made according to the rules of voting and if not coerced) must stand. Consequently, capricious choices must be respected: if, as Martin Redish says, a voter chooses a candidate based on the colour of his tie, who are we to argue?[104] These problems become apparent if we ask: even if the ambitions of the plurality project were realised, would the goals sought be achieved? By doing so, we see good reason for serious doubt about the viability of the plurality agenda.

The ostensible aim to increase the number of owners is a misleading description of the plurality agenda's ambitions. There could be one owner, ten, a thousand, but all would be business owners with rights to quiet enjoyment of their property, with ambitions of generating profit, and with obligations to their shareholders. It is not clear why the plurality agenda assumes that an increased number of owners in a free market would want to supply consumers with a greater viewpoint diversity in the race to meet unsatisfied consumer wants if there was no profit in such diversity. In fact, some advocates recognise this, but use this race for profits as the basis for criticism: that the press, by prioritising profits over plurality, robs audiences of a quality product that they value.[105] Indeed, Baker says so explicitly: 'a major cause of media dysfunction reflects market incentives to focus maximally on the bottom line rather than on quality and media that people value.'[106] But this ideal, apart from being ostensibly contradictory (for how can it be said audiences 'value' quality journalism if the market favours the 'inferior' product?), is illusory, for the market shows no signs of operating in this way. Instead, the market for diverse (highly intellectualised) opinion is less profitable than the market for sensationalism, as history shows, and current practice reflects. Those diverse viewpoints are there, but they must be sought out, for the pluralistic title does not have the marketing power (nor, apparently, the goods) to attract the greatest possible audience.

Some commentators – Edwin Baker, for example – have called for 'maximum feasible dispersal of media ownership' to achieve these plurality goals.[107] Dispersing ownership to achieve these goals (the greatest readership of the greatest range of opinions) can only achieve temporary success; the problematic behaviour is only disrupted, not prevented. Newspapers chase profits. If the most profitable market is in low value sensationalist journalism, then that is where owners will drive the business. But competition drives less efficient enterprises out of business until an equilibrium is reached – and that means a limited number of titles.

---

[104] Martin Redish, 'The Value of Free Speech,' (1982) 130 *University of Pennsylvania Law Review* 591, 619.

[105] See, eg, BH Bagdikian, *The Media Monopoly* 6th edn (Boston, Mass: Beacon Press, 2000); RW McChesney, *Rich Media, Poor Democracy* (Chicago, University of Illinois Press, 1999); Curran, (n 99).

[106] CE Baker, *Media Concentration and Democracy* (Cambridge, Cambridge University Press, 2006), 163.

[107] Ibid, 163.

Moreover, there is also reason to doubt, in an age where information travels quickly, that the market could sustain a sufficient number of daily national titles to achieve genuine plurality. Nicholas Kaldor and Robert Nield once proposed taxing, on a sliding scale, advertising revenues, to redistribute revenue amongst less profitable newspapers.[108] Even if external sources of income (external to the market) supported diverse journalism, so that unpopular or minority viewpoint publications were sustained, what would be the point? The plurality project is audience, not speaker, orientated. It is not ultimately concerned with sustaining diverse titles, but in their consumption. The imperative is educational: to benefit audience interests in realising the diversity of viewpoints. It depends upon being heard or else it is pointless. What is the social value in artificially preserving a product that the market rejects? How does plurality serve its societal goals if those alternative voices are never heard?

SRT advocates also claim that greater respect for editorial autonomy secures greater plurality, by neutralising, or else diminishing, owner interference with newspaper content. We find this view in, for example, Randall Bezanson's work.[109] Editorial autonomy, he says, is valuable because it is 'activity that reflects independent choice of information and opinion of current value, directed to public need, and borne of non-self-interested purposes.'[110] But this fetishization of editorial autonomy misses the point. An insistence on editorial autonomy cannot guarantee re-enactment of the Lord Thomson-Harold Evans dynamic.[111] 'Editorial autonomy' is but a euphemism for idealistic philanthropy. Yet such editors may be rare; indeed, an independent editor can be expected to pursue profitable journalism, which aligns with interests of the newspaper's readership, and agrees with the newspaper's worldview. It seems naïve to think an editor would join a newspaper to alienate its readership, destroy its profits, and undermine its position in the market, all in the name of principle.

Most importantly, the plan for dispersal is doomed by the sanctity of property. Whereas the state can prevent mergers, it cannot dismantle empires. Yet the project to dilute media ownership generates a paradox, for as Bollinger reminds us, it is important to have 'organizations large and powerful enough to be able to effectively monitor and check the authority of the state' – this cannot occur, he says, with dispersed community of 'isolated individuals or small organizations, however much each may be committed to high-quality journalism.'[112]

---

[108] Royal Commission on the Press, *Report* (Cmnd 1811), 1962, 93–95; see further CE Baker, *Advertising and a Democratic Press* (Princeton, Princeton University Press, 1994), 93–95.

[109] See, eg, RP Bezanson, 'The New Free Press Guarantee', (1977) 63 *Virginia Law Review* 731; 'The Atomization of the Newspaper: Technology, Economics and the Coming Transformation of Editorial Judgments about News', (1998) 3 *Communication Law and Policy* 175; 'The Developing Law of Editorial Judgment' (1999) 78 *Nebraska Law Review* 754;

[110] Bezanson, 'The Developing Law of Editorial Judgment', ibid, 856.

[111] See H Evans, *Good Times, Bad Times* 3rd edn (London, Phoenix, 1994).

[112] LC Bollinger, *Uninhibited, Robust, and Wide Open* (Oxford, Oxford University Press, 2010), 109–110.

Consequently, we must see that the ambition of the press ownership debate is about the qualities of the owner, not the quantity of them. This is clearly revealed in Baker's argument that dispersal promotes a 'more egalitarian distribution of power within the public sphere reflecting normative premises of democracy'[113] and preserves 'democratic safeguards ... against undemocratic, potentially demagogic abuse of power and safeguards in the form of likely better performance of the media's watchdog role.'[114] This ambition can be achieved without any change to the number of owners. Even if only one owner existed, plurality could be achieved if that owner produced a range of titles providing different points of view or, even, one title which provided separate columns labelled 'fact' and 'opinion' and the broadest range of opinions were captured. The pluralism project is about wanting owners to pursue philanthropic causes first and profits second (or, ideally, not at all). For this reason, the ownership debate is pursued no further, in this book, because it is the ethics debate in a different (and much less persuasive) form.

Admittedly, the belief that consumer-demand will generate viewpoint plurality has been much criticised by SR theorists. Owen Fiss, for example, thought it nonsense to say the public gets what it wants from the market; it gets what is on offer.[115] Since newspapers want to maximise profits, cheaply produced news is attractive and advertiser viewpoints on content are important.[116] Likewise, Cass Sunstein has argued that the libertarian expectation of the state's absolute regard for the sanctity of property generates its own form of censorship by limiting who may speak and what ideas are deliberated.[117] A growing appreciation of this sort of view explains why, for example, the rhetoric of public inquiries, in the UK, has changed from an absolute belief in market forces to something much more pragmatic. In 1949, the Royal Commission on the Press, believed that 'free enterprise is a prerequisite of a free Press.'[118] As Curran has argued, this treats press freedom as 'the property right of proprietors to conduct their papers as they [see] fit subject to the law.'[119]

B. Impartiality

Another, radical aspect of SRT is the idea that social responsibility necessitates press impartiality – of the sort that applies in a broadcast regulation context. We see this argument in the work of, for example, Sunstein,[120] and also in Fiss – for, having argued that content regulation by the state is not only justifiable but also

[113] Baker, (n 106), 163.
[114] Baker, ibid, 163.
[115] OM Fiss, *Liberalism Divided* (Boulder, Colorado, Westview Press, 1996) 144.
[116] Ibid, 143–145.
[117] Sunstein, (n 37), 249–250.
[118] (N 63), 682.
[119] Curran and Seaton, (n 57), 304.
[120] Sunstein, (n 37), 108–114.

necessary if (and only if) it will 'enrich public debate'[121] (because, Fiss says, the state has a 'duty' to 'preserve the integrity of public debate … not to indoctrinate … but to safeguard the conditions for true and free collective self-determination'),[122] he goes on to say that newspapers ought to be subject to the same fairness doctrine that US broadcasters were until the late 1980s. He draws support for this claim from the US Supreme Court's decision in *Red Lion Broadcasting Co*,[123] which found the doctrine – requiring broadcasters to provide a balanced and fair discussion of matters of public importance (and devote a reasonable period of time to that discussion) – to be not only compatible with the First Amendment, but also necessitated by it. The Court held that audience interests were paramount; that the public had a 'right' to receive 'suitable access to social, political, esthetic, moral, and other ideas and experiences.'[124]

Nevertheless, despite its constitutionality, the Federal Communications Commission discontinued the fairness doctrine in 1987, for the simple reason that it was unworkable in practice. Even the elementary became complicated. Of course, the reasons for this are not hard to see. Public interest matters do not manifest as something neat and unitary, for they branch out, in all directions, to further topics and sub-issues. The question, for the FCC, of whether each issue had gained sufficient attention became devilishly difficult to determine. One such case involved a programme about air traffic congestion which claimed private pilots were a major safety hazard. Private pilots were depicted as inexperienced and reckless and commercial pilots as experienced and responsible. This portrayal generated complaints. Initially, the FCC concluded that the programme breached the fairness doctrine because it failed to present the pro-private pilot position sufficiently. The decision was overturned on appeal by the full panel of the FCC who concluded that such micro-level dissection of programming made the fairness doctrine 'unworkable.'[125] Instead, the FCC said that the general *thrust* of the programme was determinative. Since that was traffic congestion, the discussion of sub-issues did not present a fresh requirement to reapply the test. Yet in subsequent decisions, the 'thrust' principle was not applied consistently and, instead, the FCC would revert to semantic decision-making, leading one commentator to despair that its reasoning had become too unpredictable.[126] Consequently, as another commentator observed, programmers could not anticipate whether they were acting compliantly or not.[127]

---

[121] Fiss, *Liberalism Divided*, (n 115), 19.

[122] Ibid, 20.

[123] *Red Lion Broadcasting Co v FCC* 395 US 367 (1969).

[124] Ibid, 390.

[125] *National Broadcasting Co* 19 Rad Reg 2d (P & F) 137 (1970) discussed in SJ Simmons, 'The Problem of "Issue" in the Administration of the Fairness Doctrine' 65 *California Law Review* 546 (1977).

[126] Simmons, ibid, 553.

[127] H Geller, 'Mass communications policy: where we are and where we should be going' in J Lichtenberg, *Democracy and the Mass Media*, (n 36), 290, 300.

These problems with the fairness doctrine are well-known and the subject of both criticism and lampooning. A cartoon in the *New Statesman* in 1981, depicting a television studio debate, joked: 'And to ensure a balanced and impartial discussion of the latest government measures I have with me a government spokesman and a wild-eyed Trot from the lunatic fringe.'[128] Indeed, the practical failure of the fairness doctrine led Powe to conclude that 'the broadcast experience with a regulated First Amendment offers the best evidence that a free press must be an autonomous press.'[129] Aside from the immense practical challenges, it conflicts with the strong constitutional presumption that government adopt a policy of content neutrality when regulating speech. As Schauer has argued, 'state action to enhance speech is simultaneously state action to suppress speech' because when the state says what must be said, it is, 'by implication', saying what must not be said.[130]

A less radical but still onerous alternative is Jerome Barron's suggestion of a 'right of access' to the media (both broadcast and printed press), which would give minority voices the chance of sharing ideas with the widest audience.[131] Echoing AJ Liebling's oft-cited quote 'freedom of the press is guaranteed only to those who own one',[132] Barron thought it illusory to say the best ideas would find acceptance in the marketplace of ideas. In modern times, this claim might have less significance given the ubiquity of social media, but his overall concern that the media controls *influential* debate still has resonance. That the media can exclude commentary that alienates audiences or advertisers remains a problem as does his concern that newspapers bound only by a voluntary scheme affording a 'right of reply' can present information in a biased and unbalanced way.[133] Consequently, one can understand why he should say that the Supreme Court in *New York Times v Sullivan* had 'missed a splendid opportunity to declare a constitutional duty to publish editorial advertisements.'[134] For him, as for Robertson (presumably), this interference with private property would be justified as a quid pro quo for the special immunity that the decision gave to the press in defamation actions (ie, that actual malice must be proved for the action to succeed; a high threshold to reach).

Barron's idea has never been fully realised, for several reasons that need not concern us here. But, the more diluted form, of requiring newspapers not to publish substantially inaccurate or misleading information secures the same ends, usually by means of an obligation to correct inaccuracies and/or provide opportunities for reply. These devices, which are important in interpersonal disputes between press and victim, also serve teleology, at least in principle, by providing an opportunity

---

[128] R Lowry, 'Wild eyed trots', *New Statesman*, 23 January 1981.
[129] Powe, (n 43), 294.
[130] Schauer, (n 11), 127.
[131] Barron, (n 39).
[132] AJ Liebling, *The New Yorker*, 14 May 1960.
[133] Barron, (n 39), 338–341.
[134] Ibid, 340–341.

to correct errors and misrepresentations relating to democratic participation and power-monitoring (albeit, in practice, rights of reply tend to be limited to personal attacks against individuals). Admittedly, the success of the accuracy clause is variable, not least because it relies upon an uneasy distinction between fact (regulatable) and value judgments (not regulatable). Nevertheless, commentators on both sides tend to have faith in this provision. As Thomas Gibbons has said, an 'absolute conception' of accuracy is unrealistic and unnecessary; all that is a required is a professional judgement 'which is the product of honest and sincere aspirations toward finding and presenting facts, manifested in procedures which are accepted as establishing veracity for practical purposes.'[135] These powers of recrimination (or, if it is not oxymoronic, to compel self-recrimination) can be extended to publications of adverse defamation decisions or regulatory adjudications.

Yet adherents offer no proof to support what is clearly an empirical claim. Where is the causal connection that links the phenomenon of high journalistic standards with superior democratic experience? There can be none, for to achieve this goal would be to interfere with individual autonomy.[136] Citizen engagement with the political process or, for that matter, newspaper reading, cannot be compelled – and neither can citizens be coerced or cajoled into better political thinking or the capacity for higher intellectual thought. Thus, even if newspapers still determine – or otherwise strongly influence – the political agenda, how are we to calculate the relationship between the informed and the ill-informed voter compared to the newspaper reader and non-newspaper reader? What impact can the best newspaper content have on ignorance when the causes of ignorance are manifold, including economic, social and environmental conditions? Moreover, what about reader autonomy? Let us say a newspaper prints some far-fetched claim 'Asylum Seekers are stealing donkeys for food'[137] and later, after regulatory intervention, prints an apology and correction, along the lines of 'Following regulatory action, we admit that this story was a fabrication ....' The rational reader attains no benefit from regulatory intervention because she never trusted the story and the irrational reader attains no benefits because she does not trust the regulator and thinks the newspaper has been unfairly censored on the grounds of political correctness.

V. Conclusion

The divergence in regulatory objectives, observable in practice, combined with the discernible gap between the rhetorical aim to realise the teleological ends of press freedom and the absence of an enforcement mechanism to achieve it,

---

[135] T Gibbons, *Regulating the Media* 2nd edn (London, Sweet & Maxwell, 1998), 99–100.
[136] See ch 8.
[137] This is a real story which Lord Justice Leveson discusses in his report, (n 1), 672, [8.47].

reflects the deep schism at a theoretical and policy level between those on the left – the SR theorists – and those on the right – the libertarians (and those with principled objections to coercive independent press regulation). Despite universal agreement about the teleological basis of press freedom, commentators are deeply divided about the means of securing these ends. This is inevitable given the idealism on both sides, which manifests in the belief in civic-mindedness, on the left, and the market, on the right. Both sides are prevented from striking the fatal blow to their opponent's argument because both must admit the press is special and that this exceptionality must be borne in mind to solve the riddle inherent in realising that teleological good. Of the two, SR theorists struggle most, for they stake their position on teleology with greater commitment than the libertarians. The failure to show *how* this commitment is to be secured in practice, has meant that unwavering principle has given way to awkward compromise.

Given these dogmatically-entrenched positions, it is little wonder that self-regulation has emerged as both the only compromise available and the most unsatisfactory of all outcomes, for, in the absence of meaningful sanctions to penalise breaches of the code, and the willingness to use them, it is neither one thing nor the other. But the problem is not easily overcome, for the teleological view of press freedom permits few real alternatives. Whilst the aversion to coercive measures through government interference is, in the main, exaggerated, fears about the regulation of press quality are not. These fears are justified by some of the more radical schemes that SRT promotes, such as forcing plurality upon disinterested readers and the insistence on press impartiality. Likewise, any measures constraining newsgathering and expression that are too onerous risk damaging the press's commercial survival, and thus, financial independence from government. Similarly, any measures that are too uncertain or too imposing may chill the great debate, rather than enhance it: as RonNell Andersen Jones puts it, we should beware the 'risk that [the press] will underestimate [their] rights and fail to contribute in meaningful and protected ways to the marketplace of ideas, out of fear that they might exceed … unclear boundaries.'[138] These logical constraints lead the debate, inevitably, to an unsatisfactory conclusion, both at an intellectual and practical level.

Nevertheless, despite these justified concerns, I shall argue for the legitimacy of coercive independent regulation. This is driven by the fact that meaningful press regulation – of the sort that will, in Leveson's words, cure or else prevent 'real harm to real people'[139] – is essential. Regardless of falling readership across the sector generally, newspaper continue to persecute old victims and root out new ones.

---

[138] R Andersen Jones, 'The Dangers of Press Clause Dicta', 48 *Georgia Law Review* 705, 722–723 (2014).

[139] Ie, not just so-called 'celebrities' – or the upper echelons of society – but *every* level of society; anyone who happens to fall under press scrutiny from time-to-time. Leveson, (n 1), 50, [2.2].

To put it mildly, there remains an absolute imperative for a meaningful regulatory solution. Something must be done.

The search for a solution must begin by re-examining the teleological conception – not only is it the source of the restrictions on regulatory design, but also it is the subject of remarkably little academic scrutiny. In all of our vast and rich literature on press freedom, its exceptionalism is rarely, if ever, questioned. It strikes me that this inquiry is both overdue and profitable, as Part 2 shows. To put it another way, the problem of harmful press malfeasance will not be solved by retaining the analytical framework imposed by the teleological view. We may make ingenious discoveries that allow incremental change, but there will be no real breakthroughs because of the severe constraints that teleology imposes. If the press is to serve its duties to public education and act as the fourth estate, then meaningful press regulation is unrealistic. No matter how this is dressed up or tampered down, this conclusion is inescapable. Consequently, if we are to realise meaningful change, in which press victims are better protected, then something must give. We must revisit and re-evaluate even our most deeply-engrained intuitions about the press and our relationship with it, of which teleology is key.

The following argues that this approach is productive because, on closer inspection, we find that our fundamental premises about press freedom are, in fact, what John Stuart Mill would call 'dead dogma'. Through constant repetition of the phrase, without constant speculation about its premises, we have lost sight of the essential meaning of press freedom. This was apparent in Chapter 1, where we saw that the ideological attachment to press freedom that still informs our thinking had lost its credibility with the demise of the party newspaper and the emergence of a truly independent, business-minded press. It may be true, as Dacre asserts, that there are 'thousands of decent journalists' who are motivated by a deontological (duty-based) spirit, of a sort that would make Immanuel Kant beam with pride, to 'give voice to the voiceless and expose the misdeeds of the rich, the powerful and the pompous,'[140] but this is clearly worthless as a safeguard. As will become most apparent in Part 2 (where Kant's deontology will play an important role), the question of the press's essential nature – whether it is teleological or not – is pivotal to the ultimate question of what can be done about press misdeeds (and of identifying what counts as a 'misdeed'). It will be argued that the teleological view of press freedom is unsustainable. To be clear, although my reasons for pursuing this argument – to legitimise coercive independent press regulation, is driven by a sort of civic-minded concern for others – its justification is not sentimental, since my opposition to the teleological view is its incompatibility with normative legal theory. With this obstacle removed, both the reticence of SRT toward mandatory regulation and the principled objection to it in the libertarian camp falls away. It is to this central argument that we now turn, in Part 2.

---

[140] Dacre, (n 89).

PART 2

Right

3

Duty

I. Introduction

This Part deconstructs the teleological conception of press freedom. Two ideas are revealed to be central to it: that the press has a 'duty' to do things (the subject of this chapter) and that the press has a 'responsibility' to do things (the subject of Chapter 4). The aim, in both this chapter and the next, is to scrutinise the arguments that sustain the use of these onerous terms. What justifies imposing obligations of 'duty' and 'responsibility'? This investigation is vital to the overall aims of the book. If SR theorists (and libertarians) are right that the press is bound by these obligations, then the state is entitled to use the coercive force of law to realise the performance of them, or otherwise penalise non-performance. In both chapters, we shall scrutinise the compatibility of the teleological conception with the positive law, (that is, the law on the books), of the UK, and by reference to the Strasbourg jurisprudence (ie, the case law of the European Court of Human Rights ('ECtHR')), as well as normative legal theory.

In legal discourse, the term 'duty' is commonly understood by the relationships that John Austin[1] and later Wesley Newcomb Hohfeld[2] attributed to it, from their analysis of the positive law, (in England and, in Hohfeld's case, the US). Briefly, they found that the state is justified in imposing a duty if its terms mirror some corresponding right enjoyed by another. That is, A has a right to legal recourse if B fails to perform his obligations toward her. These obligations may be mandatory by law (ie, imposed by the criminal law or the civil law, such as the law of tort) or else result from voluntary agreement, as in contract law and the law of trusts. Conversely, the absence of a duty-right relationship is taken to mean coercion is not justified; that, instead, there is a relationship of liberty-no right between the parties: A has the liberty to act and B has no right to interfere, even if B dislikes that activity intensely. It should be said that this relationship also corresponds to that which Immanuel Kant and, later, John Stuart Mill described (discussed below).

According to this relationship, then, the imposition of a scheme of coercive, independent press regulation upon the recalcitrant press is justified if its sole

---

[1] J Austin, *The Province of Jurisprudence Determined* (first published 1832) (New York, Prometheus Books, 2000).
[2] WN Hohfeld, *Fundamental Legal Conceptions* (New Haven, Yale University Press, 1919).

purpose is to uphold the duties that the press owes to the rights-holder. It is a feature of SRT, though, to describe these duties in such broad terms as to include not only the sort of victim rights recognised by the positive law, in, say defamation or privacy law,[3] but also, more broadly, to include societal rights to a quality press. We see this clearly, for example, in the work of William Hocking, a member of the Hutchins Commission, who said: '[t]he work of the press is, in a sense, a public trust':[4] it 'has responsibilities to the general spread of information which presents analogies to those of a ... trustee',[5] by which he meant its alleged public function to educate, check on power, and enable meaningful democratic participation. Similarly, in his report on press ethics and culture, Leveson referred to the 'duty of the press to hold power to account'[6] and located this duty in the Strasbourg jurisprudence.[7]

Yet, as we have already seen, in Chapter 2, both the Hutchins Commission and Leveson were against the enforcement of these alleged obligations by means of law, albeit Leveson was more in favour of it than the Hutchins Commission.[8] This might have been simply a matter of expedience, but I shall argue that it also signals a fundamental problem in legal analysis. For the duty-right analysis cannot justify the teleological conception of press freedom that both SR theorists and libertarians advocate. To demonstrate this, the chapter is divided into two parts. Section II examines the positive law, as found in the Strasbourg jurisprudence as well as the UK and US law. It shows that, despite judicial language to the contrary, there is no identifiable duty that would justify imposing an obligation upon the press to serve the public good. Whilst the courts often speak of press freedom in lofty terms, as public educators, the public watchdog, and the facilitator of informed democratic participation, they do not mean to shackle the press with the onerous task of performing these duties. Instead, they mean that *when* the press acts in the public interest, the social value of this expression justifies protection *despite* the harm it causes. Thus, the term 'duty' is used to articulate the contingent aspects of the negative right to press freedom. But, even if I am wrong on that point, and, in fact, both legislators and judges *do* believe the press is under such a duty, my overarching claim in this part is that normative legal theory cannot support this imposition either. If this societal right exists, then it ought to be defensible in terms familiar to the language of rights, which the liberal tradition provides us with. I shall show, in Chapter 5, that this societal right is unjustifiable in these terms. For now, in this chapter, in section III, I scrutinise the compatibility of what commentators

---

[3] See discussion in ch 7.

[4] WE Hocking, *Freedom of the Press: A Framework of Principle* (Chicago, University of Chicago Press, 1947), 150.

[5] Ibid, 225.

[6] Lord Justice Leveson, *An Inquiry into the Culture, Practices and Ethics of the Press: Report* (HC 780, 2012), 1495, [8.7].

[7] Ibid, 1848, [2.18]; 1863, [2.71]; and 1884, [3.104].

[8] The Commission on Freedom of the Press, *A Free and Responsible Press* (Chicago, University of Chicago Press, 1947), 1–19.

sometimes call the 'moral justification' for this societal right-duty construct. In doing so, I focus on the sophisticated argument that Baroness Onora O'Neill has advanced which, in short, claims that this duty could be imposed upon the press, despite the absence of a corresponding right, as a matter of Kantian ethics. It will be argued that this rightless-duty claim is unsustainable because whilst Kant's ethical philosophy allows us to label non-performance of the duty principle as morally wrong, his political philosophy is clear that ethical violations can have no legal consequences. Thus, despite O'Neill's claims, the absence of a corresponding right to the duty principle renders it impossible to enforce.

II. Duty as a Legal Claim

Ostensibly, the notion that the press has a public duty to serve is well-established in the Strasbourg jurisprudence. For example, it is quite common to see it said that:

> … the press plays an essential role in a democratic society … its duty is … to impart – in a manner consistent with its obligations and responsibilities – information and ideas on all matters of public interest …[9]

Derivatives of this principle appear in many of the regulatory codes used in mainland Europe. The Danish Pressenævnet refers to the press's duty 'to publish information correctly and promptly' (the Österreichischer Presserat, Norway's Pressens Faglige Utvalg, the Press Council of Ireland, the Deutscher Presserat, and the Raad voor de Journalistiek of Belgium and of the Netherlands, all use the term 'duty' in their codes of conduct), the Swedish Allmänhetens Pressombudsman justifies the obligations it imposes upon the press by reason of 'the role played by the mass media in society and the trust of the public of these media', whilst the Belgian Raad voor de Journalistiek speaks of 'the public's right to know the truth' (Finland's Julkisen Sanan Neuvosto uses a similar expression).

Despite its ubiquity (and perhaps because of it) these so-called duties of the press and rights of the public have escaped serious academic scrutiny. Given the theme of Chapters 1 and 2, this is unremarkable, for both terms adhere to the orthodox, teleological conception of press freedom. Yet, it is strange that the notion of 'duty' is not discussed more, especially since, ostensibly at least, it purports to impose an onerous commitment upon the press. We should enquire, more than we do, what the Strasbourg jurisprudence means by this statement. Typically, in the Hohfeldian and Austinian tradition, we think of duty as the correlative of right and as a pattern of conduct that either should or should not be engaged in against the rights-holder. Where that duty is breached, the rights-holder may appeal to the law to impose sanctions. These duties exist as a matter of private law (eg, contract,

---

[9] *De Haes and Gijsels v Belgium* [1998] 25 EHRR 1, [39].

tort, trusts), public law (eg, police duties)[10] and criminal law (eg, theft, assault and battery, and murder). In all instances, the coercive force of the law can be deployed to secure the right, punish the duty-breaker and/or compensate the rights holder.

The ECtHR consistently deploys the language of duty-right in its description of press freedom. For example, in *Axel Springer v Germany* it said of the press:

> ... its duty is nevertheless to impart – in a manner consistent with its obligations and responsibilities – information and ideas on all matters of public interest. Not only does the press have the task of imparting such information and ideas; the public also has a right to receive them. Were it otherwise, the press would be unable to play its vital role of "public watchdog".[11]

But this statement is misleading. For what *is* the mechanism by which rights-holders can enforce this so-called right?

Scrutiny of the case fact-patterns, though, suggests that, despite the contrary implication, the ECtHR does not mean duty-right in the Hohfeldian/Austinian sense. Or at all. Instead, the expression 'duty' is but an affectation or a rhetorical device by which to capture – and engage with – the nature of press freedom. This becomes apparent when we consider the three different contexts in which the duty-right expression arises. These categories relate to the defensibility of the press speech on moral grounds compared to legal grounds. Thus, the first involves cases where the speech is both morally and legally justifiable. The second, where the speech is controversial morally, but is nevertheless protected by the law. The third, where the speech is both morally and legally unjustifiable or, alternatively, where it is, or might be, morally justifiable (because it exposes acts of immorality) but not legally protected.

The first category relates to private law claims brought against the press. *Axel Springer* concerned newspaper articles in *Bild* that reported the arrest and conviction of X for a drug-related offence. By their own admission, *Bild* was fascinated by the story because X was a well-known actor in a popular crime drama, who had portrayed a high-profile police officer for several years. X complained that his personality rights had been infringed under German law and was granted damages and an order preventing further publication. According to the German Court, the story subject matter was not sufficiently serious to justify the interference with his rights. The ECtHR disagreed; they found that *Bild*'s free speech rights had been violated because the interference was not necessary in a democratic state. Applying the duty-right principle to the facts, the Court said, 'this duty extends to the reporting and commenting on court proceedings which ... contribute to their publicity and are thus consonant with the requirement under A6(1) that hearings be public.'[12] This, then, is a statement of the rule of law. Essentially, the interference

---

[10] Although the notion of ministerial responsibility would appear to fit this pattern, it is a matter of convention rather than law.

[11] *Axel Springer v Germany* [2012] EMLR 15, [79].

[12] Ibid, [80].

was disproportionate because *Bild* had been punished for drawing attention to a matter that was, or ought to have been, publicly knowable. The ECtHR said '[i]t is inconceivable that there can be no prior or contemporaneous discussion of the subject matter of trials, be it in specialised journals, in the general press or amongst the public at large';[13] the public 'have an interest in being informed … about criminal proceedings.'[14]

The second category involves objectionable speech that appears, superficially at least, immoral or else morally repugnant. In these cases, the duty-right principle acts as a rhetorical device to justify legal protection. In other words, these cases involve speech that is defamatory, conflicts with public morals, or threatens the authority of the judiciary – and so is ripe for interference – the Court has used the duty-right principle to explain why Article 10 should succeed despite the speech being harmful. For example, in *Bergens Tidende v Norway*,[15] newspaper articles drawing attention to serious medical malpractice amounted to a matter of public interest which ought to be protected despite seriously damaging the reputation of the surgeon complained of. Similarly, in *Bladet Tromso v Norway*,[16] it explained why newspapers were entitled to cite official reports verbatim without independent fact-checking, even though such publication may cause greater reputational harm than the report itself. In *Jersild v Denmark*, the Court used the duty-right principle to excuse press dissemination of racist views held by a group of disaffected Danish teenagers. Despite the underlying racism being profoundly contradictory to democratic values, state interference violated Article 10 because societal exposure to this phenomenon served the first, important step in addressing it.[17] In *De Haes and Gijsels v Belgium*, the domestic court had found that articles attacking judicial handling of an incest case amounted to 'personal insults' and contributed nothing to public debate. The ECtHR used the duty-right principle to articulate the importance of robust criticism, even of the judiciary. Whilst they accepted that courts must 'be protected from destructive attacks that are unfounded' to ensure 'public confidence' in the judicial system, that was not the case here; the evidence obtained was thorough and the allegations serious. Consequently, the Court endorsed the applicants' view: 'It is not for the press to usurp the role of the judiciary, but in this outrageous case it is impossible and unthinkable that we should remain silent.'[18] Thus, the device is used to defend the expression despite its objectionable nature. The decisions are never difficult to defend in free speech terms, and often amount to the conclusion that whilst state interference furthered a legitimate aim, it was not proportionate (necessary in a democracy society) to that aim given the importance of the speech at stake.

---

[13] Ibid, [80].
[14] Ibid, [96].
[15] *Bergens Tidende v Norway* (2001) 31 EHRR 16, [51].
[16] *Bladet Tromso v Norway* (2000) 29 EHRR 125, [66] & [73].
[17] *Jersild v Denmark* (1995) 19 EHRR 1 [33]–[37].
[18] *De Haes*, (n 9), [39].

The final category involves cases where the speech cannot be protected in law but may (or may not be) morally justifiable. Thus, in these cases, the ECtHR uses the duty-right principle to explain why press freedom has not been violated as a matter of law. For example, in the landmark decision in *Von Hannover v Germany*, the Court found that privacy-invading expression which did no more than satisfy public curiosity was ripe for state interference.[19] Here, the duty-right phrase was used by the Court to distinguish authentic from inauthentic instances of public interest expression. The candid reporting of a famous person's private life – especially one who exercises no official function – was not an instance of 'public watchdog' activity.[20] Consequently, even though the public has 'a right to be informed' and even though this can extend to the private life of public figures, public figures are entitled to pursue their own version of the good life without constant press scrutiny. Likewise, in *Editions Plon v France*, the ECtHR accepted that even though the duty-right principle was at stake in a book that breached medical confidentiality, the domestic court was justified to interfere with it, temporarily at least. This book revealed that former French President, François Mitterand, had concealed his cancer diagnosis from public knowledge. Although the ECtHR accepted that this information engaged 'the public's right to be informed about any serious illnesses suffered by the Head of State, and the question whether a person who knew that he was seriously ill was fit to hold the highest national office',[21] the temporary ban recognised his family's grief and suffering (although this did not justify a permanent ban).

In summary, the duty-right principle seems to stand for the following proposition. *When* (but only when) the press is disseminating information of public interest, interferences are generally unacceptable (are not necessary in a democratic society) because the societal value of public interest expression outweighs the corresponding impact on either private interests (such as reputation or privacy) or other social values (such as community cohesion, national security, public safety or the administration of justice), even if the moral claim to protection is doubtful. What is vital, then, to the duty-right principle is the presence of public interest expression. This is apparent in the phrase: 'Were it otherwise, the press would be unable to play its vital role of "public watchdog". In other words, if the public's right to receive *certain* information was not afforded special recognition by the Court, then the press could not serve the public interest by acting as a public watchdog. But this presupposes that public interest expression is at stake. This explains why the Court has said repeatedly that 'an initial essential criterion is the contribution made by photos or articles in the press to a debate of general interest'[22] because if there is no such contribution then the duty-right principle has

[19] *Von Hannover v Germany* (2005) 40 EHRR 1.
[20] Ibid, [63]–[65].
[21] *Editions Plon v France* (2006) 42 EHRR 36, [44].
[22] *Von Hannover*, (n 19), [60]; *Axel Springer*, (n 11), [90].

no application. Combined, then, these cases stand for the principle that if certain allowances for excessive public interest expression are not tolerated then democracy loses. But rather than being evidence of a teleological basis for press freedom, it articulates the orthodox liberal principle that harm is a necessary but not sufficient reason for interfering with rights.

Even so, does this not mean the ECtHR has created, *in effect*, a special privilege for the press, in exchange for special responsibilities? After all, in *Thorgeirson v Iceland*, the Court said that 'Regard must therefore be had to the pre-eminent role of the press in a State governed by the rule of law.'[23] What does this mean if not to carve out a special place for press freedom? In *Bladet Tromso*, it was more explicit:

> By reason of the "duties and responsibilities" inherent in the exercise of the freedom of expression, the safeguard afforded by Article 10 to journalists in relation to reporting on issues of general interest is subject to the proviso that they are acting in good faith in order to provide accurate and reliable information in accordance with the ethics of journalism.[24]

It might be said that this is an unequivocal statement which connects, explicitly, the benefits of journalism with the burden of ethics. Admittedly, this is a plausible interpretation but, ultimately, a misleading one, for several reasons. First, it does not evidence – and cannot be used to evidence – the existence of an obligation imposed upon the press as an institution, for the principle is applied according to the category of expression at stake, not the identity of the speaker. In other words, we see it applied to other, 'non-press' speakers. For example, in *Steel & Morris v United Kingdom* – a case involving public protesters engaged in pamphleteering, the ECtHR repeated this statement and added: 'the same principle must apply to others who engage in public debate.'[25] It went on to say:

> It is true that the Court has held that journalists are allowed "recourse to a degree of exaggeration, or even provocation" … [but] it considers that in a campaigning leaflet a certain degree of hyperbole and exaggeration is to be tolerated, and even expected.[26]

Thus, although the context of duty-right principle is often journalistic, it is not the case that the principle is intended to differentiate press freedom from individual freedom of expression. As the Court said in *Editions Plon v France*:

> These principles also apply to the publication of books or pieces of writing other than those which are to be published, or have been published, in the periodical press, in so far as they concern matters of public interest.[27]

---

[23] *Thorgeirson v Iceland* (1992) 14 EHRR 843 [63].
[24] *Bladet Tromso*, (n 16), [65].
[25] *Steel & Morris v United Kingdom* [2005] EMLR 15, [90].
[26] Ibid, [90].
[27] *Editions Plon*, (n 21), [43].

Similarly, in *Magyar Helsinki Bizottsag v Hungary*, it said (concerning access to information):

> The manner in which public watchdogs carry out their activities may have a significant impact on the proper functioning of a democratic society. It is in the interest of democratic society to enable the press to exercise its vital role of "public watchdog" in imparting information on matters of public concern ... This does not mean, however, that a right of access to information ought to apply exclusively to ... the press. [The Court] reiterates that a high level of protection also extends to academic researchers ... and authors of literature on matters of public concern. The Court would also note that given the important role played by the Internet in enhancing the public's access to news and facilitating the dissemination of information ..., the function of bloggers and popular users of the social media may be also assimilated to that of "public watchdogs" in so far as the protection afforded by Article 10 is concerned.[28]

It is understandable, then, that in 1992, the ECtHR should attach especial significance to the 'pre-eminent role' of the press in democratic society. The printed and broadcast press *were* the only means of mass communication. Plainly, this is no longer true – hence the ECtHR's more recent recognition of the greater role the internet plays. But the vehicle of distribution is not, and has never been, the ECtHR's primary concern. Whereas the means of dissemination is important, it is the *category of expression* that animates the decision-making. *If* public interest expression is at stake, *then* any interferences with it requires the strictest scrutiny. Thus, the duty-right principle makes no claims about the press as an institution; it essentially approximates special treatment for public interest expression, *regardless of the speaker's identity*.

But what about the functional understanding of the term 'press'? For it might be argued that these cases show the obligation exists outside the historic or institutional understanding of the press and applies to anyone who exercises comparable functions.[29] This is an interesting point (and one that will be explored more fully in the next chapter) but not a compelling one, at least as it relates to the notion of duty. For it seems that all the ECtHR is signalling in these cases, involving both press and non-press, are the limited circumstances in which it is prepared to condone serious and unfounded attacks on reputation. In this way, it is not saying that the speaker must comply 'with the ethics of journalism' constantly to benefit from Article 10 protection, for the imperative is hypothetical not categorical. Instead, it is saying that if a person wishes to rely upon what the English call the public interest defence to defamation claims, then it must comply with the 'ethics of journalism.' Moreover, it is important to notice that here the phrase 'ethics of journalism' is but a shorthand for a specific legal standard, which finds its greatest expression in *Reynolds v Times*

---

[28] *Magyar Helsinki Bizottsag v Hungary*, app no 18030/11, [168], http://hudoc.echr.coe.int/eng?i=001-167828.

[29] See, eg, P Coe, 'Redefining 'media' using a 'media-as-a-constitutional-component' concept' (2017) 37(1) *Legal Studies* 25, 37–41 and 50–53.

Newspapers Ltd[30] and the list of factors that Lord Nicholls said was indicative of 'responsible journalism'. This included the steps taken to verify the information, the reliability of the source, the urgency of disclosure, whether comment was sought from the claimant, the tone of the discussion, and the circumstances of publication.[31] It seems to me that this is what Lord Hoffmann meant when he said, in the later case of *Jameel v Wall Street Journal Europe Sprl*:[32]

> Just as the standard of responsible care in particular areas, such as driving a vehicle, is made more concrete by extra-statutory codes of behaviour like the Highway Code, so the standard of responsible journalism is made more specific by the Code of Practice which has been adopted by the newspapers and ratified by the [then] Press Complaints Commission. This too, while not binding upon the courts, can provide valuable guidance.[33]

In other words, the Court was satisfied that the standards adopted by the industry to demonstrate sound practice represented the standard that it too required to be demonstrated before it would tolerate a serious interference with the reputational rights of others in the name of public interest expression. Effectively, it demonstrates the proportionality principle in action: that the dissemination of inaccurate, reputation damaging information of public interest, is defensible because the speaker took all reasonable steps to avoid the error before publication. If it were otherwise – if the ECtHR were creating special privileges in exchange for special duties – we should expect them to ring-fence this arrangement, so that other speakers were excluded (otherwise the arrangement could hardly be described as special) or, alternatively, impose these burdens (these 'ethics of journalism') on every occasion where the Article 10 right is relied upon. And yet, we do not see the courts do this, either at Strasbourg level or at national level.

The logical inference to be drawn from this tension is that the word 'duty' is used wrongly by the courts. This usage cannot be redeemed by thinking of it as a way of describing a constraint upon press freedom. For although the right to freedom of expression under Article 10 of the ECHR is described as subject to 'duties and responsibilities', all that this expression means is the duty or responsibility to adhere to the law. If the term 'duty' is an inaccurate description, why does the ECtHR continue to use it? A partial explanation may be that it is intended to operate as a sort of moral apologia; that what the ECtHR is really saying is that the press is not morally culpable for distributing public interest expression even though it damages reputations, is offensive, or tends to corrupt, ie, it is only doing its *duty*. In this way, the expression conveys the sense that the limits of human rights have not been exceeded because the speech is immoral (and, therefore, that the immorality of speech is not a sufficient justification to make it illegal).

---

[30] [2001] 2 AC 127.
[31] Ibid, 205.
[32] [2006] UKHL 44.
[33] Ibid, [55]. I am grateful to Jan Oster for the suggestion that I engage with Lord Hoffmann's statement.

Accordingly, it seems to me, that the Strasbourg Court is hiding behind the venerability of these terms – 'duty' and 'right' – to shield itself from criticism and add a veneer of respectability and legitimacy to expression that is ostensibly unappealing. These words convey a sense of necessity that might not be conveyed by their absence, for otherwise the priority for harmful speech appears, or may appear, doubtful. Nevertheless, these words are inaccurate; there is no 'right' that the public can rely upon to hold the press to account where it fails to perform these 'duties' adequately, and, consequently, no duty that can be imposed upon it. There is no evidence to support the necessary implication, of this duty-right construct, that the ECtHR believes Article 10 *can* be used to coax, chastise, or rebuke the press for failing to serve the public good. Accordingly, we cannot treat the language of 'duty-right' literally.

This is also true of the UK judiciary's attitude, for although it sees the necessity of prioritising public interest expression above individual rights, in certain circumstances, it is not wedded to the 'duty-right' description in the same way that its Strasbourg colleagues are. Indeed, in the High Court decision of *Richard v BBC*,[34] (a case concerning the misuse of private information tort) we see the Court criticise this terminology:

> While I wonder with respect whether "duty" is quite the right word, I do not consider these descriptions of the function of a free press (which cannot as such be doubted) assist the debate at this stage in the reasoning. The freedom of expression recognised in Art 10 is clear. The question is how it is balanced against a right of privacy. That debate is not assisted by a reference to a "duty" to publish. The balancing exercise invokes more refined concepts than that.[35]

Nevertheless, we see, within this quote, the unrecognised tension between the Court's apparent endorsement of the teleological conception (ie, the press has a 'function … which cannot as such be doubted') and its failure to see the logical conclusion of this endorsement must be recognition of the public's entitlement to *enforce* such 'rights' against the press.

Of course, this is not to say that the Court *should* grant such a right. Instead, it is to say that the Court should be more reflective about the meaning of these terms – including the suggestion that the press has a 'function' (it should also seriously reconsider the idea that this function 'cannot be doubted'). As a description, the expression is tolerable, but not as a normative statement. It is unnecessary for the Court to use such terms. For what both the Strasbourg and national courts are trying to convey is the priority of public interest expression when press freedom and individual rights collide. This seems to be the point that Leveson makes when he says the 'duty to act as a "public watchdog"' calls for 'a narrow construction of any limitations on freedom of expression.'[36] In other words, public interest

---

[34] *Richard v BBC* [2018] EWHC 1837.
[35] (N 34), [274].
[36] Leveson, (n 6), 1848, [2.18].

expression has a higher value than individual rights when the interference with them is necessary and proportionate. Certainly, this principle describes the UK court's approach in press freedom cases.[37]

Another reason why the ECtHR might persist with the language of press 'duties' and public 'rights', despite its descriptive inaccuracy, may lie in the nature of the Strasbourg jurisprudence itself. The ECtHR is a supranational court of review, rather than appeal. Its decisions do not bind national courts.[38] Its role, therefore, is supervisory: it ensures that a member state's reasons for interference with Convention rights are compatible with the body of principles found in the Strasbourg jurisprudence.[39] This is achieved primarily by asking whether the interference with the Convention right was proportionate and necessary in pursuance of a legitimate end.[40] Whereas the Court sets the minimal standards for rights, and sketches out their parameters, it is for member states to make sense of these in light of local conditions. In short, therefore, the ECtHR asks not whether the Member State, or its national court, acted as the ECtHR would have on the same facts, but whether that state has developed and applied a body of principles that are compatible with the ECtHR's own understanding of those principles. Thus, a secondary function of the Court is to articulate those general principles which animate the Convention rights. Whilst the ECtHR recognises no principle of *stare decisis* (ie, it is not bound by its previous decisions), it does, for reasons of transparency and consistency, maintain and transpose those principles from case to case, and context to context.[41] So it is that the Strasbourg jurisprudence is a body of abstract principles that the ECtHR then applies to the facts when scrutinising the Member State's reasons for interference.[42] Importantly, these abstract principles are static and repeated from case to case such that they have become 'totemistic' and in grave danger of embodying John Stuart Mill's warnings about dead dogma.[43] This is important to mention here because we should recognise that the meaning of these principles are not routinely examined by the courts, nor necessarily engaged with, beyond these ritual repetitions. In that sense, it is understandable that the Court has not revised its duty-right principle now that it is established.

Yet, the sense that the duty-right principle is a rhetorical prop by which to emphasise the significance of public interest expression when it is at stake – even

---

[37] See, eg, P Wragg, 'The Benefits of Privacy-Invading Expression' (2013) 64(2) *Northern Ireland Legal Quarterly* 187.

[38] See, eg, the wording of s 2, Human Rights Act 1998 and the decision in *R (Animal Defenders International) v Secretary of State for Culture, Media and Sport* [2008] UKHL 15, [37].

[39] See, eg, *Bédat v Switzerland* (2016) 63 EHRR 15, [48, iii].

[40] See A Barak, *Proportionality* (Cambridge, Cambridge University Press, 2012).

[41] See further, eg, B Hale, 'Argentoratum Locutum: Is Strasbourg or the Supreme Court Supreme?' (2012) 12(1) *Human Rights Law Review* 65, 68–71.

[42] See, eg, J Christoffersen and MR Madsen, *The European Court of Human Rights between Law and Politics* (Oxford, Oxford University Press, 2011); R Schütze, *European Constitutional Law* 2nd edn (Cambridge, Cambridge University Press, 2016), 429–468; MW Janis, RS Kay, and AW Bradley, *European Human Rights Law* 3rd edn (Oxford, Oxford University Press, 2010).

[43] See P Wragg, 'Mill's Dead Dogma: The Value of Truth to Free Speech Jurisprudence' [2013] *Public Law* 363.

when it harms the interests of others – can be found outside the European context, for we see it even in US case law. For example, in *Mills v Alabama*, the court found that: 'the Constitution specifically selected the press … to play an important role in the discussion of public affairs. Thus, the press serves and was designed to serve as a powerful antidote to any abuses of power by governmental officials …'[44] Or, as was said in *New York Times Co. v. United States*:

> The Government's power to censor the press was abolished so that the press would remain forever free to censure the Government. The press was protected so that it could bare the secrets of government and inform the people. Only a free and unrestrained press can effectively expose deception in government. And paramount among the responsibilities of a free press is the duty to prevent any part of the government from deceiving the people and sending them off to distant lands to die of foreign fevers and foreign shot and shell.[45]

Like the ECtHR, the US courts recognise that freedom extends to abusive speech: 'In an ideal world, the responsibility of the press would match the freedom and public trust given it. But from the earliest days of our history, this free society, dependent as it is for its survival upon a vigorous free press, has tolerated some abuse.'[46] And, as it also said:

> For better or worse, editing is what editors are for; and editing is selection and choice of material. That editors – newspaper or broadcast – can and do abuse this power is beyond doubt, but that is no reason to deny the discretion Congress provided. Calculated risks of abuse are taken in order to preserve higher values. The presence of these risks is nothing new; the authors of the Bill of Rights accepted the reality that these risks were evils for which there was no acceptable remedy other than a spirit of moderation and a sense of responsibility – and civility – on the part of those who exercise the guaranteed freedoms of expression.[47]

Yet, as with the Strasbourg jurisprudence, the US courts have consistently refused to recognise either special privileges or special burdens for press freedom.[48] This suggests that it too does not mean the term 'duty' or 'responsibility' in a literal

---

[44] *Mills v Alabama* 384 US 214, 219 (1966).

[45] *New York Times Co v United States* 403 US 713, 717 (1971).

[46] *Rosenbloom v Metromedia, Inc* 403 US 29, 51 (1971).

[47] *CBS v Democratic Nat'l Comm.*, 412 US 94, 117 (1973).

[48] See, eg, *Citizens United v Fed. Election Comm'n*, 558 US 310, 352 (2010) (noting that the US Supreme Court has 'consistently rejected the proposition that the institutional press has any constitutional privilege beyond that of other speakers'); *Austin v Mich. Chamber of Commerce*, 494 US 652, 691 (1990); *Houchins v KQED, Inc* 438 U.S. 1, 16 (1978) (holding the First Amendment guarantees the press 'no special right of access … different from or greater than that accorded the public generally'); *Saxbe v Wash. Post Co.*, 417 US 843, 850 (1974) ('[N]ewsmen have no constitutional right of access to prisoners or their inmates beyond that afforded the general public.'); and 857 ('[t]he guarantees of the First Amendment broadly secure the rights of every citizen' and the Court rejects any interpretation that 'create[s] special privileges for particular groups or individuals'); *Associated Press v NLRB*, 301 US 103, 132 (1937) (holding that the press receives 'no special immunity from the application of general laws'). See also CE Baker, 'The Independent Significance of the Press Clause Under Existing Law' (2007) 35 *Hofsra Law Review* 955, 962, who notes it is a 'commonly suggested view that freedom of the press does not provide for special rights.'

sense, but as a proxy signifying the greater value of public interest expression over individual rights.

Perhaps I am wrong. Perhaps judges and legislators around the world *do* believe that the press has a duty, but have simply not considered the significance of that word sufficiently to recognise that the duty-right construct is the logical outcome of using that word. Perhaps, the ECtHR does not use the terminology 'duty-right' as a rhetorical prop at all; perhaps, they genuinely believe this duty-right exists and, if asked, would either find in favour of any member of society that sought to hold the press to their obligation to serve the public or, alternatively, would acknowledge that the term had been expressed unreflectively and so would refine it so as to restrict its reach.[49] Yet even if it exists, as a matter of positive law, the question of its justifiability, in theoretical terms, remains. As noted in the introduction, it will be argued across Part 2, that this societal right to demand performance of the teleological conception is unjustifiable as a matter of normative legal theory. Chapter 5 does much of the heavy lifting in this respect. In the final section of this chapter, I challenge the view, common in SRT, that even if the duty to serve the public does not exist as a matter of law, the moral obligation to do so somehow has the quality of law, such that the public, by means of the state if necessary, can demand its performance.

III. Duty as a Moral Justification

The source of the Hutchins Commission's duty claim is notable for both its contrived and ultimately inconsistent nature. According to it, humankind is 'burdened' with the duty to share ideas with each other ('He owes it to his conscience and the common good').[50] This manifests in a public 'right' to these ideas.[51] From this idiosyncratic and unlikely foundation, it constructed the obligations of the press toward the public, such as to impose positive obligations: 'an idea shall have its chance even if it is not shared by those who own or manage the press'; 'the press is not free if those who operate it behave as though their position conferred on them the privilege of being deaf to ideas which the processes of free speech have brought to public attention.'[52] Quite obviously, there are multiple problems with this conception, albeit there is no need to identify them all, but two are striking: first, the distinction between press speech and non-press speech collapses under the weight of this analysis and, secondly, how are we to reconcile the notion of a public 'right to receive' with the capitalist ideal that initiative and innovation are marketable goods, for which the originator is entitled to financial reward for her discovery? Let us not try to resolve the second, since, presumably, SRT adherents would seek

---

[49] I am grateful to David Rolph for prompting this thought.
[50] Hutchins Commission, (n 8), 8.
[51] Ibid.
[52] Ibid, 9.

to insert some caveat to render the (public) right qualified by the creator's right to remuneration. But, the first is not so easily dispensed with, for the inclusion of the non-press within this obligation is explicit:

> the indispensable function of expressing ideas is one of obligation – to the community and also to something beyond the community – let us say the truth. It is the duty of the scientist to his result and of Socrates to his oracle; it is the duty of every man to his own belief.[53]

Nevertheless, the Hutchins Commission imbued the press with a greater range of duties than it did individual expression despite the common source.[54] A partial explanation for this, of course, is the greater reach of the mass communication powers of the press compared to the individual. Certainly, the sort of obligations that the Hutchins Commission wished to impose upon the press relate to the distribution of information (we see this in its 'requirements' for the press: to deliver 'a truthful, comprehensive, and intelligent account of the day's events in a context which gives them meaning'; to act as 'a forum for the exchange of comment and criticism'; to 'present' and 'clarify' society's 'goals and values'; to provide 'full access to the day's intelligence').[55]

Yet, there is an awkward overlap between individual and press speech rights. For, although it rehearses the familiar idea that these obligations stem from the press's role in facilitating public discussion, it says that 'the original source of supply for this process [public discussion] is the duty of the individual thinker to his thought.'[56] With that in mind, it is understandable that the Hutchins Commission, fractured by internal division,[57] could only agree that this provided ethical grounds to criticise nonteleological press speech but no moral justification for coercive realisation of press teleology. Thus, although the ethical right to press freedom is lost when publishers resort to deceptive practices, the legal right remains inviolate. 'From the moral point of view, at least, freedom of expression does not include the right to lie as a deliberate instrument of policy.'[58] Expanding on this, they said, '[i]t is not even desirable that the whole area of the responsible use of freedom should be made legally compulsory, even if it were possible.'[59] It could hardly say otherwise, without unwittingly endorsing the state's right to compel 'thinkers' to make their thoughts publicly available which, quite apart from destroying the patents market, would be Orwellian in the extreme.

Although this compromise may be intellectually satisfying, as an ethically sound reason for persuading publishers to change, it is hopeless as a practical solution. It relies entirely upon the goodwill of publishers to improve solely because

---

[53] Ibid, 8.
[54] Ibid, 20–29.
[55] Ibid.
[56] Ibid, 9.
[57] FS Siebert, T Peterson, and W Schramm, *Four Theories of the Press* (Chicago, University of Illinois Press, 1956), 75.
[58] Ibid, 10.
[59] Ibid, 10–11.

it is the right thing to do. Here we see the tension between ethics and law. Our abilities to interfere with the decision-making of others is much more constrained in ethics than it is in law. At most, the identification of ethical wrongness of action gives rise only to a 'right' to criticise. In other words, it means that we have good reasons to say that the actor should change. To give the briefest example, ordinarily, we would say that A's decision to donate money to charity X is morally good. But our position might change if X was known to be a fraud or a front for terrorism, etc. Such knowledge would provide ethical grounds for criticising A's actions. According to the liberal tradition, such castigation is morally defensible, for we are always entitled to criticise the immorality of others and seek to persuade them to alter their behaviour. We are not, however, entitled to employ coercive measures to achieve that aim unless we satisfy the harm principle. The fact that A's behaviour is immoral is not enough. Thus, if A is fined for financially supporting X, then further justification is required to demonstrate the legitimacy of this coercion. The Hutchins Commission did not adequately perceive this problem, and certainly, to the limited extent it did, could not overcome it. Essentially, their criticisms of the press were framed almost exclusively in ethical terms and did not transcend to the level of law. We see this difficulty when we examine the simultaneous publications by Commission members William Ernest Hocking[60] and Zechariah Chafee Jr.[61]

Of the two, Hocking seems to have been convinced that the logic of the teleological view justified state intervention to secure it (albeit, intervention of a limited kind). For him, the state's guarantee of press freedom had been provided for a reason – a 'free press is free *for* the achievement of those goals of press service.'[62] This, he said, entitles the public to demand an 'adequate press'.[63] Consequently, he did feel able to express press freedom in Hohfeldian/Austinian terms: 'We say that the public has a right to an adequate press and that the press has a duty to be adequate.'[64] The public, therefore, is entitled 'to be served with a substantial and honest basis of fact for its judgments of public affairs'[65] and to insist that 'the press must now take on the community's press objectives as its own objectives.'[66] The existence of the duty-right relationship, Hocking concluded, allowed the government to interfere with press freedom as 'the residuary legatee of responsibility for an adequate press performance.'[67] This intervention would be justified, according to Hocking, to achieve four objectives: first, to 'make rules and conditions for a fairer game,'[68] because such interference affects 'no honest freedom of the

[60] Hocking, (n 4).
[61] Z Chafee, *Government and Mass Communications*, Vols I and II (Chicago, University of Chicago Press, 1947).
[62] Hocking, (n 4), 226.
[63] Ibid.
[64] Ibid.
[65] Ibid, 170.
[66] Ibid, 226.
[67] Ibid.
[68] Ibid, 183.

players; it improves the game for them and the onlookers.'[69] Second, 'the state may extend the scope of present legal remedies, if a given type of abuse amounts to "poisoning the wells of public opinion".'[70] Third, 'the state may itself enter the field of news supply, not to compete with or to displace, but to supplement the yield of private agencies.'[71] Finally, 'the state may make a strictly limited use of censorship' where expression amounts to 'diseducation.'[72] Here he had in mind 'obscene' expression (and was thinking beyond simply newspapers) 'if obscenity always offended, it would need no censor; it is when obscenity seduces that it needs a censor.'[73]

These interventions are problematic as a matter of law. The first is a fancy piece of word play, which aims to mimic the language of law without being translatable to it. Since the 'game', so to speak, is the 'function' that SRT imposes upon the press, the justification is specious, for it has no relevance unless and until the imposition of that function upon the recalcitrant is justified. Similarly, the hypothetical intervention in the third argument to secure greater plurality is flawed for the same reasons. The fourth reason is justifiable, ostensibly at least, but not for the paternalistic reasons inherent in the term 'diseducation' and the suggestion of correction that it implies; instead, it is only if the harm principle is satisfied.

Indeed, it is only because the harm principle is implied that his second reason for intervention – the 'poisoning' of public opinion – comes closest to being justifiable as a matter of law, but even then, on more limited grounds than Hocking advances. Although his reasoning speaks clearly to the liberal tradition in part – 'if an injury to private reputation justifies limiting free expression by laws of libel and slander, an injury to the integrity of the news, certainly not less serious, would equally justify legal remedy'[74] – the consequence of this raises a problem that he does not clearly perceive, let alone overcome. For, ordinarily, if A injures the reputation of B then the normal rule is that damages are an adequate remedy. Yet Hocking, in common with other SR theorists, has no interest in compensation; he wants to use the law to limit (or reframe) press autonomy. What he wants is for journalists to be re-educated so that they always act for good. Accordingly, he recognises that intervention is pointless if it does more harm than good,[75] but thought there should be an enforceable right to insist on corrections of 'demonstrable falsehood' and to increase transparency by extending the law of fraud to 'include instances of concealed purpose or concealed authorship in news statements or discussions of opinion.'[76] This is all very salutary, but does not address the problem of the recalcitrant publisher who refuses to take their teleological duty seriously.

---

[69] Ibid.
[70] Ibid, 186.
[71] Ibid, 188.
[72] Ibid, 191.
[73] Ibid.
[74] Ibid, 186.
[75] Ibid.
[76] Ibid, 187.

For this reason, Hocking's ultimate solution to the problem is limited. Although, as we saw in Chapter 2, he hints darkly that government should intervene if the press refuses to adopt these society-orientated standards, he is maddeningly obscure about what form this should take because, surely, he does not *want* intervention, nor does he see the value of it. Consequently, he is left with a jumble of conflicting aims:

> The press must remain private and free, *ergo* human and fallible; but the press dare no longer indulge in fallibility – it must supply the public need. Here, again, there is no perfect solution. But the important thing is that the press accept the public standard and try for it. The legal right will stand if the moral right is realized or tolerably approximated. There is a point beyond which failure to realize the moral right will entail encroachment by the state upon the existing legal right.[77]

Chafee is more cognisant. He notes: 'the mere absence of governmental restrictions will not make newspapers and other instrumentalities of communication play their proper part in the kind of society we desire.'[78] Despite this, he is also, by his own admission, 'fragmentary and tentative'[79] about the form this positive intervention should take since this is, he says, 'almost unexplored territory.'[80] The problem of using coercive force is, as he notes, that 'legal experiments, once started, cannot be stopped the moment they show signs of working badly.'[81] Ultimately, though, he fails in the same way as Hocking: the sort of government intervention he thinks is justifiable does not satisfy the Hohfeldian/Austinian duty-right principle. Thus, he recommends increased anti-trust laws to tackle the tendency toward monopolisation and concentrated ownership[82] but is sceptical about the efficacy of measures to tackle inaccuracy, partisanship and vulgarity.[83]

The problems experienced by the Hutchins Commission, and Hocking and Chafee specifically, are significant. The moral justification for using coercion to enforce a moral duty-right principle is deeply flawed – indeed, Chapter 5 shows that the problems are insurmountable. As will be seen, there, the notion of a societal right to demand performance of the (alleged) press function, and the corresponding duty to perform it, cannot be justified using the language of rights given to us by the liberal tradition. In short, it is unjustifiable as a matter of normative legal theory because we cannot utilise the conventional language of harm to defend this imposition. This failing leaves SRT with a serious problem – one that it has yet to overcome. In the remainder of this section, I will scrutinise what, I think, is the best and most plausible means of bridging this gap, which is provided to us by Onora O'Neill in her impressive body of work on press freedom

---

[77] Ibid, 230.
[78] Chafee, (n 61), 471.
[79] Ibid, 474.
[80] Ibid, 680.
[81] Ibid, 699.
[82] Ibid, 700.
[83] Ibid, 717–719.

and responsibility. Although she does not refer to the Hutchins Commission, or its publications, in her work, she argues, like Hocking, that the public has a right to an adequate press.[84] By grounding her claim on the Kantian understanding of duty, she presents a most interesting alternative to Hocking's argument. Briefly, she avoids the problems associated with justifying this societal right to demand performance by simply removing it, and so argues for the enforceability of a right-less duty.

The basis for this duty-only construct can be found in *A Question of Trust*, in which O'Neill sets out two essential features of the press: that it has 'no licence to deceive' and that the information it provides must be sufficiently transparent that audiences can judge its veracity. She refers to these as obligations of accessibility and assessability, which, she says, ought to frame the accuracy provisions in any prospective press regulatory code, so that readers can better know the origin of information and form judgements about its reliability and relative significance to civic society.[85] These ideas dominated her evidence to the Leveson inquiry, in which she said that better press standards could be realised only through greater transparency about the source of its information, the extent and nature of payments to acquire it, the existence of any conflicts of interests that the story implicates, etc.[86] To her way of thinking, these requirements are not especially onerous (a view that others share).[87]

The reason why these provisions are so important, she says, in terms which echo Hocking's view, is that 'if the media mislead, or if readers cannot assess their reporting, the wells of public discourse are poisoned.'[88] Like Hocking and Chafee, O'Neill expresses press teleology in duty-right terms:

> The received wisdom on press freedom assumes that freedoms and rights can be free-standing. In fact, there are no rights without counterpart obligations. Respecting obligations is as vital for communication as for other activities.[89]

By this, she means the press has no right to freedom of expression (or communication, as she calls it) unless it accepts its obligation to communicate *responsibly*. Specifically, this includes an obligation not to deceive readers. The link to Kant is lightly sketched:

> ... obligations not to deceive are more closely connected to Kant's ... conception of autonomy. Kantian autonomy is a matter of acting on principles that can be principles for all, of ensuring that we do not treat others as lesser mortals – indeed victims – whom we may disable from sharing our principles.[90]

---

[84] https://webarchive.nationalarchives.gov.uk/20140122192219/http://www.levesoninquiry.org.uk/wp-content/uploads/2012/07/Witness-Statement-of-Professor-Baroness-ONeil.pdf, [5], [8], and [9].

[85] O O'Neill, *A Question of Trust*, (Cambridge, Cambridge University Press, 2002), 92–100.

[86] O'Neill, Leveson witness statement, (n 84).

[87] See, eg, T O'Malley and C Soley, *Regulating the Press* (London, Pluto Press, 2002), 189.

[88] O'Neill, *A Question of Trust*, (n 85), 91.

[89] Ibid, 96.

[90] Ibid.

We find a richer exploration of Kantian thought elsewhere in her writings.[91] These speak clearly to the view that modern liberalism treats rights solely as entitlement-fulfilment. This is wrong, she says, because it neglects the Enlightenment view that the conception of the good is more about *obligation* than *entitlement*. This changes the perspective of the ethical dilemma – what *ought* I to do? – since it is not a matter simply of *acting compatibly with rights*, but of doing *what is right*. O'Neill's comments in *A Question of Trust* echo Kant's claim that actions, to be morally right, should be 'universalizable', treat others as ends, not merely as means to an end, and be acted upon not for pleasure or satisfaction but simply because it is the right thing to do (it is one's duty).[92] Accordingly, Kant says, duty is not a hypothetical imperative ('if I want this, then I must do that'); it is a categorical imperative ('I must'). To ensure that reason is not corrupted by baser instincts, the decision to act must be driven by nothing more than the realisation that this action is the right thing to do. These features of Kantian deontology (that is, duty-based action) alter our perception of autonomy: the Kantian actor has both limited choices and limited ambition to live anything other than an ascetic life.

According to O'Neill, this Kantian framework, when translated to a press context, allows her to say that the object of tolerating speech is not self-expression but communication; that we should judge content based not on what it does for the speaker, but what it does for the audience. Thus, whereas individuals *express* themselves (their personality), the press (and broader media) *communicate* (they pass on information and ideas). This obligation, therefore, is onerous. Like Hocking and Chafee, she connects communication with democracy. Clearly, the state that prohibits free communication is no democracy; yet for O'Neill, Hocking and Chafee, it is not that democracy must further communication, but that communication must further democracy. Consequently, the conditions of communication are equivalent to, and must be seen through, the conditions for democracy. Not only must all be allowed to participate, but also none arbitrarily excluded. All voices must be tolerated equally; communication which is not based 'on principles ... shared by all'[93] is wrong. Since press failure to uphold inclusive communicative practice is itself insidious (Orwellian, she says), damaging to democratic values, and censorious, there is a need to intervene. Since rights-based theories cannot justify such interference, a deontological account is called for and the imperfect obligations she describes (of acting from duty) enforced.

Her Kantian framework, though, does not transcend to law. In an important sense, O'Neill's early work has no serious pretensions to do so. For example, her

---

[91] O O'Neill, *Acting on Principle* 2nd edn (Cambridge, Cambridge University Press, 2013); *Constructions of Reason* (Cambridge, Cambridge University Press, 1989).

[92] I Kant, *Groundwork of the Metaphysics of Morals*, (first published 1785), M Gregor and J Timmermann (eds), revised edn (Cambridge, Cambridge University Press, 2017).

[93] O O'Neill, 'Practices of Toleration' in J Lichtenberg (ed), *Democracy and the Mass Media* (Cambridge, Cambridge University Press, 1990), 166.

contribution to Judith Lichtenberg's influential *Democracy and the Mass Media*, in which she articulates her idea of communication, describes the features of an ethical press.[94] In this, she provides no more than an account of what the press ought to do. In other words, she is describing an ideal form of the press, in the same way as Habermas does.[95] Read out of context, her claims here are confusing because there are times when O'Neill uses the word 'must' when the word 'should' is more appropriate (albeit it is simpatico with her deontological viewpoint), eg, when she says '... we can *specify* what is needed for communication ... We can *insist* that it should aim to be interpretable and judgeable by its audience' (emphasis added).[96] In the context of what she says, of criticising the failure of the modern press to act with greater transparency and integrity, 'specifying' and 'insisting' are empty words. What O'Neill means, though, is that there are sound reasons to say the failure to do this is morally blameworthy. Her contribution to the discourse is important when reduced to the claim that these obligations are 'fundamental' to ethical questions (in their purest sense) about the gathering of news and newspaper content.[97]

The picture is made murky, though, because O'Neill wants to have her cake and to eat it. She wants to make the ethical claim (which she does and well) but also to say that failures of these Kantian duties should have actual consequences. This she cannot do because, as she accepts, her argument is an articulation of imperfect (not perfect) obligations[98] – of the sort that gratuitous promises are. If I promise my sons to spend more time at the weekend with them and not on writing this book, and then break that promise, I am a bad parent and they are entitled to castigate me, but that is it. On the other hand, if I spend my working week indulging my children and ignoring my book, I am a bad employee and my employer is entitled to do more than simply feel aggrieved. Imperfect obligations and perfect obligations are entirely different. O'Neill recognises the problem – 'sometimes [imperfect obligations] are said to be more indeterminate than perfect obligations; sometimes they are said to be obligations that cannot justly be enforced by law' – but assumes she has evaded it by concluding 'I shall reserve the term "imperfect obligation" simply for those obligations ... that cannot have correlative rights *because no determinate right-holders are identified*, since the allocation of the performance of the obligation is left to the discretion of its bearer.'[99] O'Neill, essentially, sidesteps the issue of non-enforceability by a neat distraction: rather than show that imperfect obligations are enforceable, she examines the objection that

---

[94] O O'Neill, 'Practices of Toleration', ibid, 155–185.
[95] J Habermas, *The Theory of Communicative Action, Vol. 1: Reason and the Rationalization of Society*, T McCarthy, trans, (Cambridge, Polity Press, 1984); *The Theory of Communicative Action, Vol. 2: The Critique of Functionalist Reason*, T McCarthy, trans, (Cambridge, Polity Press, 1987); *Between Facts and Norms*, W Rehg, trans, (Cambridge, Polity Press, 1996).
[96] O O'Neill, 'Practices of Toleration', (n 93), 172–173.
[97] Ibid, 180.
[98] Ibid, 161.
[99] Ibid.

they are not. Finding that the concern is essentially one of unfettered censorship (because 'no "laundry list" of forbidden topics, words, or languages can be enforced without coercing communicators'),[100] she argues that the concern is exaggerated, misleading (because speech is regulated either through law or commercial practices), and unrealistic ('no society can institutionalize zero-regulation of public discourse').[101] Accordingly, since some form of regulation is inevitable, the most desirable is that which maximises the democratic values of inclusiveness, transparency, and accountability.[102] This is so because there is 'little prospect of discovering how the media ought *generally* be regulated by appealing to a supposed ideal of noninterference.'[103]

This diversion into the misunderstood character of press regulation is no answer to the problem that imperfect obligations are not enforceable (because they lack rights-holders). O'Neill, though, seems to think the problem *is* avoided because the lack of rights-holders is exactly her point: modern liberalism is too fixated on rights and not attentive enough to the pursuit of good. This sounds as if it might neatly segue into a discussion of Alasdair MacIntyre's *After Virtue*[104] which lamented exactly this point – but MacIntyre's point was simply that the triumph of individual autonomy over Aristotle's teleological view of the self, robbed the world of the ethical language by which to settle even the simplest moral disputes. It was not a claim, as O'Neill's is, or seems to be, that modern liberalism is too selfish and needs deontology to solve the problem.

The issue, here, is significant and compounded by what is a corruption of Kantian principle. Specifically, the main plank of O'Neill's position – that this interpretation has authenticity *because* it is product of Kantian thought – collapses because this is not true: it is *not* faithful to Kantian thought. Kant's work clearly shows a rigid division between ethics and law. The one cannot be subsumed within the other. The categorical imperative of the moral law says, in one form or another, that moral choice is determined by what one could will all to do, universally, in a manner that treats others '*as an end and never merely as a means*.'[105] Yet Kant's Universal Principle of Right (which governs the legitimacy of state action) says '[a]ny action is *right* if it can coexist with everyone's freedom in accordance with a universal law, or if on its maxim the freedom of choice of each can coexist with everyone's freedom in accordance with a universal.'[106] This is a very different sort

---

[100] Ibid, 177.

[101] Ibid.

[102] Ibid, 178.

[103] Ibid.

[104] A MacIntyre, *After Virtue* (first published, 1981) (London, Bloomsbury, 2011).

[105] Kant, *Groundwork*, (n 92), [4:429], emphasis in original. See AW Wood, *Kantian Ethics* (Cambridge, Cambridge University Press, 2008); CM Korsgaard, *Creating the Kingdom of Ends* (Cambridge, Cambridge University Press, 1996). See, further, H Reiss, *Kant's Political Writings* (Cambridge, Cambridge University Press, 1970).

[106] I Kant, *The Metaphysics of Morals* (first published 1797), L Denis (ed), M Gregor, trans, (Cambridge, Cambridge University Press, 2017), [6:231]. Emphasis in original.

of obligation. Ethics demands that the actor is motivated by duty alone: 'that lawgiving which makes an action a duty and also makes this duty the incentive is *ethical*.'[107] This, though, is not true of law: 'when one's aim is not to teach virtue but only to set forth what is *right*, one may not and should not represent that law of right as itself the incentive to action.'[108] In law, the incentive to act is external to ethics. That incentive is based on 'inclinations' and 'aversions'.[109]

These different reasons for acting lead to a profound difference in enforcement. Only 'juridical lawgiving' (ie, law) is enforceable through coercion (a term which Kant defines as external constraint (*äußere zwang*) or a 'hindrance or resistance to freedom').[110] Although 'all duties, just because they are duties, belong to ethics',[111] external constraint can be imposed only if 'the law … and the duty corresponding to it from the doctrine of right' exists.[112] The duties imposed by ethical lawgiving are imposable only by internal constraint (*zwang*). As Lara Denis puts it: ethical lawgiving 'is the constraint exercised upon one's choice by one's own will, through the thought of duty' whereas juridical lawgiving is the 'constraint exercised by another's choice through one's aversions.'[113] The difference between ethical lawgiving and juridical lawgiving thus illustrates the two different projects that the Enlightenment thinkers had in mind. Whereas morals are the study of how one should act in accordance with the good life, ethics is the perfection of the self in that search and law (and politics) is the perfection of the state in relation to the self. Both, therefore, are about freedom: the freedom to realise the good life as an autonomous human being. We must recognise that the self must *want* to be good; it cannot be forced. Force is legitimate only to secure the freedom of others.[114] In other words, we cannot compel 'goodness', we can only penalise wrong-doing. This notion is, of course, central to Mill's political philosophy, especially his arguments in *On Liberty*.[115] For example, he says: 'It is part of the notion of duty in every one of its forms that a person may be rightfully compelled to fulfil it. Duty is a thing which may be exacted from a person as one exacts a debt; unless we think that it might be exacted from him we do not call it his duty.'[116] Mill, here, follows Kantian principle,[117] for Kant is explicit in *The Metaphysics of Morals* that the right of human beings is a perfect duty, a duty of right, which can be enforced (through coercion); the end of human beings is an imperfect duty, a duty of virtue, which

---

[107] Ibid, [6:219].
[108] Ibid, [6:231].
[109] Ibid, [6:219].
[110] Ibid, [6:231].
[111] Ibid, [6:219].
[112] Ibid, [6:220].
[113] Ibid, 24.
[114] See Kant, *Groundwork*, (n 92), [4:387]–[4:392].
[115] JS Mill, 'On Liberty', in JM Robson (ed) *Collected Works of John Stuart Mill, vol XVIII*, (Toronto, University of Toronto Press, 1977).
[116] JS Mill, 'Utilitarianism' in JM Robson (ed) *Collected Works of John Stuart Mill, vol X*, (Toronto, University of Toronto Press, 1969), 246.
[117] Ibid, 246–247.

cannot be enforced.[118] Juridical lawgiving, Kant says, cannot be 'mixed with any precepts of virtue.'[119] Thus, Mill says, 'In the more precise language of philosophic jurists, duties of perfect obligation are those duties in virtue of which a correlative right resides in some person or persons; duties of imperfect obligation are those moral obligations which do not give birth to any right.'[120]

With this in mind, let us return to O'Neill's claim about Kantian obligations and the enforceability of imperfect obligations: 'Kantian thought – unlike that of many modern self-styled Kantians – makes the category of obligation more basic than the category of rights.'[121] She defends this position by saying: 'Needless to say, the relation between obligatory action and good will is not the instrumental relation between right action and good results familiar in utilitarian thought.'[122] This, though, is Kant's duty of virtue, not his duty of right. Her explanation, therefore, applies only to ethics, not law. O'Neill's mistake is to assume that ethical lawgiving can cross over into juridical lawgiving. When she argues for 'an older and wider view of the liberal tradition in which rights are not fundamental' – which she describes as 'the Kantian form of liberalism [in which] ... rights are not unimportant or dispensable but ... embedded in the broader perspective of obligations'[123] she makes a fatal category error. For when she says that modern liberalism is too preoccupied with rights and should adopt more Kantian thinking, she misleads. Kant's ethical lawgiving only provides a way of criticising the uses of press freedom as an ethical matter. It is, therefore, legitimate for us to say that the press should act differently. But that is the end of its use. We cannot take the next step, to say that the press can be *made* to act more ethically unless we can convert the obligation from the language of ethical lawgiving into the language of juridical lawgiving. In this, we must focus exclusively on the language of rights, as Kant himself did. In this way, we see that O'Neill is wrong when she says:

> We can then ask whether obligations that lack corresponding rights should be enforced, by legal or other sanctions ... Some rights theorists will deny that the question arises, because their *supposed* principle for constructing human rights divides acts exclusively into violations of others' rights and permitted uses of their own right to liberty, and thus leaves no room for other, imperfect obligations ...[124]

This *supposed* principle is not arbitrary, it is Kant's! And Kant could simply not support this conclusion.

We cannot rescue O'Neill's analysis by adopting Hannah Arendt's perspective on *The Metaphysics of Morals*: that, being written at the end of his career, it was the product of seriously diminished mental capacity or else not intended by

[118] Kant, *The Metaphysics of Morals*, (n 106), [6:240].
[119] Ibid, [6:232].
[120] Mill, (n 116), 247.
[121] O'Neill, 'Practices of Toleration', (n 93), 157.
[122] Ibid, 181.
[123] Ibid, 157–158.
[124] Ibid, 176 (emphasis added).

him to be taken seriously.[125] For even without this work, Arendt finds a sufficient amount of material in his other writings to reconstitute at least the basic premises of Kant's political philosophy described above. For example, if we look at, say, 'On the Common Saying: "This May be True in Theory, but it does not Apply in Practice"'[126] we see features that anticipate those key aspects of *The Metaphysics of Morals* that we have been relying on. This paper, in which Kant defends a 'concept of duty', clearly distinguishes '*morality* in general, … the welfare of each *individual man*' from '*politics*, … the welfare of *states*.'[127] In his description of the ideal social contract he anticipates his later arguments:

> Man's *freedom* as a human being [means] … no-one can compel me to be happy in accordance with his conception of the welfare of others, for each may seek happiness in whatever way he sees fit, so long as he does not infringe upon the freedom of others to pursue a similar end … ie, he must accord to others the same right as he enjoys himself.[128]

Since all are equal before the law, 'no-one can coerce anyone else other than through the public law.'[129] Consequently, 'all right consists solely in the restriction of the freedom of others, with the qualification that their freedom can co-exist with my freedom within the terms of a general law.'[130]

In classic liberalism, those rights are discernible by the harm principle and so require, as a minimum, the prevention of harm. We shall return to the harm principle shortly. First, we should consider why rights are important to law – and to Kant. In doing so, we should recall that Kant is not a man out of time; he was a product of, and great contributor to, the Enlightenment. One of its ambition was to realise the implications of Christianity for political philosophy. For, as Siedentop explains, Christianity represented a profound break from the ancient world by recognising the individual, not community, as the unit of measure for judging moral action. Thus, the individual replaced the tribe, the family, and the city-state as the ultimate end of society.[131] Unshackled from their *telos* (of serving the family, or Rome, etc), human beings became masters of their own destiny; they had no externally imposed, or imposable, purpose, only that which they chose for themselves. Transposed to political philosophy, this necessitates inalienable rights to equal treatment before the law, freedom, property-ownership, etc, etc. Although Kant's moralism is decidedly ascetic, his political view encouraged a different sort of autonomy to thrive. In *Was ist Aufklärung? (What is Enlightenment?)*, Kant says

---

[125] H Arendt, *Lectures on Kant's Political Philosophy*, (Chicago, University of Chicago Press, 1992), 7–9.
[126] I Kant, 'On the Common Saying: "This May be True in Theory, but it does not Apply in Practice"' (first published 1793) in H Reiss (ed), *Kant's Political Writings*, (n 105).
[127] Reiss, ibid, 63.
[128] Ibid, 74.
[129] Ibid, 75 (See, further, JG Murphy, *Kant: The Philosophy of Right* (London, Macmillan & Co Ltd, 1970)).
[130] Ibid, 75–76.
[131] See, eg, L Siedentop, *Inventing the Individual* (London, Penguin Books, 2014).

the 'motto' of Enlightenment is '*Sapere aude!*' (dare to know or dare to be wise). It is to think for oneself and reject the 'laziness and cowardice' that causes humankind to accept the judgements of others without critical scrutiny. If we reflect on that sentiment alone, we see that O'Neill's (and SRT's) solution to press freedom problems would not satisfy Kant because it would only encourage this laziness and cowardice: it would tempt readers to conclude no scrutiny was required; all the hard, intellectual work had been done for them and they need only act on the results. This only makes it harder, as Kant puts it, 'for each separate individual to work his way out of the immaturity which has become almost second nature to him. He has even grown fond of it and is really incapable for the time being of using his own understanding, because he was never allowed to make the attempt.'[132] Hence Kant's conclusion: the duty of all humankind is to think for themselves.[133]

O'Neill implies that the modern press generates a practical impediment to realising this ideal state of *Sapere aude* because 'at present the public have few reliable ways of detecting whether reporting is deceptive or not.'[134] Hence, she claims that the press is obliged to address the problem by providing information that is reliable. Yet this betrays the sentiment of *Sapere aude*, for it is an evasion of individual responsibility. The problem is not that the information provided by the press is susceptible to error or deliberate distortion; the problem is that *all* information is susceptible to such. In other words, the injunction to 'be wise' is an exhortation to develop scepticism; to adopt positions on matters beyond our expertise that reflect our limited understanding; to modify our views when new intelligence is received. For it is only by recognising the fallibility of inherited knowledge that one can achieve wisdom. The road to wisdom though is not to be found in the self-entitled demand for accessible and assessable information, for that is bound to encourage entrenched and dogmatic ways of thinking.

Nevertheless, it is the legal, rather than psychological or sociological, nature of O'Neill's position that is most significant. The problem she does not – and cannot overcome is that of justifying the enforcement of a rightless duty. Indeed, when we scrutinise her justification for this, we see that the 'right' is not removed at all, but simply recast. For, despite all she says to criticise the non-applicability of Mill's harm principle, she herself relies upon it to defend the enforceability of the duty. Her point is that a truly autonomous press that can disregard minority viewpoints, present information inaccurately, and conceal self-interest in partisan expression *harms* democratic values.[135] Accordingly, she says, 'toleration in democratic polities requires us to identify modes of regulation that best enable communication ... for all.'[136] Her ultimate point is *consequentialist*: if readers cannot trust newspaper reports then 'the wells of public discourse are

---

[132] I Kant, 'An Answer to the Question: What is Enlightenment?' (first published, 1784) in H Reiss (ed), *Kant's Political Writings*, (n 105), 54.
[133] Ibid, 55.
[134] O'Neill, *A Question of Trust*, (n 85), 97.
[135] O'Neill, 'Practices of Toleration', (n 93), 170–176.
[136] Ibid, 180.

poisoned.'[137] O'Neill, then, does not seek to do away with consequentialism but, instead, recalibrates what counts as sufficient to trigger liability. It is ironic, then, that despite rejecting it as analytically inadequate, O'Neill ultimately relies upon traditional liberal principle to convey both the legitimacy and the urgency of her point. The rightless duty is, in fact, a right-duty after all.

This failing also signals the fatal error in SRT. By framing the press's obligations in ethical terms, it seeks to overcome what it cannot defeat in libertarianism: that the state cannot enforce the teleological conception of press freedom by using its coercive powers without undermining, or otherwise weakening, that teleological claim. Superficially, at least, recourse to Kant's ethical philosophy seems to offer the perfect solution, for here we find, or seem to, the linguistic lever that would compel 'good' behaviour in the press: the 'must' that insists people are 'ends' not 'means', etc, etc. Yet, ultimately, this offers no more than false hope, for SRT cannot deploy the language of Kant's categorical imperative to achieve its ends without radically altering the foundation of Kant's ethics, for the 'must' in the ethical realm is always internally-driven and can never be imposed externally, by someone or something other than the self. Whereas those external to the self are always entitled to criticise an individual's behaviour, they cannot compel compliance with their vision of the 'good', for the self has exclusive domain over this performance. Accordingly, we see that the duty-right construct is not the device by which to demand that the press do good.

IV. Conclusion

The notion of a societal 'right' to a quality press on the basis of 'duty' is deeply flawed. The duty-right terminology, at least as it is understood in legal discourse, cannot be found in the positive law – at least, not on a convincing basis. For although the Strasbourg jurisprudence (unhelpfully) speaks of a 'public right to know' and a corresponding 'duty to impart information', the case law provides no evidence that this is an enforceable right in the conventional sense of the expression. Indeed, we find no evidence, at the supranational or national level (when we examine the case law of the UK and US) of a claim-right to command the press to do good (to act in the public interest). Yet, even if it did exist, in the positive law, we should still need to justify it as a matter of normative legal theory. As we have seen, SRT struggles to do so – and, as Chapter 5 will show, cannot do so, for reasons that are rooted in the language of rights, as it is understood in the liberal tradition. It seems that the Hutchins Commission, at least, recognised something of this problem, given their eventual admission that the 'duty' to serve the public only existed as a moral obligation. The breach of this obligation, though, as we have also seen, provides us with no more than a moral right to criticise the actions

---

[137] O'Neill, *A Question of Trust*, (n 85), 91.

and inactions of the press. It does not provide any justification to deploy coercive measures to ensure the duty is performed (or penalise non-performance). O'Neill's strategy for resolving this problem, by means of a right-less duty, ie, a duty-only construct, fails on its own terms, for Kantian ethics cannot serve her argument to render the moral obligation legally enforceable. This leaves her with nowhere to go but the familiar language of harm, which underpins the liberal conception of the rights-duty construct.

Consequently, in the search for a principled basis for coercive independent press regulation, the term duty has limited application. It cannot be used to justify the teleological conception of press freedom because we cannot say the press owes society at large a duty to do good. If we are to discover a rational reason, then, we must depart from the SRT and libertarian view that the notion of duty serves this purpose. Our next step is to revisit the secondary line of argument that O'Neill provided in *A Question of Trust*; that rights cannot exist without obligations.[138] Rather than the right of others to impose duties upon the press, this alternative presupposes that the right to press freedom is lost where the press acts irresponsibly. Intuitively, this chimes with the notion of responsible journalism, which is popular in the academic literature and apparent in case law globally. This is the subject of the following chapter.

---

[138] O'Neill, *A Question of Trust*, (n 85), 96.

4

Responsibility

I. Introduction

In this chapter, the word 'responsibility' is taken to mean something different to 'duty'. Although this is an idiosyncrasy that SRT (and, in fact, the Council of Europe) employs, it calls for explanation since, ordinarily, we treat the two as interchangeable, which of course they are. Here, the term 'responsibility' signals a rights-limiting or rights-directing function; that the right to do something depends upon it being done in a specific manner or form. In this way, I utilise Hart's legal analysis – specifically, that which he called 'role-responsibility' – to distinguish obligations that are constant from those that are contingent – or, what Hart called 'liability-responsibility'.[1] Thus, the obligations (I will avoid calling these 'duties' to avoid confusion, albeit it is perfectly sound to do so) arising under the role-responsibility model are due to status, eg, because we are an employee, parent, or professional (and last as long as that status does). These regulate our behaviour in furtherance of our role: our actions, inactions, and interactions. The difference, then, between these sorts of obligations and those arising through liability-responsibility is this: they only come into existence when the conditions for liability are satisfied. In other words, an individual is responsible for the actions (or inactions) that caused or resulted in legal wrong. Accordingly, although all law can be thought of as behaviour-limiting or behaviour-modifying, it should be clear that Hart's role-responsibility notion is more prescriptive: these are the behaviours we *must* comply with to serve our role, without jeopardising that underlying status.

According to Theodore Peterson this sort of responsibility informs the 'major premise' of SRT: 'freedom carries concomitant obligations; and the press, which enjoys a privileged position under our government, is obliged to be responsible to society for carrying out certain essential functions of mass communication in contemporary society'.[2] As we shall see, it is not only Peterson who says so. Neither is it a term that is confined simply to the academic literature. We see it used,

---

[1] HLA Hart, *Punishment and Responsibility: Essays in the Philosophy of Law* (Oxford, Oxford University Press, 1968), 210–237.

[2] FS Siebert, T Peterson, and W Schramm, *Four Theories of the Press* (Chicago, University of Illinois Press, 1956), 74.

quite abundantly, in the positive law. Article 10(2) of the European Convention on Human Rights utilises a sort of role-responsibility interpretation when it says that the right to freedom of expression 'carries with it duties and responsibilities', which, ostensibly, are used to limit the scope of the press freedom right. For example, in *Bédat v Switzerland*, the European Court of Human Rights ('ECtHR') said that the safeguard afforded by the Article 10 right to journalists reporting public interest matters was 'subject to the proviso that they act in good faith in order to provide accurate and reliable information in accordance with the tenets of responsible journalism.'[3] As we saw in Chapter 3, it is doubtful that this statement is intended to create an enforceable societal right, but it does suggest, superficially at least, the existence of a rights-limiting or rights-directing function.

Yet we should also note, what for SR theorists at least, is an attractive ambiguity in Hart's role-responsibility notion, for when we speak of the responsible journalist, we may intend to identify a legal responsibility, a moral responsibility, or an innominate sort, depending upon what advantage we happen to think obfuscation will serve. For example, Peterson's sense of the term is clearly meant in the legal sense. But when John Merrill says that 'the responsible journalist … want[s] … to *use* freedom in a positive, constructive, and ethical way for the creation of pockets of value, goodness, stability, and happiness that did not exist before',[4] he means it in the moral sense. The significance of this, of course, is that, as we saw in the last chapter, a breach of one's moral responsibility justifies criticism of that event and, although that moral claim may inform a subsequent normative claim that the law should be reformed so as to punish such a breach, there is no necessary connection between the two, since a person may be legally responsible but not morally blameworthy (as in laws that impose strict liability) and vice versa.[5] This does not mean that moral criticism is invalid, of course, but it does mean that a finding only of moral responsibility is insufficient to justify the use of coercion to enforce it.

This chapter scrutinises the merits of interpreting the teleological conception according to the role-responsibility analysis. It asks how the imposition of this sort of rights-limiting or rights-directing responsibility upon the press would be justified using this notion. The answer may seem simple: that the responsibility arises by virtue of the role itself: that because the press has this role, it must fulfil it according to certain standards, as the parent, doctor, or trustee must. Yet, as we saw in the last chapter, this sort of argument does not work, unless we can show why the press *must* fulfil this role. The duty-right construct that explains the obligations imposed upon the parent, doctor, or trustee just does not apply to the press. Instead of asking whether the rights of others might justify the teleological conception of press freedom (and, thus, a scheme of coercive independent

---

[3] *Bédat v Switzerland* (2016) 63 EHRR 15, [50].

[4] JC Merrill, *The Dialectic in Journalism* (Baton Rouge, Louisiana State University Press, 1989), 240.

[5] See, eg, Hart, (n 1), and HLA Hart, *The Concept of Law* 2nd edn (Oxford, Oxford University Press, 1994).

press regulation to enforce that conception), this chapter asks whether there is something about the press freedom right itself that would merit recognition and enforcement of the conception instead. I consider three candidates in this chapter. The first, discussed in section II, asks whether we might say performance of the teleological function is the tacit product of a bargain with the government, in which the press receives special privileges to assist performance of its role in exchange for the promise that it will meet certain quality standards. In section III, I ask whether, instead, we might say that the power and prestige of the press justifies the imposition of these minimum standards; that since the public places trust, or some level of trust, in it, regulation is justified to ensure that that trust is not misplaced. Finally, in section IV, I ask whether the press is a profession, or quasi-profession, such that regulation would be justifiable given that other professions are regulated. Whilst each of these arguments has merit, none are compelling: none provide a sufficient justification for enforcement of the teleological conception of press freedom.

II. Burdens for Benefits

Peterson's idealisation of a hypothetical exchange between state and press, in which benefits are traded for burdens, finds expression in Judith Lichtenberg's classic account of press freedom:

> If press institutions or their agents have special rights, it is because the people as a whole have granted them; if the people have granted them, it is because doing so is to the benefit of us all.[6]

This suggests a specific understanding of the role-responsibility notion: that legal liability ought to follow when rights are not exercised in accordance with the responsibilities attached to them. It is, therefore, a different perspective on the duty-right dynamic discussed in the last chapter; that, rather than external constraints upon the right to free speech, these responsibilities create internal ones. This interpretation, then, adds detail to O'Neill's bare claim, mentioned in the previous chapter, that there are 'no rights without counterpart responsibilities.'[7] It also accords with the Hutchins Commission's conclusion that the imposition of additional responsibilities upon the press 'are not in their nature subtractions from freedom but, like laws which help to clear the highways of drunken drivers, are means of increasing freedom, through removing impediments to the practice and repute of the honest press.'[8] Moreover, according to Geoffrey Robertson, not only

---

[6] J Lichtenberg, 'Foundations and limits of freedom of the press' in J Lichtenberg (ed), *Democracy and the Mass Media* (Cambridge, Cambridge University Press, 1990), 128.

[7] O O'Neill, *A Question of Trust* (Cambridge, Cambridge University Press, 2002), 96.

[8] The Commission on Freedom of the Press, *A Free and Responsible Press* (Chicago, University of Chicago Press, 1947), 127–128.

is the imposition of burdens legitimate, but also these burdens are transcendental. As part of his attack, in 1983, on the conclusions of the third Royal Commission on the Press, he argued that, the press should be given special access to government information (there was no Freedom of Information Act in 1983) and, in exchange, special burdens should be imposed (and contained in the same legislation): 'there is no reason why the press should not be given corresponding duties to ensure that factual errors are corrected, that privacy is not invaded in order to obtain stories of no importance, and that certain ethical standards are generally observed.'[9] Here, then, we see the imposition of general burdens that would arise regardless of whether the privilege, ostensibly justifying them, is being exercised or not.

This sort of arrangement, though, is not something the courts seem enamoured with. The special treatment of press speech compared to individual freedom of speech is not something they are prepared to countenance. For example, in *AG v Observer Ltd*[10] the House of Lords held:

> The media have greater powers of disseminating information [more] widely than other people have, but it has not been suggested by any party to this appeal that the media have any special privileges in law in the matter of freedom of speech. They have the same rights of free speech as anyone else, subject to the same constraints.

Similarly, as noted in the previous chapter, the ECtHR refused to accept the UK Government's claim that individual freedom of expression is different from press freedom,[11] and has further found that any special privileges that exist under Article 10 relate to the category of speech at stake, not the identity of the speaker.[12] In the US, the Supreme Court has 'consistently rejected the proposition that the institutional press has any constitutional privilege beyond that of other speakers'[13] – not least because '[w]ith the advent of the Internet and the decline of print and broadcast media, moreover, the line between the media and others who wish to comment on political and social issues becomes far more blurred.'[14]

The situation is more complicated when we turn to statute. For Robertson, the existence of special privileges in this context was obvious, for he saw them everywhere. The press, he said, is subject 'to special legal regimes ... [In] copyright, contempt, defamation, court reporting, rehabilitation of offenders, official secrecy, elections, local council meetings, matrimonial proceedings, race relations – to name but a few – ... special provisions [apply] only to the media.'[15] Indeed, such

---

[9] Ibid.

[10] (1990) 1 AC 109, 201.

[11] *Steel & Morris v United Kingdom* [2005] EMLR 15, [90].

[12] *Magyar Helsinki Bizottsag v Hungary* app no 18030/11, [168].

[13] *Citizens United v Federal Election Commission* 558 US 36 (2010).

[14] Ibid.

[15] G Robertson, *People Against the Press* (London, Quartet Books, 1983), 157–158. It is also sometimes said the UK press 'benefits' from VAT exemption. This benefit is hard to discern, for all the exemption means is that the cost of the newspaper to the buyer is less than it might be otherwise. Thus, removing the exemption prejudices the buyer rather than the newspaper – unless it could be said the buyer would not have bought the newspaper had VAT been chargeable. This policy, though, is not for the benefit of

was his conviction that he claimed it 'patently absurd' that the Commission should conclude that the UK press had no special privileges; the position was 'riddled with mistakes.'[16] Given how emphatic the claim is, it is unsurprising that other commentators have been unable to resist repeating, and so endorsing, Robertson's view.[17] But is it as compelling as Robertson and others find it to be?

First, the underlying factual claim of a special regime is doubtful, for the provisions that Robertson alludes to protect types of *speech* rather than the types of *speaker*. Thus, section 5 and 10, Contempt of Court Act 1981, section 4, Obscene Publications Act, the development of the breach of confidence action in equity, the libel defence of qualified privilege, the Rehabilitation of Offenders Act 1974, and section 171 Copyright, Designs and Patents Act 1988 are concerned with the qualities of the expression at stake, not the identity of the speaker. To this list, we could add section 32, Data Protection Act 1998 and section 4 Defamation Act 2013. Of these speech provisions, only section 30(2) Copyright, Designs and Patents Act 1988 comes close to resembling special press protection. Unlike the others, it does, at least, refer to news reporting. Yet even this is not a press-only provision; it provides a 'fair dealing' defence to a copyright infringement claim to *anyone* using the work for the 'purposes of reporting current events.' Admittedly, the European provisions, such as the General Data Protection Regulations 2018 contains an exemption for 'journalistic activities', in Article 85, but this is a functional not institutional description. It is not only the press or someone identifiable as a 'journalist' that can benefit from this right (as the European Court of Justice found when it applied the exemption in circumstances where a private individual uploaded to YouTube a recording of police officers conducting their duties at a police station).[18] Also, the exemption does not operate as an absolute protection for journalistic speech – it must still be shown that the invasion of privacy was not outweighed by the public interest in publication, thus, even here, it is the quality of the speech, not the identity of the speaker, which counts.[19]

It seems to me that this analysis holds true even in those rare occasions where the press appears to be privileged over ordinary individuals.[20] The most obvious example of this is in the public proceedings context of, say, the court room, local government meeting, Parliament, etc. Thus, even though, in the UK, members

---

the press per se (since it applies to books, magazines and journals). It is intended to benefit audiences through the promotion of literacy (see *News Corp UK Ltd v HMRC* [2018] UKFTT 0129 (TC), [17], which also confirms that the exemption does not apply to online subscriptions (mysteriously)).

[16] Ibid, 158.

[17] See, eg, T O'Malley and C Soley, *Regulating the Press* (London, Pluto Press, 2000), 181–182.

[18] *Buivids v Datu Valsts Inspekcija* [2019] 1 WLR 4225.

[19] See *Satakunnan Markkinaporssi Oy v Finland* (2018) 66 EHRR 8 and *Stunt v Associated Newspapers Ltd* [2018] EWCA Civ 1780.

[20] Eg, s 37, Children and Young Persons Act 1933 permits the court to exclude the public and retain the press when a child or young person is giving evidence in cases involving indecency. Similarly, s 25, Youth Justice and Criminal Evidence Act 1999 provides that the court may exclude the public and all members of the press, bar one sole representative, when children give evidence in sexual offences proceedings.

of the press are entitled to use social media to report court proceedings without permission whereas members of the public must ask,[21] it strikes me that this is a matter of expediency rather than signalling a principled difference – that, say, the press is more responsible than members of the public are. This view is consistent with the general pattern of public access to government proceedings, for despite Robertson's assertion to the contrary, UK law, generally, provides the press with no greater access to public meetings than ordinary members of the public have.[22] In court hearings, the general position is that both the press and public have equal rights to attend hearings as a matter of open justice.[23] The Court of Appeal has said previously that, irrespective of the 'importance of the role of the press', it would 'not be right as a general rule to distinguish between excluding the press and other members of the public.'[24]

Of course, SR theorists might say that the existence of other rights-holders, beyond the traditional press, does not disprove the argument, but merely revises it. That, instead, of special rights existing only for the institutional press, ie, newspapers, they also apply to the functional press, ie, it captures individuals when they mimic the press function by distributing information of public interest. In this way, SR theorists would say, the press exceptionalism argument remains intact. Although I see the point being made, I am not convinced by its logic. For, by changing the focus from speaker to speech, the exceptionalism claim is not only diluted, it is defeated. In this way, SRT is forced to abandon its central tenet that the press is *different* to the non-press. For the justification that Onora O'Neill's deploys, which Leveson endorsed, that press freedom is different because 'press organisations are not human beings with a personal need to be able to self-express',[25] clearly *cannot* apply to citizen journalists and other non-press speakers given that they *are* human. Moreover, aside from this justificatory issue, the argument raises all manner of logistical problems. Is the individual performing a one-time press-function to be deprived of protection if she fails to meet these quality standards? If she does receive protection, is she then bound to continue in this role?

---

[21] Lord Judge, *Practice Guidance: The Use of Live Text-Based Forms of Communications (including Twitter) From Court for the Purposes of Fair and Accurate Reporting* [2012] 1 WLR 12, [10] – legal commentators also benefit from this presumptive permission. I am grateful to Peter Coe for drawing my attention to this note.

[22] Eg, the Local Authorities (Executive Arrangements) (Meetings and Access to Information) (England) Regulations 2012 does not distinguish journalists from non-journalists; it provides a right under regulation 4(6) for anyone wanting to report proceedings to be 'afforded reasonable facilities for taking their report.'

[23] *AG v Leveller Magazine Ltd* [1979] AC 440, 449–50.

[24] *R v Re Crook (Tim)* (1991) 93 Cr App R 17, 24. It also said, 'There will often be other members of the public, such as the family of a defendant, victims of the alleged crime and others having a direct concern in the case with as much interest in the proceedings and as good a claim to be present as the press. It could cause a real sense of grievance if they were excluded while representatives of the press were allowed to be present,' ibid.

[25] Lord Justice Leveson, *An Inquiry into the Culture, Practices and Ethics of the Press: Report* (HC 780, 2012), 62, [3.3]; O'Neill, *A Question of Trust*, (n 7), 94. See discussion in ch 5.

Secondly, even if we pursued the idea that special privileges for the press *function* existed (ie, anyone disseminating public interest expression), rather than for the institutional press, or, even if we concluded that Robertson was right and there *is* a special regime in place, we should still need to *justify* the claim that the press can be burdened with special responsibilities guaranteeing adequate standards of public service. This, of itself, raises two complications: i) if there is an exchange, of burdens for benefits, then the nature of this exchange is puzzling, for it represents the granting of a specific privilege (arising when certain conditions are satisfied), in exchange for a general responsibility to serve the public good; ii) even if we overcome that issue, another serious problem remains. For there is already an exchange at work in this hypothetical grant of special privileges. The reason the press is given them (be that the institutional or functional press) *is* the benefit that society receives when that privilege is exercised.

These are related points which illustrate the asymmetric nature of the purported exchange. Neither is easily overcome; indeed, they are insurmountable. Consider the first sub-problem: the exchange is not simply presented as a conditional arrangement concerning the exercise of privilege x – that the privilege is contingent upon x being performed according to condition y. It is, instead, the grant of a privilege subject to a separate arrangement, which imposes conditions regardless of whether privilege x is performed or not. For example, in the UK, section 4 of the Defamation Act 2013 is a conditional privilege, for it provides those who publish defamatory statements with a defence if they can show that the information was of public interest, and they adhered to the rules of responsible journalism in obtaining and disseminating it. Here we see the formula at work: the right to rely upon this defence is contingent upon certain conditions being fulfilled. Indeed, this is true of the other so-called privileges: they are contingent upon conditions being met before they can be relied upon.

Relatedly, if the press is given special protection under section 4 of the Defamation Act 2013, when it publishes defamatory material of public interest, it is because society at large benefits from this arrangement. This bargain is one of private benefit for the press (avoidance of liability) exchanged for public benefit for society (receipt of public interest information). Here, is the reality of the second sub-issue. When we scrutinise the other so-called privileges, we see that there is, already, an exchange at work. When the press reports on court cases, or local/central government proceedings, the public benefits from this information as does the government (since open government aids civic participation). When journalists protect sources, the source receives the benefit (as the ECtHR acknowledges, 'Without such protection, sources may be deterred from assisting the press in informing the public on matters of public interest')[26] and, moreover, society benefits from a system that provides whistleblowers with the confidence to alert

---

[26] *Goodwin*, (n 28), [39].

them to public and/or private sector problems. Similarly, society benefits from these privileges which allow newspapers to raise matters of public interest, even though publication breaches the rights of others (in defamation, privacy law, etc).

My point is not simply that this represents a bad bargain (although undoubtedly it does), but that the imposition of some overarching burden (to meet minimum quality standards) is *not* the corresponding element of the exchange. It is an additional element that lacks consideration. To say, as Peterson and Lichtenberg do, and Robertson implies, that this contingent privilege is provided in exchange for a material, constant obligation to do good, is to impose a transcendental burden upon an arrangement that is already burdensome (privileges can be relied upon only when underlying conditions are met) and beneficial to the grantor (society benefits when the press uses these privileges). We cannot say, then, that the imposition of a transcendental burden to perform the teleological ends of press freedom to an adequate level is simply the corresponding promise to the promise to provide these privileges. We should have to find some fresh consideration that would justify this additional burden of acting responsibly in a general sense requires some sort of fresh consideration. This is a problem that cannot be solved, for, the simple truth is: there is none.

There are further problems with the 'benefits for burdens' analysis that, although incidental given that we cannot solve the problem of insufficient consideration to support it, are nevertheless noteworthy. For, it strikes me, some of these 'privileges' are nothing of the sort. For example, Robertson describes the protection of journalistic sources under section 10, Contempt of Court Act 1981 as a privilege.[27] This is seriously misleading, for what *is* the benefit that the press receives that would justify calling this arrangement a *press* privilege? It is not the journalist but the source and wider society that benefits from this protection. We see this clearly in statements by the European Court of Human Rights about the value of such provisions: 'Protection of journalistic sources is one of the basic conditions for press freedom' and that 'the vital public watchdog role of the press may be undermined and the ability of the press to provide accurate and reliable information may be adversely affected.'[28] Admittedly, there may be pragmatic advantages to the journalist in protecting her source, but whether we can say, with Jan Oster, that these constitute real benefits, because 'it protects the journalist, whose reputation may be negatively affected by the disclosure in the eyes of future of potential sources',[29] is doubtful.

---

[27] The passage of time has proven at least part of this assertion to be false, for what Robertson called the journalistic 'privilege of declining to answer courtroom questions which would reveal the identity of a source, when 'ordinary citizens' would be guilty of contempt for a refusal to answer', Robertson, (n 15), 158, is certainly not true today, assuming it ever was, as the House of Lords confirmed when it held that the right extends to non-journalists as well, see *Secretary of State for Defence v Guardian Newspapers Ltd* [1985] AC 339, 348 and *Hourani v Thomson* [2017] EWHC 173 (QB).

[28] *Goodwin v United Kingdom* (1996) 22 EHRR 123, [39].

[29] J Oster, *Media Freedom as a Fundamental Right* (Cambridge, Cambridge University Press, 2015), 89.

Moreover, commentators sometimes exaggerate the burdens attaching to the benefit, notably when discussing the 'responsible journalism' defence in defamation law (ie, qualified privilege or what is now section 4, Defamation Act 2013).[30] As mentioned in the previous chapter, the phrase 'responsible journalism' is slightly misleading, for it implies something peculiar to journalism, whereas what it actually connotes is a sort of plea in mitigation – that the publisher took all reasonable steps to avoid or else minimise the chances of publishing something untrue, which includes assessing the seriousness of the allegation, the steps taken to verify it, the quality of the source, the urgency of dissemination, the steps taken to contact the claimant for comment, etc.[31] Likewise, the UK practice that privileges the press in the court room is premised on the presumption that they do 'not pose a danger of interference to the proper administration of justice in the individual case.'[32] The implication of this (although it is not explicitly stated) is that the privilege may be revoked if the press abuses it (by jeopardising the right to a fair trial).

Furthermore, SRT's treatment of this 'benefits for burdens' sometimes lacks practical significance: there is an unreality about it. Consider this statement from Oster, who says, in the context of the qualified privilege type defence that the ECtHR applies '... the media not only has an obligation towards potential victims of its publications, but also towards its audience in general, to publish *prudently researched* information.'[33] Whereas Oster must be right about the former, I am not convinced about the latter. Certainly, I do not see anything in either the privilege itself or the law generally that would support the imposition of this sort of broader obligation. For without undue interference with the claimant's reputational right, there is no case for the press to answer. In that case, what does it mean to say the press has these larger obligations, extending beyond the victim of reputational injury? It is not simply that the positive law deprives us of an opportunity to subject victimless inaccurate speech to judicial scrutiny, although, of course, this is true. It is that there is no underlying normative justification that would allow us to say that the court should do so. Whereas it is true that accurate speech is socially valuable, the only potentially actionable wrong is the breach of contract claim that the reader might have if it were a term of his contract with the publisher that the information was prudently researched. But even then, the outcome of that claim is unlikely to be an order for specific performance relating either to the offending article or all future articles since damages (the cost of the newspaper) would be adequate. And if the reader remains unsatisfied, she can take her business elsewhere.

---

[30] See *Tonsbergs Blad AS v Norway* (2008) 46 EHRR 40, [89] and discussion in Oster, ibid, 180–186. See also s 4, Defamation Act 2013 and *Economou v de Freitas* [2019] EWCA Civ 2591.

[31] See *Reynolds v Times Newspapers Ltd* [2001] 2 AC 127, 205. See also *Jameel v Wall Street Journal SPRL* [2006] UKHL 44; *Economou*, ibid.

[32] (N 21), [10].

[33] Oster, (n 29), 182.

Finally, we should have regard to the larger problem that SRT's benefits for burdens analysis creates. For if we condone the state creating benefits for the press with the expectation of something in return, we do not secure press freedom, we jeopardise it. An insidious atmosphere is created, in which the government may insinuate that press privileges will be removed if the press displeases it. What is given can be taken away. Even the *threat* of removing privileges could achieve the same end. In this way, we risk recreating the conditions for punishing sedition, or blasphemy, or anything else that the state finds unpleasant. For these reasons, we should be deeply distrustful of any branch of government granting privileges in expectation of reciprocal burdens. This point is well-known to liberalism and US scholarship. It explains why John Stuart Mill described such government power as 'noxious' and 'illegitimate' even when its intentions are noble and 'at one with the people'.[34] It also explains the deep-rooted distrust that Americans have in their government's capacity to act always for good or make the right distinctions between good and bad.[35]

If, then, we are to impose burdens upon the press, to serve the public, then we should look elsewhere for our justification. SRT provides this alternative in Peterson's criticisms of the twentieth (and, by extension, twenty-first) century press: that it has 'wielded enormous power for its own ends' (in which 'owners have propagated their own opinions, especially in matters of politics and economics, at the expense of opposing views') and that its standards have slipped, especially in its concentration on the 'superficial and sensational',[36] which has tainted its image as an authoritative voice. Consequently, we see here elements of the role-responsibility analysis – that there is something about the press as a 'role model' for, in Peterson's words, 'providing information, discussion, and debate on public affairs; ... enlightening the public ...; [acting] as a public watchdog against government'.[37] This, then, is a claim that justifies, ostensibly, burdens upon the press so as to monitor its use of power as well as preserving its prestige and professional status. The following sections explore the legitimacy of this prospective justification.

III. Responsibilities Curbing Misuse of Power

In William Hocking's view, the press's status, as both a trusted and powerful source of information, justifies the imposition of minimum standards upon it. This must be so because otherwise:

> the disservice which incompetence armed with the present instruments of communication can inflict on the consumer, might well add to the doubt whether freedom of the

---

[34] JS Mill, 'On Liberty', in *Collected Works of John Stuart Mill, vol XVIII*, JM Robson (ed), (Toronto, University of Toronto Press, 1977), 229.
[35] See, eg, F Schauer, *Free Speech: A Philosophical Enquiry* (Cambridge, Cambridge University Press, 1982).
[36] Peterson, (n 2), 78.
[37] Ibid, 74.

press means or should mean freedom to all on equal terms to the use the powers of the press without so much as an automobile license.[38]

Hocking, then, sees the press like the car driver: in need of regulation to ensure responsible use of the power vested in them. Clearly, this position is informed by the press's perceived purpose, but it is not justified – or not only justified – by that. Instead, these arguments seek to draw legitimacy from the supposed influence of the press over popular opinion. Thus, it is said, for example, that although the press cannot determine what people think, it is 'stunningly successful' in deciding what they think *about*.[39] 'They can elevate men from obscurity to national prominence within a week. They can reward some politicians with national exposure and ignore others.'[40] By the same token, they can ignore or neglect serious issues until they wither away from national consciousness and the political agenda.[41] This authority may well be waning, although, according to Nick Davies, it remains significant because it drives the broadcast and internet press agenda and substantially influences government thinking.[42] Consequently, the argument goes that this profound influence (or, as some have it, undue influence),[43] over politics, morals, culture, and the general outlook of society, requires the press to act responsibly. This sense that the press ought to act in a specific way – that is, *responsibly* – is suggestive of Hart's notion of role-responsibility. Hart describes this conception of responsibility in terms that suggest the relationship between proper action and actor is one of both habit and social expectation:

> whenever a person occupies a distinctive place or office in a social organization, to which specific duties are attached to provide for the welfare of others or to advance in some specific ways the aims or purposes of the organization, he is properly said to be responsible for the performance of these duties, or for doing what is necessary to fulfil them.[44]

It is clear, from the SRT literature, that, if we follow this approach, the method of both identifying and defending the imposition of these obligations upon the recalcitrant press relates to the press's perceived power, prestige, and professionalism. All three, therefore, are taken to be characteristic of the press, and, thus, good reasons for regulation. For the purposes of discussion, this section focuses on the power (and prestige) argument and the following tackles professionalism.

---

[38] WE Hocking, *Freedom of the Press: A Framework of Principle* (Chicago, University of Chicago Press, 1947), 83.

[39] BC Cohen, *The Press and Foreign Policy* (Princeton, Princeton University Press, 1963), 13.

[40] Spiro Agnew, former Vice-President (1969–1973), quoted in T Burns, 'The Organisation of Public Opinion' in J Curran, M Gurevitch, and J Woollacott (eds), *Mass Communication and Society* (London, Edward Arnold, 1977), 59.

[41] BH Bagdakian, *The Media Monopoly* 6th edn (Boston, Beacon Press, 2000), xxvii–xxxi.

[42] N Davies, *Flat Earth News* (London, Chatto & Windus, 2008).

[43] Eg, Bagdakian, (n 41); RW McChesney, *Rich Media, Poor Democracy* (Chicago, University of Illinois Press, 1999); N Chomsky, *Media Control* 2nd edn (New York, Seven Stories Press, 2002).

[44] Hart, (n 1), 212.

Press power, as a reason to regulate, is spoken of in two distinct senses (which are often unhelpfully blurred together). The first is that the power of the press to influence its readers (or, as Bollinger puts it, 'the ability to command an audience more or less exclusively')[45] is of itself reason to impose responsibilities. It is common to see it said, as Jan Oster does, that because the press is the 'gatekeeper' between information and public knowledge, and has the power to shape and direct public thinking, this power is 'abused' when newspapers publish matters of a 'private or even intimate' nature and when it misleads.[46] This concern bleeds into the second critical use of the term 'power', which is the power of the owner to use press influence for their own purposes (see Peterson's criticisms of the press in the previous section). This kind of use of power can take several forms. For example, it may be that the owner has a specific worldview that the newspaper should adopt (this is the criticism usually levelled at Rupert Murdoch, for example). It can also suggest the use of power to attack political and business opponents for commercial advantage as well as to shield commercial partners from criticism for the same reason. This use of power is perfectly understandable. Since newspapers are themselves corporations with shareholders to satisfy and capital to protect (and grow), there are powerful incentives to avoid anything that jeopardises its investment and its revenue streams. Clearly, any negative reporting that relates to advertisers, shareholders, and investors is bad for business. There is anecdotal evidence for this sort of behaviour. In 2015, Peter Oborne resigned as chief political commentator for *The Telegraph* because, he said, the paper had failed to properly report a banking scandal involving a key advertiser and so had performed 'a form of fraud upon its readers' (something the newspaper strenuously denied).[47]

The concern also extends to press coverage of politics. As Curran argues:

> Critical scrutiny of government can also be blunted by political partisanship ... [particularly] when the parties of the right are in government and the press, as [it is] in most of Europe, is overwhelmingly right-wing. Although conflicts can occur between right-wing papers and right-wing governments, the tendency is for criticism to be reined in out of partisan and patriotic loyalty. In extreme cases, this can result almost in the suspension of critical judgement.[48]

This leads to, or can lead to, the sense that when there is this 'excess of power in the media, one perspective on knowledge is dominant.'[49] Moreover, it generates the fear that this influence may be so great as to cause 'unsound propositions [to] replace sound ones.'[50] Since the press (and the broadcast media) controls not only

---

[45] LC Bollinger, 'Public Regulation of the Media' in J Lichtenberg (ed), *Democracy and the Mass Media*, (n 6), 362.

[46] Oster, (n 29), 33–34, 37.

[47] www.opendemocracy.net/ourkingdom/peter-oborne/why-i-have-resigned-from-telegraph.

[48] J Curran, 'Mass Media and Democracy' in J Curran and M Gurevitch (eds), *Mass Media and Society* (London, Edward Arnold, 1991), 88.

[49] T Gibbons, 'Freedom of the press: ownership and editorial values' [1992] *Public Law* 279, 286.

[50] A Kenyon, 'Assuming Free Speech' (2014) 77(3) *MLR* 379, 382.

the agenda but also the duration and intensity of debate on that agenda, it has the power to determine the quality of public discussion on specific topics.[51]

In this way, the press acts 'responsibly' when this influence or command over an audience is used appropriately and for 'good reasons'. So, for example, it could be argued that this sense of responsibility informs the common claim that the press must provide accurate information because inaccurate information is inherently 'bad'. It also explains Oster's claim that the press must 'always act in good faith'.[52] On this basis, to do otherwise would, to use the colourful imagery of O'Neill[53] and Hocking,[54] 'poison the well of public opinion'. We see something of this reasoning in the responsibility clause of the Canons of Journalism, adopted by the American Society of Newspaper Editors, in 1923, which says that 'a journalist who uses his power for any selfish or otherwise unworthy purpose is faithless to a high trust'. This understanding of responsibility clearly envisages a sort of relationship between newspaper and reader and, indeed, press industry and civic society, as a position of trust, akin to that found in a solicitor and client, doctor and patient, or parent and child relationship. Indeed, Hocking is explicit that this is, in fact, the case: 'the press is more closely like a public utility in private hands. It is still more like a system of private schools undertaking through personal initiative to perform a function which is distinctly a public concern.'[55]

On this basis, then, regulation is required to monitor this imbalance of power and keep it in check. This justification is superficially appealing because it captures both the stoicism of the categorical imperative and the liberalism of the harm principle. It provides, or seems to, the sort of reason that law craves – the prevention of undue harm (in this case, the abuse of power and the violation of professional standards) – whilst also providing an alternative basis to liberalism (and libertarianism) that is rooted in socialist/Marxist thinking. Yet, there are major problems with this argument, that are not recognised in the literature. The first is empirical. The assertion that the press has great financial power is usually treated as axiomatic. Whereas historically, that claim may have been accurate, the reduction in hardcopy sales at least raises questions about its continuing veracity. Whilst it may still be true that the nationals are powerful, this has not been the case for regionals for quite some time. But, nevertheless, the notion of power as influence needs greater scrutiny, for even if the popular newspapers have significant financial resources, the connection between resources and influence is not certain. We must recognise that, through the changing nature of 'newspaper' consumption, especially the emergence of online-only readership, financial success no longer equates to either high reading figures or authority over the populace's political thinking. For example, the most profitable news entity in the UK is the Daily Mail

---

[51] OM Fiss, 'Free Speech and Social Structure' (1985) 71 *Iowa Law Review* 1405, 1415.
[52] Oster, (n 29), 45.
[53] O'Neill, (n 7).
[54] Hocking, (n 38).
[55] Ibid, 174.

and General Trust plc ('DMGT'), which owns the *Daily Mail*, the *Mail on Sunday*, the *Metro* (a free newspaper operating as a monopoly on public transport) and the *MailOnline*, and which reported revenues of nearly £2 billion in 2016. The *Daily Mail* is the third most popular national title (behind *The Sun* and the *Metro*) and yet, as with all newspaper titles (except the *Metro*, which is free), its circulation figures continue to plummet alarmingly. In 2011, at the time of the Leveson inquiry, it boasted a circulation of over 2 million readers. By January 2018, that figure had dropped to 1.3 million. But even this easily eclipses its rivals, for the *Daily Mirror* had only about 580,000, in January 2018, *The Times*, 400,000, and *The Guardian*, the only serious left-leaning national title left, a mere 137,839.

For the DMGT, then, an increasing part of its revenue – some 17 per cent in 2016 – is from its online presence, which produced profits for the first time in 2016 (online profitability itself being a rarity in the industry). Yet despite being part of the same group, and sharing corporate identities, the *Daily Mail* (in print) and the *MailOnline* do not share the same raison d'être. Whereas the print version is characterised by a general loathing for immigrants, the poor, the different, and anything thought to drain the resources of public services, the *MailOnline* is principally a source of fashion and celebrity gossip. Accordingly, although the target demographic may be the same in social and economic terms, the audience's interests in engaging with the material is not, and it would not be surprising to find that readers of one are uninterested in, perhaps even wholly ignorant of, the contents and aims of the other. Similarly, given the format of online news, it is much easier to read selectively, in ignorance of other content. This is much harder to say of the hardcopy format, for although a consumer may not read every article in detail, they are likely to scan, at least, the headlines. Consequently, when we see that the *MailOnline* is the most visited website, we cannot say that this means all its stories are seen, much less read.

This pattern, then, suggests that we can no longer blithely refer to power as some homogenous concept. Financial power, power to attract readers, and the power to influence political opinion (as opposed to cultural opinion and opinions about oneself) are surely splintered and separate (and separating) facets of the modern press. Although it may always have been apocryphal (see Chapter 1), at least historically there seems to be some basis for claiming that newspapers could influence the outcome of elections. It has become banal, by now, to mention *The Sun's* infamous headline of April 1992 'It's the Sun Wot Won It' as proof of the newspapers power to sway the electorate, and certainly Rupert Murdoch would like us to believe that his personal animus against the Labour Party at that time could be so decisive. And, of course, the press's broadly pro-Brexit strategy, which paid dividends in 2016, also adds nicely to the legend (albeit a report published by the Digital, Culture, Media and Sport Committee attributes this success to the scale of online campaigning rather than the press).[56] Yet the counterclaim,

---

[56] Digital, Culture, Media and Sport Committee, 'Disinformation and 'fake news': Final Report', HC 1791, 18 February 2019.

that this is simply the press tapping into the national mood, rather than the other way around, has gained more credibility (if it needed it) given the disastrous snap general election in the UK of 2017, in which Theresa May's Conservative Government, buoyed by unfailing support by the right-leaning press (which is an overwhelming percentage of the total), believed it would gain a huge majority in the House of Commons, but, instead, came spectacularly unstuck as it lost its previous, narrow majority and faced the prospect of a minority government until an expensive agreement with the Democratic Unionist Party of Northern Ireland gave it the bare majority it needed.

The second difficulty with the argument for power-based responsibilities is SRT's treatment of the term 'abuse'. For it is tolerably clear that SRT *wants* the press to be powerful because only a *powerful* press can perform the functions that SRT has in mind for it: to influence civic society positively and be sufficiently powerful, financially and reputationally, to match the resources of those who misuse private or political power.[57] In SRT, then, 'abuse' equates to speech or actions that work against the purposive sense of press freedom it has in mind. And yet this is deeply problematic – in a way that SRT does not sufficiently recognise let alone address – because this notion of abuse is incompatible with property rights. An organisation cannot be engaging in wrongdoing when it uses its property lawfully, but in a manner others dislike. When we scrutinise SRT's criticisms about 'abuse of power', we see that they do not fit the language of rights at all and that the concept of 'abuse' it relies upon is a term of art that attacks the prioritisation of capitalist interests over societal interests. Indeed, much of the criticism is in the vein of the socialist/Marxist critique of press freedom that was popular in the 1970s and has remained with us since. In fact, much of it comes from that era.

Consider the example that Robert McChesney provides, of the News Corp executive who, in the act of dismissing for producing a critical investigative report about the locality, said: 'we paid $3 billion for these TV stations. We will decide what the news is. The news is what we tell you it is.'[58] This, for McChesney, represented an abuse of power because the act was both 'anti-democratic' in its effect on audiences and in its attack on journalistic autonomy. According to him, such uses of private property represent a 'crisis for democracy generated by a corporate-dominated, commercially marinated media system.'[59] We find this view expressed often. Francis Williams, for example, complains that 'the freedom of the press does not exist in order that newspaper owners should grow rich.'[60] Barbara Ehrenreich calls it 'the mind-numbing materialism of our unaccountable

---

[57] See, eg, RP Bezanson, 'The New Free Press Guarantee' (1977) 63 *Virginia Law Review* 731, 735; Curran, (n 48), 86. MJ Gerhardt, 'Liberal Visions of the Freedom of the Press' (1992) 45 *Vanderbilt Law Review* 1025, 1029; LC Bollinger, *Images of a Free Press* (Chicago, University of Chicago Press, 1991).

[58] RW McChesney, *Rich Media, Poor Democracy* (Chicago, University of Illinois Press, 1999), 275.

[59] Ibid, 274–275.

[60] F Williams, *Dangerous Estate* (Cambridge, Patrick Stephens Ltd, 1957), 251.

and corporate-dominated media.'[61] Likewise, Curran has it that speech which serves capitalist interests at the expense of 'the people' is an abuse of power.[62] This line of argument, especially that which attacks the 'corporate-state nexus' decries, in overtly Marxist terms, the corporate press as a means of keeping the masses subdued.[63] It is, then, a complaint about capitalism's uninterest in enlightenment and the dominance of right-wing ideologies in press speech. So, to say that this conception of abuse conflicts with property rights is to miss the fact that this is entirely the point: the criticism of the corporate press is deep-rooted in an overriding attack on the lingering bourgeoisie obsession with property.

Admittedly, SRT is not saying that wealth creation is always an impermissible motivation for owning a newspaper. But there is, nevertheless, an awkwardness or disconnect with reality, for our legal system, economy, and society is avowedly capitalistic. There is a discernible sense in the SRT literature that not only are the pursuit of wealth and truth incompatible objectives, but also that the press's chief priority always ought to be the greater good – of furthering social progress and enlightening the masses. In this way, the pursuit of material wealth and financial success is incongruous.[64] For these commentators, it is only the pursuit of a better society that counts and that this obligation to do good binds not only owners but also the journalists and editors who work for them. Accordingly, Bertrand says, 'the number one target of professionals must be, not to increase the revenues of the firms they work for, but to serve better the various minorities that make up the public.'[65] Williams goes further: since journalists not owners are 'the legatees of history ... they have both a professional and public duty to look after their inheritance.'[66] This, says others, such as Gibbons, creates an obligation upon the state to provide greater protection for editorial autonomy[67] or upon the owner to inculcate an 'internal democracy' within the newspaper itself.[68] Of course, even if one could overcome the property rights issue, it would remain necessary to show how, in practical terms, this would make a difference since both arguments presuppose that the editor and journalists who work for the newspaper are naturally servile and timorous. That, but for overbearing ownership, they would adopt more liberal, socialist, and generally left-wing positions on the issues of the day. This may be so, although there is no proof, and it is hard to believe that journalists

---

[61] B Ehrenreich, 'The World We Share' in RW McChesney & J Nichols (eds), *Our Media, Not Theirs* (New York, Seven Stories Press, 2002), 10–11.

[62] J Curran, *Media and Power* (London, Routledge, 2002), 231–232.

[63] See especially McChesney & Nichols, *Our Media, Not Theirs*, (n 61), and N Chomsky, *Media Control*, (n 43).

[64] See discussion in previous chapter.

[65] C Bertrand, *Media Ethics & Accountability Systems* (New Brunswick, Transaction Publishers, 2000), 151.

[66] (N 60), 265–266.

[67] Gibbons, (n 49).

[68] S Holland, 'Countervailing Press Power', in J Curran (ed), *The British Press: A Manifesto* (London, MacMillan Press Ltd, 1978), 94, and N Ascherson, 'Newspapers and Internal Democracy' in Curran (ed), *The British Press*, 124.

who are so principled but cowed would choose to work for that title. Moreover, for every Harold Evans or Ben Bagdikian, there is a Paul Dacre or a Col Allan (formerly editor of *New York Post*).

But overcoming the property rights issue is a greater obstacle than SRT commentators realise. Williams, for example, misses this point entirely when he says newspaper owners have no entitlement to use newspapers to 'grow rich'. Although he pays lip-service to capitalism – 'free enterprise is a valuable bulwark of a free press' – he sees the property rights of press owners, compared to other business owners, as materially different: 'the freedom of the press differs from, and ought always to be recognised as greater than, the simple freedom of an entrepreneur to do what he pleases with his property.'[69] This is because, he says, newspapers belong not to owners but to 'the community'. Moreover, owners have 'obligations' to the past, present and future that they cannot escape, and which constrain their freedom of action: 'for newspapers would never have known independence if earlier men had not been ready to sacrifice themselves for principle' and 'the press is as much a custodian of national freedom and the qualities of civilisation as Parliament or the courts.' Thus, the press 'cannot turn its back on these obligations without reducing its stature.'[70]

The rhetorical elegance of Williams's position is undone by its own flawed logic. All citizens owe their present freedom to previous conflicts; all liberty was hard-fought, often won by bloodshed. We do not say, though, that individual autonomy is constrained by some obligation to live meaningful lives consequently. And if we impose this obligation on one set of business owners – the press – why not all others, who equally owe their freedom to the sacrifices made in their name? All private property must be in the same position. Williams, though, says:

> those who control or write for newspapers have no more right to claim immunity from the historical responsibilities of their office on the excuse that these responsibilities come between them and commercial advantage than have members of Parliament or judges; the position of all three ... are analogous.[71]

This, though, conflates the exercise of political power with the interest in it (which, anyway, all businesses have), whilst ignoring the public nature of political institutions that is entirely absent in the privately-owned press. Indeed, we must recognise that the comparison between the private press and public office holders is extremely thin. At root, Williams's position is that newspapers can be run as trusts, which forsake the pursuit of profit for the greater good.[72] This is all very salutary, and, in fact, in the UK, the *Guardian* and *Observer* operate under such a trust, but entirely irrelevant to the argument. That newspapers can so operate does not mean they must, or even should.

---

[69] Williams, (n 60), 264.
[70] Ibid, 251.
[71] Ibid, 251.
[72] Ibid, 252–253.

The third reason why the power argument is unconvincing is that, ultimately, it relies upon the harm principle to justify its position – that unchecked press power is unduly *harmful* to civic interests. We see the problem clearly in, for example, Judith Lichtenberg's argument that the property rights of the press are compromised by its civic function. Taking a wider perspective than Williams, she argues that this differential treatment is not only because the press is special but also that *all* property rights are qualified to some extent: 'hardly ever can one do with one's property exactly what one pleases.'[73] In support, Lichtenberg refers to the restaurant owner who, she argues, cannot refuse service on grounds of race, and also several US cases protecting the right to speak or distribute literature on private property.[74] These lead her to conclude: 'It does not suffice, then, simply to assert the property rights of publishers and editors against all claims to regulate the press' since 'it does not explain why newspapers and other media organizations should be immune from regulation when other businesses are not.'[75] But, in defending this position, Lichtenberg is forced to rely upon the harm principle. This is significant but fatal to SRT's claim to distinctiveness, which resides in its absolute rejection of liberalism as an adequate explanation of press freedom. So far as SRT is concerned, there are legitimate reasons to interfere with press freedom unrecognised by the harm principle. Yet, the examples that Lichtenberg provides do not demonstrate what this alternative principle is. On the contrary, these interferences are justified only because the harm principle is at work. We do not have to look too hard to see that state coercion of the racist restauranteur is justified by harm. It is easily explainable on the Kantian grounds that:

> if a certain use of freedom is itself a hindrance to freedom in accordance with universal law (ie, wrong), coercion that is opposed to this (as a hindering of a hindrance to freedom) is consistent with freedom in accordance with universal laws, that is, it is right.[76]

Thus, the state's interference is not simply justified on the positivist grounds that this sort of racism is outlawed, but on the principled grounds that denying one category of people access to services on the grounds of their race is to deny their humanity and treat them as subhuman. It is, therefore, the exercise of one freedom (of providing services) to deny others their freedom (to be treated with dignity and respect).

In the private-property free speech cases, Lichtenberg argues that the decisions turn on the extent to which the corporation operates as a 'municipality' since, in those cases, 'it assumes the obligations with respect to free speech that fall to

---

[73] Lichtenberg, (n 6), 115.
[74] Ibid, 116–119.
[75] Ibid, 120.
[76] I Kant, *The Metaphysics of Morals*, L Denis (ed), M Gregor, trans, (Cambridge, Cambridge University Press, 2017), [6:231].

public bodies.'[77] Thus, in *Marsh v Alabama*,[78] a company which owned the land on which the town stood could not prevent the distribution of religious literature. Specifically, the Supreme Court found that 'the more an owner, for his advantage, opens up his property for use by the public in general, the more do his rights become circumscribed by the statutory and constitutional rights of those who use it.'[79] It was not simply that the company provided *some* community space but that, in effect, it owned the entirety of that space. To deny the citizens of that community the opportunity to 'act as good citizens' and be 'informed' on all issues would be wholly unconstitutional; there was no other place they could go to exercise those freedoms.[80] In cases where the US courts have found for companies despite owning land used municipally, it has been because protestors and speakers have been able to communicate elsewhere.[81] Thus, these principles speak clearly to the deprivation of freedoms by others: the hindrance of a hindrance of freedom. These cases, though, do not show that property rights are qualified by free speech considerations. Instead, they show that when private property is used as a form of public forum then constitutional rights cannot be allocated selectively. Indeed, we should be wary of drawing general propositions from a case like *Marsh*. It needs to be seen for what it is: a peculiar case. Although Lichtenberg is not wrong to say it shows private property rights may have to bend to public rights, the proposition is misleading. It was not simply that the property had a municipal function, but that it represented the *totality* of municipal space available to citizens. The Supreme Court was faced with the prospect of an entire community being deprived of its constitutional rights in respect of its township. If the distribution of religious of religious literature could be outlawed, then so too could, say, the sale of newspapers criticising the company's administration of the town.

This argument has no application to the press, for newspapers are not municipalities. Press owners do not invite the public to use its facilities. Despite Jerome Barron's elegant argument to the contrary, the public has no right of access to determine newspaper content.[82] This is true as a matter of normative principle and doctrinal positivism.[83] This has important ramifications for, say, the public's 'right to know' which refers to no more than those occasions when the state cannot stand between speaker and audience to prevent information being disclosed. It does not provide, though, any entitlement by the audience to the product of the speaker's labour nor to command that labour. The audience has no right to demand that the speaker speaks, investigates, or acts. The fact that the press has the capacity to do

---

[77] Lichtenberg, (n 6), 118.
[78] 326 U.S. 501 (1946).
[79] Ibid, 506.
[80] Ibid, 508–509.
[81] *Central Hardware v NLRB* 407 US 539 (1972) and *NLRB v Babcock & Wilcox* 351 US 105 (1956) discussed in Lichtenberg, (n 6), 117–118.
[82] JA Barron, *Freedom of the Press for Whom?* (Bloomington, Indiana University Press, 1973).
[83] *Miami Herald Pub. Co. v Tornillo* 418 US 241 (1974).

so is insufficient, just as the grocer, butcher, and baker have no obligation to feed the starving even when it is in their capacity to do so.

IV. Professionalism and the Dualism of Responsibility

The final role-responsibility type argument concerns professionalism. Briefly, it claims that the status of the press as a role-bearer in civic society produces sufficient justification for both state and non-state intervention. Responsibility, therefore, in this sense, means the responsibility to act professionally, which carries with it the obligation to meet certain minimum standards. Thus, the Canons of Journalism, in the US, have been described as 'the newspaperman's quest for professional status.'[84] Admittedly, the press industry is not altogether comfortable with professionalisation since journalists fear 'the label might imply that someone has power to decide who is a journalist or to set standards.'[85] For commentators, though, professionalisation of the press is attractive since it provides a means of 'reconciling market flaws with the traditional conception of the democratic role of the media' since '... at its core is a seductive idea: professionalism means that the journalist's first duty is to serve the public.'[86]

When we examine these arguments, though, we see clearly what is otherwise apparent throughout SRT's discussion of responsibility. That the term 'responsibility' is used ambiguously, so as to signify, at times, Kant's ethical lawgiving and, other times, his juridical lawgiving (which was discussed in the last chapter). In this way, we see that the term has a dual quality. As noted in the introduction, Hart, himself, recognised this ambiguity clearly. It is apparent in the colloquial sense in which we describe, say, role-models. For, when we scrutinise the expression, we see that there are two types. There are those that the law recognises, either directly through statute or common law or indirectly through a regulatory body. Roughly speaking, this category captures those in a position of trust, such as the parent, doctor, teacher, politician, etc. Accordingly, the obligation to do the right thing is externally determined. And there is the other sort of role-model, whose title is imposed by the community on anyone whom we suspect others will seek to emulate. For example, when we say that artists, actors and actresses, sportsmen and women, or any other type of celebrity are role-models, especially to young people, we mean to say that people in this group should adopt higher moral standards than others and be mindful constantly of how others perceive their actions. Although the community articulates these standards, the choice to comply with

---

[84] WL Rivers and W Schramm, *Responsibility in Mass Communication* revised edn (New York, Harper & Row, Publishers, 1969), 239.
[85] DA Anderson, 'Freedom of the Press' (2002) 80 *Texas Law Review* 429, 475.
[86] Curran, (n 48), 99.

them or not is internally-regulated by the supposed role-model alone. Thus, the incentive to act responsibly – to do the right thing – is personal. This duality often lurks in SRT's use of the term.

To demonstrate this, I want to pause, for a moment, to scrutinise the work of William L Rivers and Wilbur Schramm whose approach to the professionalisation of the press represents a microcosm of SRT thinking. Let us begin with this statement: 'the basic responsibility of mass communication is to turn out the highest-quality product it can, which *requires* that it develops an awareness of the depth and breadth of the public's needs and interests.'[87] As a purely ethical claim, this is unremarkable: the good journalist, editor, and owner wants to satisfy their readership by producing their best work. As a legal claim, though, it is more problematic, for it begs the question of why that is so. As noted above, if it is a consumer claim – that purchasers pay for this standard – then the legal solution to this does not assist SRT's aims, for all the law would say is that, at best, the purchaser is owed the contract price for the 'defective' goods. In other words, law will not realise this standard directly, it will only compensate the breach of contract. Nevertheless, let us ask which meaning of responsibility Rivers and Schramm intend in this passage – is it ethical or juridical? From what follows, it is not entirely clear, and although, at times, they separate ethics from law, it is a muddled attempt, which leads to obfuscation. For Rivers and Schramm discuss strategies for *enforcing* this obligation by means of, first, self-regulation (which they discount) and, secondly, professionalisation (which they think more promising). In criticising self-regulation, they lament its inability to enforce quality standards, and conclude 'the responsibility of mass communicators is a higher horizon than can be reached through codes of conduct.'[88]

In their (lengthier) examination of professionalisation, the ethical is blended with the juridical. Accordingly, although they say 'finally, we can hope for the beginnings of self-criticism',[89] their strategy relies upon coercive means. These are to be realised by means of the 'critical apparatus' that press self-regulation lacks but which exists in the regulatory model used on professionals. Consequently, they endorse Walter Lippmann's claim that developments (then) in self-regulatory practices mark 'only the first beginnings of the equivalent of bar associations and medical societies which set intellectual and ethical standards for the practice of the profession. Journalism, we might say, is still an under-developed profession.'[90] But these professional bodies, as we shall see, are organs of coercion, which have the power to discipline and, ultimately, suspend those who do not comply with their standards. Rivers and Schramm, though, advocate the use of such measures, either by the regulator or the newspaper owner, to purge the industry of 'bad' journalists.

---

[87] Rivers and Schramm, (n 84), 238.
[88] Ibid, 238–240.
[89] Ibid, 245.
[90] Ibid, 246.

For they say, 'it is hardly heretical to suggest that a profession seeks to purify itself. Medicine and law have long tried to purify their ranks'[91] and 'the employer can help professionalize by upgrading their staffs.'[92] In this way, the discussion has the superficial appearance of ethical lawgiving, thinly masking the insistence on juridical lawgiving underneath.

I detect a similar problem in Hocking, when he discusses the rationale for regulation generally:

> [w]henever an institutional activity affects a general need, there is a public concern that the effect be favorable rather than detrimental. One begins to speak of a "right" of the public to have its news; this language has no necessary legal implications – a moral right lifts its head to announce an answering responsibility on the part of the institution.[93]

There is a reliance here on the language of law – that these obligations are, ultimately, enforceable. It is also apparent in Peterson's summary of the Hutchins Commission's conclusions: 'Media operators and owners are *denied* the *right* of publishing what pleases themselves. Free expression being a moral *right*, they are *obligated* to make sure that all significant viewpoints of the citizenry are reported in the press' (emphasis added).[94] And in Francis Williams claim that 'the journalist ought to accept and *ought to be required to accept* standards of professional integrity *morally not less mandatory* than those of the barrister, the solicitor or the doctor' (emphasis added).[95] Thus, these commentators smuggle the language of law (eg, talk of coercion and legal consequences) into propositions about ethics (eg, what one ought to do).

Thus, the duality of responsibility is problematic because when SRT says the press ought to act responsibly because of its role (either because it has this alleged professional status or is otherwise powerful), it means, and can only mean, ethical lawgiving (unless the claim is justified by the harm principle). This claim needs unpacking in the context of professionalisation, for there have been some attempts within the SRT literature, as we have seen in Rivers and Schramm's work, to claim the press is equivalent to the established professions, and so should be regulated for the same reasons. Edward Gerald, for example, has defended this on the basis that journalists enjoy the same level of autonomous decision-making as the solicitor, accountant, or doctor, and that this autonomy manifests in a sense of collective pride about the standards of journalism and, therefore, a shared concern to secure its reputation.[96] Francis Williams, meanwhile, argues that the journalist's professional responsibilities are equivalent to the traditional professions because 'the

---

[91] Ibid, 247.
[92] Ibid, 242.
[93] Hocking, (n 38), 167.
[94] Peterson, (n 2), 101.
[95] Williams, (n 60), 268.
[96] JE Gerald, *The Social Responsibility of the Press* (Minneapolis, University of Minnesota Press, 1963), 180.

preservation of the strictest ethical and professional standards in the press is no less important to society than in their case.'[97]

The comparison between the press and the traditional professions, though, is a false one. First, the dynamic between doctors, solicitors, etc, and those they work for is materially different compared to the press. The press operates at arms-length to the ultimate consumer, through its intermediaries. Indeed, it does not *know* its audience nor need to know them, except to the extent good business practices requires it to do so. Nevertheless, the poorly-read and well-read newspaper have the same obligations toward its ultimate consumers, and those are contained squarely within the transactional relationship. There is no position of trust and no intimate relationship that characterises the parent/child, doctor/patient or professional/client relationship, ie, no physical or mental vulnerability or inequality of knowledge between the professional and the person contracting with them.

Secondly, and relatedly, there is no special nexus of harm that would animate the imposition of professional standards. This arises from the position of trust which is peculiar to professional relationships and the parent/child dynamic. We can characterise these relationships in several ways. For example, there is usually a discernible vulnerability in the patient/client/child, which the law recognises. Although this is more pronounced in the case of the child compared to the client, crucially, it is not altogether absent in the client. This reflects the disparity in experience, knowledge, and expertise between the two parties. It also reflects the limitations in the exercise of choice that the weaker party has, which this imbalance creates. In the parent/child relationship, the liberty-limiting nature of this relationship is pronounced, although the doctor/patient relationship may be analogous, particularly where the surgeon is performing an operation on the patient, who, literally has no control over the surgeon's actions. But even in the solicitor/client or accountant/client relationship, the weaker party must cede an identifiable element of control to the professional if they are to act on her behalf. Whereas the client must provide the instruction to act, those instructions are informed by the solicitor's advice. All of this speaks to an impaired sense of autonomy in the subjugated party.

This dynamic simply does not translate to the press/audience relationship. There is no sense in which it can be said the audience is in a position of vulnerability relative to the press. This is not to dispute that readers will 'trust' newspapers and believe that what they read. Neither is it to dispute that the press 'knows more' than the public, or may have better access to, say, politicians, etc, than the reader. But we cannot say that this makes the reader vulnerable, for the reader has no right to the press's best endeavours to act in their best interests (unlike those other professions). We must, then, recognise that the law imposes liability on those in positions of trust, especially the professions, because of the serious effect that violation of their obligations causes. This includes death, serious injury, trauma, loss of

---

[97] Williams, (n 60), 268.

liberty, incarceration, bankruptcy, etc. In the worst cases of negligence, then, the adverse consequences are ruinous. When newspapers fail their readers, nothing so contiguous or dramatic occurs.

Similarly, we must seriously doubt the group dynamic that Gerald alludes to and which, if it did exist, would drive self-regulation as it does in the professions. For example, whereas the overall reputation of the group is unaffected when there are isolated incidents of poor service by a small number of professionals, the situation is different when poor service is endemic since frequent incidents are bound to impact adversely on the group's reputation as a whole. This can have a damaging direct effect on group members (eg, by driving up the cost of professional indemnity cover) as well as an indirect effect by causing users to seek alternative service providers in different markets, ie, if the legal services are thought to be poor in one region (or country), a user might use services from a different region. This dynamic just does not apply to the press. There is not the same sensitivity to poor reputational status (albeit there might be some risk of losing market share to a rival sector on the basis of poor quality). Moreover, the consequences of professional malpractice are different – or require different reflections. In serious cases of medical negligence, for example, it is in the public interest that the practitioner has her licence revoked. But the idea of 'revoking' a journalist's 'licence to practice' is not only odd but downright Orwellian.

Finally, we should recognise the error of labelling legally enforceable norms as 'ethical'. It creates the erroneous impression that the scope of potential regulatory provisions is all that can be called ethical. Although there is bound to be some overlap, not all ethical duties can be legally enforceable norms. The most obvious example of this duality is medicine's most well-known ethical injunction: to do no harm. Clearly, this is legally enforceable. The use of the term ethics as a proxy for regulatable conduct confuses two separate systems of organising principles. Ethics is the means of critiquing human action and our conceptions of both the good and the good life. But, although we may criticise the actions of others in the strongest terms, we cannot enforce our judgement without transcending to the realm of law. Oster recognises this point clearly when he says, 'a violation of media ethics can only be vindicated in a court if the ethical command has been absorbed into a *legal* obligation.'[98] The palette of potential regulatory provisions is narrower, therefore, than it may otherwise appear.

V. Conclusion

When we say that the press is responsible, we must recognise the ambiguity of the phrase. SRT plays upon this ambiguity to its own advantage. It seeks to

---

[98] Oster, (n 29), 47.

smuggle purely ethical concerns into the domain of legally-enforceable norms. Its strategy, though, is flawed because ethics and law are, and must be, kept separate. Responsibility, in Hart's sense of liability-responsibility, is a legitimate and sufficient reason to impose obligations upon the recalcitrant press. Since it must uphold its legal responsibilities, coercion is unobjectionable when it fails to. SRT, though, has sought to misuse this sense of liability-responsibilities to impose restrictions upon the press related not only to the exercise of certain rights but also more generally to say that the fact of having differential rights to the public is, of itself, sufficient reason to impose greater responsibilities upon it. This claim fails as a matter of positivism for, when we look, we do not find these special rights in law, and neither do we find special obligations.

The notion that, in exchange for special privileges, the press can be held to minimum standards fails on several grounds. First, it is doubtful that the press, at least institutionally, has these special privileges. Even if we resort to the alternative – that the institutional press might not have them, but the functional press (ie, those occasions the non-press, as well as traditional press, perform press functions) does – the problem remains. The nature of the exchange is asymmetric and lacks consideration. SRT is trying to impose a transcendental burden upon the press for which there is nothing given in return. For, when we evaluate the nature of the hypothetical exchange in these supposed privileges, we see that there is already a burdensome quality, in that the specific privilege is contingent upon certain obligations being performed in the exercise of it, for example, the adherence to the principles of responsible journalism to receive the benefit of protection under section 4 of the Defamation Act 2013. Alternatively, we see that the 'benefits' of the privilege go both ways: the press receives a private benefit (protection from liability) and society receives a public benefit (by receiving public interest information). Consequently, SRT's 'benefits for burdens' analysis is irredeemably flawed: there would need to be some extra benefit provided to the press to satisfy this transcendental burden to act 'responsibly'. Finally, even if we could overcome all of these problems, we should be more fearful of this sort of exchange than SRT appreciates: for no one – the institutional or functional press – should be beholden to the state for providing these privileges.

SRT, then, needs an alternative justification for this cross-cutting programme of responsibilities. It seeks to do so, although unsuccessfully, on the related premises that either the press is too powerful to remain unregulated in this way or its (supposed) professional status alone justifies a scheme of regulation comparable to that which applies to the traditional professions. Yet, in both instances, SRT fails to provide a distinctive, coherent justification for these claims, leaving it with no choice but to resort to the harm principle instead. In this way, for example, it becomes an argument that excessive or unchecked press power causes undue harm to the individuals affected by it or the democratic interests of wider civic society. As a justification for interference with press freedom, it is sound enough – but it is not a *distinctive SRT reason*. Moreover, there seems to be no recognition within SRT scholarship of this inadvertent reliance upon liberalism (ie, this failure to differentiate itself from liberalism) when the power argument is deployed. Instead, the strategy seems to be that an argument based not only upon power but also power combined with institutional prestige or the notion of professionalism is sufficient to produce alternative grounds to liberalism for regulation. Furthermore, the imposition of professional status upon the recalcitrant press is equally problematic, first, and foremost, because professional regulation depends upon the harm principle for its justification and, second, because the press does not bear serious comparison to the traditional professions.

Accordingly, although SRT seeks to use the term 'responsibility' to combine the stoicism of the categorical imperative with the familiarity of the harm principle, it cannot do so without becoming a thinly-disguised application of traditional liberal thought – and, in doing so, its claim to reject the liberal solution to press malfeasance fails. Consequently, we are left with no other conclusion that the only conception of responsibility viable for regulatory purposes is Hart's liability-responsibility. Thus, it is only the consequentialism of liberalism, not deontology or teleology, that can animate the parameters of legitimate regulation. This has significant implications for the type of regulatory provisions that may be enforced (as Part 3 will demonstrate). But liberalism, as a justification for press freedom, is deeply unfashionable. Moreover, as we shall see in the next chapter, there are several commentators who argue it simply cannot apply to the corporate press. These arguments deserve our attention. Moreover, we must understand how the harm principle applies to press freedom. This is the subject of the next chapter.

5

Accountability

I. Introduction

The essential claim of the book is this: the imposition of independent coercive press regulation upon the press is compatible with press freedom if it does no more than hold the press to account for unduly breaching the rights of others. Words like 'duty' and 'responsibility', when applied to the press, must have a meaning that is limited to this accountability context: that the press has a duty not to unduly interfere with the rights of others and that it has a responsibility to make good the legally-enforceable losses that it causes or else to comply with injunctions not to breach the rights of others. This accountability model of press freedom, therefore, adheres to the moral limits of law that we find in the liberal tradition and, especially, John Stuart Mill's seminal essay *On Liberty*:[1] that freedom of thought and opinion should be tolerated because of its pivotal role in 'truth-discovery' (by which Mill meant societal progress and individual self-improvement), unless it causes sufficient harm to warrant interference. The aim of this chapter is both to outline and defend the accountability model that will be applied, in Part 3, to common and prospective regulatory provisions. In doing so, it also defends Mill's argument from truth.

For some, the application of Millian principle to press freedom will be controversial; for others, prosaic. Indeed, given how well-known Mill's argument is, some will wonder what one more discussion could possibly add. Counter-intuitively, though, this sentiment provides more, not less, reason to explore its meaning and interrogate our understanding of it.[2] Many myths about *On Liberty* have grown stubborn roots. Familiarity has certainly bred contempt. For commentators assume that, given both its vintage and the superabundance of critical commentary, there is nothing new left to say about it nor ways of rehabilitating it from its perceived failings. This, though, is a mistake. It may lead to the sort of superficial readings that can, and have, generated these entrenched misconceptions. As Alan Ryan notes, many readers have been too easily seduced by Mill's

---

[1] JS Mill, 'On Liberty' in JM Robson (ed) *Collected Works of John Stuart Mill*, vol XVIII, (Toronto, University of Toronto Press, 1977).
[2] Famously, Mill himself recognised the importance of rehearsing familiar arguments in contemporary contexts when he begged his reader's indulgence in 'one discussion more.' Ibid, 227.

clear and plain prose; they do not appreciate that Mill is a 'difficult writer' whose 'clarity hides complicated arguments and assumptions that often take a good deal of unpicking.'[3] As CL Ten has pointed out: '*On Liberty* is a more complex piece of work than is generally supposed.'[4] But Mill's argument from truth cannot be properly understood without a close textual reading of both *On Liberty* and his wider work. Thus, although much has been said, not everything worth saying has been, and, of what has, there is much that is good and convincing, and much that is not. Whereas in political commentary and moral philosophy, many of these misinterpretations have been addressed (and Mill defended), the same cannot be said of the legal literature, especially that concerning freedom of speech. Indeed, the orthodox view among these academics seems to be that there is little to salvage from the wreckage.

There are several reasons for this hostility. For example, it is not uncommon for commentators to dispute the applicability of Mill's argument from truth, as an expression of autonomy and self-fulfilment, to the corporate press.[5] Onora O'Neill speaks for these commentators when she says Mill's defence of speech is inapplicable because 'freedom of expression is for individuals, not for institutions.'[6] Indeed, O'Neill has championed this claim most vociferously.[7] Although it is demonstrably wrong, it must be taken seriously given Lord Justice Leveson's endorsement of it in his report on press ethics and culture.[8] More generally, there is much hostility in the academic literature toward *On Liberty* – in keeping with the popular distrust of liberalism as a political creed – which, of itself, necessitates some defence of its application here. The opprobrium meted out to it can be traced back to Mill's time. His contemporaries were broadly united against him. For some, he went too far. Mill's fear of a 'tyrannous majority' at large impeding individuality was generally considered specious.[9] Thus, Thomas Babington Macaulay accused him of 'crying "Fire!" in Noah's flood.'[10] For others, he did not go far enough. James Fitzjames

---

[3] A Ryan, *The Making of Modern Liberalism*, (Princeton, Princeton University Press, 2012), 257.

[4] CL Ten, *Mill On Liberty* (Oxford, Oxford University Press, 1980), 144.

[5] See, eg, J Charney, *The Illusion of the Free Press* (Portland, Bloomsbury, 2018), xv and ch 4; J Rowbottom, *Media Law* (Oxford, Hart Publishing, 2018), 7–11; and J Oster, *Media Freedom as a Fundamental Right* (Cambridge, Cambridge University Press, 2015), 33.

[6] O O'Neill, *A Question of Trust* (Cambridge, Cambridge University Press, 2002), 94.

[7] See *A Question of Trust*, ibid, 92–95; 'It's the newspapers I can't stand', *Philosophy at Cambridge (Newsletter of the Faculty of Philosophy)* Issue 2, May 2005; 'Ethics for Communication?' (2009) 17(2) *European Journal of Philosophy* 167, 168–169; https://webarchive.nationalarchives.gov.uk/2014012219 2219/http://www.levesoninquiry.org.uk/wp-content/uploads/2012/07/Witness-Statement-of-Professor-Baroness-ONeil.pdf [2(b)]; 'Regulating for Communication', Foundation for Law, Justice and Society, Policy Brief, 31 July 2012, 4; 'The Rights of Journalism and the Needs of Audiences' in J Lewis and P Crick (eds), *Media Law & Ethics in the 21st Century* (Basingstoke, Palgrave Macmillan, 2014), 39–40.

[8] Lord Justice Leveson, *An Inquiry into the Culture, Practices and Ethics of the Press: Report* (HC 780, 2012), 63–63.

[9] See discussion in G Himmelfarb, *On Liberty and Liberalism* (New York, Alfred A Knopf, Inc, 1974), 143–168.

[10] Ibid, 162–163.

Stephen, for example, thought the liberal agenda would flourish only if lesser men were 'driven into a dictated form of virtue.'[11] The antagonism has only grown since then. Not only is liberalism still dogged by the sort of curious label Maurice Cowling gave it in the 1960s: of being 'carefully disguised intolerance' and of being 'a peculiarly exclusive, peculiarly insinuating moral doctrine.'[12] But also *On Liberty* has been so deeply and roundly criticised as to be almost discredited as a serious scholarly work. Gertrude Himmelfarb thought it contradicted by Mill's other works,[13] Lee Bollinger called it 'Pollyannaish' in its treatment of truth,[14] while John Rawls considered it paradoxical since it would require 'the oppressive sanctions of state power' to keep society 'united on a form of utilitarianism' to sustain it.[15] And this from scholars broadly sympathetic to his aims.

Clearly, Mill's liberalism is not without difficulty. Yet the aim, in this chapter and the book overall, is not to defend *On Liberty* absolutely but to demonstrate that his argument from truth is not only a plausible but the most persuasive basis for a coherent account of press freedom. This chapter, therefore, aims to show that contrary arguments may be overcome, as well as to demonstrate the misconceptions that have influenced those hostile to Mill's position. So that these misconceptions may be challenged, it is necessary to remind ourselves of what Mill said. The next section tackles this point by identifying the key elements of the free speech claim in *On Liberty* and considering how each of these is often misunderstood. This discussion is developed in section III, by challenging the common misconception that Mill's argument expects rationality to be a constant feature of civic life. Section IV continues this theme by articulating the mid-level principles which constitute the accountability model of press freedom. Finally, section V challenges O'Neill's objection that since Mill's argument defends free speech as an aspect of individuality it cannot apply to the corporate press.

II. Mill's Argument from Truth

Surely, the most egregious and stubborn misconception about *On Liberty* is to interpret it as no more than an argument that unimpeded debate eradicates error in popular debate. Lee Bollinger, for example, speaks for many when he reduces the argument from truth to the proposition that 'the truth will always win out'[16] whilst Bernard Williams, although more guarded, repeats its essence when he labels Mill unduly 'optimistic' in thinking freedom of speech 'must assist the

---

[11] MS Packe, *The Life of John Stuart Mill* (London, Secker & Warburg, 1954), 404.
[12] M Cowling, *Mill and Liberalism* (Cambridge, Cambridge University Press, 1963), xiii.
[13] Himmelfarb, (n 9).
[14] LC Bollinger, *The Tolerant Society* (Oxford, Oxford University Press, 1986), 74.
[15] J Rawls, *Justice as Fairness: A Restatement* (Cambridge, MA, Harvard University Press, 2001), 34.
[16] Bollinger, (n 14), 74.

emergence of truth.'[17] Similarly, Frederick Schauer questions whether Mill's theory 'accurately portrays reality': 'It does not follow as a matter of logical entailment that truth will be accepted and falsehood rejected when both are heard.'[18] We see it also in O'Neill's work: 'Despite Mill's eloquence,' she says, 'it is unlikely that freedom of the press and freedom of expression always produce optimal results.'[19] That this curious interpretation has endured is as frustrating as it is bewildering given that Mill is at pains to point out in *On Liberty* itself that such claims as these are utter nonsense.[20]

In fact, there is nothing 'optimistic' in what Mill says, for his argument does not depend upon the human capacity to progress or to accept truth when presented with it. It is, he says, 'a piece of idle sentimentality that truth, merely as truth, has any inherent power denied to error, of prevailing against the dungeon and the stake. Men are not more zealous for truth than they often are for error ...'[21] Instead, he presents an entirely negative claim: if we want to discover truth, societally and individually, then the optimal legal and ethical conditions that would enable it are those which are tolerant of non-conformity and the capacity to challenge orthodoxy. In short, to suppress information and ideas, because we think them false, is an unproductive strategy ill-befitting civilised society. It may be that Isaiah Berlin is right when he complains that history shows that 'fiery individualism' grows even in the coldest of political and cultural climates,[22] and, therefore, that liberty is not a necessary condition for it. But that is beside the point. Mill is discussing the optimal conditions for truth-discovery, not the minimum.

To understand this, Mill says, we must see that the formation, development, and refinement of opinion relies upon the power of reason. If, but only if, an individual is permitted to reason from the premises of an opinion, then they will discover its truth (or untruth). Conversely, if they are prevented from doing so, or do not bother to, then what they acquire is no more than 'a prejudice, a belief independent of, and proof against, argument.'[23] But this 'is not the way in which truth ought to be held by a rational being. This is not knowing the truth. Truth, thus held, is but one superstition the more, accidentally clinging to the words which enunciate a truth.'[24] We will only know truth if we are free to challenge, to contest, to deny the opinions that others hold to be truths. Unless we can do that, whatever knowledge we gain will be brittle and worthless.[25] We will not be able to defend

---

[17] B Williams, *Truth and Truthfulness* (Princeton, Princeton University Press, 2002), 212.

[18] F Schauer, *Free Speech: A Philosophical Enquiry* (Cambridge, Cambridge University Press, 1982), 25.

[19] O'Neill, 'Practices of Toleration' in J Lichtenberg (ed), *Democracy and the Mass Media* (Cambridge, Cambridge University Press, 1990), 158.

[20] Mill, *On Liberty*, (n 1), 238–239.

[21] Ibid, 238.

[22] I Berlin, *Four Essays on Liberty* (Oxford, Oxford University Press, 1969), 128.

[23] Mill, *On Liberty*, (n 1), 244.

[24] Ibid.

[25] Ibid, 231–234.

our views to others, for we will have no means of explaining *why* it is the truth, beyond asserting it as such:

> However unwillingly a person who has a strong opinion may admit the possibility that his opinion may be false, he ought to be moved by the consideration that however true it may be, if it is not fully, frequently, and fearlessly discussed, it will be held as a dead dogma, not a living truth.[26]

In this way, we see that *On Liberty* is a claim about reason and its battle with conformity. As KC O'Rourke put it: 'the general thrust ... is to urge people to value freedom rather than constraint, individuality rather than social conformity in human affairs.'[27]

Yet Mill's conception of mankind as eternally rational has produced the enduring prejudice that he is naïve and, thus, this quaintness has no place in our modern, secular, cynical society because, commentators say, people are irrational. This, of itself, is bewildering. Mill says nothing different to Aristotle in the *Nicomachean Ethics*: that humankind is defined by its *capacity* to reason and, thus, the good life is reached when reason and passion exist in harmony.[28] Indeed, despite the claims of elitism, much of *On Liberty* is spent in defending acts of irrationality. But Mill's point is that the ideal society utilises policies founded upon reason not passion – and thus seeking to force others to accept information and ideas that are unpalatable to them is profoundly unsound and pointless. This view has endured beyond Mill. We find it, for example, in Friedrich Hayek's *Road to Serfdom*[29] and Berlin's 'Two Concepts of Liberty'.[30]

Another egregious misreading of *On Liberty* is that he desires absolute freedom of speech. This stems from commentators reading one of the opening passages in Chapter II (where his argument from truth is substantially but not exclusively located, as superficial readings of *On Liberty* conclude) too literally, where Mill says that the silencing of opinion is a 'peculiar evil' and that:

> If all mankind minus one, were of one opinion, and only one person were of the contrary opinion, mankind would be no more justified in silencing that one person, than he, if he had the power, would be justified in silencing mankind.[31]

This does not mean, as Bernard Williams suggests, that 'the appeal to liberty ... [means] anyone can say or ask anything.'[32] It seems tolerably clear that the term 'opinion' is meant to convey a specific meaning, ie, the product of introspection.

---

[26] Ibid, 243.

[27] KC O'Rourke, *John Stuart Mill and Freedom of Expression* (London, Routledge, 2001), 118.

[28] Aristotle, *The Nicomachean Ethics* (Oxford, Oxford University Press, 2009).

[29] FA Hayek, 'The Road to Serfdom', in B Caldwell (ed), *The Collected Works of FA Hayek*, vol II, (First published, 1944) (Chicago, Chicago University Press, 2007).

[30] I Berlin, 'Two Concepts of Liberty' in *Four Essays on Liberty* (Oxford, Oxford University Press, 1969), 118.

[31] Mill, *On Liberty*, (n 1), 229.

[32] Williams, (n 17), 213.

We see this in Mill's brief description of opinion as something which belongs to the 'inward domain of consciousness' like conscience, thought, feeling, and sentiment.[33] The distinction between opinion and, say, discussion or expression is not negligible, for it indicates that Mill did not seek to protect all speech from state interference. It is a phrase he had used previously in contradistinction to fact: in a discussion on libel, Mill noted that 'the truth or falsehood of an alleged fact, is a matter, not of opinion, but of evidence.'[34] The difference remains important in libel law, but not only there. In defending his claim that 'society is justified in enforcing at all costs' those 'conditions' of society that each person can be made to bear her share of, the distinction between opinion and fact becomes important.[35] Whereas, in the court room, he thought it right that a person may be 'compelled ... to give evidence,'[36] he thought it a gross invasion of liberty that they could not do so unless they declared their belief in God.[37] Mill also uses the distinction as an exception to his arguments in favour of tolerating speech for its contribution to truth for, as he admits, the study of mathematics would not benefit from constantly tolerating error.[38] Consequently, Gertrude Himmelfarb must be wrong when she says Mill advocates 'the principle of *absolute* freedom of discussion.'[39]

But this distinction between opinion and fact (or something other than opinion) only goes so far. Mill is not saying, for example, that classification as fact rather than opinion renders speech fair game for suppression or the speaker fit for punishment. It must be shown that there is some enforceable obligation that would otherwise justify coercion, as with the compelled witness testimony example. Here, the distinction Mill makes between self-regarding and other-regarding conduct becomes important. For although opinion is usually classified as self-regarding – and so belongs to the 'very simple principle' that *On Liberty* advances, it can cross the divide to become other-regarding and so within the state's 'jurisdiction' to interfere when the harm principle is satisfied. Likewise, the dissemination of untruthful information presented as fact can also fall within the self-regarding category and, whilst there may be no obvious reason to protect such speech, there remains every reason to protect the speaker who causes no harm by disseminating it.

Consequently, the distinction between self-regarding and other-regarding calls attention to the nature of causation. For the fact of receiving speech cannot be taken, of itself, as absolute proof of the causal event. As Mill puts it, the expression of opinions 'affects others, only with their free, voluntary, and undeceived

---

[33] Mill, *On Liberty*, (n 1), 225.
[34] JS Mill, 'Law of Libel and Liberty of the Press', *Westminster Review*, Apr 1825, 291.
[35] Mill, *On Liberty*, (n 1), 276.
[36] Ibid, 225.
[37] Ibid, 239.
[38] Ibid, 244.
[39] Himmelfarb, (n 9), 33 (emphasis added).

consent and participation.'[40] In this respect, Mill's view is no different to Kant's conclusion that:

> A person is "authorized to do to others anything that does not in itself diminish what is theirs, so long as they do not want to accept it – such things as merely communicating his thoughts to them, telling or promising them something, whether what he says is true and sincere or untrue and insincere (*veriloquium aut falsiloquium*); for it is entirely up to them whether they want to believe him or not."[41]

Both statements provide an important explanation of, or qualification to (depending upon one's point of view), the notion of causation. Specifically, they capture the priority of reason as the primary determinant of when the state should intervene in human interactions. So long as humankind is free to rationalise and determine her own choices, the state should remain impartial and has, as Mill would say, 'no business' in interfering.

This clarification helps explain the difference between self-regarding and other-regarding activities. For Mill, this distinction is the engine of his 'very simple principle' that 'the only purpose for which power can be rightfully exercised over any member of a civilized community, against his will, is to prevent harm to others. His own good, either physical or moral, is not a sufficient warrant.'[42] If the recipients of opinions and (ostensibly) factual information, are free to act upon the information or not, as a matter of choice (ie, they are not coerced into doing so), then the state has no right to prevent them from doing so. Acting upon this information is, of itself, a self-regarding act. Likewise, if recipients disagree with that information – if they find it offensive, impertinent, or unhelpful – then they are free to disregard it. But they can no more use coercion to suppress it than the state could. Yet, crucially, this does not mean that they *cannot* disagree. On the contrary, Mill insists that anyone who disagrees with an opinion is always entitled to criticise it: it is only through the 'complete liberty' of full and frank exchange – 'of contradicting and disproving our opinion' – that both society and individuals improve: it is 'the very condition which justifies us in assuming its truth for purposes of action; and on no other terms can a being with human faculties have any rational assurance of being right.'[43] Whilst society is never justified in suppressing speech it dislikes, it is always entitled to try to persuade the holder that she is wrong. Speech that is other-regarding is not entitled to absolute protection, but instead may be interfered with when it harms others.

For James Fitzjames Stephen, Mill's distinction between self-regarding and other-regarding was nonsensical. It was, he said, the difference between 'acts which happen in time and acts which happen in space.'[44] Modern commentators

---

[40] Mill, *On Liberty*, (n 1), 225.
[41] Ibid.
[42] Ibid, 223.
[43] Ibid, 231.
[44] JF Stephen, *Liberty, Equality, Fraternity* (First published, 1873) (Indianapolis, Liberty Fund Inc, 1993), 231.

will often say that speech becomes other-regarding as soon as it concerns public or social matters. Alternatively, they might say, as Kent Greenawalt does, that Mill 'overstates his case' when he argues government suppression is a false assumption of infallibility because 'suppression might correspond with a cynical scepticism about any truth, with a belief that, fallible as it is, government is likely to judge more accurately than a dissident minority, or with a conviction that, true or not, some ideas are too destructive of a social order to be tolerated.'[45] None of these positions recognises the purpose or extent of Mill's harm principle. To take Greenawalt's example: Mill would say that the expression of false information – even that which the government has good reason to suppose is false – does no harm to anyone unless they choose to allow it to by, for example, failing to exercise good judgement. But that analysis does not apply where the speech is, as Greenawalt says, 'too destructive of a social order to be tolerated.' What is the difference? It is in the *source* of the harm. If an individual lacks, or fails to engage, the critical qualities necessary to detect false information (and so avoid acting upon it to her detriment), then the 'plea', such as it is, for government protection (for the state to prohibit or penalise such speech) is a plea for protection from oneself: it is to say, save me from my own gullibility. If, on the other hand, the recipient cannot defend themselves from the harm of the expression by their own means (by simply ignoring it, or distrusting it, or verifying it using other sources), then it becomes other-regarding and so there is a prima facie claim for state intervention. We see Mill acknowledge as much in Chapter IV, where he says that the state's 'authority' over the individual arises when that person, being part of a society, fails to 'observe a certain line of conduct towards the rest',[46] namely, where that individual breaches the rights of others: 'as soon as any part of a person's conduct affects prejudicially the interests of others, society has jurisdiction over it, and the question of whether the general welfare will or will not be promoted by interfering with it, becomes open to discussion.'[47] For example, since an individual cannot prevent herself from the harm of Thomas Scanlon's 'misanthropic inventor', who discovers the process for making nerve gas from 'gasoline, table salt, and urine',[48] simply by ignoring either him or the people he passes the information onto, she is entitled to expect the state to intervene on her behalf.

Of course, the harm principle itself has been the subject of vigorous and sustained criticism. It is often dismissed as an unprincipled means of determining liability, or labelled, as one commentator put it: 'catastrophically' unworkable.[49] Cass Sunstein speaks for most, it seems, when he says it invites ad hoc decision-making: 'under the pressure of the moment, there will be temptations for judges

---

[45] K Greenawalt, 'Free Speech Justifications' (1989) 89 *Columbia Law Review* 119, 130–131.

[46] Mill, *On Liberty*, (n 1), 276.

[47] Ibid.

[48] T Scanlon, 'A Theory of Freedom of Expression' in RM Dworkin (ed), *The Philosophy of Law* (Oxford, Oxford University Press, 1977), 159.

[49] DA Dripps, 'The Liberal Critique of the Harm Principle' (1998) 17 *Criminal Justice Ethics* 3, 10.

to find the harms great (or small) in particular cases'[50] and use this fact to deny protection to speech. These criticisms are examined below (section IV), but, as a preliminary, we should note that they usually overlook the fact that, in *On Liberty*, Mill describes harm as a necessary *but not sufficient* reason to interfere.[51] So, for example, the conclusion that liberalism justifies coffee being prohibited, because it is harmful, is a wildly inaccurate assessment of Mill's argument.[52] The identification of harm is merely the first step in the argument for prohibition. Moreover, as JC Rees has shown, this is a fundamental misreading because Mill does not deem everything that affects others to be other-regarding, only those things which affects *the interests* of others.[53] We can see the difference between effects and interests clearly through HLA Hart's example of the devout believer who thinks homosexuality is wrong. That person, says Hart, may well claim to be deeply affected simply by the *thought* of homosexuality being legal but cannot claim that his or her interests are affected consequently.[54] Mill made a similar point:

> a religious bigot, when charged with disregarding the religious feelings of others, has been known to retort that they disregard his feelings, by persisting in their abominable worship or creed. But there is no parity between the feeling of a person for his own opinion, and the feeling of another who is offended at his holding it.[55]

Although the term 'interests' needs defining, for now we can think of it in Hayek's sense as the question of 'whether the actions of other people that we wish to see prevented would actually interfere with the reasonable expectations of the protected person.'[56]

From this, we see that *On Liberty* is a claim about the importance of liberty to personal self-improvement and its related impact on societal progress. Many commentators, though, have criticised the apparent reliance upon rationality that this claim involves. Frederick Schauer's complaint that 'the argument from truth presupposes a process of rational thinking ... the theory weakens or dissolves when the process does not obtain'[57] and that it 'rests on an assumption about the prevalence of reason, for which the argument offers no evidence at all, in the face of numerous counter-examples from history'[58] is representative. Since this chimes with the complaint, examined in previous chapters, that SRT raises about the modern press (that it dupes readers into believing untruths and so vitiates the

---

[50] CR Sunstein, *Democracy and the Problem of Free Speech* (New York, Free Press, 1995), 150.

[51] Mill, *On Liberty*, (n 1), 224.

[52] Dripps, (n 49), 10.

[53] JC Rees, 'A Re-Reading of Mill On Liberty' (1960) 8(2) *Political Studies* 113.

[54] HLA Hart, *Law, Liberty, and Morality* (Oxford, Oxford University Press, 1963), 46–47.

[55] Mill, *On Liberty*, (n 1), 283.

[56] FA Hayek, 'The Constitution of Liberty' (first published, 1960) in R Hamony (ed) *The Collected Works of FA Hayek, vol XVII*, (Chicago, University of Chicago Press, 2011), 212.

[57] F Schauer, *Free Speech: A Philosophical Enquiry* (Cambridge, Cambridge University Press, 1982), 30.

[58] Ibid, 33.

quality of public debate), these claims deserve further consideration, which the next section does.

III. Liberty, Rationality, and the Press

There is, throughout the academic literature, a sort of sneering jocularity at Mill's supposed sanguinity. We see it even in the celebrated *Collected Works of John Stuart Mill* from the University of Toronto Press, in which Alexander Brady, in the introduction to volume XVIII, claims that the argument 'rests also on Mill's supremely confident faith in man's rationality.'[59] Yet Mill's argument rests on no such thing; to think that is to misunderstand him entirely. *On Liberty* is not about rationality; it is about autonomy. It examines the justifiability of coercion to prevent or else punish acts that society thinks are wrong. The rationality, of either the act or the actor, is irrelevant. It is the *consequences* of those actions that are determinative. It is only when the harm principle is satisfied that coercion is justified. If it is not, then all we may do is criticise or seek to persuade the actor to our way of thinking. In saying this, Mill is not saying that the actor will respond to rationality or, even, that the actor is *capable* of so responding. All he is saying is that this is the only *legitimate* means of challenging our strong moral concerns about the actor's behaviour. In modern times, we have seen just how great this challenge is, in our attempts to persuade the misogynist, the fascist, the racist, the homophobe, and the transphobe that their bigoted ways are wrong. The rise of demagoguery shows how poorly these attempts have succeeded. But what is the alternative? We can use the law to prohibit acts of violence toward minorities, but we cannot punish the thought itself that drives these bigots. Neither can we erase its perverse, pervasive influence; we cannot exorcise these evils away. The most we can hope for is that by inculcating the liberal outlook into our children during their schooling they will become resistant to this disease. Yet, once adulthood is reached, the state's power to direct learning ends. This is true even, though, as Mill says: 'in many cases, though individuals may not do the particular thing so well, on the average, as the officers of government, it is nevertheless desirable that it should be done by them, rather than by the government, as a means to their own mental education.'[60] Of course, Mill's hope that society should recognise continual self-improvement as synonymous with the good life is just that: a hope. This is why he quotes William von Humboldt in the preface to *On Liberty*: 'The grand, leading principle, towards which every argument unfolded in these pages directly converges, is the absolute and essential importance of human development in its richest diversity.'[61]

---

[59] A Brady, 'Introduction' in *Collected Works of John Stuart Mill*, vol XVIII, (n 1), lii.
[60] Mill, *On Liberty*, ibid, 305.
[61] Ibid, 215.

Consequently, we should recognise that rationality is a goal – an ambitious one at that – and the only means by which we can encourage this delicate flower is to provide fertile ground, through comprehensive education, intellectual nourishment by means of diverse opinion, and the sort of space that only a tolerant society can provide. Thus, the parameters of liberty are configured around these conditions. Of course, we can say that Mill championed rationality ethically, for he thought the good life was to be achieved by means of intellectual development. Yet he had no intention to render this a condition or an impediment in juridical lawgiving; it is merely an indication of his own ethical lawgiving. Moreover, he made no claims about the likelihood of rational decision-making prevailing in society. Unlike Milton, who thought truth would always triumph over falsehood when the two grappled,[62] Mill had no delusions about the allure of falsehood, as we have seen. A common mistake is to think Mill the later day incarnation of Milton, as O'Neill does when she says Mill endorsed Milton's quixotic claim that 'Truth will emerge victorious' when confronted by falsehood.[63] According to her, Mill employs 'the same line of argument … [when] he argues for 'the clearer perception and livelier impression of truth, produced by its *collision with error*.'[64] Yet Mill does no such thing. He clearly recognised that truth was often persecuted and sometimes suppressed for long periods.[65] His comment forms part of a discussion which asks why society should ever have to bear the dissemination of demonstrable falsehoods. To silence that expression, says Mill, is a 'peculiar evil', for if society is wrong, and the opinion is correct, then society loses. Yet, even if society is right, then the repetition of falsehood can be a useful educational tool for illustrating how the truth is confused with error.[66] In other words, error is not wholly without value, for it has this descriptive power which helps illustrates truth. In fact, this is exactly the method used in this paragraph: a falsehood has been repeated in order to reveal truth. If the state, or the publisher, prevented me from repeating these falsehoods, simply because they are false, I should have no means of signalling the error – and, in fact, if these falsehoods could never be mentioned, then the opportunity would be lost to diminish the prospects of their rediscovery in the future. This is why Mill says that this sort of practice leads eventually to dead dogma. We know that certain things are right, and certain things wrong, but if we cannot ask why – if we cannot satisfy our intellectual curiosity – then the reasons become lost and society is robbed of the opportunity to later correct any corruptions that creep into the myth.

It is this process, of self-reflection and intellectual curiosity, that is the most vital part of Mill's claims about liberty generally and free speech specifically. For without this, the goal of individuality, viz-a-viz self-realisation, cannot be realised.

---

[62] J Milton, *Areopagitica* (1644).
[63] See O'Neill, 'Regulating for Communication', (n 7), 3.
[64] Ibid, emphasis in original.
[65] Mill, *On Liberty*, (n 1), 237–243.
[66] Ibid, 229.

Whilst it would be wrong to reduce his philosophy to a sort of restatement of Stoicism,[67] nevertheless, these passages are reminiscent of that school of thought, especially the virtue of constantly striving to become the best possible version of oneself. But, more importantly, we see recognition that failure is both normal and to be expected. The individual that embraces this virtue 'becomes more valuable to himself, and is therefore capable of being more valuable to others. There is a greater fulness of life about his own existence, and when there is more life in the units there is more in the mass which is composed of them.'[68]

Perhaps Himmelfarb is right to criticise the image that Mill presents of the lone, spirited individual against the homogenous society when, as she says, it is surely more 'accurate to speak of the individual *versus* another individual or other individuals?'[69] This, at least, captures the complexity of disagreement, for it is rarely simply heterodoxy versus orthodoxy, but often a multitude of contested ideas, competing for supremacy. Of course, this is not to say that society is essentially a sort of civilised form of the Hobbesian paradigm of all against all, but rather a battle of ideas, played out in front of an audience. Yet, I do not think Mill was oblivious to this contest. Instead, I think he intended his dichotomous approach to describe not the ideas themselves but the qualities of the actors in this contest, as well as the audience members: that society is comprised of the 'developing' and the 'undeveloping', which is to say, those that embrace liberty for the benefits it provides for self-fulfilment and those who 'do not desire liberty, and would not avail themselves of it.'[70] This, then, translates, in the context of the free speech paradigm, to at least four different audience types:

1. The individual committed to a life of constant self-improvement whose progress is hindered by society's undue interferences.
2. The individual, either committed to a life of constant self-improvement or not, who seeks to interfere with the lifestyle choices of those whom she perceives as failing to live rationally or else is living poorly.
3. The individual who despises non-conformity and may have a desire to enforce conformity or punishment non-conformity.
4. The individual who neither despises non-conformity nor appreciates the liberty of seeking self-improvement.

---

[67] Although Mill was clearly sympathetic to Stoicism (and Epicureanism), particularly in its adulation of the higher faculties. See, eg, 'Utilitarianism' (first published, 1861), 211, 212, 218, 221, and 'Whewell on Moral Philosophy' (first published 1852), 176, in JM Robson (ed), *Collected Works of John Stuart Mill*, vol X, (Toronto, University of Toronto Press, 1985); See also 'Public and Parliamentary Speeches', in JM Robson and BL Kinzer (eds), *Collected Works of John Stuart Mill*, vol XXVIII, (Toronto, University of Toronto Press, 1988), 247; 'The Spirit of the Age, III' [Part 2], *Examiner*, 13 March 1831, 162–3, in AP Robson and JM Robson (eds), *Collected Works of John Stuart Mill*, vol XXII, (Toronto, University of Toronto Press, 1986), 279; 'Inaugural Address Delivered to the University of St Andrews', 248 and 'The Subjection of Women' (first published, 1869), 266 in JM Robson (ed), *Collected Works of John Stuart Mill*, vol XXI, (Toronto, University of Toronto Press, 1984), 248.

[68] Mill, *On Liberty*, (n 1), 266.

[69] Himmelfarb, (n 9), 15.

[70] Mill, *On Liberty*, (n 1), 266–267.

Even within these audience types, there is fluidity, for an individual may move between different categories at different times in her life.

When we transpose the arguments from *On Liberty* to the press freedom context, we can put these different mindsets to good effect to describe press actors, the objects of their journalism, and their readerships. For within the complex and diverse range of all potential stories are those that cherish individuality, those that abhor it, criticise it, praise it, encourage it in others and castigate those who would so encourage it. Likewise, we see the diversity of newspaper audiences in their potential responses, from those that engage critically with the newspaper stories, regardless of their political leanings, and so disregard what they perceive to be wrong or unconvincing, follow what they think useful and wise, and reserve judgement on that which they are unsure of, to those that do not and so misunderstand what they read, or react emotionally, or fervidly, or do nothing at all. It would be a mistake then to conclude, as some commentators have, that we can describe audience behaviours in static, binary terms and en masse: that audiences are simply rational or irrational.

Commentators tend to treat *On Liberty* as if it were only about situations a) and c): that it does no more than castigate unthinking conformity and defend self-reflective non-conformity. For, despite Mill's depiction of the 'developing' and the 'undeveloping', he does not reduce the problem to some simplistic model, as if it comprises nothing more than some epic battle between the two. Thus, *On Liberty* is not a competition between the 'enlightened' individual against the 'unenlightened' world (or, for that matter, heterodoxy versus orthodoxy) but rather the interaction between these four competing mindsets. In this way, it is a rich and nuanced argument. Moreover, it is as critical of the 'right-minded' as it is the 'ignorant', especially people that seek to coerce others due to their poor lifestyle choices. Accordingly, those that accuse Mill of 'elitism' should acknowledge, more than they do, his vociferous critique of the paternalistic type b) person. For in *On Liberty*, he attacks those who say the law should prohibit gambling, drunkenness, idleness, or even uncleanliness on the grounds that such vices are 'injurious to happiness', 'a hindrance to improvement' and serve no purpose in the pursuit of the good life. Such attitudes, says Mill, are indefensible.

He even anticipates the criticism that correcting such vices coercively does not affect autonomy because 'experience has shown not to be useful or suitable to any person's individuality.'[71] He responds by defending the (so-called) irrational agent whose disreputable behaviour hurts no one's interests but her own by arguing that a policy of intervention serves no purpose. This argument applies equally to the type a) person, for we should recognise that the rational agent, who seeks to be guided only by reason, will make mistakes and act irrationally or do things that others think disreputable or wrong. The argument, then, is also a plea for the opportunity to learn from one's mistakes. But *learn* is the operative word.

---

[71] Mill, *On Liberty*, (n 1), 280–281.

To force the agent to act is to reduce them to a state of perpetual childhood and will learn nothing valuable from the experience.[72] Moreover, the state will be unable to defend its actions:

> Let not society pretend that it needs, besides all this, the power to issue commands and enforce obedience in the personal concerns of individuals, in which, on all principles of justice and policy, the decision ought to rest with those who are to abide the consequences.[73]

Similarly, Mill recognises no power of the state nor the tyrannous majority to compel the type d) person to act rationally or embrace the positive effects of liberty upon their lifestyle.

Why would he do so – why would he defend this sort of self-destructive lifestyle – if, as Schauer says, he thought humankind permanently and constantly rational or was, as Alan Haworth says, elitist[74] or, as Cowling has it, a sort of 'moral totalitarian'?[75] The tawdry habits of the irrational agent ought to be of no interest to him; indeed, on this account, we ought to find him saying, explicitly, that only the *rational* agent is immune to coercive interference for his own good. Indeed, Cowling's description of Mill as someone who says 'that there is *a* doctrine, one doctrine, defining the nature of happiness and the means to achieve it, and that that doctrine is binding'[76] is mystifying. Whereas liberalism establishes a bedrock upon which social interactions must be conducted, it is neutral about what constitutes the good life since this is entirely a matter for the individual to discover. As KC O'Rourke reports, more recent commentators, such as John Skorupski and John Gray, have criticised this neutrality in Mill as being incompatible with utilitarianism: surely, they argue, individuality must give way to the greater good?[77] But, as O'Rourke sees, Mill's utilitarianism is more subtle and complex than Bentham's and his father's ever was – external notions of what makes for happiness, contentment, and self-fulfilment have no meaning unless embraced by the individual themselves.[78] This is why Mill says:

> The only freedom which deserves the name, is that of pursuing our own good in our own way, so long as we do not attempt to deprive others of theirs, or impede their efforts to obtain it. Each is the proper guardian of his own health, whether bodily, or mental or spiritual. Mankind are greater gainers by suffering each other to live as seems good to themselves, than by compelling each to live as seems good to the rest.[79]

---

[72] Mill, *On Liberty*, (n 1), 282.
[73] Ibid, 282.
[74] A Haworth, *Free Speech* (Oxford, Routledge, 1998), 27.
[75] Cowling, (n 12), xii.
[76] Cowling, (n 12), 33.
[77] See discussion in O'Rourke, (n 27), 122.
[78] Ibid, 121–124.
[79] Mill, *On Liberty*, (n 1), 226.

Of course, as we have seen, this does not mean Mill himself was neutral on what constituted the good life. Like the Stoics and the Epicureans, he thought the secret was to cultivate the higher faculties – that it is 'better to be a human being dissatisfied than a pig satisfied; better to be Socrates dissatisfied than a fool satisfied.'[80] But, as noted already, this was his view of ethics, not law. Moreover, he saw no point in using paternalism (which he likened to despotism) to improve the ethics of others.[81] What would be served by *forcing* people to accept ideas that they reject or to see the value in liberty when they have no interest?

> To be held to rigid rules of justice for the sake of others, developes *(sic)* the feelings and capacities which have the good of others for their object. But to be restrained in things not affecting their good, by their mere displeasure, developes *(sic)* nothing valuable, except such force of character as may unfold itself in resisting the restraint. If acquiesced in, it dulls and blunts the whole nature.[82]

The point has obvious significance for press freedom. SRT, in reviling right-wing newspaper coverage, has not shown how the strategy of coercive regulation would produce the outcomes of enlightened thinking that it holds dear. For why would the type d) person react favourably to the compulsion of newspaper coverage on certain topics, or more balanced coverage, when she is largely ambivalent toward reason? Likewise, what benefit will this strategy have in changing the outlook of the type c) or even type b) person who is, or is not, rational but loathes those who do not follow his own ideals? Applying Millian principle, we see that no one is entitled to interfere with either the freedom of the press or its ardent readers for propagating intolerant views, including those that champion conformity and castigate non-conformity, anymore than they can interfere with the unengaged individual who sees no value in self-improvement. We cannot hope to change their opinion meaningfully by preventing them from holding and expressing these unenlightened perspectives.

Such an intervention would be paternalistic, which Mill argues is always a wrongful reason to act. David Brink has questioned the persuasiveness of such an absolute rejection.[83] What about successful paternalism? By this, Brink means situations where the actor is thankful for the intervention, either immediately or at some later point in time. The example that Brink has in mind – of X physically impeding Y to prevent her stepping out onto an unsafe bridge – has no correlative in a newspaper context. Nevertheless, it is a valuable means of better understanding why Mill is hostile to paternalism. To illustrate the point, we should see that Brink's example is not a convincing one, for Y's autonomy has not been *denied* through coercion, so much as *delayed*. If Y knew of the danger, intending to commit suicide, for example, then she is free to continue despite X's intervention.

---

[80] Mill, *Utilitarianism*, (n 67), 213.
[81] Mill, *On Liberty*, (n 1), 299.
[82] Ibid, 266.
[83] DO Brink, *Mill's Progressive Principles* (Oxford, Oxford University Press, 2013), 150–151.

If Y did not know of the danger, then there has been no interference with her autonomy, for she would not have used the bridge otherwise. Paternalism, then, is not simply a matter of intervening but rather of denying agency to the actor, for it removes the individual's right to decide for herself.

The fact that a paternalistic intervention might prevent harm does not detract from its incompatibility with liberalism. Its unpalatability resides in the fact that it represents the negation of the agent's autonomous decision-making in favour of the supposed superiority of the intervenor's. It is this interference that is most troubling, for if the paternalistic agent did not more than share her views about the recipient's best interests, liberty would be preserved. But when paternalism is acted upon, it becomes an intolerable restraint that sacrifices individuality. As Berlin put it:

> to threaten a man with persecution unless he submits to a life in which he exercises no choices of his goals; to block before him every door but one, no matter how noble the prospect upon which it opens, or how benevolent the motives of those who arrange this, is to sin against the truth that he is a man, a being with a life of his own to live.[84]

This explains why Mill equated paternalism to despotism. It is also why the SRT agenda to improve the quality of press speech through regulation is so deeply problematic. When SRT theorists say that the public needs a press that furthers democratic participation, they may be right. But when they seek to use the coercive force of law or regulation to achieve this goal, they make despotism their end. But to fully appreciate this, we must look beyond the paternalistic intervener's intentions and think only about the effect.

This is difficult because the intentions of SRT are eminently reasonable and the problem not always clear. Consider, Onora O'Neill's claim that the imposition of obligations upon the press to provide information that is both accessible and assessable in terms of its veracity benefits society at large:

> If we can't trust what the press report, how can we tell whether to trust those on whom they report? An erratically reliable or unassessable press may not matter for privileged people with other sources of information, who can tell which stories are near the mark and which confused, vicious or simply false; *but for most citizens it matters.*[85]

Whilst O'Neill says censorship is an impermissible solution to this problem, what she proposes instead is little removed from that if it is to be effective. If we follow her comments – that the press has 'no licence to deceive', that they should 'distinguish comment from reporting', and that there should be 'penalties for recirculating rumours others publish without providing evidence'[86] – through to their logical conclusion, then we arrive at a system of regulation that has much in common with censorship. But O'Neill misses the point. There can be no *effective* solution

---

[84] Berlin, (n 30), 127.
[85] O'Neill, *A Question of Trust*, (n 6), 90–91.
[86] Ibid, 93–100.

precisely because her prognosis is wrong. If we were to create institutions that monitor the assessability of information – to check its veracity and connotations – we would simply displace the problem that O'Neill identifies, for having this sort of monitor does not solve the trust problem, it simply introduces another, well-known one: *Quis custodiet ipsos custodes?*

But it is O'Neill's diagnosis that is the major problem, for the question is not why can the public not trust the press, but why *would* the public trust the press? Given her pessimistic conclusion that the great many (the unprivileged) cannot consult alternative sources of information, we see Mill's concern about the fostering of belief and prejudice – dead dogma not living truth – in conduct that promotes passive learning. Trust is the conscious substitution of suspicion with faith. Vigilance is replaced by acquiescence. Obliviousness instead of cognizance. Packe summarised Mill's position well when he said: 'Truth unchallenged withered into commonplace. Thought was vital only when it was created, not received. More deadly even than violent persecution was "the deep sleep of a decided opinion".'[87] This explains Mill's conclusion that perpetual paternalism – that is paternalism which extends into adult life – damages social and individual progress: 'intellect and judgment of mankind ought to be cultivated.'[88] It is not trust but *distrust* that will stimulate this development. The US jurisprudence and literature is much more attuned to this principle. For example, Schauer has argued, persuasively, that the most convincing interpretation of the free speech guarantee is its role in nurturing this fundamental political principle: that it is based largely on:

> a distrust of the ability of government to make the necessary distinctions, a distrust of government determinations of truth and falsity, an appreciation of the fallibility of political leaders, and a somewhat deeper distrust of governmental power in a more general sense.[89]

We must see, then, that 'successful paternalism' in a newspaper context is a misnomer, for, as the O'Neill example shows, what SRT seeks to achieve is optimal reasoning in its readership, not by cultivation of the mind, but by directing, restraining, even controlling, the type and quality of information provided. But coerced 'reasoning' is not reasoning, it is the product of dictatorship.

In her Reith lectures, O'Neill argued for 'a more robust public culture, in which publishing misinformation and disinformation, and writing in ways that others cannot hope to check, are limited and penalised.'[90] In other words, as the term 'penalised' necessitates, a regulatory culture in which only reliable information is published – 'writing that seeks truth, or (more modestly) tries not to mislead.'[91] But the ostensible positives of this approach are, on Mill's analysis, illusory, for

---

[87] Packe, (n 11), 402.
[88] Mill, *On Liberty*, (n 1), 244.
[89] Schauer, (n 18), 86.
[90] O'Neill, *A Question of Trust*, (n 90), 92.
[91] Ibid, 93.

this would lead to no better result than the inculcation of dogmatism. It would not encourage but diminish the analytical faculties of readers who, having become accustomed to the practice that newspapers do not print untruths for fear of sanctions, are given to receiving information passively. The prospect of dead dogma not living truths is exacerbated by the greater space limitations that the newspaper format imposes compared to, say, the textbook or monograph.

Moreover, a perpetual state of trust undermines the value of disagreement, which is vital to liberalism. Ideas need to be tested, even ones we intuitively agree with, if they are to be sufficiently robust. And if we disagree, we should try to persuade the other person to change their mind. Mill makes this clear when setting out his 'one very simple principle': 'These are good reasons for remonstrating with him, or reasoning with him, or persuading him, or entreating him, but not for compelling him, or visiting him with any evil in case he do otherwise.'[92] This is a strategy Mill thought valuable, for it reflected his own experiences of forming, refining, discarding, and defending opinions. Again, the ignorant view of Mill is that he is himself an automaton: a product of some freak experiment in which his father James deprived him of contact with anything but the Utilitarian thought of Jeremy Bentham. This is but half-truth, for whilst his childhood was certainly exceptional, the real Mill is the product of intense self-development – a self reconstituted from the devastation of a profound nervous breakdown in his early twenties, which caused all the thinking of his earlier self to be re-examined and subjected to the hostile environment of those who vehemently disagreed. For individuals as diverse in their interests as Auguste Comte, Henri de Saint-Simon, Gustave d'Eichthal, Samuel Taylor Coleridge, Thomas Carlyle, James Fitzjames Stephen, and, of course, his wife Harriet, challenged, and often displaced, the views he had acquired in childhood from Jeremy Bentham and his father. This explains why he embraced the Hegelian sense of the dialectic: 'Truth, in the great practical concerns of life, is so much a question of the reconciling and combining of opposites.'[93]

This is important to emphasise, for it is sometimes said Mill was intolerant of opposing ideas and that his ideal society was 'morally homogeneous',[94] led by 'intellectual elite [providing] systematic indoctrination',[95] and that *On Liberty* is about protecting 'the elite from domination by mediocrity' and thus 'does not offer safeguards for *individuality* [per se].'[96] This is plainly untrue, as the above discussion adequately demonstrates. To this we can add CL Ten's point, which he sets out in his refutation of these claims: a liberal remains a liberal despite vehement disagreement with others and the desire to show them the error of their ways.

---

[92] Ibid, 224.
[93] Mill, *On Liberty*, (n 1), 254.
[94] Cowling, n 12, 28.
[95] Ibid, 38.
[96] Ibid, 104, emphasis in original.

What separates a liberal from a non-liberal is that 'these doctrines and standards should not be imposed on others who should be free to choose for themselves.'[97] Accordingly, when non-liberals complain bitterly that they are entitled to their opinion, as if this phrase has magical properties that terminates all dissent, they forget that so is everyone else, and that includes the right to tell them their opinion is garbage.

Himmelfarb, though, in her book *On Liberty and Liberalism*, thought she detected inconsistency in Mill's attitude toward distrust. In an earlier series of articles, entitled 'Spirit of the Age', published in 1831 (almost 30 years before *On Liberty*), Mill seemed firmly against the value of disagreement[98] and expressed an opinion that seems more closely related to O'Neill's: that the ideal state would be one 'in which the opinions and feelings of the people are, with their voluntary acquiescence, formed *for* them, by the most cultivated minds, which the intelligence and morality of the times call into existence.'[99] For Himmelfarb, this is anathema: 'so far from being an absolute good, freedom of discussion appeared, in these articles, as at best a very mixed good, at worst a necessary evil.'[100] In her view, we cannot dismiss this as evidence of the unrefined Mill who had not yet escaped the shackles of his strict Utilitarian upbringing (although it is not clear why this must be so). Nevertheless, even if one takes this Mill to hold the same views as the one that wrote *On Liberty* the two positions are not as irreconcilable as Himmelfarb suggests. Most significantly, this earlier Mill is not disclaiming reason; on the contrary, he argues that all should exercise their powers of reason 'as far as [it] will carry them, and cultivate the faculty as highly as possible.'[101] By doing so, reason will provide the analytical tools to enable individuals to determine the persuasiveness of an expert's opinion for themselves and, where it does not (if, for example, the level of expertise required is beyond them), then it will enable them, as a second best, to know whether to put their faith in that person's authority. This is perfectly compatible with a state of distrust – for distrust does not mean disbelief but rather active engagement with sources of information. It develops the discipline of scrutinising information, consulting alternative sources or, if that is not practical, the suspension of judgement: that information is treated with caution and, if acted upon, it is in the knowledge that it may be wrong. Indeed, this seems to describe what most of us do intuitively when, for example, we engage with expert opinion on climate change. Few of us have the requisite technical knowledge to know for sure whether climate change is real or not, but most of us are persuaded by the views of experts that it is because we engage our powers of reason when examining the arguments for and against. Admittedly, Mill's critics

---

[97] Ten, (n 4), 148.
[98] Himmelfarb, (n 9), 36–39.
[99] Ibid, 41.
[100] Ibid.
[101] Ibid, 40.

might say that this is elitism. But there is nothing inconsistent in his belief that the rational person would lend weight to the views of authorities on subjects beyond her knowledge and lived experience. The novice that takes up fishing looks to the expert at the lake; the student looks to their supervisor on how to write a dissertation; the election campaigner who wants to know the most efficient method of covering a neighbourhood consults the binman. What is elitist about this?

But we must see this consensus-building in context. Respect for the intellectual thought of others is itself a product of reason. It is to see that expertise is superior to intuition and ignorance. But this does not supplant the value of disagreement. In this context, this quality emerges as a healthy scepticism for all forms of knowledge – or rather the need to check even the conclusions of experts for signs of error. Respect but not total submission. In other words, the preservation of will. Admittedly, one weakness in Mill's thought is that this overriding aim should be achieved through artificial disagreement should unanimity be achieved. This, perhaps, places too much faith on the power of reason to overcome passion in any context and neglects the Socratic truth that the wise person knows that she knows nothing for certain. Constant disagreement on ethical issues, including what we would now call political questions, seems not only likely but inevitable. For even on a question as fundamental as justice we see disagreement stretching back to antiquity, from Plato's *The Republic* to, in modern times, Rawls's *Theory of Justice*.[102] And even though we may think Rawls had it more or less right, still that did not prevent Amartya Sen publishing, in 2009, *The Idea of Justice* – his essential reworking of Rawls's theory – to critical acclaim.[103]

IV. The Accountability Model Outlined

The qualification that harm must relate to interests is important but, without more, does little to diminish SRT's claims. Indeed, it would seem to give it greater purchase, given that its central claim is that impoverished standards of press speech *harm* society's interests in democratic participation and the public interest in a robust press.[104] This is why O'Neill says:

> if powerful institutions are allowed to publish, circulate and promote material without indicating what is known and what is rumour, what is derived from a reputable source and what is invented, what is standard analysis and what is speculation, which sources may be knowledgeable and which are probably not, they *damage* our public culture and our lives.[105]

---

[102] J Rawls, *A Theory of Justice* revised edn (Oxford, Oxford University Press, 1999).
[103] A Sen, *The Idea of Justice* (London, Penguin, 2009).
[104] See, eg, discussion in Sunstein, (n 50), 93–119; RW McChesney, *Rich Media, Poor Democracy* (Chicago, University of Illinois Press, 1999); T Aalberg and J Curran (eds), *How Media Inform Democracy* (London, Routledge, 2012).
[105] O'Neill, *A Question of Trust*, (n 6), 95.

As seen in previous chapters, SRT would describe this harm as that done to drown out minority voices; to distort, exaggerate, and, in some cases, invent materials relevant to democratic participation in pursuit of personal vendettas and self-serving agendas. Moreover, the expression 'harm to interest' seems significantly engaged, if we accept the validity of the SRT claim that 'the expanse of our knowledge of public affairs must come from the mass media. There simply are no practical alternatives.'[106]

The key to Mill's liberalism, though, is to be found not in isolation, by plumbing the depths of the terms 'harm' and 'interests', but by understanding the overall scheme of legitimate interference that he sketches out for us. Specifically, we must see that harm as the setback of interests means a violation of rights (otherwise our understanding of the distinction between 'affected by harm' and 'interests affected by harm' is not much advanced). For instance, a traffic jam harms my interest in being on time for work; losing out to a competitor in a job interview harms my interest in paid employment; a divorce harms my interests in the financial security in two incomes. All this may be true, but I cannot claim to have a *right* to travel unimpeded by traffic, or to success in job interviews or in personal relationships. Examined this way, we see that the key to understanding the harm principle is not in further and better definitions of 'harm' but in what counts as a protected, or protectable, 'right' as a matter of liberty. Consequently, we do well to think of 'harm' and 'interests' in the same manner that Joel Feinberg does: as a placeholder to indicate a range of activities which are denied protection by the liberty principle because of their adverse consequences.[107] In this way, we will find precision not in the terms 'harm' and 'interest' themselves but only in the context in which they are used.

By doing so, we can overcome another common criticism of Mill: that *On Liberty* provides insufficient examples of when coercion relating to speech is justified.[108] There are only two. The first relates to the failed prosecution for seditious libel against Edward Truelove, a radical publisher, who, in 1858, had published a pamphlet by William Edwin Adams, another radical, entitled 'Tyrannicide: is it justifiable?'[109] The prosecution was 'ill-judged', Mill argued, because the pamphlet was not harmful but merely offensive (the government's case had been that it was 'immoral'): 'there ought to exist the fullest liberty of professing and discussing, as a matter of ethical conviction, any doctrine, however immoral it may be considered' unless the words constitute an 'instigation' to the act of assassinating a political leader and 'a probable connexion' between the act and the speech exists.[110]

[106] WL Rivers and W Schramm, *Responsibility in Mass Communication* revised edn (New York, Harper and Row, 1969), 14.

[107] J Feinberg, *Harm to Others* (New York, Oxford University Press: 1984), 31–36.

[108] See, eg, Himmelfarb, (n 9), 58–59; Haworth, (n 74), 28–31.

[109] Referred to in FE Mineka and DN Lindley (eds) *Collected Works of John Stuart Mill,* Vol XVI (Toronto, University of Toronto Press, 1972), 1262, letter 1074, fn 1.

[110] Mill, *On Liberty,* (n 1), 228, fn 1.

The second is the well-known corn-dealer example. As with the rest of *On Liberty*, its meaning suffers when presented in summary form and, since the discussion that follows places great emphasis upon it, it is worth setting out in full:

> No one pretends that actions should be as free as opinions. On the contrary, even opinions lose their immunity, when the circumstances in which they are expressed are such as to *constitute their expression a positive instigation to some mischievous act.*

> An opinion that corn-dealers are starvers of the poor, or that private property is robbery, ought to be unmolested when simply circulated through the press, but may justly incur punishment *when delivered orally* to an excited mob assembled before the house of a corn-dealer, or *when handed about* among the same mob in the form of a placard.

> Acts, of whatever kind, which, without justifiable cause, do harm to others, may be, and in the more important cases absolutely require to be, controlled by the unfavourable sentiments, and, when needful, by the active interference of mankind.

> The liberty of the individual must be thus far limited; he must not *make himself a nuisance to other people.* But if he *refrains from molesting others* in what concerns them, and *merely* acts according to his own inclination and judgment in things which concern himself, the same reasons which show that opinion should be free, prove also that he should be allowed, without molestation, to carry his opinions into practice at his own cost.[111]

Unsurprisingly for a passage so sparse and yet so important, it has received multiple interpretations. Himmelfarb, for instance, saw it as a simple example of the distinction between 'action' and 'speech': it is 'one instance in which discussion constituted a direct and practical call to action … not a symbolic or potential call to action.'[112] Alan Haworth concluded similarly, though he thought the distinction unsustainable since, to his mind, speech must be a category of action. Instead, he argued, it demonstrated that irrational speech fell outside the zone of absolute protection: 'whatever the orator in the 'corn dealer' example is doing it is not behaving like a good seminar group member; presenting propositions for careful consideration by other rational agents, weighing the views of others in the balance, and so on.'[113] Gray, meanwhile, thought it showed nothing more than 'the improbability of autonomous thought in 'excited mobs',[114] whereas for O'Rourke it demonstrated that 'individuality also entails responsibility for one's own actions' so that a person can be punished if she 'exploits a situation in which people are likely to act without reflection, and others are harmed as a consequence.'[115]

These interpretations suffer to the extent that they are selective and disjointed from both the tyrannicide example and a holistic interpretation of Mill's position on liberty. The formula is set out in the tyrannicide example: there must be

[111] Mill, *On Liberty*, (n 1), 260, emphasis and breaks to the text added.
[112] Himmelfarb, (n 9), 58.
[113] Haworth, (n 74), 31.
[114] J Gray, *Mill on Liberty: A Defence* 2nd edn (London, Routledge, 1996), 105.
[115] O'Rourke, (n 27), 131.

some form of encouragement or provocation to commit the act, the act itself has happened, or is likely to, and there is a sufficient connection between the two events. We are looking, then, for an act that breaches, or will breach, the rights of others which occurred because of prior encouragement or provocation. Mill wants us to understand the context as an instigation to a mischievous act because here it is done deliberately or recklessly to endanger the life and/or property of the corn-dealer. He is not saying that the holding of a placard in every instance *is* such an act. Neither is he claiming special immunity for the press, as the tyrannicide example makes plain since that, in some instances, can also be understood as such an instigation. The distinction then is between speech that compromises a person's physical safety, and that of her property, and trenchant criticism.

What is important, then, is the speaker's strategy, inferable in the words themselves. If the speaker is advocating lawful means of addressing the problem, then the speech is protected by liberty.[116] Thus, in the corn dealer example, the connection would disappear if the speaker said: 'the corn-dealer is starving us, and to show our dismay, I want you to join me in sitting down in protest.' Gray might be right that autonomous thought is unlikely in the 'excited mob' but if, having heard these words, it still attacks the corn dealer or vandalises his property, then the cause is not the speech. In other words, it is the delivery of an opinion that champions, or can be understood as championing, reprisals upon the corn dealer that justifies the interference with speech.

If, however, the speaker is advocating unlawful means, then the speech may not be protected, nor if it is recklessly indifferent to provoking unlawfulness, but *only* if the speaker has the probable means of achieving the unlawful ends. This is a point that is often neglected in interpretations of Mill: it seems to be assumed that the words used by the speaker are innocent enough since there would be no problem if printed. It may be that Mill had in mind David Hume's injunction that ideas distributed through the press cannot never incite violence because they are read 'coolly and alone': there is no one from which to catch the 'contagion' to riot.[117] But this would be to accept Haworth's dubious thesis that Mill was an elitist only interested in protecting higher order speech. Yet other passages in *On Liberty* give the lie to this assertion, for Mill had, on the page before no less, said that 'law and authority' have 'no business' in restraining 'unmeasured vituperation', nor 'offensive attacks', nor polemics,[118] nor 'intemperate discussion, namely invective, sarcasm, personality, and the like.'[119] A more promising interpretation, then, is that Mill wants us to understand the words as inflammatory, irrational, unfair: the corn-dealer is *starving* us *deliberately*; he is no better than a common *thief*; all property owners are *thieves*. These are not hypothetical

---

[116] Mill, *On Liberty*, (n 1), 260–262.
[117] D Hume, *Essays Moral, Political and Literary* (first published 1741) (London, Grant Richards, 1903), 11, fn 1.
[118] Mill, *On Liberty*, (n 1), 259.
[119] Ibid, 258.

ideas, plucked from thin air; these *are* Mill's views. His conclusions that the Corn Laws starved the poor and that the landed gentry did not deserve the income they derived from land they did not work can be seen in *Principles of Political Economy* (first published,1848), and, later, in *England and Ireland* (1868). These were set out reasonably enough, but in his earlier work he had presented them much more polemically. For instance, in 1834, in William Johnson Fox's *Monthly Repository*, he wrote of the Corn Laws:

> The time of calm discussion is gone by, and that of agitation must commence. The people are convinced, they are now to be stimulated. Reason is satisfied; the appeal must now be (however little the word may be relished) to passion. Injustice was never hurled from its throne by men who remained cool. The people must show that when they are wronged they can be indignant, and that the deliberate profession of a determined purpose to persevere in wronging them, can only be expiated by the complete loss of political influence.[120]

Is this, as Haworth would have us believe, the behaviour of a 'good seminar group member'? Is it, as O'Rourke might say, the actions of a responsible advocate? Does it provide, as Himmelfarb suggests, a clear example between immune speech and prosecutable action? Is it, as she might also say, simply a symbolic call to action? We see now, more clearly, the problem that Mill wants us to see of why delivering this sort of opinion to the excited mob or handing it out on placards is materially different to publishing it when unaware of our audience.

This side of Mill's character is not prominent in the commentary on *On Liberty*. Perhaps it should be. Perhaps, seen through the lens of this more vitriolic Mill, his arguments might be liberated from the qualities that commentators attribute to him. For commentators have been too quick to dismiss Mill as the timid college professor of Haworth's imagination, or the mouthpiece of Harriet, as Himmelfarb has it,[121] or as supremely naïve in thinking humankind capable of constant, uniform progress, as Gray does[122] – and, consequently, to imbue his argument with these same weaknesses, rendering them either too soft or too cerebral to capture reality. These appraisals overlook the stubborn Mill who disowned his mother and his sisters for their cold treatment of his wife,[123] the vengeful Mill who, for two years, doggedly pursued the death penalty for Edward John Eyre, who orchestrated a massacre of indigenous people in Jamaica,[124] and the passionate Mill who championed rights for women despite being castigated, ridiculed, and ignored constantly in both Parliament and the popular press.[125] This Mill was not some naïf with a lovely view of his fellow man nor someone easily

---

[120] Mill, 'The Debate on the Corn Laws', 8 March 1834, in JM Robson (ed) *Collected Works of John Stuart Mill*, vol VI, 183–184.

[121] Himmelfarb, (n 9), 257–272. See criticism of Himmelfarb's argument in Ten, (n 4), 156–166.

[122] See 'Postscript' in Gray, (n 114), 130–158.

[123] R Reeves, *John Stuart Mill: Victorian Firebrand* (London, Atlantic Books, 2007), 214–217.

[124] Packe, (n 11), 470.

[125] Reeves, (n 123), 413–448.

cowed. He was bold, cunning, and determined. He understood well enough the power of ideas. He was not, then, concerned to protect timorous speech but bold, challenging, irreverent speech – of the type that he deployed from time to time and which he suffered.

The freedom to express even intemperate opinions interferes with the freedom of others only when it constitutes 'molestation' of their rights. A vivid, modern example illustrates the point. In April 2015, controversial columnist Katie Hopkins called for gunships in the English Channel to tackle immigration.[126] After expressing her inability to feel pity for those that drowned attempting the crossing, she compared them to 'cockroaches', and said they should be returned and have their boats burnt. Aside from confirming what is already known, that Hopkins is a despicable human being, the article cannot be said to constitute 'a positive instigation to some mischievous act'. It did not, for example, advocate violence toward migrants. It did claim that asylum seekers and illegal immigrants – that is, those that smuggle onboard Britain-bound trucks – were a 'plague of feral humans' who were turning British towns into 'festering sores' and receiving benefits 'shell[ed] out … like Monopoly money'. But here as well there is no overt advocacy of violence or other unlawful means to tackle the problem (as she sees it). Moreover, Hopkins is not addressing a specific group, who might receive this as an incitement to act.

The fact-pattern of *Green Corns Ltd v Claverley Group Ltd*[127] illustrates my point. Here, the defendant newspaper published a series of articles hostile to the claimant care home association's plans to buy properties in the local vicinity to house troubled, vulnerable teenagers. These articles, published between February and April 2005, contained the exact location of these homes. Overall, they conveyed the impression that: these care homes were populated by sex offenders; that, since they were close to primary schools, local children were at risk; that an incident like the vicious machete attack that took place at a nearby nursery in 1996 may be repeated; that local house prices would suffer, and local businesses fail. Consequently, angry residents began to protest outside the named properties – once, the atmosphere was so frightening that the police had to be called to spirit away a 15-year-old resident and his carers to safety – and several of them were vandalised. Despite this, the newspaper campaign continued, apparently buoyed by the claimant's decision to cancel their plans for some of these houses following these acts of violence. The claimant's claim that the publication of specific addresses constituted an actionable misuse of private information was upheld by the High Court. In its view, although the discussion of these care homes generally was a matter of public interest, the exact location of them was not; that the newspaper had not empowered 'the people' to 'influence events by lawful means' but, rather,

---

[126] K Hopkins, 'Rescue boats? I'd use gunships to stop migrants', *The Sun*, 17 April 2015.
[127] [2005] EWHC 958 (QB).

had enabled them to compel 'another to abandon lawful activities under threat of harassment or violence': in other words, 'the opposite of democratic' protest.[128]

What distinguishes the Hopkins example from the *Green Corns* case is the absence of the discernible 'angry mob'. In *Green Corns*, the defendant publisher knew, or ought to have known, that a group of angry, militant residents were acting on the information that they had provided. As the claimants told the court, they had received no attacks on their properties prior to the first article, published in February 2005.[129] Moreover, those attacks took place at the addresses published in the defendant newspaper. Consequently, then, the facts show that the various stories – written in powerful, emotive language – had created an incendiary atmosphere in the local community. Each new article acted as a catalyst to violence. The Hopkins story does not fit this pattern. First, it is written as a personal reflection about her apparent lack of empathy, in which both she and the object of her ire are presented as inhuman:

> No, I don't care. Show me pictures of coffins, show me bodies floating in water, play violins and show me skinny people looking sad. I still don't care. Because in the next minute you'll show me pictures of aggressive young men at Calais, spreading like norovirus on a cruise ship.

Second, it is not providing encouragement: the defendants in *Green Corns* had indulged in a sort of gleeful boasting that their actions were achieving results: the claimant was changing or cancelling plans to buy houses because of its actions.[130] Third, since it did not name specific towns, the Hopkins article was not identifying, and therefore not inciting, a specific group of British people who had been 'wronged' by the government's immigration policy.

But even if such a group did emerge post-publication the connection between speech and whatever act they might commit would be too remote to attribute to Hopkin's vitriol – assuming that she published nothing further to encourage them to commit some unlawful act. Mill refers causation in these terms:

> But with regard to the merely contingent, or, as it may be called, constructive injury which a person causes to society, by conduct which neither violates any specific duty to the public, nor occasions perceptible hurt to any assignable individual except himself; the inconvenience is one which society can afford to bear, for the sake of the greater good of human freedom.[131]

Clearly, the 'greater good' he refers to is equally prospective and uncertain – so why should we tolerate xenophobia and not tackle it whenever it arises? To understand this, we must see that Mill, if he had the Hopkins example before him, would not say that xenophobia is good – for small-mindedness is always ethically

---

[128] Ibid, [105].
[129] Ibid, [29].
[130] Ibid, [106].
[131] Mill, *On Liberty*, (n 1), 282.

wrong – but that the way to tackle xenophobia effectively is through more, not less, discussion. History entitles us to be sceptical about this claim: as Alexander Bickel said, society has lived through too much to believe it.[132] Schauer might say that this is one of those times when 'generally, but not always, the expression of unsound opinions causes greater harm than the expression of sound opinions.'[133] And yet whilst our intuition is to interfere with hateful speech, like Hopkins's, perhaps we should follow Oliver Wendell Holmes's view, that democracy:

> is an experiment, as all life is an experiment. Every year if not every day we have to wager our salvation upon some prophecy based upon imperfect knowledge. While that experiment is part of our system I think that we should be eternally vigilant against attempts to check the expression of opinions that we loathe and believe to be fraught with death, unless they so imminently threaten immediate interference with the lawful and pressing purposes of the law that an immediate check is required to save the country.[134]

In this way, when we interfere with speech based on consequence not content, we do not need to find it valueless, we only need to find it powerless. We protect the speech of people like Hopkins not because it deserves to be, but because we see that it moves no one to act upon it, at least not to the extent of immediate, impulsive violence.

Yet, whereas these examples demonstrate the significance of causation, they do not provide a complete answer. Since harm is a necessary but not sufficient reason to interfere with speech, it must be shown that the rights of others are not only affected but also *unduly* affected. For instance, in *Green Corns*, the court accepted that a discussion about the provision of care homes is a matter of public interest that ought to be protected despite the interference with privacy rights that it may cause.[135] But, it concluded, the precise location of those care homes was not a matter of public interest, but one of private interest to local homeowners.[136] Talk of private interests instead of public ones provides an artificial dynamic. But clearly the decision in *Green Corns* was correct. What the court might have found instead was that the actions of the newspaper amounted to coercion: that it sought not to persuade but to force the claimant to abandon its plans through bullying and intimidation. This is not to say that the defendants were orchestrating riots but that the inflammatory nature of their reports and the provision of precise locations were tantamount to incitement to act for what Mill would call some 'mischievous' end. Neither is this to deny that residents are entitled to have their say on the provision of such care homes in their community. But, by acting as they did, the protestors and vandals had usurped the function of democratic participation, and the defendant newspaper had, through its reckless actions, encouraged

---

[132] A Bickel, *The Morality of Consent* (New Haven, Conn, Yale University Press, 1975), 71.
[133] Schauer, (n 18), 28.
[134] *Abrams v US* 250 US 616, 630 (1919).
[135] *Green Corns*, (n 127), [97].
[136] Ibid, [99].

them to do so. Thus, we are entitled to interfere with press speech when it crosses the divide between 'individual independence and social control'.[137]

Translated to the press regulation context, this need not mean that the regulator is limited to protecting only those rights found in the positive law. In *On Liberty*, Mill had argued that freedom from coercion extended to 'certain interests, which, either by express legal provision or by tacit understanding, ought to be considered as rights'.[138] He provides a little more detail on this later, where he describes 'acts injurious to others' as:

> Encroachment on their rights; infliction on them of any loss or damage not justified by his own rights; falsehood or duplicity in dealing with them; unfair or ungenerous use of advantages over them; even selfish abstinence from defending them against injury – these are fit objects of moral reprobation, and, in grave cases, of moral retribution and punishment.[139]

In *Utilitarianism*, in a discussion about the meaning of justice, he defined rights as 'something guaranteed to him by society' and 'something which society ought to defend me in the possession of'.[140] But Mill only ever hints at what he means by this: later on, echoing the central theme of *On Liberty*, he describes justice as 'the moral rules which forbid mankind to hurt one another (in which we must never forget to include wrongful interferences with each other's freedom)';[141] and, elsewhere, that this includes 'acts of wrongful aggression, or wrongful exercise of power over some one' and 'wrongfully withholding from him something which is his due'.[142] On this point, Mill held the same view as Kant, who had said, in *The Metaphysics of Morals*, that a purely empirical inquiry into the notion of rights was 'like the wooden head in Phaedrus's fable … [something] that may be beautiful but unfortunately it has no brain'.[143] In the Kantian scheme, rights, as external duties that one must observe,[144] are either natural (and derived from *a priori* principles) or acquired (and derived from 'the will of a legislator')[145] and the former are further sub-divided into innate and acquired rights. Of these, Kant's notion of innate right foreshadows an important aspect of Mill's argument from truth: there is only one innate right, he says, which is freedom: this, he defines as 'independence from being constrained by another's choices'.[146] Like Mill, Kant sees this as having three parts: equality, autonomy, and freedom of speech.

---

[137] Mill, *On Liberty*, (n 1), 220.

[138] Ibid, 276.

[139] Ibid, 279.

[140] Mill, *Utilitarianism*, (n 67), 250.

[141] Ibid, 255.

[142] Ibid, 256.

[143] I Kant, *The Metaphysics of Morals* (first published 1797), L Denis (ed), M Gregor, trans (Cambridge, Cambridge University Press, 2017), [6:230].

[144] Ibid, [6:237].

[145] Ibid.

[146] Ibid, [6:238].

From these observations we can derive some principled limits to the regulator's capacity to implement rules outside the positive law. Interferences with speech or conduct are justifiable only if there has been an act of wrongdoing which causes harm to the victim. In other words, the regulator's code of conduct must comply with the harm principle: the justification must be to safeguard the freedom of others; it must not be paternalistic (because it would make the press better or more civic-minded); or to prohibit offence to others; and must protect speech that respects the persuasion/coercion dichotomy. These rules may protect the innate freedom of others – their equality, autonomy, and freedom of speech – but only if innate press freedom is protected. In other words, the press is entitled to say whatever it wants so long as that speech 'does not in itself diminish what is theirs.'

Whilst this discussion clarifies some important features of Mill's argument from truth, and helps triangulate 'undue harm' as the area between 'offence', 'paternalism', and 'persuasion', it remains too abstract to demonstrate the range of legitimate regulatory provisions. For that, Part 3 applies the principles set out here to concrete examples. Prior to that discussion, though, it is necessary to refute the popular, but baffling, claim that Mill's argument from truth cannot apply to press freedom.

V. Liberty and the Press

In his report on press ethics and culture, Leveson agreed with Baroness O'Neill's view that:

> John Stuart Mill's argument from *On Liberty*, that freedom of speech serves a central function in promoting individual autonomy and self-fulfilment ... has no direct relevance to press freedom because, put simply, press organisations are not human beings with a personal need to be able to self-express.[147]

Owing to what she describes as an 'unfortunate convergence of terminology',[148] freedom of expression, as Mill understood it, and as it applies to the press are two separate concepts. Sometimes, the fault for this 'simple error' is blamed upon 'contemporary commentators' who, she says, fail to see that Mill's argument only applies to *individuals* not organisations[149] – as if Mill himself had excluded the press from his argument. Other times, she says that Mill was equally deluded in thinking the press could benefit from the liberty argument.[150] This indecision makes the strategy for engaging with her work slightly harder, because, of course, Mill did apply his argument to the press. But we need not quibble with O'Neill

---

[147] Leveson Report, (n 8), 62, [3.3].
[148] O'Neill, 'The Rights of Journalism and the Needs of Audiences', (n 7), 40.
[149] See O'Neill, Witness statement and 'Ethics for Communications', ibid.
[150] O'Neill, 'It's the newspapers I can't stand', ibid.

over this. Her overall point is that to apply the argument from truth to press freedom is an error which 'leads to confusion, and claims about media freedom based on this error have no value.'[151] Although, in other respects, she has adjusted her position over the years, O'Neill has been faithful to her claim that Mill's argument from truth protects self-expression (ie, expressions of individuality) whereas press freedom protects only something which she calls 'communication'. This is the view she set out in Judith Lichtenberg's book *Democracy and the Mass Media*, summarised in her BBC Reith Lectures of 2002 (entitled *A Question of Truth*), glossed in her evidence to the Leveson inquiry, and has repeated since in various other minor publications.[152]

O'Neill's argument from communication is straight-forward enough, although it relies on some rocky foundations. In her article for Lichtenberg, entitled 'Practices of Toleration', she asks why we tolerate freedom of expression. Her answer is that we tolerate individual expression because it is self-regarding, and therefore harmless, and because it needs no audience. She notices that 'rights approaches to speech and expression insist on rights to express opinions, but deny that there are rights to communicate' and explains that 'this is because advocates of freedom of expression doubt whether anyone has rights to have an audience or to be understood, or to be published by presses others own.'[153] But then, she moves in a different direction, claiming that the press, on the other hand, is 'important, especially in democracies ... mainly because they are organs of communication.'[154] This is confused or else confusing, for it mistakes an empirical claim for a normative one. Newspapers do have audiences (their readers) but so do some individuals – and newspapers can no more demand an audience than the individual can. Nevertheless, O'Neill proceeds to the conclusion that since the press is communicative (it has an audience), it has what she calls 'communicative obligations', which include 'noncoercion' and 'nondeception'.[155] These, she says, are perfect obligations, ie, enforceable by the state.

There are several problems with O'Neill's position on press freedom. In Chapter 3 we considered – and dismissed – her central claim that newspapers are under an enforceable duty to serve a public function. There is no need to rehearse those arguments here, although we should recognise that this teleology is also an important difference for O'Neill between press freedom and individual freedom of expression – that whereas press freedom is teleological, individual speech rights are non-teleological.[156] Instead, we shall focus on her claim that newspapers

---

[151] O'Neill, Witness statement, ibid.

[152] See, eg, O'Neill, 'Practices of Toleration', (n 19), 163–176; *A Question of Trust*, (n 6), 96–100; 'It's the newspapers I can't stand', ibid, 1 & 8; Witness Statement, ibid, [1]–[5], especially; 'Regulating for Communication', ibid, 5–6; 'Ethics for Communication?', ibid, 167–170.

[153] O'Neill, 'Practices of Toleration', (n 19), 165.

[154] Ibid, 166.

[155] Ibid, 170.

[156] O'Neill, Witness statement, ibid.

cannot benefit from the anti-paternalism principle that is central to Mill's conception of liberty. There are several elements to her position on this and each needs to be tackled. The starting point is O'Neill's claim that journalism is not about self-expression. Sometimes, this is presented as a sort of existential claim: since the press is a series of corporate bodies 'they are not selves in the relevant sense'[157] and, therefore, the argument from truth cannot apply because 'the need to protect individuality applies only to beings that *can* express themselves.'[158] Other times, it is presented as a normative claim: 'Powerful institutions, including media organisations, are not in the business of self-expression, and should not go into that business.'[159] And on others still, it is presented as a sociological or consumer claim: 'readers, listeners and viewers don't need media that 'express themselves': they need media that meet at least minimal standards for adequate communication with intended audiences.'[160]

The claim that the press is not human and therefore does not need the protections given to humans to safeguard its autonomy is, certainly at face value, quite baffling. The corporate structure of a newspaper is no more than a convenient vehicle for organising its financial obligations. If a newspaper was run as a partnership, would it suddenly become a 'self'? The whole argument quickly leads to some odd conclusions, for, by the same logic, we would be forced to say that a nation is also not a self in the relevant sense and yet we still speak sensibly enough of nations having the right to self-determination as an aspect of individual autonomy. The content of newspapers is not mechanically produced: it is the product of human thought and comes from beings that *can* express themselves. But let us think of O'Neill's objection not as one of possibility but preference: that, ideally, newspapers should not be self-expressing. This requires us to engage more fully with what O'Neill has in mind when she refers to this thing called 'self-expression'. The sense one gets from 'Practices of Toleration' is that O'Neill regards self-regarding expression as something introspective, personal, and self-absorbed: that it is, above all else, harm*less*. This is confirmed by her later work where, for example, she summarises Mill thus: 'it is an argument for freedom for individuals to express themselves, providing that their self-expression is innocuous.'[161] For reasons that are obvious from the discussion above, this is a gross misstatement of Mill's harm principle. But let us take it at face value and pursue it through to its conclusions. Let us pretend that newspapers are not in the business of self-expression nor that the audience, or wider society, wants it to self-express. What then?

Immediately, we encounter a problem that O'Neill does not anticipate. If newspaper content is not about self-expression, then it is a sort of mechanical process in which audiences are provided with 'accessible, assessible and intelligible'[162] content

---

[157] Ibid.
[158] Ibid.
[159] O'Neill, 'The Rights of Journalism and the Needs of Audiences', ibid, 40.
[160] O'Neill, Witness statement, ibid, [5].
[161] O'Neill, 'Regulating for Communication', ibid.
[162] O'Neill, Witness statement, ibid, [5].

that audiences can utilise in both their private and public decision-making. In this way, newspapers become reduced to the role of disengaged conduit, passing information back and forth. Yet, for the most part, this is not the role that O'Neill has in mind for the press; she wants it 'to be free to seek truth and to challenge accepted views',[163] to engage in 'wide-open, robust debate',[164] to represent a diverse range of viewpoints. To do so, the journalist must make decisions about the persuasiveness of the arguments, brevity (and levity), and their intelligibility given the diverse intellectual abilities of her readership. In short, she must engage her powers of reason. How is she to do so if the protections afforded to reason by Mill's argument from truth do not apply to her?

But, of course, O'Neill is not saying that Mill's argument has no relevance to the press (albeit at times this *is* what she says), but that Mill's claim does not provide the complete answer[165] because the responsibilities she imbues in press freedom means that the press must act as a conduit in some circumstances: to provide audiences with the diverse views *of others*. The journalist, recognising that she is not an 'oracle of truth or authority beyond question', must 'neither *mislead* by assuming bogus authority nor *silence* others by undermining their standing and capacities to respond.'[166] Ultimately, then, it is not for the journalist to exercise her reason to devise these viewpoints, but to disseminate more widely the thought of experts.

In this view we might see something of Mill's opinion in 'Spirit of the Age', but we are talking at cross-purposes if we think what Mill says is equivalent to what O'Neill is saying. When Mill says that reason will cause those with less expertise to follow the views of those with more, he is not saying that those people have an *obligation* to agree with, let alone repeat, what those authorities think. But O'Neill is. She says that the journalist should forsake her own views in favour of those of her audience: that she 'should assume and reveal [her] own fallibility';[167] she should not provide her own viewpoints but reveal and prioritise those of her audience instead.[168]

O'Neill's strategy, here, is difficult to discern, once we start to scratch the surface of her argument. We quickly see that there is paradox. On the one hand, she denies that Mill's argument from truth has relevance to the press, whilst on the other maintaining truth-discovery is the *only* rationale that matters. In her 2009 article, 'Ethics for Communication?', she reaffirmed her consistent view that the press cannot benefit from the truth-seeking justification because they lack the requisite 'discipline' (which she identifies as 'experiment, careful inquiry, fact checking, and many others'). And yet O'Neill's scheme, which she set out in 'Practices of

---

[163] O'Neill, *A Question of Trust*, (n 6), 93.
[164] Ibid, 94.
[165] O'Neill, 'Practices of Toleration', (n 19).
[166] Ibid, 171.
[167] Ibid, 173.
[168] Ibid.

Toleration', summarised in *A Question of Trust*, and embellished in her evidence to the Leveson inquiry all point toward the inculcation of this discipline as a prerequisite for journalism – that speech is accessible, assessable and intelligible. It is an essential part of her teleological claim about press freedom that the press has an 'epistemic responsibility' to its readers.[169] How is one to characterise these obligations if not as truth-discovery?

The problem is not so much that O'Neill's strategy is not apparent so much as that it is not defensible. It is readily apparent that she thinks Mill's truth-discovery argument provides a much greater range of protection than the sort of freedom she thinks the press deserves. Her position is, then, much more faithful to a sort of Meiklejohnian reading of the First Amendment clause: that the free speech guarantee protects only that which enables democratic participation. It is a regular theme in her work that individual speech is innocuous, eccentric, and probably false but this is fine because such speech is, of itself, harmless.[170] Whereas, when expressed by the press, that same speech becomes sinister, dangerous, and corrupting.[171] Not only are these claims mere assertion, they ignore an important aspect of Mill's argument which goes apparently unnoticed by O'Neill. For Mill had no interest in advancing an argument that would protect only innocuous, pointless speech. The problem is the limited and limiting basis on which O'Neill reads Mill as a manifesto for self-expression. Self-expression, O'Neill says, is 'often obscure, uncivil or inaccurate, but even when it fails in these ways usually causes little harm'[172] and 'Other acts of self-expression fail to communicate for various reasons: some are eccentric, unintelligible or egocentric to the point of obscurity.'[173] She is, therefore, presenting self-expression as the *antithesis* of communication: eg, 'Communicative acts may be inaccessible to intended audiences for a range of reasons. Some may be *unintelligible* because intended audiences cannot follow what is communicated: even if satisfactory as acts of self-expression, they inevitably fail as communication.'[174]

In this way, self-expression and communication are distinguished by their orientation (one is inward-facing, the other outward) and their production (self-expression is singular, communication is collective). But this makes little sense once we begin to interrogate the ideas. Mill's notion of individuality depends not on isolation, but interactivity. How else is the individual to refine their own ideas without sharing them or having the opportunity to interrogate the thoughts of others? Indeed, this collaborative quality is so important to Mill's theory that Himmelfarb concluded the argument from truth had nothing to do with individuality: that the

---

[169] O'Neill, 'It's the newspapers I can't stand', ibid, 1.
[170] O'Neill, 'Ethics for Communication?' ibid, 169; 'Regulating for Communication', ibid; *A Question of Trust*, (n 6), 94.
[171] Ibid.
[172] O'Neill, 'Ethics for Communication?', ibid, 169.
[173] Ibid, 168.
[174] Ibid, 175, (emphasis in original).

suppression of just one opinion 'deprives the whole of the human race.'[175] This interpretation of self-expression, as something interactive, is apparent in more modern thinking. For example, we see Karl Popper[176] and Jeremy Waldron[177] emphasise disagreement as a positive, *worthy* feature of progressive society (for it is only through this openness to challenge that real progress is made). And, in Jürgen Habermas[178] and Joseph Raz,[179] we see the importance of validation to self-expression. This comes only through the active non-judgmental acceptance of the community to diversity, not simply from some begrudging or dismissive tolerance of the type O'Neill has in mind. It cannot be that the value of individual freedom of expression, then, is in allowing people to be 'silly, irrelevant, or plain crazy.'[180]

The reason for O'Neill's strategy is, of course, perfectly clear. She wishes to distinguish individual freedom of speech from press freedom so that burdens can be imposed on one without interfering with the other. As she says: 'If the media were in the business of self-expression, they (like individuals) would be liberated from requirements to communicate effectively, accurately or in ethically acceptable ways.'[181] But the distinction is artificial – and, in an important sense, unnecessary. For although O'Neill is most concerned with improving democratic participation, she also fears the power of the press to harm others unduly. For example, she says: 'Freedom of expression for the media (or for other powerful organisations) cannot be justified as [innocuous]: on the contrary it can be harmful to the less powerful'[182] and 'if powerful organisations enjoy more-or-less unconditional rights of self-expression they are likely to harm and injure.'[183] This *is* an important reason to interfere with the free speech rights of the press – but it is also a reason that Mill himself emphasises. There is *always* legitimate reason to interfere with *unduly* harmful speech. We do not need to construct a new narrative solely around the press to realise this.

VI. Conclusion

The essence of the accountability model is this: the press has an obligation to make good, not do good. When the press breaches its obligations, then it should be made to compensate its victims. A scheme of coercive independent press regulation is

---

[175] Himmelfarb, (n 9), 24.

[176] K Popper, *The Open Society and Its Enemies*, vol 1 (London, Routledge, 1945); *The Open Society and Its Enemies*, vol 2 (London, Routledge, 1945).

[177] J Waldron, *Law and Disagreement* (Oxford, Oxford University Press, 1999).

[178] J Habermas, 'Morality and Ethical Life: Does Hegel's Critique of Kant Apply to Discourse Ethics?' in R Beiner and WJ Booth (eds), *Kant & Political Philosophy: The Contemporary Legacy* (New Haven, Conn, Yale University Press, 1993), 323.

[179] J Raz, 'Free Expression and Personal Identification' (1991) 11 *Oxford Journal of Legal Studies* 303.

[180] O'Neill, *A Question of Trust*, (n 6), 94.

[181] O'Neill, 'Ethics for Communication?', (n 7), 169.

[182] Ibid.

[183] Ibid.

perfectly legitimate if it aims to do no more than this. The scope of permissible regulation, then, concerns determining when the rights of others are unduly breached. This arises when an agent engages in wrongdoing that causes harm to a victim. This is a matter of identifying harm to rights which, although not restricted to purely legal rights in a positivist sense, nevertheless cannot extend to protection from offence or interferences to appease paternalism. These elements, therefore, translate to the simple formula of wrongdoing-causation-harm.

The superiority of Mill's argument from truth is its complete absence of content bias. Mill had no interest in stacking ideas to determine protection. Unlike later authors like Alexander Meiklejohn, Mill did not say that political expression was more important than any other.[184] Neither does he confine speech's importance to this one, narrow area of existence. For Mill, classification into 'important' and 'unimportant' speech is anathema: it would be the paternalism principle in action. To understand Mill, then, we must see the evils of paternalism in the way that he does. Paternalism leads to no good because: a) no one is qualified to make these decisions; b) those that pretend they are (those that assume infallibility) will reduce the art of expression to tedious pedantry; c) relatedly, they will sap creativity, innovation, and initiative in the press; and d) their agenda, even if well-meaning, will fail, for no autonomous being can be made to accept information and ideas as truth unless they are free to contest its premises without the threat of coercion (fines or imprisonment) hanging over them. *On Liberty*, then, is about the limits of government power in the formation of character. It is about controlling what individuals think about themselves, those around them, the world at large, and their place in it. This is the 'one very simple principle' that Mill sought to highlight.

Whereas this chapter has been important in outlining the accountability model, it has only established a broad framework for identifying the legitimate parameters of coercive independent press regulation. It has said little yet about what these parameters are. In this way, it has said little about what the accountability model *is*. This is the task of the following Part.

---

[184] A Meiklejohn, *Political Freedom* (New York, Oxford University Press, 1965).

PART 3

Regulation

6

Society

I. Introduction

The primary (although not the only) obligation that the press owes the public, according to SRT, is to provide accurate information. Since newspaper content informs the news agenda of other mediums (eg, broadcast and online) as well as the political agenda in government,[1] this obligation is owed not only to readers but society at large. Accuracy, of course, is essential to good journalism. Nobody would dispute that. But, in not only SRT but the wider communication studies, legal, and political literature, the provision of accurate journalism has transmogrified from a feature of press freedom to a function, from a choice to a condition. Both the Royal Commission of the Press of 1947–1949,[2] echoing Wilson Harris[3] and CP Scott,[4] and the Hutchins Commission,[5] claimed accurate reporting was the press's primary purpose. Specifically, the Royal Commission charged the press with falling 'short of the standard achieved by the best, either through excessive partisanship or through distortion for the sake of news value.'[6] It did not, the Royal Commission said, meet the 'need for public instruction' on increasingly complex public affairs nor did enough 'to encourage its public to accept or demand material of higher quality.'[7]

The obligation to provide accurate information is a constant feature of press regulatory codes across Europe and in the UK. In that respect, the obligation seems uncontentious. Nevertheless, despite its ubiquity, it shall be argued that this arrangement deserves greater scrutiny than it receives; that it *is* a controversial obligation.

To see this, we should begin by recognising its duality. Obviously, accurate reporting can be understood as a personal right, which seeks to protect an individual's reputation. Indeed, the fact that accuracy provisions can be (and are) read

---

[1] See N Davies, *Flat Earth News* (London, Chatto & Windus, 2008).

[2] Royal Commission on the Press, 1947–9, *Report*, (Cmnd 7700), [384].

[3] W Harris, *The Daily Press*, (Cambridge, Cambridge University Press, 1943), 9–10.

[4] CP Scott, 'A Hundred Years' in *CP Scott 1846–1932: The Making of the Manchester Guardian* (London, Frederick Muller Ltd, 1946), 161–162.

[5] The Commission on Freedom of the Press, *A Free and Responsible Press* (Chicago, University of Chicago Press, 1947), 117–118.

[6] Royal Commission on the Press, 1947–9, *Report*, (Cmnd 7700) [677].

[7] Ibid, [680]–[681].

down, by regulators themselves sometimes, to stand for no more than a sort of defamation law equivalent, allied with the fact that such clauses are not enforced by coercive means, might explain why they encounter such little resistance in both the popular and academic commentary. The other interpretation of the accuracy clause is as a civic measure: a guarantee that published information can be relied upon, by readers and third-parties, to inform their public (and private) decision-making. For ease, this sort of accuracy 'obligation' will be referred to as 'third-party accuracy'. This treatment of accuracy is vital to the realisation of SRT. If newspapers are to fulfil their supposed constitutional function, then the information they provide must be reliable. Leveson described it as 'the foundation stone on which journalism depends.'[8] Whilst he accepted that the press of 2012 faced serious commercial pressures, he could not accept that this justified a 'race to the bottom' in terms of quality standards.[9] In this, he echoed the sentiments of the American Society of Newspaper Editors who, in the Canons of Journalism of 1923, thought sincerity, truthfulness, and accuracy the cost of the 'good faith' that readers signal through their purchase.

Can we use regulation to protect society from inaccurate press speech? This is the focus of this chapter. As will be seen, the imposition of a third-party accuracy standard to secure this civic function is deeply problematic. We have already seen the problems of relying upon notions of 'duty' and 'responsibility' in Chapters 3 and 4. If accuracy is an ethical obligation, then it is one only a newspaper can select for itself. Since no one external to the newspaper can force the obligation on it, then its mere presence in a regulatory code is unjustified. But SR theorists might argue – in fact, they do – that inaccurate information is regulatable on the 'accountability' grounds described in the previous chapter: that inaccurate information *harms* readers and wider society. It will be argued that this claim is unsustainable. If accuracy is regulatable on harm grounds, it is only as a consumer problem, not a civic one. These are separate issues that cannot be conflated. We cannot regulate speech based on its public good. This insight presents difficulties for the regulation of accuracy that are not easily overcome. Yet, this does not mean that the regulator has no role to play in improving public discourse, as will be seen.

II. The Meaning of Accuracy

Our first task, I will suggest, is to rein in our ambitions for third-party accuracy clauses. They cannot achieve all that we would want for them, nor all that SRT has in mind. This is unfortunate because greater accuracy in public debate is

---

[8] Lord Justice Leveson, *An Inquiry into the Culture, Practices and Ethics of the Press*, HC 780, November 2012, 673.

[9] Lord Justice Leveson, *An Inquiry into the Culture, Practices and Ethics of the Press, Executive Summary and Recommendations*, (HC 779, 2012), 6, [18].

much needed, presently. The inexorable rise of populism and anti-intellectualism in Western society is a cause of great concern. That politicians can lie so openly, and with so little apparent consequence, is the hallmark of totalitarianism, not liberal democracy.[10] In the UK, we have seen this, vividly, in the manipulation of the public debate on the merits of leaving the European Union.[11] The consistent warnings from experts that leaving would be disastrous to the British economy and social stability, were, according to Michael Gove MP, worthless: Britain had had enough of experts.[12] Of course, Brexit is merely a symptom, not a cause, of populism and anti-intellectualism. It is apparent across Europe, in Geert Wilders's Partij voor de Vrijheid in the Netherlands, Marine Le Pen's Front National in France, Recep Tayyip Erdoğan's Turkey, Viktor Orbán's Hungary, Heinz-Christian Strache's Austrian Freedom Party, the New Flemish Alliance in Belgium, the Danish People's Party, the Swiss People's Party, the Law and Justice party of Poland, Alternative for Germany, the UK's failed, morally bankrupt, populist party United Kingdom Independence Party, and, of course, in the United States of America's Donald Trump's 'Make America Great Again' presidency.[13]

Populism, in its recent resurgent form, has been canny in exploiting new technology and social media to inflame wild conspiracy theories – from the Birther movement to the influence of George Soros on world politics. But its continuing success is down to anti-intellectualism, for if the inconvenient truth cannot redress the balance by *proving* these conspiracies to be nonsense, then how can they fail? As Alan Wolfe has said, popular hostility toward climate change science illustrates the point:

> if we cannot agree that the breaking off of an Antarctic iceberg as large as the state of Delaware is something we should worry about, how could we ever disprove that the US government is engaged in a secret plot to take away the guns of God-fearing ordinary Americans or that 9/11 was an inside job?[14]

So it is that emotions, feelings, and belief have replaced reason, logic, and scepticism as the basis of wisdom. It is not that these people are no longer rational, as some commentators are quick to conclude, but that rationality is bounded: it extends only so far as instincts, traditions, and loyalty will allow, and where there is conflict, it is the latter that dominates. This has led some commentators to conclude that greater paternalism is the solution: to ensure that the bad public decision-making that follows from this mindset cannot cause permanent or serious damage to democratic values and institutions.[15] For these commentators,

---

[10] See H Arendt, *The Origins of Totalitarianism* (first published 1951) (London, Penguin Books, 2017).

[11] See discussion in P Coe, '(Re)embracing social responsibility theory as a basis for modern speech: shifting the normative paradigm for a modern media' (2019) 69(4) *Northern Ireland Legal Quarterly* 403.

[12] H Mance, 'Britain has had enough of experts, says Gove', *Financial Times*, 3 June 2016.

[13] See discussion in J Müller, *What is Populism?* (London, Penguin Books, 2017).

[14] A Wolfe, *The Politics of Petulance* (Chicago, University of Chicago Press, 2018), 99.

[15] See, eg, PEN America, *Faking News: Fraudulent News and the Fight for Truth*, (2017, PEN America).

then, the guarantee of accurate journalism is vital to their goal.[16] Let us scrutinise the justifiability of this strategy.

We should start by recognising that inaccurate reporting is hardly new.[17] Yet, what we know from the Leveson inquiry and other sources, is that newspapers will sometimes deliberately or recklessly publish false information. Richard Peppiatt told the inquiry that, whilst at the *Daily Star*, he had been encouraged to write false stories so as to meet unrealistic publishing targets. These ranged from the facile (about Katie Price's marriage) to the inflammatory (that taxpayer money was being spent on 'Muslim only' toilets).[18] Sadly, this is not an isolated example. Leveson received intelligence that the problem of fabricated stories, and sources to support them, was a widespread issue in the industry. Sometimes, these stories are invented or embellished to further a newspaper's worldview on certain issues, eg, that 'immigrants are taking over, Muslims are a security threat.'[19] Nick Davies, in *Flat Earth News*, identifies the *Daily Mail* as the prime culprit for this sort of manipulation. Its success – it is the most successful newspaper in the UK – is due to its 'urgent desire to feed its readers with the world they want to believe in'[20] – a world where multiculturalism has failed and the relationship with ethnic minorities is complicated: '... the *Mail* can embrace people from ethnic minorities providing they are respectable, short-back-and-sides people, who are trying to be British in a traditional way.'[21] This has resulted in unethical but financially reward-ing journalism:

> [t]he difficulty for the *Mail* is that in its relentless pursuit of [its] commercial agenda [to please its readers at all costs], it has developed a striking willingness to cut the corners of journalistic integrity, to inject the facts with the falsehood and distortion which will please its readers. And if that involves publishing a few clarifications or even paying occasional damages, so be it.[22]

Such has been the importance of this strategy that news which conflicts with or otherwise undermines its readers' worldview is positively ignored. An example of this, as Davies reports, are the various reports and studies conducted over several years which show that immigration, including successful asylum seeker applica-tions, has boosted the economy demonstrably, from freeing up capital through the purchase of expensive London properties (allowing wealth to move to the regions), to keeping inflation down, to increased tax collection, and the net gain

---

[16] See, eg, T Allberg and J Curran, *How Media Inform Democracy* (Oxford, Routledge, 2012); C Ireton and J Posetti (eds), *Journalism, 'fake news' and disinformation: A handbook for journalism education and training* (Paris, UNESCO, 2018).

[17] P Bernal, 'Fakebook: why Facebook makes the fake news problem inevitable' (2018) 69(4) *Northern Ireland Legal Quarterly* 513.

[18] https://webarchive.nationalarchives.gov.uk/20140122175653/http://www.levesoninquiry.org.uk/wp-content/uploads/2011/11/Witness-Statement-of-Richard-Peppiatt.pdf.

[19] Leveson, (n 8), 671.

[20] N Davies, *Flat Earth News* (London, Chatto & Windus, 2008), 372.

[21] Ibid.

[22] N Davies, *Flat Earth News* (London, Chatto & Windus, 2008), 370–371.

(in tax receipts) to the public purse.[23] These stories have not appeared in the *Daily Mail* because 'the readers wouldn't like it'.[24]

Although there is substantial evidence, both in the UK[25] and the US,[26] that readers are disillusioned with newspaper speech, and think it generally untrustworthy, Davies's work reminds us that trust is not simply about receiving information that is actually correct but receiving information that *appears* to be correct. What we must see, then, is that certainly, but not only, *Daily Mail* readers are fantasists who *want* to see the world in a specific way, according to the prejudices and stereotypes that they have in mind. Consequently, we cannot be sure that a tougher accuracy regime would correct their myopia.

The minimal changes made to self-regulation in the UK since Leveson's report was published[27] have not resolved the problem. Even a quality title like *The Times* is not immune. In August 2017, it published a story entitled 'Christian child forced into Muslim foster care', which, in inflammatory terms, claimed that the child had been subjected to a shocking ordeal. The tone of the report is apparent from both the title and first sentence: 'A white Christian child was taken from her family and forced to live with a niqab-wearing foster carer in a home where she was allegedly encouraged to learn Arabic.'[28] It said that the placement was against the family's wishes, that the girl had 'begged' social services to remove her because her carers did not speak English, would not let her eat bacon, ridiculed Christianity, and called European women 'stupid and alcoholic.' The story was riddled with inaccuracies. These resulted from insufficient fact-checking and over-reliance upon the mother's versions of events – testimony that an experienced reporter ought to have discounted or otherwise heavily caveated. It later transpired, in the subsequent care proceedings,[29] that the council had removed the child because of her mother's alcoholism and drug-taking and due to the bouts of domestic violence that plagued the mother's relationship with the child's father. Her carers were chosen because the child's maternal grandparents were Muslim, and therefore, it was concluded that a Muslim community was most appropriate for her. Indeed, the grandparents were eventually granted custody of the child and an order made for the child to live with them in their country of origin. When press reform campaigners Brian Cathcart and Paddy French objected to the multiple inaccuracies in the story,[30]

---

[23] Ibid, 377–379.

[24] Ibid.

[25] Tom Gibbons discusses this evidence in 'Building Trust in Press Regulation: Obstacles and Opportunities' (2013) 5(2) *Journal of Media Law* 202, 204–205.

[26] https://www.knightfoundation.org/reports/indicators-of-news-media-trust. See also N Newman, *Journalism, media, and technology trends and predictions 2018* (Oxford, Reuters Institute for the Study of Journalism, 2018).

[27] See discussion in ch 2.

[28] A Norfolk, *The Times*, 28 August 2017.

[29] The judgment is discussed by B Cathcart, '"Muslim fostering": Times journalism utterly discredited', *Inforrm*, 8 September 2018.

[30] The nature of this complaint is set out in B Cathcart and P French, *Unmasked: Andrew Norfolk, The Times Newspaper and Anti-Muslim Reporting – A Case to Answer*, (London, Unmasked Books, 2019).

their complaint was substantially dismissed by IPSO on the grounds that they were third parties; only those personally affected by the inaccuracy were entitled to complain.[31]

The story is a useful example of both the nature of press inaccuracy and its social consequences. First, the story plays to three popular tropes in British reporting: immigrants 'taking over' (the alleged inability to speak English is key), Islamophobia, and hostility toward social services.[32] Secondly, it was utilised by militant far-right campaigners, Tommy Robinson and Britain First,[33] following its reiteration on the front-page of the *Daily Mail*,[34] which called for a public inquiry. We know from the Leveson inquiry that newspaper inaccuracy has been significant in helping far-right groups to disseminate hate speech.[35] Matters have not improved since. Miqdaad Versi, of the Muslim Council of Britain reported, in April 2018, that over the preceding 18 months, he had obtained corrections relating to over 40 inaccurate stories in major newspapers about Muslims.[36] He had no doubt that this rampant Islamophobia was self-perpetuating: 'stories that play on the public's fears and feed their prejudices are popular, especially at a time when more than half of British people see Islam as a threat to western liberal democracy.'[37]

Given this pattern, it is understandable that campaigners would want to see tougher accuracy standards apply not only to stories which name specific individuals but those that spread falsehoods about groups and controversial issues such as climate change or the alleged benefits of leaving the European Union.

Some commentators have argued that the ideal accuracy standard is unrealisable because it requires complete objectivity.[38] Although we might disagree, we should nevertheless recognise the difficulties inherent in imposing an accuracy standard. Even if we accept, as we should, that inaccuracy is inevitable given the speed with which newspapers are produced (not to mention the financial rewards of exclusives), even the lesser obligation that reporters *aim for* accuracy raises problems. For one thing, all news is 'value-laden.'[39] Indeed, a common complaint about accuracy standards concerns what newspapers do *not* say as much as what they do: at the Leveson inquiry, participants complained about the absence of positive stories about minorities,[40] which is something Nick Davies also highlighted in

---

[31] https://www.ipso.co.uk/media/1719/unmasked-hacked-off-rebuttal_.pdf.

[32] See discussion in Leveson report, (n 8), 486–489; see also Cathcart and French, (n 30).

[33] J Grierson, 'Muslim fostering row: how the Times and Mail gave a skewed portrayal', *The Guardian*, 1 Sep 2017.

[34] V Allen and E Harding, *Daily Mail*, 29 August 2017.

[35] Leveson, (n 8), 670, [8.39].

[36] M Versi, 'Islamophobia not an issue in the British press? You've got to be kidding', *The Guardian*, 27 Apr 2018.

[37] Ibid.

[38] See discussion in D McQuail, *Media Performance* (London, Sage Publications, 1992), 187–188.

[39] M Kieran, 'Objectivity, impartiality and good journalism' in M Kieran (ed), *Media Ethics* (London, Routledge, 1998), 24.

[40] Royal Commission on the Press, (n 6), 487, [3.18].

Flat Earth News.[41] Yet, as Leveson recognised, newspapers are entitled to publish information selectively, even if, in doing so, this leads readers to gain a distorted image of the world at large, in which stereotypes go unchallenged.[42] This eventuality is compounded by another feature of press freedom that Leveson emphasised at several points in his report: the right of newspapers to be partisan. He applied this phrase not only to party political bias but also to what he called 'agenda journalism', which he defined as a 'fusion of fact and comment'.[43] Although Leveson was content that this admission of rights status for biased journalism did not undermine the obligation to report accurately – an obligation he saw clearly in SRT terms ('the press have a responsibility to ensure that the public are accurately informed so that they can engage in the democratic process')[44] – we might question his reasoning. A newspaper may publish nothing but accurate information and still provide such prejudiced comment as to leave the unwitting reader with an inaccurate picture of the world. As CP Scott put it: '... there are cases in which nothing is so misleading as the bald fact.'[45]

This leads us to the real problem: in a third-party context, what do we mean by accuracy? This is something Leveson did not define – at least not in any detail. He was content to leave this to the regulator to work out, as if it were a semantic matter.[46] Yet, when we look to the literature, we see that it is not. Moreover, we see that, ironically, commentators themselves do not speak with precision when they describe the accuracy obligation. In its most nebulous form, we see accuracy described grandly as an obligation to present the world as it is. For example, Wilson Harris (former editor of the Spectator) put it thus in 1943:

> It is a question of giving – or endeavouring honestly and persistently to give, for in this matter there can be no full attainment – an accurate, adequate and faithful picture of life as a whole, in which things intrinsically important are represented as important and things intrinsically trivial as trivial.[47]

Taken literally, Harris's vision would be disastrous for newspapers, for the proportionality standard that he articulates would mean that even 'serious' stories would be reduced to a few lines of copy given how little they impact on everyday lives. For life 'as a whole', in the twenty-first century, is good and much of what occupies the mainstream press is but a minor inconvenience in the grand scheme of things. Indeed, Harris's definition has acute implications that seem to have escaped him, for if the test of seriousness and triviality is, as he says, determined by comparison to life-as-it-is then things that we would intuitively consider serious become

---

[41] Davies, (n 20), 371–379.
[42] Royal Commission on the Press, (n 6), 490, [3.28].
[43] Ibid, 688, [9.56].
[44] Ibid.
[45] CP Scott, 'The Function of the Press' (1931) 2 *Political Quarterly* 59, 60.
[46] Royal Commission on the Press, (n 6), 1763.
[47] Harris, (n 3), 13.

trivial and vice-versa. For, given how little it actually touches upon the real lived experience, even murder becomes trivial. Moreover, it would end variety, for those issues that do affect life are fairly constant. Thus, content would be dominated by the threat of climate change. As this implies, content would be repetitive: yesterday, climate change was the main threat to our way of life, today, climate change is the main threat to our way of life. And it would be mundane: for the trivial issues that constitute life would have to be a constant feature. Harris's definition, then, would have a profound and deleterious effect on freedom of speech.

Harris also argues that accuracy means impartiality: 'no matter how violent or extreme the convictions a paper holds, the sole place … for their expression is in its leader columns. The news columns must by their impartiality and objectivity supply the reader with dependable data by which he can forms his views by himself …'[48] Of course, in his day, this objective was more readily achievable, for reports – say, of parliamentary proceedings – were separated, physically, from comment and opinion, which appeared in the leader columns. Nevertheless, this sense of accuracy as impartiality or objectivity is common in the literature. Matthew Kieran, for example, has previously argued, along SRT lines, that if the press is to fulfil its purpose 'in covering such matters appropriately, it seems to follow that the media must be impartial in their approach in order to arrive at and report upon what is, in fact, the case.'[49] Others argue that this notion of accuracy cannot be achieved because it relies upon neat distinctions between fact and opinion. This is problematic, they say, because journalism is a synthetic blend of objectivity and subjectivity, of 'the world 'out there' *and* … the subjective world 'in here' … of the scientist and the poet.'[50] More prosaically, Chris Frost assesses accuracy by two qualities: the standard of verification applied and the journalist's intentions. All that can be expected by the reader is that the journalist provides 'an honest presentation of the information they have gathered, checked as best they can, together with its sources …'[51]

These different views show us how the literature interprets the term 'accuracy' by reference to words like 'objectivity', 'impartiality', and 'truth'. Yet accuracy, objectivity, impartiality, and truth are four *different* standards and although it is understandable why commentators might think them synonymous, they are not. Instead, we should think of these four terms as belonging to two sets, for objectivity and impartiality are related, as are truth and accuracy. When we scrutinise each of these pairs, and consider the relationship between the first term (objectivity, truth) and the second (impartiality, accuracy), we see that whilst the first is an absolute, the second is not. For Arendt, in her reading of Kant's political work, objectivity and truth are metaphysical terms which require an absence of

---

[48] Harris, ibid, 9–10.

[49] Kieran, (n 39), 23. See also C Bertrand, *Media Ethics and Accountability Systems* (New Brunswick, Transaction Publishers, 2000), 47.

[50] JC Merrill, *The Dialectic in Journalism* (Baton Rouge, Louisiana State University, 1989), 92.

[51] C Frost, *Journalism Ethics and Regulation* 3rd edn (Harlow, Pearson Education Limited, 2011), 84.

judgement.[52] Thinking along those lines, we begin to see the difficulties, if they are not readily apparent already, of using the terms 'objectivity' and 'truth' to describe the journalistic task. Even the simple act of relating events leads the journalist towards subjectivity because she must convey information in terms that the reader will understand. In doing so, she is bounded by her own life experiences, as well as the reader's. Moreover, of these two, the latter is determinative: if she does not translate the issue or event to the language of the reader, comprehension is imperilled. Yet the mere act of translation compromises the dissemination of nuanced issues which, of itself, threatens the possibility of comprehending truth. This is especially significant in the areas of science and law.

Similarly, we should recognise that information can be impartial and accurate without being objective and true. For example, imagine that a scientific study claims that climate change has ended but the scientific community, as a whole, strongly disputes its findings. Now imagine that a newspaper article reports extracts from the study, and the bare fact of the scientific community's denial, but offers no comment on the report's veracity. Whilst we can say that this description of events is impartial (it takes no sides) and accurate (these events have happened), 'truth' and 'objectivity' depends upon knowing which of these conflicting accounts is right. In this, we must recognise a serious flaw in SRT's position. For it does not want simply impartiality and (factual) accuracy; it wants readers to have the means to determine the better claim – the most persuasive of the opposing positions – in the debate. This requires the newspaper, at the very least, to provide readers with the analytical toolkit by which to make a decision about its persuasive, or else, if that is too onerous on the press or, more likely, the reader, to offer a sound opinion. In doing so, though, the press *must* be partisan. There is a further reason why the provision of this analytical toolkit may be unrealisable, and that is the problem of policing the quality of journalistic sources. For, as we know, journalists are entitled to protect their sources. Whilst this protection is not absolute it is treated as special. Section 10, Contempt of Court Act 1981 recognises the journalist's right to conceal their source's identity without legal punishment, unless the court is satisfied that the refusal unduly threatens national security, public safety, or the administration of justice. These conditions are not easily met.[53] Consequently, it is normal for journalists to report the views of sources without naming them. Yet, as Leveson reported, these sources are sometimes invented.[54] Unless we are to compromise the journalist's right to protect her source, there can be no guarantee that fictitious sources are not used.

Thus, even though it is indisputable that 'accurate' information is socially valuable, for both public and private decision-making, the regulatory task of ensuring newspapers provide such is deeply problematic. Not only is the standard

---

[52] H Arendt, *Lectures on Kant's Political Philosophy* (Chicago, University of Chicago Press, 1992), 72–77.

[53] See, eg, *Goodwin v United Kingdom* (1996) EHRR 123.

[54] Leveson, (n 8), 674–680.

difficult to define, but also there is a discernible disconnect between the ambitions of SRT and its realisation. Objectivity and truth are not identical standards to impartiality and (factual) accuracy. For what SRT wants is for citizens to appreciate where the stronger arguments lie so that these can inform policy. Regulating on this basis, though, presents serious challenges, as the next section recognises.

III. The Harm of Inaccuracy

Ostensibly, the most plausible justification for regulating newspaper accuracy concerns the harm done to public and/or private decision-making by inaccurate information. This would fit the framework that Chapter 5 outlines on press accountability – superficially, at least. This sort of harm analysis is readily identifiable in the SRT literature. As we have seen in previous chapters, it is central to Onora O'Neill's claim that the press has no 'licence to deceive'.[55] It underpins the Hutchins Commission's conclusions that an inaccurate press is 'dangerous'[56] and that 'not only positive misdeeds but omissions and inadequacies of press performance have now a bearing on general welfare'.[57] The crux of the argument is best expressed by O'Malley and Soley: since 'accurate information is a prerequisite for arriving at informed political and social judgements' then the public should be 'protected' from the 'damaging consequences' that misinformation and disinformation have.[58] Indeed, such is the intuitive appeal of this claim that its logic seems undeniable.

The harm, then, is to the political process. Nick Davies expresses it this way when discussing the impact of the *Daily Mail*'s inaccurate reporting, in a passage that is worth quoting in full:

> In so far as it is simply making moral judgements about what is important, its work is entirely legitimate. In so far as it allows its special relationship with inaccuracy to distort those issues, it clearly is not. In that case, the effects of the *Mail*'s professional foul is not merely to mislead its readers about the state of the world but to distort the whole political process.[59]

But how does it *distort* the political process? According to Davies, this is done in two ways: first, other newspapers, and the media more generally, will follow

---

[55] O O'Neill, *A Question of Trust* (Cambridge, Cambridge University Press, 2002), 83–100.

[56] The Commission on Freedom of the Press, *A Free and Responsible Press* (Chicago, University of Chicago Press, 1947), 115.

[57] Ibid, 124.

[58] T O'Malley and C Soley, *Regulating the Press* (London, Pluto Books, 2000), 145. The same logic is apparent in the Hutchins Commission's report, see, (n 56), 118 and 124.

[59] N Davies, *Flat Earth News* (London, Chatto & Windus, 2008), 389; see, also, discussion in T Gibbons, 'Freedom of the Press: ownership and editorial values' [1992] *Public Law* 279.

the *Daily Mail's* lead and so repeat these inaccuracies and distortions, which gives them further credibility. Secondly, consequently, politicians will listen carefully to the *Daily Mail*, and so act upon what it says.[60]

In the liberal tradition, the fact of harm is not sufficient to justify coercion. As we saw in Chapter 5, harm is a necessary but not sufficient reason to interfere. Ordinarily, the law insists that the harm is *caused* by the wrongdoing. This is something that SR theorists overlook. For example, O'Malley and Soley argue that penalising press inaccuracy is analogous in principle to the prohibition of inaccuracy in wider consumer contexts. Thus, they note that the Sale of Goods Act 1979 (now supplemented by the Consumer Rights Act 2015) 'protects customers from being misled by traders.'[61] There is also the Consumer Protection from Unfair Trading Regulations 2008 and the Business Protection from Misleading Marketing Regulations 2008, which regulate, for example, the accuracy of advertisements and aggressive trading practices. Yet, the law is not triggered simply because the information is inaccurate, as O'Malley and Soley's analysis implies. It is because this defect *causes* demonstrable harm. Goods that do not correspond to their description, for example, cause damage to, or even destruction of, property[62] and/or physical harm through, for example, allergic reactions.[63]

To be analogous, therefore, we must show that inaccurate newspaper information *causes* harm to the democratic process. The fact that it is sub-optimal to that process is not enough, for there are numerous ways in which other sources of information that citizens use for public and private decision-making are similarly defective. We do not hold mainstream publishers, internet providers, or, indeed, actors in casual conversation accountable for the reliability of the information they provide even though that information may influence the agent's actions or inform their opinions. Why not? Because to do so would be ridiculous, not only due to the practical impossibility (how do we police casual conversations?) but also the positively Orwellian connotations of doing so. Yet this realisation should give us greater pause for thought about imposing the accuracy obligation upon newspapers than it seems to.

As we have seen, SRT maintains, or seems to, that press speech is different from other types, especially individual freedom of expression, but presumably novels, textbooks, and poetry, for example, because, unlike those forms, it has a teleological basis. That claim, though, does not satisfy the causality point. The recipient of press speech is an autonomous agent. The information contained within newspapers is provided on non-coercive grounds. No one is forced to read a newspaper or act upon its contents. Consequently, the reader has a choice. She can choose to believe what she is told or she can choose not to. Or she can choose healthy scepticism: she will believe it until such time that she has reason to doubt it.

---

[60] Davies, ibid, 389–390.
[61] O'Malley and Soley, (n 58), 145.
[62] See, eg, *Ashington Piggeries Ltd v Christopher Hill Ltd* [1972] AC 441.
[63] See, eg, *Grant v Australian Knittings Mills Ltd* [1936] AC 85.

In claiming, as O'Malley and Soley do, in the above quote, that accurate information benefits the democratic process and inaccurate information damages it, agent autonomy is unaccounted for.

The SRT literature seems cognisant of this problem, but not entirely persuasive in proving causality. For example, as part of a broader argument, David Strauss has argued that manipulative lying robs the recipient of their autonomy and, therefore, can be interfered with because it is tantamount to coercion (and, he says, 'in one respect lying is worse than outright coercion, because it is more insidious: the victim does not even know that he or she has been taken over and is being manipulated').[64] This sort of claim appears in the House of Lords decision in *Animal Defenders International*, in which the court found that restrictions on political advertising are justified by the harm they cause: 'The risk is that objects which are essentially political may come to be accepted by the public not because they are shown in public debate to be right but because, by dint of constant repetition, the public has been conditioned to accept them.'[65]

Whereas this argument might have intuitive appeal, it deserves more scrutiny than it receives. For it treats the fact of a phenomenon (treating press speech uncritically) as proof of causality and, in doing so, attributes agency for that phenomenon to the *wrong* cause. The fact of, at best, temporary disengagement of the critical functions, at worst, gullibility, is not sufficient, for it is a decision internal to the autonomous agent – it is her choice. There must be something about the newspaper's behaviour. Can we say, with David Strauss, that lying is, itself, a form of audience manipulation which *does* compromise autonomy, in a manner that is tantamount to coercion? Surely, that sets the bar too low. In fairness to Strauss, his example is really about the dynamics of intimate relationships. Spousal and familial relationships have a powerful emotional element that does not compare to the arms-length transaction between publisher and newspaper purchaser, and we cannot pretend otherwise. Can we really say that a newspaper reader responds because they must? Because they are robbed of alternatives to action? We should admit the very real possibility that when readers believe newspapers it is because they choose to do so, which means their autonomy is not absent, but actively engaged. As Nick Davies implies, readers are likely to believe the inaccurate information because it accords with their own worldview. In this sense, their autonomy is validated. Indeed, this explains the commercial success of the *Daily Mail*: it tells its readers what they want to hear. Clearly, this speaks to a failure, on the part of the reader, to engage the critical faculties, but this failure, of itself, is proof of autonomy: when Hayek claimed 'the whole argument for freedom, or the greater part of the argument for freedom, rests on the

---

[64] DA Strauss, 'Persuasion, Autonomy and Freedom of Expression' (1991) 91 *Columbia Law Review* 334.

[65] *R (on the application of Animal Defenders International) v Secretary of State for Culture, Media and Sport* [2008] UKHL 15, [28].

fact of our ignorance and not on the fact of our knowledge',[66] he recognised that autonomy was as much about making the wrong choices as making the right ones. The fact that, say, the *Daily Mail* reader chooses to believe the inaccuracy does not mean that she would modify her outlook if presented with the correction.

Moreover, the historic reason for this factual causation is much less convincing in the digital era. The Hutchins Commission's view that the consumer had a right to demand 'adequate and uncontaminated mental food' from newspapers was premised on the claim that '[he] can get what he requires only through existing press organs'.[67] Clearly, this is no longer true, assuming it ever was. In 2002, Onora O'Neill tried to give it fresh impetus by reimagining it as a class claim: 'an erratically reliable or unassessable press may not matter for privileged people with other sources of information, who can tell which stories are near the mark and which confused, vicious or simply false; *but for most citizens it matters*'.[68] The nature of 'privilege' here is not entirely clear, for it seems to imply that wealth and intelligence are causally linked, which is plainly untrue. Nevertheless, the advent of social media has provided the means of overcoming any such disadvantage, at least to the extent it is caused by wealth. Admittedly, the problem of disinformation has not been overcome, but that cannot be blamed on privilege.

Further, the advent of new technologies combined with the ubiquity of social media platforms has also addressed the concern that the US Supreme Court raised in *Cox Broadcasting Corporation v Cohn*: that 'in a society in which each individual has but limited time and resources with which to observe at first hand the operations of his government, he relies necessarily upon the press to bring to him in convenient form the facts of those operations'.[69] Consequently, not only can the public observe government at work, through the live streaming, say, of Parliament, but also it can interact directly with government through its various websites. Further, the public can access a wide range of resources through the internet which provide the means of verifying the information that both the government and the press supplies it with. For example, there are independent fact-checking services such as Full Fact in the UK (fullfact.org) and FactCheck.org and PolitiFact in the US. There is also the Euromyths blog, compiled by the European Commission, which debunks myths about the EU propagated by the UK Eurosceptic press.[70] In light of resources like this, it cannot be said that the public is necessarily reliant upon receiving accurate information from the press. The public is not *forced* to rely upon press speech. It *chooses* to.

This difference is important. We simply cannot say that the press *causes* the public to hold particular views. Remember, according to Davies, the opposite is

---

[66] PG Klein, *The Collected Works of FA Hayek, vol IV: The Fortunes of Liberalism* (Indianapolis, Liberty Fund, 1992), 6–7.

[67] (N 56), 125.

[68] (N 55), 90–91 (emphasis in original).

[69] 420 US 469, 491–92 (1975).

[70] https://blogs.ec.europa.eu/ECintheUK/euromyths-a-z-index/?fbclid=IwAR3WE3fo7LUzLq4o-lwf31EFL-itgHINN-LoW5ZOLISAMvu8HU9mVCEfuBc.

true: the content in a newspaper like the *Daily Mail* is *caused* by its readers' attitudes (at least, as the *Mail* perceives them to be). But is the claim true? Is the
press, instead, manipulating the public through misinformation and disinformation? Certainly, the press wants to have this sort of influence. As we saw in
Chapter 5, the press likes to propagate the myth that it controls election results.
But given the arms-length nature of the transaction between press and reader, it
is hard to accept that the press has this sort of power. Whilst David Hume's view
that 'we need not dread' the press because the reader 'reads ... alone and coolly'
is no longer persuasive (assuming it ever was), there remains something in his
reasoning that even if that reader 'should ... be wrought up to never so seditious
a humour, there is no violent resolution presented to him by which he can immediately vent his passion.'[71] Here, again, we see the argument that if a reader acts
on information presented to her in a newspaper, it is because she has chosen to
act, not because she has been compelled to act. If she has chosen to do so on
inaccurate or insufficient evidence, then the responsibility for this is hers alone.

Yet SRT seems to presuppose that causality is established because the actor is
entitled to disengage her critical functions and, instead, rely upon the information she receives because it is the press's duty to supply her with it. Put this way,
the scenario resembles negligent misstatement under *Hedley Byrne & Co Ltd v
Heller & Partners Ltd*,[72] ie, the obligations that the law imposes on the statement-
maker when she knows the recipient will act on it to their detriment. Yet this
obligation is contingent upon a duty of care existing between statement-maker
and recipient. We saw in Chapter 3 why the imposition of this sort of duty is
not feasible. Nevertheless, let us interpret that duty not in tortious terms – as an
obligation that the state imposes – but in contractual terms – as an obligation that
the parties have freely entered into.[73] This, then, is not a duty that society at large
could impose, only one that the reader, as a representative of society, could.

Even so, we should still struggle to find, even as between the speaker and the
reader, 'an expression of a legally meaningful intention to incur an obligation'[74]
to provide reliably accurate information, which would justify the imposition
of the duty. It is not enough to find commitments to accuracy in a newspaper's
editorial policy (see below). The obligation would need to relate to the adverse
consequences of being wrong – and that is something newspapers do *not* say.
Indeed, we find evidence in IPSO adjudications, of the opposite attitude: that the
press does *not* expect readers to believe everything they say. For example, we see
the *Daily Telegraph* claiming that Boris Johnson (prior to being Prime Minister),
writing in his regular column, was not, and could not be, taken seriously by

---

[71] D Hume, 'Of the Liberty of the Press' in *Essays Moral, Political and Literary* (London, Grant
Richards, 1903), 11 (n 1).

[72] [1964] AC 465.

[73] JAW Grover and OF Sherman, 'Equivalent to contract? Confronting the nature of the duty arising
under *Hedley Byrne v Heller*' (2019) 135 (Apr) *LQR* 177.

[74] Ibid, 179.

readers because the MP was so well-known for being 'comically polemical', even though the offending article purported to rely upon survey results to support its wild claims (a claim that IPSO wholly rejected).[75]

Moreover, even if a (contractual) duty of care could be established, the reliance on the statement-maker's skill or knowledge must be *reasonable*. Typically, negligent misstatement claims arise in an employment context, where an employer relies upon a defective reference about a prospective employee to their detriment. At the risk of oversimplification, where the employer has no other sources of information about a person apart from that reference, they are at the sort of disadvantage that has no real parallel in a press context. Most significantly, we would be unable to establish an equivalent proximate relationship between the newspaper and the reader to demonstrate the sort of voluntary assumption of responsibility that the court found to be pivotal to its decision in *Hedley Byrne*.[76] In *Caparo Industries plc v Dickman*, the Court of Appeal was careful to exclude liability for statements 'put into more or less general circulation'[77] which may be relied upon, even foreseeably relied upon, by 'strangers … for any one of a variety of a different purposes which the maker of the statement has no specific reason to anticipate.'[78] Consequently, the Court has consistently held that negligent misstatement liability must be limited to both a foreseeable class and a foreseeable type of transaction, both of which the defendant has anticipated in advance.[79]

To be clear, the point of this comparison is not to say that newspapers ought to be liable in negligence or negligent misstatement for inaccurate information. Instead, it is to consider the standard we see elsewhere in the positive law for imposing accountability for inaccuracy. This shows that, as a matter of civil law, the law requires there to be sufficient proximity, both in the relationship between statement-maker and recipient and in the nature of the information disseminated, before it will impose liability. The court is concerned to see that the offending statement is either advice or something like advice (ie, information that will be used for a specific purpose) and that the specific transaction for which it is to be used is *known* by the defendant. Thinking about press accountability for inaccurate information along these lines helps focuses our mind on two important, and related, issues: of why a reader should be entitled to rely upon that information and why a newspaper should be liable for that reliance. Of course, as Chapter 1 makes clear, the positive law's treatment of a legal issue is not determinative, but, in this case, it is instructive, not least for its compatibility with the liberal principle that harm is a necessary but not sufficient reason for coercive interference.

This is important when considering inaccuracy. We know that readers believe what they hear. We know that certain newspapers, such as the *Daily Mail*, depict

---

[75] IPSO ruling, 00154–19 *Stirling v The Daily Telegraph*, 4 April 2019.

[76] See, (n 72), 529–530.

[77] [1990] 2 AC 605, 620–621.

[78] Ibid.

[79] Eg, *Hedley Byrne*, (n 72); *Caparo Industries plc*, (n 24); *Playboy Club London Ltd v Banca Nazionale del Lavoro SpA* [2018] UKSC 43.

the world as they think their readers wish to see it. We also know, from evidence to the Leveson inquiry, that minority groups – a common target of vitriolic diatribes in the popular press – suffer real and serious abuse from people who believe these inaccuracies: those people that think Muslims are terrorists, that asylum seekers, single mothers, trans people, etc, are a drain on the NHS, that immigration is bad for the economy. We can conclude, therefore, that inaccurate information can be seductive to narrow-minded people, if it accords with their preconceived ideas about the world. We can accept, then, that readers *act* upon newspaper information, even inaccurate information. Yet because newspaper audiences are not captive, nor limited in space and time to act upon that information, and newspapers cannot compel readers to act upon the information they distribute, we cannot demonstrate a sufficient nexus between newspaper and reader or newspaper and general public to justify *accountability* for inaccuracy. Consequently, we cannot say that inaccurate newspaper information *causes* harms to specific groups or society at large in a legally meaningful and interesting sense that would justify interference.

Further, even if we could overcome all of these obstacles to show that society or simply readers (as representatives of society) are entitled to accurate information, there are severe limits to what law can do to realise this obligation. Most importantly, it cannot provide anything like a *guarantee* that this obligation will be fulfilled. For, in regulating the consumer bargain, the primary remedy is damages, not specific performance.[80] In other words, even if we could say that, as part of the consumer transaction, newspapers promised to provide the purchaser with 'accurate' information, the remedy for the disappointed consumer would be compensation for their loss. This amount is limited to the transaction cost. Whilst it would be accurate to say that this promise obliges the newspaper to provide accurate information, it would be misleading to describe it as a guarantee, for there would be no way for the disappointed consumer to demand the shortfall in quality is made good. The reason for this lies in an important feature of the common law that non-commercial law commentators often overlook, which is that it guards against any sort of order for specific performance which smacks of subjugation. In *De Francesco v Barnum*, the High Court recalled that it ought not to 'compel persons who are not desirous of maintaining continuous personal relations with one another to continue those personal relations ... the courts are bound to be jealous, lest they should turn contracts of service into contracts of slavery.'[81] Moreover, it would be impossible for the courts to police this obligation by means of injunction, even if minded to do so, which is another reason why no court would issue one.[82] This renders O'Malley and Soley's comparison to statutes like the Sale of Goods Act impotent since compensation is worthless for SRT's purposes.

---

[80] *Co-operative Insurance Society Ltd v Argyll Stores Ltd* [1998] AC 1.
[81] (1890) 45 Ch D 430, 438.
[82] *Co-operative Insurance Society Ltd v Argyll Stores Ltd*, (n 82).

SRT advocates might point to section 12 of the Defamation Act 2013 in response since, ostensibly at least, this demonstrates the court's power to demand newspapers publish specific information. This provision empowers the court to order the defendant to publish a summary of the judgment against it. Yet this provision is feebler than it appears. For the court cannot dictate the wording, position, or timing of the summary as such. It can only intervene if the parties cannot agree these issues amongst themselves and, even then, it is restricted by what is 'reasonable and practicable' in the circumstances (section 12(4)). And, of course, the order to publish a summary of the judgment is justifiable in principle by the harm done to a person's reputation – which does not arise in the context we are concerned with here.

IV. The Limits of Accuracy Regulation

It follows, from the arguments set out in this chapter, and those in Part 2, that the coercive independent press regulator is not only prevented from enforcing the third-party accuracy provision, but also from including such a provision in its code of conduct, even if that clause is neither enforced nor treated as enforceable. This conclusion does not mean that SRT's goal to improve the quality of public debate through regulation is entirely redundant. Indeed, I will argue in this section that the regulator may yet play some role in policing accuracy, albeit a more limited one.

Prior to setting out this more limited role, I want to unpack the claim that even the inclusion of an *unenforceable* third-party accuracy clause is illegitimate as a matter of principle, for I suspect that this conclusion will not sit well with commentators. Even the PCC – which Lord Justice Leveson thought suffered from regulatory capture – permitted complaints about third-party inaccuracy, as does its successor, IPSO, which many commentators feel is little better. To say that these organisations, which are hardly exemplars of best regulatory practice, engage(d) in high-minded ethical practices is bound to give rise to some incredulity.

Yet, in a practical sense, the idea that third-party accuracy clauses are beyond regulatory competence is not that strange when we consider that such provisions are not universally recognised across Europe. Indeed, there are few regulators that will hear complaints from those not personally affected by a story. For example, Denmark, which has a genuinely coercive system in place,[83] requires complainants to have been personally affected by the story. Similar restrictions apply in the Netherlands, Sweden, Norway, and in Belgium (but only in the Raad voor de Journalistiek scheme, which covers the Flemish press; the Conseil de Déontologie

---

[83] See discussion in ch 2.

Journalistique, which covers the French and German press, allows anyone to complain).

A notable exception to this is the Austrian scheme, which operates two complaints systems, known as the independent procedure (das selbständige Verfahren) and the complaints procedure (das Beschwerdeverfahren). Whereas anyone can complain under the independent procedure about a breach of regulatory standards, only those personally affected can use the complaints procedure. The difference lies in the sanctions available to the Österreichischer Presserat. Under the independent procedure, newspapers are not expected to publish adverse decisions. As is typical in other regulatory schemes, the Österreichischer Presserat code of conduct says that 'it is the prime duty of journalists to aim at a maximum of conscientiousness and accuracy in their investigations, the presentation of news items, and comments in them.' The inclusion of commentary – and not simply facts – makes this a broad obligation.

Interestingly, there are several UK newspapers which commit themselves to third-party accuracy standards, albeit the scale of their commitment varies. The most committed, ostensibly at least, is *The Guardian*, the *Financial Times*, and *The Independent*. All three operate their own codes of conduct, which contain high-minded statements of principle about their ethical commitments. For example, *The Guardian*'s code explicitly recognises IPSO's claim that 'all members of the press have a duty to maintain the highest professional standards';[84] the *Financial Times*'s code begins 'It is fundamental to the integrity and success of the *Financial Times* ... that we uphold the highest possible standards of ethical and professional journalism, and that we are seen to do so';[85] and *The Independent*'s starts in a similar vein: 'It is important to us that we get things right. Our commitment to high standards is embodied in our ... Code ...'[86] *The Independent*'s accuracy provision says 'It is our primary endeavour to publish information that is accurate and will not mislead readers. You must take care not to distort information either by disingenuous phrasing or by omission.'[87] Interestingly, although *The Guardian* and the *Financial Times* are not regulated by IPSO (they are not members), both have adopted IPSO's Editor's Code of Practice as their code.[88] Consequently, they are committed, they say, to the obligations under Clause 1, which includes the obligation to 'take care not to publish inaccurate, misleading or distorted information', to correct 'significant inaccuracy ... promptly and with due prominence' and to 'distinguish clearly between comment, conjecture and fact.'[89]

These newspapers, though, are unusual. The remaining major titles restrict themselves to the bare assertion that they are 'committed to abiding by' IPSO's code of conduct. Of course, this is proof, of itself, of an ethical obligation – but

---

[84] *The Guardian*'s Editorial Code, 5 August 2015.
[85] *FT*'s Editorial Code of Practice, 1 July 2019.
[86] *Independent*'s Code of Editorial Content.
[87] Ibid.
[88] *The Guardian*, (n 84); *FT*, (n 85).
[89] Ibid.

these titles are less forthcoming in their commitment to accuracy that does not affect named individuals directly. For example, all those controlled by Reach Plc (formerly Trinity Mirror) – which is most of them (*Daily Mirror, Sunday Mirror, Sunday People, Mirror Online, Daily Express, Sunday Express* and *Daily Star*) – will only consider third-party complaints where the 'alleged breach … is significant *and* there is substantial public interest in considering the complaint.'[90] The Telegraph Media Group, which owns the *Daily Telegraph* and the *Sunday Telegraph*, similarly reserves the right to dismiss complaints 'from any person who has not been personally and directly affected by the matter complained of'[91] but, unlike Reach plc, does not specify when it *will* consider such complaints.

What is the effect of this commitment? Does it not legitimise regulation of the accuracy standard for third-party complaints? The answer is no. For it is in the nature of ethics that only the newspaper itself can regulate its actions according to its own ethics. This is not mere semantics. No external agency can without transcending the boundary between ethics and law – what, as we saw in Chapter 3, Kant called 'ethical lawgiving' and 'juridical lawgiving'.[92] It is only when the doctrine of right is engaged – when interference is required to secure the freedom of others – that intervention is justified. Consequently, since the commitment to accuracy, as it relates to third-party complaints, is a purely ethical matter, compliance cannot be achieved through external intervention. Since newspapers can be neither forced nor required to publish adverse adjudications, complainants are misled when regulators suggest members *must* comply with the requirement of third-party accuracy. As was also discussed in Chapter 3, it is unfortunate that regulatory codes of conduct are often described as 'ethical codes' in circumstances where the decision to impose the obligation is taken by an external body. This renders the term 'ethics' a misnomer.

How, then, can regulators police third-party accuracy (as was suggested earlier) whilst respecting this principle? The solution is to recast this sort of regulation as a public service rather than rule-monitoring. By recognising that newspapers promise to provide accurate information, the regulator can act as a beacon to alert readers to breaches of this promise. In effect, the regulator would then act as a neutral source of clarification. This benefits not only the inquisitive reader but also wider public debate by providing a means of authoritative rebuttal. So, for example, when a newspaper says 'German children banned from sending their Christmas wishlists to Santa … because it breaks EU privacy laws', the adverse adjudication can be used to correct the inaccuracy: the ban resulted solely from town officials, in the Bavarian town of Roth, misunderstanding the provisions of the General Data Protection Regulations and was not due to EU law.[93]

---

[90] Reach plc Complaints Policy, (emphasis added).
[91] *The Telegraph*, Editorial Complaints Policy, 9 November 2017.
[92] I Kant, *The Metaphysics of Morals* (first published, 1797), L Denis (ed), M Gregor, trans (Cambridge, Cambridge University Press, 2017), [6:219]–[6:220].
[93] IPSO ruling, 07543-18 *White v Mail Online*, 15 February 2019.

Or when a journalist reported that guidance issued to schools on how to deal with transgender issues instructed headmasters to shield children with gender dysphoria from any and all complaints – including when parents of non-transgender children object to a transgender girl watching other girls undressing whilst playing with her penis – the adverse adjudication proves the journalist invented the example; it was not taken from the guidance as he had said.[94]

This regulatory feature can be achieved by removing mention of third-party accuracy from the code of conduct and relocating it to a separate section (either on its own or else as part of a description of regulatory powers to hear complaints). It could invite members of the public to notify it of serious inaccuracy, which it could investigate, and publish its findings on its website. Yet, it would have to be made clear that it has no power to compel or direct the member to be accurate and that all the regulator can do is signal the fact of inaccuracy to society at large so that the conscientious voter can take this information into account. In this way, the regulator does no more than highlight instances of the newspaper failing to meet their own ethical standards. In this way, the Austrian independent procedure (das selbständige Verfahren) is instructive.

We can also usefully look to this and other UK and European regulators to ascertain the standard of accuracy that newspapers are expected to achieve. Two norms are especially notable. First, there is a requirement in all UK and European regulatory codes that inaccuracies must be material. Trivial inaccuracies – and even major ones that are not central to the story's purpose – will not count. Secondly, regulators do not expect perfection. Since they are most concerned with the skill of newsgathering and its presentation, they apply a sort of negligence standard. We see this clearly in the code used by the Slovakian Tlačovo-digitálna rada Slovenskej republiky (journalists must 'take care'), the Deutscher Presserat ('the publication of specific information ... must be carefully checked in respect of accuracy'), the Swiss Press Council (journalists must use 'diligence'), and the UK's IMPRESS regulator ('publishers must take all reasonable steps to ensure accuracy'). Belgium's regulator for the French and German press, the Conseil de Déontologie Journalistique, adopts a similar position, insisting that journalists should 'honestly' verify information ('Ils en vérifient la véracité et les rapportent avec honnêteté'). Consequently, it is usual to see the accuracy standard qualified by pragmatism. These caveats speak more to qualities in the journalist than solely to those in the content itself. For example, as we have seen, the Österreichischer Presserat says journalists should *aim* at accuracy, as does IPSO and Finland's Julkisen Sanan Neuvosto, whilst Ireland's press regulator uses the comparable word 'strive'. The Danish Pressenævnets says journalists should verify information 'as far as [it is] possible' to do so – and Sweden's Allmänhetens Pressombudsman uses similar phrases. The regulator, therefore, is most concerned with whether

---

[94] IPSO ruling, 06642-18 *Hill v The Spectator*, 29 January 2019.

the journalist *tried* to achieve accuracy and whether that attempt was sufficient. Belgium's regulator for the Flemish press, the Raad voor de Journalistiek, is a notable exception for its use of an absolute obligation ('a journalist must report information accurately').

This qualified treatment of accuracy means, generally, that regulators do not treat the reporting of another's inaccuracy, such as that contained in a government report,[95] as a violation of the accuracy clause. This is so even if the complainant feels that the report of this inaccuracy translates to the reader as endorsement of its veracity. We get a sense of this problem by examining adjudications on a controversial subject like climate change or immigration. The Finnish broadcaster that reported a former Maldivian President's claim that rising sea tides, caused by climate change, had forced many inhabitants to leave, was found not to have violated the accuracy clause, even though the accuracy of this view was debatable. The Finnish Julkisen Sanan Neuvosto emphasised that it could not act as a 'referee' on whether climate change is happening.[96] The Deutscher Presserat has ruled similarly. In a complaint, from the 1980s, involving three journalists, about the true political situation in East Timor, the Presserat declared it could not adjudicate since the dispute was not about facts (which were apparently unknown) but ideology. It refused to take sides in a dispute between correspondents with opposing political views.[97] We also see regulators take this sort of position in disputes over objectivity. For example, in a newspaper report that claimed Serbian refugees from East Slavonia were economic not political refugees, who travelled to Norway only because the prospects of work were better, the Norwegian Pressens Faglige Utvalg found there had been no violation because the article was clear that these were the views of the immigrants themselves (ie, those who had been interviewed).[98] The fact that this sort of reporting might lead to racial tension was irrelevant.

We see a similar approach in the UK. A complaint that a story, in the *Daily Express*, entitled 'REVEALED: Britain's immigration crisis laid bare as 12,000 asylum seekers VANISH' breached the accuracy clause was not upheld because the story clarified the source and meaning of this number. So although, as was admitted in the story, this figure represented those who missed their first interview with the Home Office but attended a subsequent interview – which gave the headline the appearance of being misleading – nevertheless, since the Home Office could not confirm that all 12,000 were now removed from the 'absconder' list, the journalist was entitled to conclude that they were unaccounted for.[99]

In this way, we see that IPSO has tended to rely upon the opinion/fact distinction to resolve many complaints about misleading stories in the press's

---

[95] See, eg, IPSO ruling, *07507-18 McDermott v The Spectator*, 21 February 2019.
[96] JSN ruling, 5365/YLE/13, 26 March 2014.
[97] Deutscher Presserat ruling, B 36/86.
[98] PFU ruling, PFU-sa 170/98, 23 March 1999.
[99] IPSO ruling, 08772-16 *Lozza v Daily Express*, 9 March 2017.

favour. For example, there are several rulings which treat climate change denial as opinion rather than fact – and so unregulatable.[100] Thus, a *Daily Mail* comment piece by Christopher Booker which dismissed the link between the increasing frequency of global heatwaves and climate change as 'hot air' did not breach the accuracy clause because the complaint was not that the journalist had published inaccurate facts but had interpreted those facts inaccurately and misleadingly.[101] The gist of the journalist's position was that global warming was not happening: that although summer 2018 had been 'abnormally hot', it was only eighteenth in the list of hottest summers in the past 350 years, and that June had been hotter in 1846 than 2018. IPSO summarised the complainant's position thus:

> … overall, the article was misleading, as it suggested that heatwaves were not becoming more frequent in the UK, and that climate change had had no impact on heatwave conditions this summer. He [the complainant] said that there was evidence available that showed that the frequency of heatwaves had been increasing across the UK in the past few decades, and that this was most likely due to global warming. He also said that using the [Central England Temperature Record] figures as the basis for evaluating and comparing heatwaves was misleading, as they only show the mean temperature for each month. The complainant said that the most appropriate way to compare heatwave conditions was to compare mean maximum daily temperatures, which would have shown that in 1976 the temperature was only higher on 17 of 61 days during June and July, compared with 2018. Similarly, he said that by using mean maximum daily temperatures, it was possible to dispute the article's claim that no other summer had compared with the temperatures of 2003, as in 2003 there were two days in excess of 30 degrees, whereas the summer of 2006 had three days in excess of 30 degrees.

By setting out the complainant's position in full, we appreciate the complexity of the climate change debate and the vulnerability of knowledge to summary form. But we also see the limitations of the accuracy clause because, in an important sense, the journalist's claim is false but not inaccurate.

Consequently, we see the regulator engaged in a game of semantics. The regulator is asked to examine the truth value of propositions and make determinations on whether, first, the journalist had provided external verification for the truth claim and, second, that that source had been reported accurately. Generally, if the proposition lacks justification, it is an opinion and beyond the scope of regulation – the reader is expected to engage their own critical faculties to realise this. If it does provide a justification, then the accuracy clause is satisfied even if that source is wrong. In this way, we see that accuracy is not truth.

There is one other effect of this limited regulatory role for third-party accuracy that we must consider. It follows from the discussion above, that the instruction to provide corrections or a right of reply is unjustifiable. It is a different matter

[100] See, eg, IPSO ruling, 01570-18 *Ward v The Sunday Telegraph*, 24 May 2018; 18693-17 *Ward v The Mail on Sunday* 6 April 2018; 01032-17 *Ward v The Mail on Sunday*, 7 July 2017.
[101] IPSO ruling, 05555-18 *Ward v Daily Mail*, 27 November 2017.

if the regulator were to recommend that the newspaper should correct the story or else provide the opportunity to reply, but it cannot insist. Presently, those UK and European regulators that do hear such complaints, reserve to themselves the 'power' to require corrections and/or rights of reply. This is not 'power' in a real sense because these regulators lack the coercive power to enforce the demand. The only European regulator that has this sort of power is Denmark – the failure to publish an adverse adjudication in the form specified by Pressenævnets is punishable by a fine or four months imprisonment under section 53(2) of the Media Liability Act 1991 – and it will not hear third-party accuracy complaints, as we have seen. Nevertheless, these regulators do instruct newspapers to publish their decisions in serious cases, and with some success. IPSO, for example, ordered the express.co.uk to publish its adverse adjudication after it had published what IPSO called a 'significantly misleading article' that falsified the findings of a poll.[102] Its central claim that UK employers were 'BRIMMING WITH CONFIDENCE' about Brexit was unsupported by the poll (which had never asked this question). IPSO directed that the adjudication should be published online:

> with a link appearing in the top 50% of the homepage for 24 hours; it should then be archived in the usual way. The headline of the adjudication must make clear that IPSO has upheld the complaint against the express.co.uk, and refer to its subject matter. It must be agreed with IPSO in advance.[103]

Similarly, IPSO has found in other cases that corrections have breached the accuracy clause where they have not been published with due prominence.[104]

V. Conclusion

In an important sense, the aims of SRT to improve greater public debate through regulatory intervention cannot be realised. First, as we have seen, the scope of a third-party accuracy clause must be limited by pragmatism. It is unrealistic to insist upon an absolute standard of accuracy. A negligence standard reflects the pressures of journalism. But also, accuracy is not equivalent to truth. A newspaper can publish information that is perfectly correct but nevertheless misrepresents the true picture. Accordingly, when a journalist like Christopher Booker claims that climate change is not happening, he is wrong. Yet when he reports official statistics accurately but draws unpersuasive inferences from them, he is beyond regulatory criticism. It is a matter for his readers whether they believe him.

Secondly, although SRT suggests that regulation is justifiable to avert the harm that misinformation and disinformation causes, it fails to realise that the press is not the *cause* of that harm, either as a matter of fact or law. Even though we

---

[102] IPSO ruling, 07925-13 *Partlett v Express.co.uk*, 26 March 2019.
[103] Ibid.
[104] See, eg, IPSO ruling, 06939-18 *Thorne v express.co.uk*, 23 January 2019.

know that newspapers publish inaccurate information which readers act upon, the newspaper does not rob the reader of their autonomy. It is a matter for them if they choose to believe it. They have simply exercised faulty reasoning by treating what appears in print as irrefutable. Normative legal theory, therefore, does not justify the regulation of a third-party accuracy clause because the link between newspaper action and harmful consequence is not established. Neither, when we look across to the positive law, can we find a parallel in consumer protection laws or negligence that would justify this sort of intervention. In the consumer context, the harm, be that physical or financial, is a direct result of the inferior product or negligent advice. But that is not the case with press speech. The two situations are not comparable. Thus, the consumer protection argument – that the third-party accuracy standard prevents readers from being misled – is a logical fallacy. Its object – to either protect public decision-making from the misinformed reader or else to protect the misinformed reader from themselves – fails to acknowledge that it is the reader who is the source of the problem.

Consequently, the regulatory role in third-party accuracy complaints must be limited. Neither the inclusion of a third-party accuracy clause in the regulatory code of conduct nor the use of enforced corrections or rights of reply is justified. But this does not mean the regulatory role must be non-existent. Instead, a regulator could perform a public service by acting as a neutral source of clarification for third-party accuracy complaints. Since, typically, newspapers claim to adhere to the accuracy standard, the regulator would be entitled to highlight those occasions in which the standard was not met. No adverse consequences for the newspaper could follow, at least not from the regulator, but the quality of public debate may be improved, in principle at least, by the availability of this impartial source.

Although this outcome does not bode well for the value of press regulation, it is unimportant, in a way. The most valuable function of regulation, according to the accountability model, is that it protects not public decision-making but the public itself, at least when the public interacts with the press. The greatest significance of regulation, then, is the protection of victims of press abuse. It is to this aspect of regulation that we now turn.

7

Victims

I. Introduction

When newspapers target people, not issues, the unwanted attention can be devastating. Lord Justice Leveson saw this clearly.[1] What he also saw was that the 'real harm' press malfeasance causes does not simply affect politicians and celebrities (ie, people that the press say are 'fair game') but 'real people'.[2] People like Christopher Jefferies: an innocent man, monstered by the press and wrongly accused of murder.[3] People like the Bowles family: hounded as they struggled to cope with the tragic death of their 11-year-old son.[4] And he saw the appalling treatment that those so-called 'fair game' people receive. People like Claire Ward: repeatedly harassed by a newspaper whilst she was an MP and threatened with the publication of damaging, false allegations about her private life – so much so that her health was seriously harmed.[5] He saw that press wrongdoing manifests not only in the information published but also – and in some ways, more importantly – in the means by which this information is obtained. It was this damage, he said, to the rights and interests of individuals who had suffered these wrongs, that ought to be at the 'heart' of regulatory reforms; that the regulator must be empowered to penalise unwarranted press intrusion, misuse of private information, seriously inaccurate reporting, and the substantial risk of serious prejudice to a fair trial.[6] It is the ambition of realising this coercive, independent form of regulation that drives the arguments in this book. The promise of meaningful press regulation will be met only once victim's rights are adequately protected.

In keeping with this ambition, the aim of this chapter is to show the compatibility of coercive measures, in a victim's rights context, with press freedom. Our exclusive focus will be on regulatory standards that deviate from the positive English law, and so provide either greater or lesser protection for rights than the law does. As will be seen, such deviations are common in the UK and

---

[1] Lord Justice Leveson, *An Inquiry into the Culture, Practices and Ethics of the Press: Report* (HC 780, 2012).

[2] Ibid, 50, [2.2].

[3] https://webarchive.nationalarchives.gov.uk/20140122175126/http://www.levesoninquiry.org.uk/wp-content/uploads/2011/11/Witness-Statement-of-Christopher-Jefferies.pdf.

[4] Leveson, (n 1), 576–579.

[5] https://webarchive.nationalarchives.gov.uk/20140122191509/http://www.levesoninquiry.org.uk/wp-content/uploads/2012/08/Witness-Statement-of-Claire-Ward.pdf.

[6] Leveson, (n 1), 1791, [6.5].

European press codes. Because we are interested only in the problems arising from those deviations, there will be no substantial discussion of those regulatory provisions that conform to the law (ie, those rights available under Arts 6 and 8 of the European Convention on Human Rights ('the Convention')). Nor will there be a comprehensive account of the code provisions and their operation in practice (there is an established literature on this subject).[7] For example, there will be no discussion of provisions relating to, say, children or victims of sex crimes.

As will be seen, the ambition of enforcing victim-orientated provisions through coercion raises distinct but separate issues depending on whether those provisions relate to content or conduct. Since the production of content could be understood as a form of conduct, these terms need defining. Intuitively, we might think it translates to the difference between published material and newsgathering activity. Even this, though, is imprecise: is the obligation to contact those accused of serious impropriety prior to publication, found in Belgium's Raad voor de Journalistiek's code,[8] a question of conduct or content? To resolve the dilemma, for the purposes of discussion, I will treat provisions like this as a content obligation on the basis that rules about the form of published material – what it must and must not contain – speak to content obligations. Rules about what might be called journalistic interactions – ie, the way journalists interact with sources and story subjects – are conduct obligations. These conduct measures operate independently of content measures; they are not contingent upon publication. Thus, for our purposes, the newspaper could breach the rules on newsgathering, even if no story about the complainant appears.[9]

Whereas many pre-existing content-related provisions readily correspond to rights found in the positive law (particularly English law), the conduct-related provisions, generally, do not. Nevertheless, it will be argued that many of these conduct provisions translate to the accountability model set out in Chapter 5 which, it will be recalled, has three elements: wrongdoing, harm, and causation. 'Wrongdoing', here, amounts to Kant's view (explored in Chapter 3) that 'whatever is wrong is a hindrance to freedom in accordance with universal laws.'[10] That standard is not met where, for example, the journalist simply fails as a human being, as when a German photo-journalist, having witnessed a truck collide with a car, sending it crashing into a lake, rushed toward the distressed, trapped driver, so that he could take photographs. Understandably, although somewhat coldly,

---

[7] In the UK, the definitive account of IPSO's practices is J Grun, *The Editors' Codebook* (London, The Regulatory Funding Company, 2016). See also, NA Moreham and Sir M Warby (eds), *Tugendhat and Christie: The Law of Privacy and the Media* 3rd edn (Oxford, Oxford University Press, 2016), 691–756; G Millar QC and A Scott, *Newsgathering: Law, Regulation, and the Public Interest* (Oxford, Oxford University Press, 2016).

[8] Raad voor de Journalistiek. December 2016. Code of Practice.

[9] There is also a legal precedent for this: *Gulati v MGN Ltd* [2015] EWCA Civ 1291.

[10] I Kant, *The Metaphysics of Morals* (first published 1797), L Denis (ed), M Gregor, trans (Cambridge, Cambridge University Press, 2017), [6:231].

the Deutscher Presserat found no violation of the code: the driver's privacy right was not substantially engaged, and there was no obligation upon the journalist to provide assistance.[11]

In this chapter, we are concerned solely with issues of normative legal theory concerning the realisation of enforceable victim's rights. The argument is geared toward a hypothetical: the justifiability of using coercive measures to enforce existing regulatory measures, found in the UK and mainland Europe. We should recognise that this is a thought-experiment. Many of the provisions we shall encounter are not enforced coercively, despite the constant language of the categorical imperative. This is true even of Denmark – the only European regulator with coercive powers – since all the Pressenævnets can do is fine the non-publication of its adverse rulings. Moreover, significantly, many regulators use codes that do not even pretend to be enforceable. For example, the Finnish code says it is 'good journalistic practice' to allow criticised parties to comment on stories about them[12] whilst the Norwegian code says 'good press conduct requires clarification of the terms on which an interview is [conducted]';[13] neither code contains mechanisms to enforce these platitudes. Thus, there is an artificiality to the criticisms to be made in this chapter: provisions deemed 'unjustifiable' are not, necessarily, unlawful per se; the point is that they would be if enforced coercively.

The chapter is divided into three parts. Section II explores the difficulties of imposing regulatory obligations, beyond the positive law on conduct-related matters, of which anti-discrimination clauses are the exemplar. Section III tackles conduct. Finally, section IV examines the public interest justification for interfering with victim rights. At first sight, the argument I employ may appear contradictory, for in section II, it will be argued that the regulator is not justified in holding the press to a tougher standard than that found in law, whilst section III, in arguing for the imposition of conduct standards that have no equivalent in law, seems to represent a departure. In fact, the argument common to both is that the regulatory standard need not be identical to that found in the positive law, but it must be compatible with it. So long as normative legal theory is satisfied (ie, the accountability model), then the regulator is justified. As will be seen, there is judicial support for this approach in both the English and Strasbourg jurisprudence.[14] Finally, given that the right to freedom of expression is at its strongest when public interest expression is at stake[15] (which Leveson also recognised),[16] any limitations on press content and conduct must speak only to *unwarranted*, not simply *unwanted*, press attention.

---

[11] German Press Council ruling, Docket 0545/18/2.

[12] Julkisen Sanan Neuvosto. January 2014. Guidelines for Journalists and Annex.

[13] Norsk Presseforbund. June 2015. Code of Ethics of the Norwegian Press.

[14] See section II, below.

[15] See, eg, *Lingens v Austria* (1986) 8 EHRR 407; *Jersild v Denmark* (1994) 19 EHRR 1; *Bladet Tromsø v Norway* (2000) 29 EHRR 125; *Jameel v Wall Street Journal Europe Sprl* [2006] UKHL 44; *Browne v Associated Newspapers* Ltd [2008] QB 103; *Axel Springer AG v Germany* (2012) 55 EHRR 6.

[16] Leveson, (n 1), 69–72.

II. Content

The regulatory codes of mainland Europe and the UK, relating to victim's rights, are often composed in terms that match the positive law. For example, Article 25 of the (misnamed) 'Rules of Ethics', used by Belgium's Conseil de Déontologie Journalistique, says '[j]ournalists respect the privacy of individuals and reveal no personal data that is not relevant to the public interest.'[17] Similarly, the Austrian code says, at clause 5.2, 'libellous or disparaging statements about a person or persons violate the Code of Ethics'[18] whilst the Irish code says, at clause 7, that court reporting must be 'fair and accurate, ... not prejudicial to the right to a fair trial and that the presumption of innocence is respected.'[19]

Some regulators, however, seek to impose tougher standards than the positive law requires (at least, as it is in England and Wales), especially in relation to privacy. The law says, in effect, that only reasonable expectations of privacy are enforceable, and then only where not outweighed by the public interest in invading that privacy.[20] Yet, for example, part IV, clause 1, of the Slovakian code prohibits the publication of *any* details of a person's private life, unless it is in the public interest to do so.[21] The Norwegian code, at clause 4.3, says that the press should 'never draw attention to personal or private aspects if they are irrelevant.'[22] The Danish code, meanwhile, at clause B.1, says 'information which *may* violate the sanctity of private life shall be avoided unless an *obvious* public interest *requires* public coverage.'[23]

Sometimes the right to reputation (where treated separately to the accuracy obligation) is also more generous than the law demands. For example, the Danish code, at A.3, says

> information which *may* be prejudicial or *insulting* or *detract* from the respect in which individuals should be held shall be very closely examined before publication, primarily by submission to the person concerned. Submission should be made so as to give the person concerned a reasonable time to reply.[24]

Similarly, the code of the other Belgium regulator, the Raad voor de Journalistiek, says, at clause 25, that '[a] journalist must not express any unfounded suspicions or accusations.'[25] Occasionally, this generosity is apparent in the fair trial clause.

---

[17] Conseil de déontologie journalistique. September 2017. Code of Journalistic Ethics.

[18] Österreichischer Presserat. June 2014. Guiding Principles for Journalistic Activities (Code of Ethics for the Austrian Press).

[19] Press Council of Ireland. June 2015. Code of Practice.

[20] See, eg, *Axel Springer AG v Germany*, (n 15); *Campbell v MGN* [2004] UKHL 22.

[21] Slovenský syndikát novinárov. June 2017. Journalists' Code of Ethics.

[22] (N 13).

[23] Pressenævnet. May 2013. The Press Ethical Rules. Emphasis added.

[24] Ibid. Emphasis added.

[25] (N 8).

For example, Germany's code, at clause 13, says 'Reports on investigations, criminal court proceedings and other formal procedures must be free from prejudice.'[26]

Sometimes, this tougher reading of press obligations manifests not in the codes themselves, but in regulatory decision-making. Surprisingly (given its propensity toward press favouritism),[27] we see it even in IPSO adjudications. Moreover, these decisions, which all involve MPs, is even more surprising given the apparent incompatibility with Strasbourg caselaw. Thus, IPSO upheld complaints concerning stories which claimed, falsely, that Scotland's First Minister, Nicola Sturgeon, had said her supposed political ally was not Prime Minister material,[28] that a Labour MP had accused the Prime Minister of lacking empathy because she was childless,[29] that a candidate had contravened the terms of his suspension from the UK Independence Party.[30] It is highly unlikely that the European Court of Human Rights ('ECtHR') would have reached the same decision, for although, as seen in earlier chapters, it speaks of a press duty to act 'in good faith and on an accurate factual basis and provide "reliable and precise" information in accordance with the ethics of journalism',[31] it has also said that politicians must tolerate greater degrees of criticism than private individuals,[32] that journalists should be given latitude where they rely upon official reports,[33] and that journalistic freedom extends to a degree of exaggeration.[34] *Salov v Ukraine*[35] illustrates how far this tolerance extends, for that case concerned an allegation, made during an election, that the incumbent President was dead and had been replaced by a doppelgänger, who was being manipulated by a 'criminal entourage'. In finding that the suppression of this material violated the applicant's free speech rights, the ECtHR said, interestingly, that Article 10:

> … does not prohibit discussion or dissemination of information received even if it is strongly suspected that this information might not be truthful. To suggest otherwise would deprive persons of the right to express their views and opinions about statements made in the mass media and would thus place an unreasonable restriction on the freedom of expression set forth in Art.10 of the Convention.[36]

---

[26] Deutscher Presserat. March 2017. German Press Code – Guidelines for journalistic work as recommended by the German Press Council.

[27] J Coad, 'IPSO Committee betrays its absolute lack of independence via its front-page policy', *Inforrm*, 15 August 2018; B Cathcart, 'IPSO: The Toothless Puppet Rolls over for its masters (again)', *Inforrm*, 20 October 2018; P Magrath, 'Bob the Builder: can IPSO fix it?' *Inforrm*, 8 November 2018.

[28] IPSO ruling, 02572-15 *Office of the First Minister v The Daily Telegraph*, 10 June 2015, which concerns this story: S Johnson and P Dominiczak, 'Sturgeon's secret backing for Cameron', *The Daily Telegraph*, April 4, 2015.

[29] IPSO ruling 01629-18 *Champion v The Sun*, 8 May 2018.

[30] IPSO ruling 05677-18 *Costello v Swindon Advertiser*, 20 December 2018.

[31] *Fressoz v France* (2001) 31 EHRR 2 [54].

[32] *Lingens v Austria*, (n 15), [42].

[33] *Bladet Tromsø v Norway*, ibid, [68].

[34] *Prager and Oberschlick v Austria* (1996) 21 EHRR 1, [38].

[35] (2007) 45 EHRR 51.

[36] Ibid.

Of course, this is not an invitation to invent information, but it does emphasise the need to justify the interference with inaccuracy.

We also see this pattern of strict interpretation in Denmark, where the Pressenævnets often reads the 'duty', in rule 1, to publish information 'correctly and promptly', in conjunction with rule 3 (which requires prior consultation with the subject about speech which '*may* be [received as] prejudicial, insulting or degrading').[37] Where the articles imply childhood neglect[38] or abuse,[39] the interpretation is unobjectionable. More troubling, though, are rulings where the inaccuracy seems entirely trivial, ie, an ex-wife had prevented an individual seeing his adult children (she had not)[40] or that large numbers of wild cats were living in an unoccupied caravan (it was occupied; they were pets).[41] The Norwegian regulator, Pressens Faglige Utvalg, also has a propensity toward strict interpretations of the accuracy clause, ie, the inaccurate report of a scuffle during a football match breached the clause,[42] as did the inaccurate claim that an actor had sneaked his partner onto set, resulting in 'turmoil'.[43] Perhaps the worst decision of this kind is by the Finnish regulator, Julkisen Sanan Neuvosto, which criticised a newspaper that had misspelt the name of an equestrienne, Mia von Schantz, three times (von Scantz, von von Schantz, and von Wendt), and her horse Zatal (Zetel). The JSN considered this a serious inaccuracy since it 'could give the reader a false impression of the rider's identity'.[44]

These cases illustrate the problem of using terms like 'significance' or 'materiality' (which is the Finnish standard)[45] to determine complaints. If those terms are not judged by the seriousness of the consequences and but that of the lexical error, then regulatory decision-making becomes mind-numbingly pedantry, as in the horseshow puff piece and the cat story. Finickity insistence upon exactitude turns well-meaning provisions into bureaucratic quibbling. Russell Wiggins, the distinguished American journalist, experienced this, having become ensnared in the fine detail of a Minnesotan retraction statute, over a story concerning one Irving Cohen. For four consecutive days, careless errors caused a non-compliant retraction to be published. After an authentic one was finally published, on the fifth day, a fellow journalist called him 'to say that he was sorry the paper had discontinued the Cohen column just when he was getting interested in it'.[46] When these purely lexical considerations dominate, or the standard of ill-consequence is taken too lightly, then tough regulatory decision-making risks derision.

---

[37] IN 23), emphasis added.

[38] Case number 12-70-00380, KEN no 9143 of 19/3/2013.

[39] Case number 17-70-01123, KEN no 9541 of 23/5/2017.

[40] Case number 13-70-00568, KEN no 9833 of 17/12/2013.

[41] Case number 13-70-00538, KEN no 9592 of 22/10/2013.

[42] PFU ruling, *Advokat Erik Rolfsen pva. klient mot Tidens Krav*, PFU-sak 277/17, 22 March 2018.

[43] PFU ruling, *Adv. Mona Danielsen pva. klienter mot Se og Hør*, PFU-sak 196/17, 27 February 2018.

[44] JSN Ruling, 6777/PL/17, 11 April 2018.

[45] See JSN Rulings, 6016/SL/15, 6025/SL/15 and 6028/SL/15.

[46] Discussed in MS Shapo, 'Media Injuries to Personality: An Essay on Legal Regulation of Public Communication' (1968) 46 *Texas Law Review* 650, 650.

Can we really criticise *The Times* (of London) for mocking the Pressenævnets's decision to protect the 'hurt feelings' of the convicted felon inaccurately described of grabbing his victim's neck instead of her body?[47] Can we blame it for fearing the deleterious effect that replication of this system in the UK would have?

The disconnect between the positive law and regulatory norms is problematic, though, only to the extent that the accountability model, outlined in Chapter 5, is not observed. In the language of both Kant and Mill, only undue interferences with freedom count, and these are comprised of three elements: 'wrongdoing' on the part of the duty-holder amounting to an interference with the right-holder's freedom, the infliction of harm to the rights-holder amounting to a serious impact upon her freedom, and a causal link connecting the two. This construct – of wrongdoing-causation-harm – provides us with a formula by which to judge regulatory provisions, and so determine what may be enforced coercively.

The meaning of 'wrongdoing' deserves some explanation, albeit I do not say this as some preliminary to articulating a theory of wrongdoing. Nor is it necessary to do so, for although the concept is complicated, and controversial,[48] the parameters of our enquiry are limited by a practical point. If the regulator is to employ a standard that differs from the positive law, then its compatibility with Article 10 must be established, should one of its members pursue judicial review.[49] Consequently, although, as we shall see, the regulator is afforded some discretion in determining its code of conduct, that discretion is limited by an important principle: the discretion cannot be exercised in a manner that undercuts Article 10 rights. Accordingly, we can say, then, that 'wrongdoing' constitutes that which falls outside the zone of 'press freedom' and into, instead, the zone of 'freedom of the press',[50] which is to say that the speech or activity interferes with the rights of others and causes them harm.

In the UK, clauses 7 and 8 of the Royal Charter on Self-Regulation of the Press provides this discretion. We see similar provisions in other press regulatory contexts such as, in broadcast journalism, under section 319, Communications Act 2003, and other countries, such as section 34(1) of the Danish Media Liability Act 1991. Thus, according to the UK High Court, 'Section 319 of the 2003 Act obliges OFCOM to set such standards for the content of programmes as appear to them best calculated to secure standard objectives.'[51] Section 34(1), for example, simply reads 'The content and conduct of the mass media shall be in conformity with sound press ethics' and it has been for the Pressenævnets to work out what those standards are. Similarly, clause 7 of the Royal Charter says that 'the standards code must ultimately be the responsibility of, and adopted by, the

---

[47] A Gilligan, 'So this is what press regulation looks like', *The Times*, 21 April 2013.

[48] See, eg, R Alexy, *A Theory of Constitutional Rights*, J Rivers, trans, (Oxford, Oxford University Press, 2010); MH Kramer, NE Simmonds and H Steiner, *A Debate over Rights* (Oxford, Oxford University Press, 1998).

[49] See, eg, *Gaunt v Ofcom* [2011] EWCA Civ 962, [11] & [36].

[50] See discussion in Preface.

[51] *Gaunt v Ofcom* [2010] EWHC 1756, [7].

[Regulator's] Board, advised by a Code Committee.' Clause 8 provides minimal information about its content, saying only that it must uphold freedom of speech, the public interest, confidentiality of sources, and the rights of individuals affected by journalistic conduct, invasions of privacy, and inaccuracy.

At both a domestic and supranational level, the courts afford the regulator this discretion due to its superior expertise in the field. In *Gaunt v Ofcom*, a case in which Ofcom upheld a complaint regarding offensive language used on air by the claimant radio presenter, the Court of Appeal held that '... although the decision whether article 10 is infringed in this case is ultimately one for the court, we should none the less "have due regard" to' Ofcom's judgement since it 'has the experience and the "feel" which the court lacks.'[52] When the case reached the ECtHR, it agreed with this reasoning, and was similarly deferential to Ofcom's 'considerable experience of balancing the parameters of potentially offensive content with the fluctuating expectations of contemporary radio audiences in the Contracting State.'[53]

If current regulatory provisions were to be enforced coercively, the greatest source of tension, concerning their compatibility with Article 10, would surely arise in respect of the discrimination clause. For example, consider IPSO's anti-discrimination clause (12): 'The press must avoid prejudicial or pejorative reference to an individual's, race, colour, religion, sex, gender identity, sexual orientation or to any physical or mental illness or disability' and that details relating to these characteristics 'must be avoided unless genuinely relevant to the story.' Ostensibly, there is tacit approval for coercive enforcement of this clause for the recognition panel, when considering an application for regulatory status, 'may but need not, take into account'[54] Leveson's recommendation that the regulator have 'the power to intervene in cases of allegedly discriminatory reporting, and in so doing reflect the spirit of equalities legislation.'[55] That said, there is nothing in clause 8 of the Royal Charter that would force a regulator to implement such a provision if it did not do so voluntarily.

Yet, as this equivocal approach signals, discriminatory language does not readily translate to legal wrongdoing. To the limited extent that the law prohibits anti-discriminatory speech, it is in the context of public order measures (speech that will incite violence) and the employment relationship (the regulation of contractual duties). There is nothing in the positive law that restricts the holding and expression of bigoted views. It is not clear why Leveson thought the 'spirit of' equalities legislation'[56] would overcome this problem, for the Equality

---

[52] Ibid, [47] & [48]. See also *R (on the application of Wildman) v Ofcom* [2005] EWHC 1573, [14].

[53] *Gaunt v United Kingdom (Admissibility)* (2016) 63 EHRR SE 15, [61].

[54] Sch 2, cl 4, of the Royal Charter on Self-Regulation of the Press.

[55] Recommendation 38. Lord Justice Leveson, *An Inquiry into the Culture, Practices and Ethics of the Press, Executive Summary and Recommendations*, (HC 779, 2012), 37.

[56] Leveson, (n 1), 1808.

Act 2010 prohibits direct discrimination but only by service providers and public authorities.[57]

It may be argued, though, that since these anti-discrimination clauses protect the dignity of those discriminated against, the sense of wrongdoing – of undermining an individual's dignity – is analogous to the protections afforded by Article 8 of the Convention. This would also provide a principled means of penalising speech that attacks named individuals without compromising the liberal sentiment that those holding illiberal viewpoints should be persuaded, not coerced, into changing their minds. This claim is not without its difficulties. Nevertheless, we can avoid, at least, some of the criticisms that, for example, Christopher McCrudden raises about 'dignity' as an open-ended, unprincipled claim.[58] We can also draw some support from the Strasbourg jurisprudence. For example, in *Aksu v Turkey*,[59] the ECtHR recognised, in principle, that the right to a private life under Article 8 was sufficiently broad enough to 'embrace multiple aspects of the person's physical and social identity'[60] and that:

> … any negative stereotyping of a group, when it reaches a certain level, is capable of impacting on the group's sense of identity and the feelings of self-worth and self-confidence of members of the group. It is in this sense that it can be seen as affecting the private life of members of the group.[61]

Similarly, in other cases, the Court has held that human dignity can be protected under Article 8.[62] Likewise, its approval in principle of Holocaust and genocide denial laws speaks to the compatibility of protecting human dignity under Article 8 with the principle of free speech under Article 10, so long as interferences are proportionate.[63]

Nevertheless, the ECtHR is quite generous toward freedom of expression, even in these circumstances. Alongside its longstanding principle that freedom of expression extends to speech that 'shocks, offends, or disturbs',[64] it has been prepared to protect political expression even in genocide denial cases, like *Perinçek v Switzerland,* and even though that speech, according to the Swiss Government, 'threatened the values underpinning the fight against racism and intolerance, infringed the rights of the victims' relatives, and [was] incompatible with the values of the Convention.'[65] Similarly, in *Aksu* itself, the Court endorsed

---

[57] Ss 29 & 31, Equality Act 2010.

[58] C McCrudden, 'Human Dignity and Judicial Interpretation of Human Rights' (2008) 19(4) *European Journal of International Law* 655.

[59] (2013) 56 EHRR 4.

[60] Ibid, [58].

[61] Ibid.

[62] See, eg, *Hachette Filipacchi Associates v France* (2009) 49 EHRR 23.

[63] See discussion in DJ Harris, M O'Boyle, EP Bates, and CM Buckley, *Law of the European Convention on Human Rights* 3rd edn (Oxford, Oxford University Press, 2014), 623–626.

[64] See, eg, *Handyside v UK* (1979–80) 1 EHRR 737, [49].

[65] See, eg, *Perinçek v Switzerland* (2016) 63 EHRR 6 [169].

the state's decision to prefer the Article 10 right of the author to make derogatory comments about the applicants.

Of course, even if we could demonstrate that discriminatory speech counted as wrongdoing, we should draw a distinction between that which targets a named individual and that which targets a homogeneous group. For the more generic the object of discrimination is, the harder it becomes to demonstrate causation. Thus, although newspapers, as Leveson saw clearly, regularly agitate racial dishar-mony and incite the 'othering' of minorities, the connection between the harm that these groups suffer, and the cause of that harm is uncertain. For, even though, we can easily evidence the practice of depicting fringe and extremist elements of the Muslim community as representative of the whole;[66] of inflating (sometimes inventing) statistics about refugees;[67] of 'monstering' trans people;[68] of vilifying social services (which jeopardises the trust vulnerable young people have in those services);[69] of distorting and desensitising the public's view of rape and violence against women;[70] of depicting women as sex objects,[71] we cannot show that this is the *cause* of the same obnoxious views that we find in ignorant people, for it may well be merely a symptom. Admittedly, this type of reporting does not help incul-cate multiculturism, tolerance, and understanding into our way of life, but that is not the test.

Moreover, the issue of wrongdoing is also complicated at this level. For the law should be careful to force the illiberal to hold liberal views. Quite obviously, this would be an intolerable interference with individual autonomy – and here we have the liberal paradox. Whilst the law can protect the rights of all so as to achieve equality, it cannot force citizens to embrace equality as a way of life. In this way, we see the limitations in the public order measures, which outlaw discrimination only to the extent violence would or could follow. Similarly, we see the tension inherent in the equalities legislation, for the legal obligation not to discriminate has raised tricky issues, as where a devoutly religious baker was ordered to pay damages for refusing to produce a cake that proclaimed 'Support Gay Marriage'.[72] Consequently, we see the law protecting one way of life, by imposing sanctions on another, and although, given a choice between the two, the liberal would prefer the reactionary attitude penalised, it is nevertheless a law that sits uncomfortably with liberalism.

Consequently, the wrongfulness of discriminatory language relates to a spec-trum of speech, which includes, at one end, language intended to traumatise a

[66] Leveson, (n 1), 486–487.
[67] Ibid, 487–488.
[68] Ibid, 488.
[69] Ibid, 489.
[70] Ibid, 489–490.
[71] Ibid, 490.
[72] *Lee v McArthur* [2016] NICA 39. See also *Preddy v Bull* [2013] UKSC 73. See further D Capper, 'Free Speech is Not a Piece of Cake' in RL Weaver et al, *Free Speech and Media Law in the 21st Century* (Durham, NC, Carolina Academic Press, 2019), 105.

specific individual or limited group. In these circumstances, the rights-claim equates to a sort of privacy right, to be left alone, as it were. At the other end, we find language expressing a dislike, maybe even a hatred of a generic group. Penalising this sort of speech seems less justifiable. It is not akin to protecting privacy rights; it is more the indoctrination of liberal thinking, and, for that reason, deeply problematic.

III. Conduct

A. Introduction

Conduct measures appear less frequently in the code provisions. Denmark's code says remarkably little about conduct. Of its 23 provisions, only one mentions conduct explicitly, and even then, only in passing. Clause B.6 says: 'At the *collection* or publication of information, the confidence, feelings, ignorance, lack of experience or lack of self-control should not be abused.'[73] The Swedish code says even less: there are *no* provisions relating to newsgathering.[74] Conversely, IPSO's code has eight measures of this type. Ireland's has seven.

Some of these conduct measures are plainly unenforceable, having no parallel in the positive law. For example, the common 'obligation' that journalists disclose their profession before conducting an interview. We find this in Belgium (in the Raad voor de Journalistiek code, clause 17), Slovakia (clause V.1), Germany (guideline 4.1), Switzerland (directive 4.1), Finland (clause 9), the Netherlands (clause B.1), and IPSO (clause 3(ii)). Sometimes this is expressed in qualified terms: the Finnish code says only that journalists are 'encouraged' to identify themselves; the Slovakian code, that journalists should not conceal their identity; whilst IPSO is more begrudging: '*if* requested, they must identify themselves and whom they represent' (emphasis added). The coercive enforcement of this clause would be hard to justify, for what *is* the interference with freedom should the hypothetical interviewee fail to appreciate the consequences of speaking candidly to her interlocutor?[75]

Other conduct measures are more easily explicable in juridical terms, relating, as they do, to harassment and intrusion. The IPSO code, for example, prohibits the use of intimidation, harassment and 'persistent pursuit', restricts the capacity to intrude where press attention is unwelcomed, and contains strict obligations on interviewing children, those suffering grief or shock, and those in hospital. It also restricts the use of clandestine devices and subterfuge to acquire

---

[73] (N 23).

[74] Pressens Opinionsnämnd. June 2018. Code of Ethics for Press, Radio and Television in Sweden.

[75] Indeed, the Norwegian Pressens Faglige Utvalg has rejected such a claim: PFU ruling, *Morten Bangås, daglig leder i Remiks Husholdning AS mot iTromsø*, PFU-sak 073/18, 29 May 2018.

information. Yet, coercive enforcement, in the UK, requires some justification since English law contains little protection from such wrongs[76] – with the notable exception of harassment claims which satisfy the test in the Protection from Harassment Act 1997. Comparable laws do exist, though, in the United States of America, Canada, and New Zealand, in the form of protection from intrusion into seclusion.[77] In the US, for example, section 652B of the Restatement (Second) of Torts (1977) imposes liability for intentional intrusion, upon the 'solitude or seclusion of another or his private affairs or concerns', that is 'highly offensive to a reasonable person.' This operates as a sort of property right that protects against unwarranted invasions of private space, such as the home or places usually treated as private, like hospitals, changing rooms or toilet facilities.[78] The remainder of this section examines the justifiability of using coercive measures to penalise journalistic interactions where a) such interaction is unwelcomed (as in scenarios involving harassment or intrusion into grief or suffering) or b) is duplicitous (as in undercover reporting).

B. Unwanted Contact

Would-be interviewees ought to have greater protection from unwanted journalistic contact than they currently receive. Their right to be left alone ought to trump the journalistic norm of persistently chasing leads, even though, on occasion, this persistence benefits the would-be interviewee and/or the wider community. In this section, I shall outline the form that this ideal protection should take (and defend this model). Briefly, I shall argue that once a would-be interviewee notifies the regulator that they wish to be left alone, the only permissible means of contacting them should be through the regulator, as an impartial conduit between the individual and the press. Thus, the following discussion has several objectives. First, it outlines the reasons for this tougher regulation of unwanted contact; secondly, it defends the notion of an individual's right to be left alone; thirdly, and relatedly, it tackles an important objection: that this would have a deleterious effect on serious investigative journalism; finally, it outlines, and defends, the 'conduit' system that I have in mind.

---

[76] Although the English common law does not formally recognise an intrusion into seclusion tort, Nicole Moreham has argued, on several occasions, that the case law shows promising signs of judicial receptivity toward developing the law in that direction: See N Moreham, 'Beyond Information: Physical Privacy in English Law' (2014) 73(2) *Cambridge Law Journal* 350, 'Liability for Listening: Why Phone Hacking Is an Actionable Breach of Privacy' (2015) 7(1) *Journal of Media Law* 155 and NA Moreham and Sir Mark Warby (eds), *Tugendhat and Christie: The Law of Privacy and the Media*, 3rd edn (Oxford, Oxford University Press, 2016) 10.82–10.92. See also P Wragg, 'Recognising a privacy-invasion tort: the conceptual unity of informational and intrusion claims' (2019) 78(2) *Cambridge Law Journal* 409.

[77] See, eg, TDC Bennett, 'Emerging Privacy Torts in Canada and New Zealand: An English Perspective' (2014) *European Intellectual Property Review* 298.

[78] See discussion in Wragg, 'Recognising a Privacy-Invasion Tort: The Conceptual Unity of Informational and Intrusion Claims', (n 76).

Most regulators recognise this right to be left alone, albeit the degree of stringency varies. IPSO is one of the more strongly worded. It has two specific clauses designed to protect vulnerable individuals – those in a state of grief or shock (clause 4) and those in hospital (clause 8). It has a general anti-harassment clause (clause 3) which states: 'Journalists must not engage in intimidation, harassment or persistent pursuit' and further, that, attempts to interview must cease 'once asked to desist', and this includes leaving the property when asked and not pursuing the would-be interviewee. Ireland's code says virtually the same. Both are notable, though, for condoning harassment (and, in IPSO's case, intimidation) where it is in the public interest to do so (which, of itself, raises an important point that I shall address shortly). Conversely, there are those that speak in vague or ambiguous terms, such as the Slovakian code, which says, part V, clause 4, 'The journalist shall show particular sensitivity and responsibility when approaching persons who have no experience of communicating with journalists', or the German code, which says, at guideline 4.2, that, when interviewing vulnerable individuals 'particular restraint is called for', or the Austrian code, which says, at clause 8.1, that 'no unfair or improper methods' should be used to gather materials, or the Dutch code which says, at B.1, that the journalist should enable the interviewee to make an 'informed decision' about whether to co-operate or not.

Yet, adjudications reveal a timorous approach that betrays the language of the categorical imperative in these clauses. IPSO is a prime example. Although its guidance describes the harassment clause as 'one of the toughest and most explicit',[79] its rulings (as well as those of its predecessor) suggest this assessment is hyperbolic. For IPSO's approach is formalistic rather than substantive. Unless the victim has been explicit, both in expressing the fact that they wish to be left alone and in stipulating the terms on which the right is exercised, then IPSO is largely unsympathetic and bound to dismiss the complaint, even though the fact of wanting to be left alone may be obvious from the complainant's conduct (such as a constant refusal to engage with questioning)[80] or the circumstances. We see this clearly in a complaint by a person called John Gordon, a bailiff, who was threatened by masked men whilst performing his duties, and so became the subject of press interest. Despite informing the press of his right to be left alone, he received a further unsolicited approach, this time at his doorstep, from a journalist who only reluctantly left when asked. IPSO condoned this intrusion because the 'new angle' that the journalist wished to pursue voided Gordon's original request.[81] Similarly, when a famous couple issued a statement through their representative that they wished to be left alone, clause 4 was not breached because the press had contacted a representative rather than the couple directly.[82] Another complainant issued a press statement, through her employer, indicating her wish to be left alone.

[79] J Grun, *The Editor's Codebook*, (The Regulatory Funding Company, 2016), 40.
[80] IPSO ruling, 06701-18 *Watson v Daily Mirror*, 11 January 2019.
[81] IPSO ruling, 08062-18 *Gordon v Sunday Life*, 29 March 2019.
[82] PCC ruling, *Gary and Danielle Lineker v The Sun*, 12 July 2013.

Nevertheless, a journalist contacted her, through the Facebook messaging service, and then proceeded to contact her mother, father, grandfather, boyfriend, and other unspecified friends and family. The PCC partially dismissed the complaint because these third parties were not mentioned in the original press release and neither had they objected when contacted.[83]

These adjudications are disappointing for they fail to recognise the wrong inherent in the journalist's intrusive conduct. The regulator ought to appreciate that such conduct is a gross invasion of privacy. For, in determining what is wrongful, the victim's autonomy ought to be determinative. This becomes clearer if we scrutinise the hypothetical interaction between journalist and would-be interviewee. Newspapers become interested in people for one of three reasons: castigation, celebration, or compassion. The would-be interviewee is either a material witness to these events, or is the subject of the story. Usually, but not always, there is no prior relationship between journalist and agent. Nevertheless, the journalist's goal is always the same: they want the information that the agent possesses. Our question, then, is ultimately, what entitlement does the journalist have to this information? Only once we have determined that question can we speak of the means that the journalist would be entitled to use to obtain it.

Here, then, we see the source of tension between journalist and victim, for journalists act as if they have a *right* to question people; as if the only question to be asked is the *extent* of that right: how far can they go to obtain the information that *they* believe they have a right to? I disagree, albeit I understand why journalists, and their supporters, would think this. For SRT engenders this entitled attitude in its view that the press has a duty to impart information which the public has a right to receive. Yet there is a distinction to be drawn here between thought and the product of thought. There is nothing problematic about the notion that the product of thought, when it manifests in a thing external to the agent (ie, a document), is something that can be demanded. We see this clearly, for example, in the MP's expenses debacle, in which, due to a journalist's persistence, evidence was extracted from the government that revealed that MPs were misusing public funds to supplement their own lifestyles, sometimes outrageously.[84] The same cannot be said of thought itself. Whereas, it is often true, undoubtedly, that a newspaper has a right to disclose certain information, and may also have a legal right to obtain certain information, there is no right to demand testimony from an unwilling witness.

In this, the term 'duty' becomes significant in distinguishing the press from law enforcement agencies. The police, for example, or the courts, have obligations to the public to discover truth and deliver justice. These duties *do* justify the imposition of coercive measures upon the unwilling witness. It cannot be said that *the press* has this duty, nor the entitlement, to prosecute for truth and justice.

---

[83] PCC ruling, *Parkyn v The Mail on Sunday*, Report 79, 5 May 2009.

[84] A Dawar, 'Timeline: MPs' expenses', *The Guardian*, 7 May 2008.

On this point, we should return to the harassment clause used by IPSO and the Irish Press Council. Both sanction the use of harassment, and in IPSO's case, intimidation, to discover truth. The ends justify the means, according to this logic. This cannot be right. For when newspapermen chased Andrew Robathan MP, and his family, as they enjoyed a family drive out, and then proceeded to conduct an impromptu interview when, traumatised by the experience, he pulled over in the hope they would pass,[85] we see the point vividly, I hope. Journalists are not entitled to what is inside our heads (the episode concluded with Mr Robathan MP inviting the two men to contact him during business hours).

Consequently, then, in determining what constitutes unlawful intrusion between the persistent interlocutor and the unwilling respondent, the press is not special. Although UK law offers only rudimentary protection from intrusion, we see this sort of right clearly in other jurisdictions, specifically the US, Canada, and New Zealand. Problematically, this tends to be limited to a sort of property right (ie, the place in which the act occurred is determinative) and subject to a sort of common standard of morality to determine what constitutes the unlawful act (ie, it must be an act that others would find 'highly offensive'). Nevertheless, despite consistent persuasive criticisms, in the academic literature[86] and the judiciary,[87] that social norms are a poor barometer (Lord Nicholls, in *Campbell v MGN Ltd*, called it a 'recipe for confusion'),[88] even in the US, intrusive press practices have been found unlawful.[89]

Moreover, the restrictive approach to determining unlawful intrusion, by reference *only* to social norms, is not normatively required, as I have argued elsewhere.[90] The wrong (intrusion) ought to be judged not only *objectively*, according to social norms, but also, and more importantly, *subjectively*, through the lens of autonomy. This represents a fact-sensitive exercise which examines the communicative exchange (in which the autonomous agent signalled her sense of intrusion to the journalist), the agent's emotional state, and the journalist's knowledge of that state. This subjectivity is vital. Consider the reasons why the PCC dismissed Andrew Robathan MP's complaint: there was no breach of clause 3, they said, because the complaint referred to a single occasion, the newspapermen had not acted in an 'overtly aggressive manner', they had not driven dangerously, and they had left the family alone once asked to do so. This sort of detached, unreal analysis takes no account of the lived experience – of being pursued by strangers for ten to twenty minutes, and of being approached by these strangers upon

---

[85] PCC ruling, *Robathan v Sunday Mirror*, 28 May 2012.

[86] See, eg, Robert C Post, 'The Social Foundations of Privacy: Community and Self in the Common Law Tort' (1989) 77(5) *California Law Review* 957, 962; Daniel J Solove, 'Fourth Amendment Pragmatism' (2010) 51 *Boston College Law Review* 1511.

[87] *Campbell*, (n 20), per Lord Nicholls, [22], per Baroness Hale, [134], per Lord Carswell, [166].

[88] Ibid.

[89] See, eg, *Miller v NBC* 187 Cal App 3d 1470 (1986).

[90] Wragg, 'Recognising a Privacy Invasion Tort', (n 76).

pulling over. This is not normal behaviour; it is unnerving and hostile. It strikes me that what the PCC describes (the absence of overt aggression) amounts to aggravating factors, that go to the seriousness of the intrusion, and not the fact of it. To illustrate the point, consider the facts of *Kaye v Robertson*,[91] in which a reporter and photographer from the *Daily Sport* inveigled their way into the room of a well-known television personality, who was recovering from major brain surgery and still experiencing the effects of anaesthesia, and proceeded to conduct an interview with him. There is no suggestion in the case report that these men were anything other than courteous in their dealings with Kaye, yet we would have no hesitation in labelling their actions intrusive and, had the law been on Kaye's side in 1990, unlawful (privacy law did not exist meaningfully in the UK until 2004).[92]

Of course, the fact that this interview took place in a hospital is significant, and evidences Kaye's vulnerability, yet it is not determinative, for the simple reason that those in hospital may be happy to be interviewed – in fact, they may want to be.[93] Harassment, then, must be judged by the sense of intimidation it evokes in the agent: the 'inducement of fear, physical endangerment, and perhaps the threat of future repercussions,'[94] as Gavin Millar QC and Andrew Scott put it. Admittedly, this standard should not be read too low, for, in a sense, all interactions with journalists are likely to be unnerving, especially those with little or no experience of them. Accordingly, we can say, with IPSO, that the act of a journalist sitting near the complainant during her husband's trial did not constitute harassment, for the feeling of intimidation must have some rational basis.[95]

Instead, the complainant must demonstrate that the journalist's actions interfere with her autonomy. We see this in the case of Mary Bale, who became notorious in 2010 after she was caught on CCTV trapping a cat in a rubbish bin. She was subjected to intense media scrutiny, of the sort usually reserved for senior politicians and major celebrities (indeed, this quickly escalated and the police, fearing for her safety, provided her with police protection).[96] She later reported to the *Financial Times* that this press attention began with a suspicious telephone call, ostensibly from an insurance firm, which asked her personal questions.[97] She became suspicious and terminated the call. Moments later a reporter from the *Sun* was at her doorstep. After declining the request for an interview, she began to receive telephone calls from two separate journalist who, she says, adopted

[91] [1991] FSR 62.

[92] See discussion in R Moosavian, 'Charting the Journey from Confidence to the New Methodology' [2012] 34(5) *European Intellectual Property Review* 324.

[93] See, eg, PCC ruling, *Hutchison v News of the World*, Report 37 and PCC ruling, *Stamp v Essex Chronicle*, 26 August 2011.

[94] G Millar QC and A Scott, *Newsgathering: Law, Regulation, and the Public Interest* (Oxford, OUP, 2016), 330, [14.72].

[95] IPSO ruling, 05686-18 *Ashford v Basingstoke Gazette*, 4 February 2019.

[96] See further, P Wragg, 'Leveson and Disproportionate Public Interest Reporting' (2013) 5(2) *Journal of Media Law* 241.

[97] MJ Hyland, 'The Trial of Mary Bale', *FT Magazine*, 25 March 2011.

the strategy of good cop/bad cop with one seeking to cajole her into compliance through various incentives and promises whilst the other sought to achieve the same end by threats ('he was trying to scare me with ideas of being besieged by reporters, etc, to try and get his exclusive'). This began shortly after 5pm and continued every 30 minutes until 11pm that night.

Here we see clearly how autonomy-impairing conduct can manifest in a sort of power dynamic, in which the journalist takes advantage of a person's vulnerability. This exploitation may be implied or else take the form of overt threats to humiliate or shame them publicly. We see this contemptible behaviour in *Mosley v News Group Newspapers Ltd*.[98] That notorious case concerned an egregious invasion of privacy, in which the claimant's outlandish sex life was graphically exposed. The journalist who wrote the story, Neville Thurlbeck, exerted pressure on the claimant's lovers to provide information. Mr Justice Eady, in the case, described the correspondence thus:

> [It] would appear to contain a clear threat to the women involved that unless they co-operated with Mr Thurlbeck (albeit in exchange for some money) their identities would be revealed on the following Sunday. He was as good as his word and attached photographs and also some extracts from their websites. This was obviously to bring home to them the scale of the threatened exposé.[99]

In the later case of *CDE v MGN Ltd*,[100] this was described by counsel as 'the standard journalistic ploy': the journalist tries to secure the co-operation of an unwilling source by telling them that the story is bound to enter the public domain regardless of their wishes and, therefore, that co-operation ensures 'some kind of control over it'.[101] In *AAA v Associated Newspapers Ltd*,[102] the Court was told that the claimant (an infant less than one-years-old) and her mother was subjected to intense media scrutiny, over a period of 12 days, because the father of the child was said to be a famous politician. The claimant's mother said: 'I was made to feel under siege by members of the press'.[103] The child's nanny said: 'We spent a lot of time sitting on the stairs': the only place that felt safe.[104]

What is not always recognised, although is well-understood by those unfortunate enough to have experienced it, is that this sort of unwanted press attention is frightening. In *AAA,* the Court was told that journalists and photographers would camp outside the family house 'until at least 11pm'; on one occasion, they 'swarmed around [the family car], shouting questions and taking photographs … The claimant was visibly distressed by this incident'.[105] They rang the doorbell incessantly, they rang the claimant's mother's mobile telephone

---

[98] [2008] EWHC 1777.
[99] Ibid, [82].
[100] [2010] EWHC 3308.
[101] Ibid, [10].
[102] [2012] EWHC 2103.
[103] Ibid, [18].
[104] Ibid, [21].
[105] Ibid, [2].

constantly, and they even stood outside the family home, shouting out from the street to the upstairs window. 'The behaviour created an atmosphere of tension and unease in the family home, it caused distress to the claimant's mother and nanny, which in turn caused distress to the claimant.'[106] This is not acceptable behaviour. Similarly, an individual complained to the Irish regulator that he had been 'effectively housebound' such was the level of harassment when he tried to leave his property. It took the intervention of the police before he could leave.[107]

As these cases also highlight, the would-be interviewee is often emotionally vulnerable. This is especially true of those suffering a bereavement, or otherwise in shock. As Moreham and Tinsley put it, 'this is not just unfortunate timing: family members are not just being approached at a bad time; they are approached because it is a bad time.'[108] Although IPSO takes this vulnerability into account, it is regrettable that it puts a time limit on grief and suffering. Thus, when the former fiancée of murdered soldier Lee Rigby – whose shocking death was the subject of intense media coverage – complained about unwanted press contact, she was told her complaint failed because too much time had passed between his death and this subsequent press contact.[109] Apart from the gross insensitivity of the decision, it is not cognisant of the fact that the only reason the press would be interested in reporting her new relationship with Rigby's former colleague is *because* of that tragedy, for apart from that, they (and presumably their readership) would have no interest in her.

This insensitivity is also apparent in other decisions. Take, for example, the IPSO ruling in *Armstrong v Edinburgh Evening News*,[110] which concerned a teenage girl who had died from brain cancer. An article entitled 'Ellie Armstrong, 14, loses brain cancer fight' appeared two days after her death. It was comprised largely of information taken from Ellie's Facebook page, including messages of condolence from her classmates. The family objected to this act, of itself, for reasons that go beyond our discussion here, albeit we might note how tone deaf both the *Edinburgh Evening News* and IPSO were to the insensitivity of this behaviour. Our focus here is on the journalist's interactions with the family. Taking the Facebook page as proof of the family's wish to communicate Ellie's death to the world at large, the journalist pestered and connived to extract further information from the family. Accordingly, Ellie's father's refusal to be interviewed was repurposed in conversations with other family members, in which the journalist sought 'clarification' on his statement from them, which clearly implied he had consented to an

[106] Ibid.

[107] Irish ruling, *O'Donoghue and the Irish Daily Star Sunday*, 15 April 2010.

[108] NA Moreham and Y Tinsley, 'The impact of grief journalism on its subjects: lessons from the Pike River mining disaster' (2019) 10(2) *Journal of Media Law* 189, 189.

[109] IPSO ruling, 02716-15 *West v Sunday Mirror* and 03071-15 *Draper v Sunday Mirror*, 5 October 2015.

[110] IPSO ruling, 03856-15 *Armstrong v Edinburgh Evening News*, 4 August 2015.

interview. In dismissing the complaint, IPSO's reasoning is revealing, for according to them, the fact of the Facebook page (which invited expressions of condolence) made the family's 'personal tragedy' ripe for public discussion. Further, the intrusion into grief or shock clause, they said, is no more than an obligation to show 'sensitivity': 'this does not create a requirement that the family must consent to publication or an absolute prohibition on journalists approaching the family for comment.'[111]

It is this attitude that ought to be challenged, for in the conflict between the agent's privacy right and the journalistic norm of tenacity, it is the agent's autonomously-made decision that should be determinative. If the agent has communicated to the press that she wishes to be left alone, then the argument is settled. In advocating this, I do not mean to suggest that persistency is always malignant or insensitive. Nor do I doubt that this persistency can be beneficial, to both the would-be interviewee or the wider community. We find an excellent example of this in the tireless work that Julie K Brown conducted to encourage the victims of Jeffrey Epstein to speak to her so that she could pursue justice on their behalf.[112] Her persistence uncovered 80 victims of sex trafficking, allegedly orchestrated by Epstein.

Nevertheless, these victims initially resisted her advances.[113] According to the analysis above, these actions by Brown amount to an ostensible breach of the hypothetical regulatory code, justifying the use of coercive measures against her paper. No doubt, this looks odd. Why should she be punished for helping these victims? My argument is not that straight-forward. I am arguing that the would-be interviewee's autonomy should be paramount. In a regulatory context, this is normal. For example, solicitors, in England and Wales, are prevented by their regulator from cold-calling even though, of course, they too could help victims achieve justice.[114] Whilst I am not arguing for the equivalent standard for journalists, I am suggesting that their interactions with would-be interviewees should be more tightly regulated than they are. Yet, in this, the regulator might serve a positive role by acting as an independent intermediary between journalist and prospect. IPSO, for example, operates a similar scheme already, whereby individuals can notify the press, through them, that they do not want to be contacted by the press about a story. The advisory scheme helps the press and, where it is involved, failure to comply is a reason to find a breach of clauses 3 and 4. Yet, I imagine the regulator acting more extensively than this, operating in a way akin to that of ACAS in the UK. ACAS, the advisory, conciliatory and arbitration service, is a non-departmental public body involved in resolving industrial relations disputes. Although independent and impartial, it can provide guidance

---

[111] Ibid.
[112] T Hsu, 'The Jeffrey Epstein Case Was Cold, Until a Miami Herald Reporter Got Accusers to Talk' *New York Times*, 9 July 2019.
[113] Ibid.
[114] Solicitors Regulation Authority Handbook, ver 21, December 2018, r 8.3.

to participants and thus act as a sort of sounding board. In this way, the compassionate investigative journalist, once denied by the would-be interviewee, might appeal to her through the intermediate.

C. Covert Conduct

The use of concealed recording devices to capture information raises both content and conduct issues. This section focuses entirely upon the conduct dimension: that is, the harms done by the fact of recording or the use of subterfuge to obtain information. It does not examine the publication dimension, which finds its parallel, in English law, in tortious claims for misuse of private information and/or the equitable claim of breach of confidence. This distinction is important because, for example, in IPSO's code, the press is constrained not only from publishing material acquired by deception but also from *obtaining* it, in the first place, without consent (clause 10(i)). Clause 10(ii) says, further, that such 'misrepresentation or subterfuge' is justifiable 'only in the public interest and then only when the material cannot be obtained by other means.' This provision, in more or less the same terms, is common in the European press codes. For example, the Dutch code says, at C1, that 'Journalists must refrain from bothering, persistently following or tailing persons for prolonged periods of time.'[115] Clause 3 of the Irish code, which calls for 'fairness and honesty' in journalistic practices, is breached when journalists obtain information 'by misrepresentation or subterfuge ...'[116] The Danish Pressenævnets, at B7 of the code, tolerates clandestine recordings only where consent has been given or 'if the interests of society *clearly* supersede the claim for protection of the individual and it is not possible, or only possible with great difficulty, to obtain the necessary journalistic evidence in any other way' (emphasis added).[117]

These are strange injunctions. In English law, there are no other circumstances in which the mere fact of covert recordings is outlawed. To say, for example, that this recognises the serious repercussions that subsequent reporting of candid expression can have misses the point: such repercussions arise from *publication* not the mere fact of being interviewed without one's knowledge. What is it, then, about this duplicitous conduct that constitutes either wrongdoing or harm? IPSO's Clause 10(i) extends beyond hidden recording devices. It captures the interception of communications as well. In *Gulati v MGN Ltd*,[118] which was the culmination of a long-running legal action against the *News of the World* for its part in the phone-hacking scandal that prompted the Leveson inquiry, the claimants were awarded substantial damages for the interception of private

[115] Raad voor de Journalistiek. June 2018. Guidelines of The Netherlands Press Council.
[116] Irish Press Council ruling, *A Woman and the Sunday World*, 16 April 2015.
[117] (N 23).
[118] *Gulati*, (n 9).

messages by the newspaper. Interestingly, in one case, damages were awarded even though the newspaper did not act upon the information it obtained. The Court noted that this award reflected 'the personal effects on him when he discovered how comprehensively his phone had been hacked over several years.'[119] Of course, there is an important distinction between the facts of this case and the injunction in the IPSO clause, for there, is *Gulati*, a sort of property dimension that does not arise in the other context. The act of accessing phone messages unlawfully is comparable to breaking into a house to read the owner's personal papers. The act of recording someone without their knowledge does not have the same quality.

It seems to be the perceived underhandedness of subterfuge and hidden recordings which best explains the rationale for these provisions. Consequently, though, they do not readily fit the wrongdoing-causation-harm construct, resembling, instead, the ethical lawgiving discussed in Chapters 3 and 4. We see this, for example, in IPSO's rules and its rulings, in which justifiability depends upon whether some greater good rescues the dishonourable nature of the overarching deception. In *Allardyce, Moloney, Curtis v the Daily Telegraph*,[120] compliance with clause 10 was said to involve three steps: first, that there must be a 'reasonable belief that subterfuge would uncover material in the public interest'; second, that 'the level of subterfuge employed was proportionate to the public interest identified'; and, finally, that 'the material required could not have been obtained by open means.' This, then, is a search for moral purity in three parts: that the motivation is righteous, the execution is restrained, and the exercise is necessary.

This deontological approach, though, is problematic. If the intentions are bad, or otherwise unconvincing, the publisher breaches the clause, even if the information revealed is socially important. The PCC ruling in *Liberal Democrat Party v The Daily Telegraph*[121] is an egregious example of this inflexibility. The *Daily Telegraph* had received intelligence of party disharmony (the Liberal Democrats were in a coalition government then) and sent undercover reporters, posing as constituents, to various MPs' constituency surgeries. They did not uncover evidence of disharmony, but they did discover that these MPs held private opinions deeply at odds with their public positions. Two such instances were especially troubling: Vince Cable, the Business Secretary, said of News Corporation's bid for BSkyB: 'I have blocked it, using the powers that I have got ... his whole empire is now under attack' and that he had 'declared war on Mr Murdoch.' Michael Moore, Secretary of State for Scotland, said of the Liberal Democrat's *volte face* on university tuition fees (their manifesto promise not to raise fees was quickly forgotten once they gained power) that the decision was 'ugly', 'horrific' and 'a train wreck';

---

[119] Ibid, [109].
[120] IPSO ruling, 13405-16 *Allardyce, Moloney, Curtis v The Daily Telegraph*, 19 October 2017, [70].
[121] PCC ruling, *Liberal Democrat Party v The Daily Telegraph*, 10 May 2011.

the party's decision to renege on their election pledge was 'the worst crime a politician can commit.' But, despite the constitutional significance of these statements, the PCC upheld the complaint. It decided that the level of subterfuge was 'high' and the gain (in public interest terms) low.

The reasoning, though, is odd. First, the PCC made much of the subterfuge ('The Commission wished to make it clear that recording individuals using clandestine listening devices without their knowledge was particularly serious and intrusive, requiring a strong public interest defence. Secretly recording a public servant pursuing legitimate public business was without question a serious matter.'). Secondly, it talked mysteriously about a perceived need to safeguard 'the democratic process' which, it said, 'was in the public interest to preserve' and which 'could be threatened if journalists were to be allowed to use hidden devices to record MPs' views, expressed within the confines of their constituency surgeries, in order to test broad claims about policy matters.' This is all very strange. Transparency is an equally important democratic value. Likewise, ministerial indiscretion is newsworthy.

Although this deontology is not replicated uniformly across Europe, we can find similar reasoning at work in other regulatory adjudications. The Swiss Press Council, for example, speaks of the need for an 'overwhelming' public interest.[122] The position in Germany is even stricter: the failure to identify as a journalist is itself a deception and can be justified only where the public interest demands it.[123] Consequently, the Deutscher Presserat has found the covert recording of an individual with extreme right-wing leanings was unjustified even though he had broadcast his extreme views in a local newspaper. It was not in the public interest to evidence his 'authenticity.'[124] The Norwegian Pressens Faglige Utvalg has ruled similarly that the secret recording of a discredited doctor, previously convicted of sexually assaulting his patients in Norway, who had subsequently moved to Germany to practice medicine, breached the code. Although it agreed that his return to medical practice was a matter of public interest, it could not condone the use of a hidden camera: 'The committee cannot see that the hidden recordings reveal significant information of social significance that was not revealed in any other way.'[125]

The perplexing nature of IPSO's deontological approach is thrown into sharp relief by its reasoning in unsuccessful clause 10 claims. IPSO dismissed the complaint in *Allardyce, Moloney, Curtis v the Daily Telegraph* because, it seems, the newspaper obtained the information it broadly expected to obtain without acting objectionably in the process. That the information it did uncover was so mundane that the best headline it could manage was 'How Sam Allardyce tried

---

[122] Geschäftsstelle Schweizer Presserat. Directives relating to the 'Declaration of the Duties and Rights of the Journalist' [July 2017] & Declaration [June 2008].

[123] German Press Council ruling, Docket B 50/96.

[124] German Press Council ruling, Docket B75/98.

[125] PFU ruling, PFU-sak 275/14 *Advokat Tony Vangen pva. klient mot Dagbladet*, 24 March 2015.

to make as much money as possible as England manager' and required heavily caveated subsequent headlines like 'Sam Allardyce business meetings could fall foul of world football's code of ethics' and 'Sam Allardyce may have breached FA rules' did not trouble IPSO.[126] In its view,

> the newspaper had uncovered evidence which could reasonably be considered to demonstrate sufficiently serious impropriety on the part of the complainants to justify publication. In particular, whilst it could not be demonstrated that Mr Allardyce had broken any FA rules, he appeared to show disregard for them and had spoken disrespectfully about them to people he had only just met.[127]

This reasoning demonstrates the stark formality of clause 10. We see that when the rules are followed, the threshold for 'public interest' is relaxed. Not only had Allardyce not broken the law, he had not broken his employer's rules. Yet, because his conduct was, in some opaque way, dishonourable, the public interest was sufficiently engaged. Conversely, where the rules are not followed, the threshold for 'public interest' intensifies. Suddenly, the impropriety abundantly evident in the statements made by both ministers is not enough. Whilst, the outcome in *Allardyce* strikes me as the right one, the reasoning is deeply problematic: it was not that the public interest outweighed the privacy concern, but that privacy was not at stake to begin with.

The rigidity of IPSO's approach to subterfuge sits awkwardly with its treatment of covert surveillance in other contexts, for as we have seen, tailing a politician for miles in the hope of a comment is acceptable (it says), as is photographing targets without their knowledge,[128] or recording an interview, covertly, if the interviewer has been open about her identity.[129] This fondness for form over substance seems inconsistent when seen through the lens of autonomy. Certainly, it does not make for a coherent theory of wrongdoing. Thinking in terms of autonomy allows us to differentiate between the realm of the 'outward' and the realm of the 'inward.' We are outward-facing when we are in-the-world. This realm is associable with words like 'public' and 'external' and 'open.' When we are in-the-world, we are displaying the self that is expected of us – the professional self, the law-abiding self, the respectable self, the tolerant self. We are conforming. We are accountable. It is when we are in-the-world that we undertake our societal roles, in the workplace, in the community, and in our interactions with others, especially those who are strangers. We do things in-the-world that we would not necessarily do otherwise. To be anything other than polite, considerate, shame-avoiding, etc, has consequences. The alternative realm – the inward-realm – is the mirror image. We are inward-facing when we are out-of-the-world. This realm is associable with

[126] (N 120), [1].

[127] Ibid, [76].

[128] IPSO ruling, 04524-18 *McAlpine v The Scottish Sun*, 13 November 2018; IPSO ruling, 02804-18 *A woman v Sunday People*, 3 July 2018; IPSO ruling, 20927-17 *Johnson v The Sun on Sunday*, 5 July 2018; IPSO ruling, 06740-17 *Palestinian Return Centre v Mail Online*, 22 August 2017.

[129] IPSO ruling, 02714-16 *Cameron v Scottish Daily Mail*, 16 September 2016.

words like 'private' and 'internal.' When we are out-of-the-world, we are displaying our true-self – this self may be identical to the expected-self but not necessarily, for this is our opportunity to rest and recharge. Thus, we may display the unprofessional self, the selfish self, the disreputable self, the intolerant self. In this, we are non-conforming. We are unaccountable. It is when we are out-of-the-world that we can reveal ourselves to ourselves and to those of our choosing. This is the realm in which we are masters-of-the-world. It is here where we have complete control over whom to share our real selves with. In this we can be rude, inconsiderate, and shameful without being judged, or judgeable, by the world.

For many, the inward realm is a physical place, eg, a home. It includes those places we label private, eg, hospital, hotel, changing room, toilet, etc. It may even be a workplace in some instances. Or it can be a state of mind, eg, relaxing on the beach or being 'on holiday'. It strikes me that this analysis – of these two realms – is a useful means of determining wrongdoing in covert conduct cases. In the *Liberal Democrat Party v Daily Telegraph* ruling, although the MP was with his/her constituent in a private place, it was not a scenario that could be labelled out-of-the-world. The MP was speaking in-the-world, to his/her constituents. Clearly, those MPs spoke in an unguarded manner, but I am not clear on why that unguardedness should not have been recorded – I say this not simply because the actors involved were MPs, but because they were in-the-world. When we are in-the-world, all of our actions are ripe for judgement. Similarly, although Allardyce was in a public place, it is not the physical location – a hotel or restaurant – that makes his statements disclosable but that, in speaking with unknown 'businessmen' (they were journalists), he was also in-the-world. Compare this with the facts of *Campbell v MGN Ltd*[130] in which Naomi Campbell was covertly recorded leaving a Narcotics Anonymous meeting. The fact that the photographs were of her in a public place was not, and ought not to have been, determinative, for, in attending the meeting, she was exposing her true self to others who had pledged to keep that true identity confidential. Thus, she was out-of-the-world both during and after the meeting. Similarly, when Princess Caroline of Monaco was photographed in public places, such as restaurants, etc, she was out-of-the-world as she formed, and developed, intimate relationships with others.[131]

Ultimately, covert conduct cases have a common theme. They are designed to catch those unguarded moments that journalists find newsworthy and wish to share. When we are in-the-world, those unguarded moments are at our own risk. This does not negate a finding of unlawful privacy-invasion if the information is later disseminated, for it may still amount to an actionable misuse of private information. It does mean, though, that if the covert conduct occurs when we are in-the-world, the journalist ought not to be penalised for recording that information covertly. For our choosing to be in-the-world must mean that

---

[130] *Campbell*, (n 20).
[131] *Von Hannover v Germany* [2005] 40 EHRR 1.

we accept our actions are observable by others. It is different, though, when we are out-of-the-world because, here, we are entitled to be unguarded and action that takes advantage of this unguardedness abuses autonomy. When we are out-of-the-world our actions are private, we our observable to ourselves and those we choose to share our true-selves with. Yet, even here, I recognise that there are instances in which the public interest in disclosing the information revealed by, especially, covert conduct justifies interference with the privacy right. It is to those circumstances I now turn.

IV. Public Interest Expression

The complexion of the code complaint changes once public interest expression is at stake. The press freedom claim achieves its zenith and the regulator must choose between two rights in tension. Given this book's overarching argument, the ultimate point is this: only press malfeasance is regulatable; press freedom is not. If the expression constitutes an instance of press freedom then the complaint must fail. Consequently, we can say, that public interest speech amounts to an act of press freedom if, but only if, the interference with the rights of others is both necessary and proportionate.

Determining what counts as 'public interest expression' can be tricky sometimes. Indeed, it is a matter that even the positive law struggles with at times. The academic literature provides only limited assistance, mainly because it has been fascinated too much by the question of what counts as public interest expression and too little by the question of what we do with it once we find it (thus, leaving unanswered the related questions of what 'necessary' and 'proportionate' means). On this point, SRT is singularly unhelpful. In its fanatical adulation of public interest expression, it is hoisted by its own petard, for all other rights claims must fall away when it is in play. Since, according to the Hutchins Commission, the audience's right to such information is based on necessity (need) not preference (want), then it cannot be deprived of it: 'the need of the consumer to have adequate and uncontaminated mental food is such that he is under a duty to get it; and, because of this duty, his interest acquires the stature of a *right*.'[132] Onora O'Neill echoes this sentiment in her evidence to the Leveson Inquiry: 'A free press is a public good because it is needed for civic and common life.'[133]

Problematically, neither the Hutchins Commission, nor the chief architect of its report, William Hocking, defined public interest expression, except in wholly euphemistic terms like 'adequate and uncontaminated mental food' or, as Hocking

---

[132] The Commission on Freedom of the Press, *A Free and Responsible Press* (Chicago, University of Chicago Press, 1947), 125 (emphasis in original).

[133] https://webarchive.nationalarchives.gov.uk/20140122192219/http://www.levesoninquiry.org.uk/wp-content/uploads/2012/07/Witness-Statement-of-Professor-Baroness-ONeil.pdf, [3].

put it, as 'something in the nature of daily bread for his mental activities as a social being and as a citizen.'[134] Moreover, it is not a term they use to describe the sort of speech they have in mind. When Hocking used the expression 'public interest', it was for the purposes of describing the newspaper's task – to disseminate information that the audience needs – rather than to define what constituted this information.[135] Thus, the press function, he said, was 'clothed by' or 'affected by' a public interest: 'the freedom of the publisher to publish becomes responsible to a specific public goal.'[136] O'Neill also stops short of defining the term: in her evidence to Leveson she uses the imprecise expression 'truth claims' which is defined by examples of what it does not include: 'music and art, puzzles and stories.'[137]

We see the same issue in the English positive law. One of the best-known definitions belongs to Lady Hale who triangulated its approximate position as somewhere between 'information which interests the public – the most vapid tittle-tattle about the activities of footballers wives and girlfriends interests large sections of the public but no-one could claim any real public interest in our being told all about it'; 'newsworthiness' (which she thought 'too subjective') and something the public 'need to know' (which she thought would be 'too limiting').[138] Although this approach has its advantages in its flexibility, its limitations become apparent when one considers that Lady Hale had, in the earlier decision of *Campbell v MGN Ltd*,[139] found that information about Naomi Campbell's drug addiction was public interest expression: 'the possession and use of illegal drugs is a criminal offence and a matter of serious public concern. The press must be free to expose the truth and put the record straight.'[140] As I have said elsewhere:

> It is understandable, perhaps, that a judge would not want to condone drug use but the criminal law treats use differently to possession and supply, and possession is usually treated as less serious. To suggest that *any* drug use is a matter of *serious* public concern surely exaggerates the issue.[141]

Here we see Lady Hale conflate several tropes to produce (what she perceives to be) a powerful argument in favour of publication. Yet her reasoning is flawed. There are many aspects to the debate on drug use that *are* of serious public concern, including the government's position on it, the police's handling of it, and even the extent of the problem – but surely an individual case of drug misuse is not one of them.

---

[134] WE Hocking, *Freedom of the Press: A Framework of Principle* (Chicago, University of Chicago Press, 1947), 166.

[135] Ibid, 167–170.

[136] Ibid, 170.

[137] O'Neill, (n 133), 3.

[138] *Jameel*, (n 15), [147].

[139] [2004] 2 AC 457.

[140] Ibid, [151].

[141] P Wragg, 'Protecting private information of public interest: *Campbell's* great promise, unfulfilled' (2015) 7(2) *Journal of Media Law* 225, 228.

In Naomi Campbell's case, the Court was also convinced that her previous denial (that she did not take drugs, unlike other models) was significant since this untruth entitled the press to 'put the record straight.' Yet this idea, of itself, is more mysterious than I think we give it credit, for it implies then when questioned by a journalist, the interviewee is obliged to tell the truth, and nothing but the truth. This elevates the moral duty to be truthful to a legal duty, as if the press is always entitled to expose false testimony. This would be intolerable. Although there will be circumstances in which the press is entitled to do so, there must be some other ingredient or quality that justifies it, otherwise, as I mentioned above, the press holds a coercive power normally reserved for the state.

As this discussion illustrates, in identifying the presence of 'public interest', personal (and, usually, paternalistic) judgements loom large. In the UK, this has led to a duality in the case law, in which sceptical and generous approaches to the conception are apparent.[142] Thus, the sceptical approach has it that the 'tittle-tattle', as Lady Hale calls it, cannot be a matter of public interest. Mr Justice Eady's view, in *CTB v News Group Newspapers Ltd*, is paradigmatic: 'As in so many "kiss and tell" cases, it seems to me that the answer, at stage two, is not far to seek.'[143] Conversely, the generous approach adopts a more expansive reading. For example, Mr Justice Tugendhat's view that public interest expression includes the 'freedom to criticise the conduct of other members of society as being socially harmful, or wrong'[144] was given its widest possible reading in the subsequent cases of *Ferdinand*[145] and *Hutcheson*[146] to justify, in both cases, privacy-invading expression about alleged extra-marital affairs.[147]

Consequently, the scale of the term has grown considerably beyond the sort of narrow, paternalistic readings that SRT seems to have in mind when it talks of information citizens should know. But this is inevitable: as Kent Greenawalt has said, 'politics is not hermetically sealed offered from other human concerns ... speech that is not explicitly political often has political implications.'[148] Similarly, Edwin Baker has argued that 'once the insight that the personal is political is fully accepted, the category of politically relevant speech could be virtually unlimited.'[149] Moreover, as Kalven reminds us, this over-inclusiveness serves an important function: 'it must be recognised ... that a reason implicit in the breadth of protection afforded speech is due to the judicial recognition of its own incapacity to

---

[142] See discussion in P Wragg, 'The Benefits of Privacy-Invading Expression' (2013) 64(2) *Northern Ireland Legal Quarterly* 187.
[143] [2011] EWHC 1232, [26].
[144] *Terry v Persons Unknown* [2010] EWHC 119, [104].
[145] *Ferdinand v MGN Ltd* [2011] EWHC 2454, [63].
[146] *Hutcheson v News Group Newspapers Ltd* [2011] EWCA Civ 808, [29].
[147] See discussion in Wragg, 'The Benefits of Privacy-Invading Expression', (n 142), 195–198.
[148] K Greenawalt, *Speech, Crime, and the Uses of Language*, (Oxford, Oxford University Press, 1989), 45.
[149] CE Baker, *Human Liberty and Freedom of Speech*, (Oxford, Oxford University Press, 1989), 26.

make nice distinctions.'[150] Consequently, the category of public interest expression grows large once the concession is made that any decision which impacts significantly on the lives of others must be subsumed within it.

Something of this enormity is apparent in the various regulatory codes across Europe. For example, IPSO provides a list of seven indicative topics:

> detecting or exposing crime, or the threat of crime, or serious impropriety; protecting public health or safety; protecting the public from being misled by an action or statement of an individual or organisation; disclosing a person or organisation's failure or likely failure to comply with any obligation to which they are subject; disclosing a miscarriage of justice; raising or contributing to a matter of public debate, including serious cases of impropriety, unethical conduct or incompetence concerning the public; and, disclosing concealment, or likely concealment, of any of the above.[151]

Controversially, it also says that there is 'a public interest in freedom of expression itself'.[152] The Slovakian[153] and Austrian[154] codes provide shorter, though similar, lists. The Norwegian[155] and Irish[156] codes provide minimal detail about the meaning of the term. Meanwhile, the Danish,[157] Finnish,[158] Dutch,[159] and Flemish Raad voor de Journalistiek[160] codes permit interferences with victim rights where the public interest is at stake, but do not define what the term means.

Yet, as sensible as these diverse definitions are, it is futile to seek to perfect the definition of the term public interest. The task is hopeless because such definitions, if they are not to be under-inclusive must be abstract, and therefore ambiguity is bound to creep in, or else will assume list form, in which case the risk of excluding some important but unforeseen type arises. More importantly,

---

[150] H Kalven Jr., 'The New York Times Case: A Note on the Central Meaning of the First Amendment', [1964] *Supreme Court Review* 191, 213.

[151] IPSO Editors' Code of Practice, 1 July 2019.

[152] Ibid.

[153] At clause 13, 'a) prevention of the abuse of public authority, b) the proper functioning of the political system and public institutions, c) protection of citizens' life, health, security and property, d) protection of morality and basic social values, e) protection of the environment, cultural monuments or cultural heritage', (n 21).

[154] Clause 10.2 says 'The term "public interest" within the meaning of this Code of Ethics for the Austrian Press shall in particular refer to situations in which publications of the facts in question might help to bring a criminal to justice, or might be desirable in the interest of protecting public security or health or preventing the general public from being misled', (n 18).

[155] Clause 1.4. says 'It is the right of the press to carry information on what goes on in society and to uncover and disclose matters, which ought to be subjected to criticism', (n 13).

[156] The preamble says 'the general principle is that the public interest is invoked in relation to a matter capable of affecting the people at large so that they may legitimately be interested in receiving and the print and online news media legitimately interested in providing information about it', (n 19).

[157] See, eg, B.1 'Information which may violate the sanctity of private life shall be avoided unless an obvious public interest requires public coverage', (n 23).

[158] See, eg, clause 9, (n 12).

[159] See, eg, C.1, 'An intrusion of privacy would be imprudent if not in reasonable proportion to the social interest of the publication', (n 115).

[160] See 'Foundation', (n 8).

it gives the wrong impression, for it suggests the task of determining exceptions to victim rights begins and ends at *defining* the term public interest. Unwittingly, it implies that public interest expression has an absolute claim to protection, like a trump card. This can lead to the conclusion that all conceivable public interest expression claims deserve protection. This sort of generous regulatory decision-making is apparent across Europe. In the Netherlands, we see the regulator permit ostensible infractions of the subterfuge clause because the object of inquiry raises a matter of public interest. Yet this can lead to disproportionate interferences, as where the allegations of cruel practices at a dog training facility was found to be sufficient: 'After all,' said the Raad voor de Journalistiek, 'it is the job of the press to expose wrongdoing [misstanden].'[161] Similarly, the Swiss Press Council deemed privacy-invading expression about the sex life of a web-based game creator to be a matter of public interest. Since the 'game' required players to act as pimps and inflict violence on prostitutes, it was important to know the creator's background, it found: 'It seems legitimate to question a character who invented a game of humiliating, torturing and murdering women, even virtual, about his sex life.'[162] In the UK, the PCC ruled that a story about a member of Scottish Parliament's young son was a matter of 'considerable public interest' which justified the accompanying invasion of privacy.[163] The story, which ostensibly breached the injunction in clause 6 (Children) that 'young people should be free to complete their time at school without unnecessary intrusion', reported that the MSP's autistic child was so disruptive that his school had had to hire a former police officer to monitor him. It also reported that the child was violent, 'out of control', and had 'battered staff and pupils.' The PCC dismissed the complaint that, despite not being named, readers could easily identify her child through the various pieces of information disclosed (it was the only school in the area with an autism unit and the photograph of the member of staff who complained was known locally to have been assigned only to one child: her son).

As these rulings suggest, the problem is not so much in defining the public interest, but in weighing it against the competing rights. Regulators lack the analytical tools that would enable them to balance the press freedom right against the victim's rights. The Irish ruling of *McHugh and the Irish Times* highlights this problem. Ms McHugh's partner was killed in a fatal drink-driving road traffic accident. The incident was described in extensive detail in the *Irish Times* – including what the Press Ombudsman called 'intimate and personal material' as well as details of his injuries, taken from the autopsy.[164] In her complaint, Ms McHugh also referenced the multiple instances of insensitive newsgathering activity, in which she,

---

[161] Rvd J ruling, 2019/2 *X, h.o.d.n. Hondenschool Y tegen BNNVARA en CCCP Televisie B.V. (Rambam)*, 14 January 2019.
[162] Swiss Press Council ruling, Nr. 56/2004 *Respect de la vie privée de l'animateur d'un site internet*, 4 November 2004.
[163] PCC ruling, *Alex Neil MSP v Scottish Sun*, 22 December 2011.
[164] Irish Press Ombudsman ruling, *McHugh and the Irish Times*, 14 April 2015.

her family, and her partner's family were approached for information.[165] The Press Ombudsman concluded that the interference with privacy was disproportionate to the public interest in this information. Yet the Irish Press Council disagreed and overturned the decision. It felt that the Ombudsman had not had enough regard to the importance of the information nor to the fact that part of the information disclosed (the autopsy) was a matter of public record (it had been discussed at the public inquest into the crash).[166]

When we turn to the English and Strasbourg jurisprudence, and examine the treatment of privacy law, we find the same problem. In both jurisdictions, the case law suggests that the judicial task is to balance the respective rights claims to determine which is weightier.[167] As I have argued elsewhere,[168] this is a pretence. Instead of balancing, all the courts do is apply a rule: if public interest expression is at stake, the privacy claim fails; if not, it succeeds. It seems to me that this outcome is inevitable. Although we can make fine distinctions when determining the strength of the privacy claim, based on the metrics we find outlined in *Murray v Express Newspapers plc*,[169] ie, the claimant's attributes, the nature of the activity, its location, the effect of privacy-invasion, etc, we cannot do the same with public interest expression. By conceiving of it as an audience-orientated right, we immediately lose the capacity to make objective determinations about its value. We are then forced back to the unsatisfactory position of using ad hoc and (typically) paternalistic judgements: '*this* sort of speech is important, *that* sort of speech is unimportant.' This is exactly the sort of problem that drives Mill's argument in *On Liberty*.

Of course, the reason why we cannot hope to grade public interest expression in any sort of reliable, objective, and systemised way is due to the nature of the thing itself. The phrase public interest is an absolute. It is not simply a means of categorising types (including speech). It is more than that: it connotes an *entitlement*. In the case of speech, it conveys the sense of an audience's entitlement to obtain, use, and exchange information of the material type. This is why we say there is a public interest in the defence budget or in knowing that the commanding officer of a Royal Navy vessel had been relieved of his duties following allegations of bullying[170] but no public interest in the codes that activate the nuclear weapons or the identities of undercover intelligence agents even though all of these examples may be classified as political. Once that is accepted, it becomes meaningless to talk of *strengths* of public interest, as if it can be plotted along a spectrum: the public interest is either engaged or it is not. It seems that Strasbourg thinks similarly: 'La Cour rappelle de plus que l'article 10 § 2 de la Convention ne laisse

[165] Ibid.
[166] Irish Press Council ruling, McHugh and the Irish Times, 22 May 2015.
[167] See, eg, *Campbell*, (n 20); *Couderc v France* [2016] EMLR 19, [82].
[168] See Wragg, '*Campbell*'s great promise unfulfilled', (n 141).
[169] [2009] Ch 481, [36].
[170] *Axon v Ministry of Defence* [2016] EWHC 787, [104].

guère de place pour des restrictions à la liberté d'expression dans le domaine du discours politique ou des questions d'intérêt général.'[171] This statement was approved by Lord Rodger in the Supreme Court decision of *In re Guardian News and Media Ltd*,[172] who paraphrased it as 'where the publication concerns a question "of general interest", Article 10(2) scarcely leaves any room for restrictions.'[173]

Abandoning the balancing analogy, though, does not mean forsaking proportionality. Quite the opposite: we should consider proportionality the only analytical tool available to the regulator (or judge) once the public interest expression claim is established. Consequently, claims should be determined according to the impact upon the claimant and not the significance of the speech. In this way, the regulator has no need to make any ad hoc judgements about the weight of the expression. Instead, the regulator should focus on the necessity of specific aspects of the privacy-invading expression and the relationship between the information disclosed and the public interest claimed. We get a sense of how this works in the hypothetical that Lord Hoffmann supplies in *Campbell*, of a politician having an affair with someone 'she appointed to public office':

> there is a public interest in the disclosure of the existence of the sexual relationship but the addition of salacious details or intimate photographs is disproportionate and unacceptable. The latter, even if accompanying a legitimate disclosure of the sexual relationship, would be too intrusive and demeaning.[174]

The proportionality task, then, is to separate detail from bare fact, so as to ask why the privacy-invading expression was required to satisfy the public interest at stake. In this way, the regulator can determine the necessity of the interference as well as the proportionality of it. This is a fact-sensitive exercise in which the publisher should justify their actions. It is, as Lord Hoffmann further remarked, a matter of determining 'whether the journalists exceeded the latitude which should be allowed to them in presenting their story.'[175]

The regulatory rulings across Britain and Europe provide a mixed picture of this proportionality principle in action. For example, the Irish Press Ombudsman dismissed a complaint that an intrusive court report breached an individual's privacy rights. The victim of an assault was distressed by the level of detail that the newspaper had provided about the assault. Applying the sort of rule outlined above, the complaint was dismissed due to the 'important part [newspapers play] in ensuring that justice is delivered in public.'[176] We see a more positive outcome in a Swiss ruling concerning Micheline Calmy-Rey (long before she was President

---

[171] 'The Court further recalls that Article 10(2) of the Convention leaves little room for restrictions on the freedom of expression in the field of political speech or matters of general interest.' *Petrina v Romania* App no 78060/01 (ECtHR, 6 April 2009), [40].

[172] [2010] 2 AC 697 [51].

[173] Ibid.

[174] *Campbell*, (n 20), [60].

[175] Ibid, [68].

[176] Irish Press Ombudsman ruling, A Father and the Northern Standard, 4 December 2017.

of the Confederation). The complaint related to several articles which repeated an unfounded but persistent rumour that Calmy-Rey must have had been having an extra-marital affair with someone in the state tax department to access certain tax data.[177] The Swiss Press Council recognised that although there was a public interest at stake – and that the need to deny a rumour could justify its dissemination, the repeated publication risked giving it an 'unmerited echo' (un écho immérité).[178]

Two rulings of the Pressens Faglige Utvalg provide further useful examples. The first concerned published images of a bank robbery, which exacerbated the distress and suffering of those employees involved. The PFU recognised that although there was a public interest in reporting the fact of the robbery, this did not require the additional publication of the disturbing images.[179] The second related to a documentary series in which a film crew followed on-duty police officers. The complaint concerned a traumatic incident, caught on film, in which a girlfriend pleaded with the police not to arrest her drunken boyfriend for disorderly conduct because this would violate the terms of their housing association agreement. Although the broadcasters had sought to anonymise the participants, through image manipulation and voice distortion, the location and circumstances made identification relatively easy. Although the PFU accepted that the documenting of police activity was in the public interest, this did not justify the resultant privacy-invasion.[180] The Dutch Raad voor de Journalistiek ruled the same way on similar facts. The complainant objected to the broadcast of bailiffs entering her home to repossess property. Since the programme exposed no wrongdoing, there was no justification for the privacy-invasion.[181]

From these examples, we see the proportionality principle in action. Once the public interest in the expression is identified, the regulator can make judgements on the extent to which the invasion of privacy, damage to reputation, or substantial risk of serious prejudice to the trial was necessary to communicate the information and whether that interference was proportionate to the press freedom right.

V. Conclusion

This chapter has covered a lot of ground. Nevertheless, it has not sought to provide an exhaustive account of victims' rights. Instead, it has aimed to do no more than sketch out the substantive principles which inform the compatibility

---

[177] Swiss Press Council ruling, Nr. 12/2003 *Publication d'une rumeur démentie*, 19 March 2003.
[178] Ibid.
[179] PFU ruling, *Handelsbanken v kommunikasjonsdirektør Lars N. Sæthre mot Sandefjords Blad*, PFU-sak 267/10, 25 January 2011.
[180] PFU ruling, *NN mot TV Norge*, PFU-sak 365/13, 29 April 2014.
[181] RvdJ ruling, *X en Y tegen de hoofdredacteur van De Deurwaarders: Betalen Of Leeghalen (RTL Nederland)*, 2016/10, 15 March 2016.

of victim-orientated provisions with press freedom and so aid the regulatory design process. Specifically, it has sought to realise the wrongdoing-causation-harm construct in a practical context. As was argued, code provisions need not replicate the positive law. But they must be sufficiently proximate that the justifications found in the positive law translate. Moreover, since victims' rights are premised on *unwarranted* rather than *unwanted* press attention, public interest expression must be protected. This does not mean that the regulator should engage in some convoluted balancing exercise to determine which rights claim is stronger. Instead, as was argued, the regulator should protect public interest expression, but only proportionately. Thus, content and conduct may be penalised where those activities exceed the limits of what is necessary to convey the public interest information at stake.

As noted in the introduction, the arguments in this book are driven by the need to protect victims from unwarranted press attention. This raises an issue that has not been discussed in this chapter. If regulators are to apply equivalent standards to those found in law, such as in defamation, the misuse of private information tort, and the Contempt of Court Act 1981, then why is coercive independent press regulation necessary? If the wronged party would obtain an adequate remedy if they pursued the claim through the courts, then how is regulation justified? It is surely for courts to decide these legal issues, not regulators. Lord Justice Leveson tackled this point, briefly, in his report. He said that the legal system is not sufficiently equipped to provide the sort of quick and satisfactory response that this sort of breach requires and, that, 'furthermore, it is unlikely to be a possible route for any other than the very rich and there is no external monitoring of compliance with civil and criminal legal requirements.'[182] This point is scrutinised in Chapter 9.

---

[182] Leveson, (n 1), 1784.

8

Readers

I. Introduction

The final group of code provisions relates to readers. Some seek to police the contract between press and reader. Others seek to protect the reader from harm. Common to both is a sense that demands are being of the reader, as well as the press; that they too are being regulated. These demands are sometimes subtle, sometimes overt. Whilst all reflect the centrality of SRT's view that newspapers are instrumental devices, serving the readers' interest in democratic participation, they go further by echoing the inherent expectation in Jürgen Habermas's work that the reader must do something *productive* with this information.[1]

These provisions do not readily lend themselves to the accountability model. This incompatibility manifests in a lack of sufficient wrongdoing and/or harm to the reader in the perceived journalistic failures. Moreover, there is a faulty conception and/or treatment of autonomy animating the overarching design of these clauses. Readers are treated not as human beings, responsible for their own judgements and lifestyle choices, but something like automatons, incapable or unwilling to engage their critical functions when receiving information, and thus in need of paternalistic intervention. This attitude, which is apparent in the Hutchins Commission's thinking, and Habermas, has been rejuvenated by the current moral panic concerning 'filter bubbles', 'echo chambers' and other (alleged) perfidious interferences with the receipt of reliable information.

II. Consumer Protection

The first subset of provisions – the smaller of the two – protects the consumer's interest in performance of the contract. Or at least, this is what it appears to do. It presupposes that certain consumer expectations have become terms. In this way, the regulator polices the contract to ensure those terms are fulfilled. In her 2009

---

[1] J Habermas, *The Theory of Communication Action*, Vols I & II, T McCarthy, trans (London, Polity Press, 1987); *Between Norms and Facts*, W Rehg, trans (London, Polity Press, 1996).

article, 'Ethics for Communication?', Onora O'Neill saw these sorts of provisions as vital to her proposed criterion of assessability:[2]

> Is a purported editorial really an advertorial? Is purported information in whole or in part misinformation, or disinformation, or infotainment? Do authors, editors, producers, publishers or owners have undisclosed financial or other interests in the matters discussed?[3]

Press regulatory codes, which speak to these concerns, are readily apparent in Europe. Accuracy clauses, which are common across Europe, are a species of this sort of provision.[4] The most onerous of these is surely to be found in the Slovakian code, which says, in part III, clause 1: 'The journalist is responsible for carefully verifying every piece of information that he/she publishes. As a rule, he/she should check the information against at least two mutually independent sources.'[5]

There are provisions which regulate conflicts of interest. In Belgium, both the Raad voor de Journalistiek[6] and Conseil de Déontologie Journalistique[7] operate such clauses. Clause 10, of the Raad voor de Journalistiek, for example, says 'a journalist must avoid conflicts of interest with persons or organisations with which he/she comes into contact in a professional context.' Austria has a similar provision, at clause 4,[8] as does Finland (clauses 4 and 6),[9] Germany (section 15),[10] Ireland (clause 2.3),[11] Norway (clause 2.2),[12] Slovakia (Part III, clauses 13, 14 and 16)[13] and Switzerland (directive 9.2).[14] Denmark has a watered-down version, at clause B.4: 'Text, sound and images generated by direct or indirect commercial interests should be published only if a clear journalistic criterion calls for publication.'[15] IPSO has a very limited prohibition, at clause 13, preventing journalists using financial information for their own gain.[16] Sweden has no such provision.

These clauses are generally concerned to avoid conflicts of financial interest, as between advertiser and investigative journalist (as opposed to say political or personal interests). Such clauses can be found in Austria (clause 11), Belgium's

---

[2] This criterion was discussed in ch 3.

[3] O O'Neill, 'Ethics for Communication?' (2009) 17(2) *European Journal of Philosophy* 167, 177.

[4] See discussion in ch 6.

[5] Slovenský syndikát novinárov. June 2017. Journalists' Code of Ethics.

[6] Clause 18, Raad voor de Journalistiek. December 2016. Code of Practice.

[7] Clause 19, Conseil de déontologie journalistique. September 2017. Code of Journalistic Ethics.

[8] Österreichischer Presserat. June 2014. Guiding Principles for Journalistic Activities (Code of Ethics for the Austrian Press).

[9] Julkisen sanan neuvosto. January 2014. Guidelines for Journalists and Annex.

[10] Deutscher Presserat. March 2017. German Press Code – Guidelines for journalistic work as recommended by the German Press Council.

[11] Press Council of Ireland. June 2015. Code of Practice.

[12] Norsk Presseforbund. June 2015. Code of Ethics of the Norwegian Press.

[13] (N 5).

[14] Geschäftsstelle Schweizer Presserat. Directives relating to the 'Declaration of the Duties and Rights of the Journalist' [July 2017] & Declaration [June 2008].

[15] Pressenævnet. May 2013. The Press Ethical Rules.

[16] IPSO Editors' Code of Practice, 1 July 2019.

Raad voor de Journalistiek (clause 10) and Conseil de Déontologie Journalistique (article 12), Finland (clause 4), Germany (guideline 15.1), Norway (clause 2.2), Slovakia (clause III.11), and Switzerland (directive 9.2). Having said that, the obligation to *disclose* financial interests arises explicitly only in the codes of Ireland (clause 2.3) and Slovakia (Clause III.14). It is common, though, for regulators to oblige newspapers to distinguish editorial from advertorial. Such provisions can be found in the codes of Austria (clause 11), Denmark (clause B.4), Finland (clause 16), Germany (section 7), Norway (clause 2.6), Switzerland (directive 10.1), Slovakia (clause III.9), and Belgium in both the Raad voor de Journalistiek (clause 11) and Conseil de Déontologie Journalistique (article 13). Less common, but in the same vein, are provisions which oblige newspapers to publish the name of sponsors who pay for press trips, etc (eg, Austria,[17] Slovakia,[18] Switzerland[19]), or, as Directive 10.5 does in the Swiss code, oblige journalists to tell readers of any boycotts or threats of boycotts by advertisers due to press speech.[20]

Although the rationale for these clauses is not always stated explicitly, they are best understood as harm-based. Admittedly, this is not universally true, for some provisions, such as IPSO's clause 13 and Conseil de Déontologie Journalistique's article 15 speak only to journalists using financial information for their own profit (which, of course, may result in no harm to consumers; indeed, they may benefit). Yet, to the extent these provisions do speak to harm, there seems to be two different types at stake. First, there is the prospect of financial harm, arising from a bad investment, say. Secondly, there is a sort of civic or public harm, which arises, eg, when alleged corporate malfeasance is not reported because it would jeopardise advertising revenue.

We might be able to construct some sort of argument that breach of such provisions represents wrongdoing, of the kind that legitimises regulation, but it would be fairly tenuous. As made clear in Chapter 3, O'Neill's argument from duty does not work and could not support an obligation of 'accessibility or assessability'. But, even if we could show wrongdoing, the greater issue is in demonstrating that sufficient harm has been *caused* by it. Just how is the reader harmed in any meaningful sense by, say, non-disclosure of sponsorship or a conflict of interest? Imagine the reader purchases a car, indulges in tourism, or invests in a company due to favourable publicity which she thought was independent but was actually due to sponsorship, or some other conflict of interest. Even if the journalist's actions amount to wrongdoing, and the reader suffers something we recognise as harm, the connection between the two is too remote. There is no proximate relationship between the reader and journalist that would justify the imposition of liability.

Surely the most challenging of these provisions to defend, certainly in terms of the accountability model, is the rule on reporting suicides minimally.

---

[17] Clause 4.5, (n 8).
[18] Part III, clause 12, (n 5).
[19] Directive 10.2, (n 14).
[20] Ibid.

This provision is apparent in Britain and across Europe.[21] The most prescriptive of these is in directive 7.9 of the Swiss code:

The media should exercise the greatest restraint in a case of suicide. Suicides can be the object of a news story:

- when it has drawn a large public attention;
- when it concerns a person of public interest. For lesser known persons, the suicide must at least have a probable relation to public affairs.
- when the deceased or his or her family inform the media;
- when it provokes public debate;
- when it gives rise to rumours and accusations.

In all cases, reporting should be limited to what is needed to understand the facts and exclude intimate and personally damaging details. In order to avoid suicides by imitation, the media should not mention any details about the method or product used.

Of course, such a clause is defensible – readily so – for the purposes of protecting families of the deceased, as an extension of the privacy and/or intrusion into grief and shock provisions. But our interest here is its justifiability as a protection of readers' interests, which manifests, as the Swiss clause says, in the risk of imitation. This rationale is expressly stated in the Austrian, Norwegian, and IPSO codes, the latter of which says, at clause 5, that 'excessive detail of [the] method used' should be avoided. In the code used by the Belgian Raad voor de Journalistiek it finds expression in the prohibition on 'positive portrayals' of suicide.

Restrictions of this type are intellectually interesting not only for the sharp distinction they make between press reporting and all other forms of communication, but also for the disconnect with the treatment of suicide in our wider cultural and historical tradition. They beg the question: why single out the press? For, when we turn to the arts, as well as history, we see that glorification of suicide abounds. Indeed, the arts has always rebelled against the Judeo-Christian view that suicide is 'sinful' and, in the Christian tradition, a barrier to salvation. In this way, the arts takes its inspiration, in the West, from the Greco-Roman tradition of suicide as a noble act, as Socrates and later Seneca showed, and, in the East, from Seppuku. This treatment surely achieved its most romantic form in *Romeo and Juliet*, and has continued to feature heavily in literature, especially in the late nineteenth century and early twentieth-century novels of Jane Austen, Emily Brontë, Joseph Conrad, Fyodor Dostoevsky, and Gustave Flaubert, to name only a few, and in the modern day works of JD Salinger, William Styron, and David Foster Wallace. Suicide is a major theme in music. We see it, for example, in the theme from M*A*S*H, which had it that 'suicide is painless' (although this was meant ironically); Filter's 1995 hit 'Hey Man, Nice Shot', which describes

---

[21] Austria, cl 12; Belgium, Raad voor de Journalistiek, guidance to cl 24; Denmark, cl B.2; Germany, guideline 8.7; Ireland, principle 5.4; Norway, cl 4.9; Sweden, cl 8; IPSO, cl 5.

R Budd Dwyer's suicide by self-inflicted gunshot in 1987 (although some say it is about Kurt Cobain); REM's 1993 song, 'Everybody Hurts'; Lana Del Rey's 2012 song, 'Summertime Sadness'; and, in the form of suicide as self-sacrifice, in Bryan Adams's chart-topping hit '(Everything I do) I do it for you.' The song, which describes the lengths the protagonist will go to demonstrate his feelings, ends with the declaration 'I will die for you', as if this is the ultimate expression of love.

Continuing the theme, suicide as self-sacrifice is positively lauded by works of fiction, especially in cinema, as not only heroic but also immortalising. What we see in *Les Misérables*, when love inspires Éponine Thenardier to throw herself in front of the bullet meant for Marius Pontmercy, echoes in reality, as when Captain Oates told the remainder of Captain Scott's ill-fated party, 'I am just going outside and may be some time', and has become a major plot device in Hollywood's biggest family films, from *Star Wars* and *Star Trek II* to *Avengers: Endgame* (twice). Indeed, we see it, albeit in highly sanitised form, in children's programmes, like Nickelodeon's *Avatar: The Last Airbender*, the Lego Group's *Lego Ninjago: Masters of Spinjitzu*, and even Nickelodeon's *SpongeBob SquarePants* when, in an episode called 'Something Smells', various characters kill themselves to escape SpongeBob's halitosis. In this way, this prohibition on glamorising suicide – to prevent, as the Belgians have it, the 'positive portrayals' – strikes me as unreal. The press is hardly the outlier here if it creates the impression that suicide is glamorous.

Any discussion, therefore, of the press's responsibilities toward suicide reporting has to recognise, and be rooted in, the context of this cultural tradition, since it must affect our analysis of the press's role in imitation. For it is only through this lens that we can have a meaningful discussion about causation. The suicidology literature, such as it is, shows there is a strong correlation between suicide reporting and imitation.[22] This is known as the Werther effect – a reference to the phenomenon of copycat suicides that followed the publication of Goethe's *The Sorrows of Younger Werther* in 1774.[23] It has been argued, for example, that the rate of suicide on the subway system in Vienna dropped substantially when newspapers changed their reporting methods.[24] A similar effect is said to have occurred when Canadian reporters did the same.[25]

---

[22] See summary of evidence in J Maloney et al, 'How to Adjust Media Recommendations on Reporting Suicidal Behavior to New Media Developments' (2014) 18 *Archives of Suicide Research* 156 (adult suicides) and SY Lee, 'Media Coverage of Adolescent and Celebrity Suicides and Imitation Suicides among Adolescents' (2019) 63(1) *Journal of Broadcasting & Electronic Media* 130 (adolescents).

[23] DP Phillips, 'The influence of suggestion on suicide: Substantive and theoretical implications of the Werther effect' (1974) 39 *American Sociological Review*, 240.

[24] E Etzersdorfer and G Sonneck 'Preventing suicide by influencing mass-media reporting: The Viennese experience 1980–1996' (1998) 4 *Archives of Suicide Research* 67.

[25] See discussion in R Cohen-Almagor, *Speech, Media, and Ethics* (Basingstoke, Palgrave Macmillan, 2001), 106–107.

Of course, researchers are not saying that excessive detail in suicide reporting causes suicides in the general population, but that those suffering from underlying conditions, such as severe mental and/or physical health problems, drug and other forms of abuse, chronic family relationships, etc, may be suggestible. Indeed, this suggestibility is said to work in both directions,[26] such that positive newspaper reporting on suicides, which encourages self-help or underlines the devastating effect that suicide has on family and friends has a significant preventative effect.[27] Consequently, the literature argues that the media generally (broadcast, online, and press) should avoid reporting techniques that might provoke imitation, such as glorification, excessive detail on method, sensationalism, and photographs of the victim. One group of commentators provide a comprehensive list of factors which they say, if followed, would lessen imitation:

- Not mentioning the name and characteristics of the suicidal person;
- Not referring to online suicide forums;
- Not mentioning an accumulation of suicidal acts at certain locations (hotspots);
- Not citing or printing photographs of suicide notes;
- Not mentioning positive consequences of suicidal behavior;
- Not mentioning suicide pacts;
- Not mentioning suicides that are close in time or space (suicide clusters);
- Referring to self-help groups.[28]

Needless to say, this is an onerous list. The strange thing about these sorts of restrictions is not only that the press would be restricted when reporting the death of Kurt Cobain, Michael Hutchence or, more recently, Robin Williams. It would be prevented, also, from even describing the visceral scene in Netflix's 2017 teen drama, *Thirteen Reasons Why*, in which the central character, Hannah Baker, is shown opening up her veins whilst taking a bath.

It is important to note, though, that the literature does not speak with one voice on causation. Although there is a broad consensus that the link between excessive detail in press reporting and the act of imitation is real, there are others who disagree. For example, one commentator – Gerard Sullivan – has said:

> most studies that have been undertaken to examine the relationship are relatively unsophisticated, either in media analysis … or in examining whether certain groups are more susceptible than others to this type of influence …[29]

As he, and other commentators, have noted, the Werther effect is not inevitable. When Kurt Cobain committed suicide in 1994, the expected increase in suicide

---

[26] See, eg, Etzersdorfer and Sonneck, (n 24), 69.

[27] JJ Mann et al, 'Suicide prevention strategies: A systematic review' (2005) 294(16) *Journal of the American Medical Association* 2064.

[28] Maloney, (n 22), 165–166.

[29] G Sullivan, 'Should Suicide Be Reported in the Media? A Critique of Research' in M Mitchell (ed), *Remember Me* (New York, Routledge, 2007), 149.

did not occur, as two independent studies, one in Canada[30] and one in Australia,[31] found. Consequently, Sullivan has derided the 'slavish loyalty to the media imitation thesis despite a lack of evidence.'[32]

If we are to enforce this sort of limitation on suicide reporting, though, then causation, even if it is established, is not enough. We should need to be satisfied that, in principle, the act of using excessive detail, glorification, and/or sensationalism constitutes wrongdoing. Recalling Kant's formulation, discussed in earlier chapters, that 'any action is *right* if it can coexist with everyone's freedom in accordance with a universal law'[33] and that coercion is legitimate where it constitutes 'a *hindering* of a *hindrance to freedom*',[34] the question we must ask ourselves is how insensitive suicide reporting interferes with the freedom of readers (excluding, of course, those connected to the victim). The answer cannot be: because it harms. Many acts cause harm – unrequited love, a failed job interview, unsuccessful tender – but we do not think them ripe for coercive regulation merely for that reason. It would be too unprincipled to say there is some general right not to be harmed. The prevention of harm is the goal of rights, but it is not the right itself. It would be akin to saying there is a right to be compensated or a right to incarcerate. These rights are contingent upon some further right being established.

What we should have to show, then, is the existence of some right that is interfered with when newspapers report insensitively about suicide. We would have to show that there is something about the vulnerability of those susceptible to suicide which gives them a right not to be triggered and that the corresponding duty not to trigger arises even though the newspaper operates in a state of continual ignorance about whether any of these rights-holders is a reader. But once we start to think in these terms, the rights claim starts to get away from us. Are we saying that the right-not-to-be-triggered applies constantly and against all, or does it only apply to press reports? Does it arise, for example, if someone other than the press shares information about a suicide with the rights-holder? These are important questions because once we have shown that the accountability model is satisfied then we have the basis for claiming coercive measures to enforce the right-duty are legitimate in that context. If the right arises against the newspaper, then it arises against the coroner, the lecturer, or the loudmouth at the bus stop, unless we can carve out principled exceptions.

What would be the basis of this right not-to-be-triggered? Perhaps it might be in privacy or maybe freedom of expression, as a sort of negative right: a right not

---

[30] DA Jobes, AL Berman, PW O'Carroll, S Eastgard and S Knickmeyer, 'The Kurt Cobain Suicide Crisis: Perspectives from Research, Public Health, and the News Media' (1996) 26(3) *Suicide and Life-Threatening Behavior* 260–269.

[31] G Martin and L Koo, 'Celebrity suicide: Did the death of Kurt Cobain influence young suicides in Australia?' (1997) 3(3) *Archives of Suicide Research* 187.

[32] Ibid, 151.

[33] I Kant, *The Metaphysics of Morals*, L Denis (ed) and M Gregor, trans, (first published, 1785) (Cambridge, Cambridge University Press, 2017), [6:231] (emphasis in original).

[34] Ibid, [6:232] (emphasis in original).

to receive certain information. The problem here, though, is that no one is forcing the purported rights-holder to receive the information – indeed, no one is forcing her to do anything. Instead, it is the purported rights-holder who is attempting to restrict the rights of others. If we can solve this problem, then perhaps we could argue that there is wrongdoing when newspapers write insensitively about suicide. But the positive law provides little encouragement. *O v Rhodes*[35] provides an analogous fact-pattern: the claimant – an 11-year-old child diagnosed with Asperger's syndrome, ADHD, dyspraxia, and dysgraphia – applied, through his mother to restrain publication of his father's (the defendant's) autobiography. O's mother feared that the book's candid and chilling account of the abuse, and repeated rapes, he suffered as a child, the alcohol and substance abuse that followed, his repeated attempts at suicide, his continuing battles with self-harm and suicidal ideation would seriously harm O if he read it (and, further, that O would read it because he idolised his father and sought out online information about him). According to a child psychologist who had interviewed O:

> the information in the book would be inappropriate for any 11-year-old child to read and have access to, but it would be even more devastating for this child, because of his difficulties in processing information: his psychological schemas are not malleable, he receives information in a literal way and is unable to conceptualise it in an alternative way, and he would view himself as responsible for some of his father's distress and an extension of his father. He is already prone to self-harm and emotional outbursts and these would probably increase.[36]

Here, then, we have a parallel scenario, where a detailed account (which the mother called excessive) will, or is likely to, cause serious harm to the vulnerable reader. But – in keeping with the hypothetical, normative discussion about the suicide clause, above – the Court struggled to identify sufficient wrongdoing in the defendant's actions to fit any of the limited causes of actions available. Claims in misuse of private information and negligence were struck out at first instance (in an unreported decision). Whereas there might have been some mileage in pursuing the claim that parents owe children an actionable duty of care in these circumstances, the privacy claim certainly had no merit, for, apart from anything else, it was not O's private information that was being *misused*. For the claim to have succeeded, therefore, a new approach to privacy would have been required to allow a claimant to recover where an actor uses their own private information in such a way as to constitute 'misuse.' Understandably, the Court was not prepared to countenance such novelty.

It also dismissed the claim, under *Wilkinson v Downton*,[37] for the intentional infliction of emotional harm. The Court of Appeal, though, disagreed, and allowed the appeal. It found that this point should go to trial.[38] For our purposes,

---

[35] [2015] UKSC 32.
[36] Ibid, [18].
[37] [1897] 2 QB 57.
[38] [2015] EMLR 4.

this is an interesting decision. At first instance, Mr Justice Bean had said that the *Wilkinson v Downton* claim could not be used in circumstances where the information disseminated was true (the defendant in *Wilkinson* had played a cruel trick on the claimant, telling her that her husband had suffered serious injuries in an accident; he had not). The Court of Appeal, though, reasoned differently, finding that, although it was 'inconceivable that the law would render all intentional statements which cause psychiatric harm actionable in damages', 'there may be many ways in which the court could draw the line between acceptable intentional statements or acts which cause psychiatric harm, and those which are actionable under this head.'[39] The question, therefore, was not whether the information was true or false, but whether the act was 'unjustified' because the speaker was not 'entitled' to make the statement.[40] Accordingly, in *Rhodes*, the Court of Appeal suggested, the fact that the defendant had promised previously, to the claimant's mother, to ensure that O was protected from harmful information could constitute such an act.[41]

The Supreme Court, though, disagreed and reinstated Bean J's decision. Their analysis of *Wilkinson*, and subsequent decisions relying upon it, concluded with the view that, since the tort secured protection against the 'wilful infringement of the right to personal safety', it depended upon the claimant establishing three parts: 'a conduct element, a mental element and a consequence element.'[42] These loosely translate to *actus reus*, *mens rea*, and causation. The conduct element, they said, 'requires words or conduct directed towards the claimant for which there is no justification or reasonable excuse.'[43] They were greatly troubled by the prospect of the tort being used to suppress freedom of speech:

> It is difficult to envisage any circumstances in which speech which is not deceptive, threatening or possibly abusive, could give rise to liability in tort for wilful infringement of another's right to personal safety. The right to report the truth is justification in itself … there is no general law prohibiting the publication of facts which will cause distress to another, even if that is the person's intention.[44]

For the Supreme Court, then, the threat to free speech principle was too grave. Applying this sort of reasoning to the suicide clause, the courts would be opposed to the prohibition of insensitive suicide reporting. In *Rhodes*, it was not merely the description of abuse that the courts found valuable, but the lived experience of the abuse victim. It was at pains to point out, though, that this did not render the test consequentialist according to the perceived value of the expression: 'in pointing out the general interest attaching to this publication, we do not mean to suggest that there needs to be some identifiable general interest in the subject matter of

---

[39] Ibid, [68].
[40] Ibid, [69].
[41] Ibid.
[42] *Rhodes*, (n 35), [73].
[43] Ibid, [74].
[44] Ibid, [77].

a publication for it to be justified';[45] and, later: 'A right to convey information to the public carries with it a right to choose the language in which it is expressed in order to convey the information most effectively.'[46] This echoes the statements we find elsewhere in the positive law. For example, in *Re X*, which concerned similar facts: an attempt to restrain, or otherwise suppress specific passages in, the biography of a child's deceased father, who was said to have engaged in 'depraved' sexual activities, 'indulged in sordid and degrading conduct, ... was obscene and drank to excess'[47] because it would damage the child if she read it. The Court of Appeal dismissed the application because even though no public interest was served by the contents itself, there was a general public interest at stake in protecting freedom of speech: 'It means freedom, not only for the statements of opinion of which we approve, but also for those of which we most heartily disapprove.'[48] Further, the Court said:

> The reason why ... the law gives no remedy is because of the importance it attaches to the freedom of the press: or, better put, the importance in a free society of the circulation of true information ... It would be a mistake to extend these so as to give the judges a power to stop publication of true matter whenever the judges – or any particular judge – thought that it was in the interests of a child to do so ... In my opinion it would be extending the wardship jurisdiction too far and infringing too much upon the freedom of the press for us to grant an injunction in this case.[49]

Likewise, in *R v Central Independent Television Plc*, another case involving a complaint about the damage that true information about a parent would cause to a child, the Court reached the same conclusion:[50]

> The motives which impel judges to assume a power to balance freedom of speech against other interests are almost always understandable and humane on the facts of the particular case before them. Newspapers are sometimes irresponsible and their motives in a market economy cannot be expected to be unalloyed by considerations of commercial advantage. Publication may cause needless pain, distress and damage to individuals or harm to other aspects of the public interest. But a freedom which is restricted to what judges think to be responsible or in the public interest is no freedom. Freedom means the right to publish things which government and judges, however well motivated, think should not be published. It means the right to say things which "right-thinking people" regard as dangerous or irresponsible. This freedom is subject only to clearly defined exceptions laid down by common law or statute.[51]

These statements speak for themselves, which is why I have quoted them in full. Freedom of speech cannot be reserved only for that which is instrumentally

---

[45] Ibid, [76].
[46] Ibid, [78].
[47] [1975] Fam. 47, 57.
[48] Ibid.
[49] Ibid, 58–59.
[50] [1994] Fam 192.
[51] Ibid, 202–203.

valuable otherwise, as these statements show, it is no freedom. Likewise, it should not be suppressed simply because it causes harm. There must be, as the Supreme Court recognised in *Rhodes*, something in the author's conduct which justifies the interference; some wrongdoing.

All three cases, but especially the latter two, emphasise one point clearly: interferences cannot be justified by arguing that the author did not *need* to write the offending passages, or that the publication would be permissible if only it was toned down. Commentators – people in general – are too quick to conclude that compromise is reasonable, and therefore justified, whenever some complaint about speech is made. What they do not readily grasp is that the pursuit of compromise, as a valid course of action, depends upon the existence of two (or multiple) rights clashing. In that context, the proportionality principle acts as a sort of compromise, as we have seen previously, such that exercising one's right may be unlawful where it unnecessarily interferes with the rights of others. Yet in situations like this, as with the suicide clauses, there is only one right at stake, freedom of speech, and neither proportionality nor compromise has any role to play.

Neither is it permissible to say, as advocates for compromise seem to argue, that interferences with freedom of speech are justified where the value of that speech is low. This sort of paternalism is incompatible with liberal principle, as both Mill and Kant understood it. Indeed, what makes the speeches in *Re X* and *Central Television* notable is the rejection of such paternalism. Thus, we see the implicit adherence to Millian and Kantian principle in their decisions. We also see the Supreme Court in *Rhodes* rejecting the chance to embrace paternalism, when they conclude that the value of the speech is immaterial to their reasoning. It must be said that this anti-paternalism is not something which generally characterises the UK positive law: there are too many instances in which courts have adopted an overtly paternalistic approach to free speech protection.[52]

Paternalism looms large in the suicide clause because, of course, even in our hypothetical discussion of rights-holder and duty-holder, we indulged in a fallacy. For, in our model, it is not the rights-holder who is asserting some right, but third parties, external to the relationship between rights-holder and duty-holder. It is they that claim the authority to interfere with speech for its effect on others. This strategy speaks to what I think is the dominant theme in reader-oriented clauses, which is the diminution, and, in some instances, outright denial, of reader autonomy to determine for themselves the value of information and the actions to be taken, if any, in light of it. Of course, to speak of suicide as an autonomous choice looks peculiar. The decision of, typically, young and healthy people, usually men, (in the UK, suicide is the greatest killer of men aged 20–49) to take their own life is something we cannot comprehend, certainly not from afar. Instinctively,

---

[52] See P Wragg, 'Separated by a Common Language: The Anti-Paternalism Principle in US and English Defamation and Privacy Law' in A Koltay and P Wragg (eds), *Research Handbook on Comparative Privacy and Defamation Law* (Cheltenham, Edward Elgar, 2020).

we would label it the height of *ir*rationality and, therefore, not something that an autonomous being would choose to do. But our attitude to suicide is not consistent, for when we encounter the terminally ill, like Diane Pretty or Debbie Purdy, only the most reactionary or staunchly religious would deny them support, or at least some measure of sympathy, in their campaign for the right to assisted suicide. Most liberals, I am sure, would secure them that right if only they could devise a scheme that could not be abused. This reaction is revealing, for, if pressed, we would say the distinction between these two cases is a matter of reason: that suicide to escape unbearable suffering is not only humane but also *rational* whereas suicide, absent such impediments, is not. This, I suspect, is because those who have not experienced serious mental health concerns do not understand the despair that sufferers endure in which suicide is an attractive and meaningful escape. This is because they do not equate mental suffering with physical suffering. In making this distinction, they impose their own moral norms upon the process – rationality extends only to physical suffering, not mental suffering. What should occur, although it may feel alien to do so, is to recognise the compromise of autonomy that takes place when this societal or external view of rationality is imposed upon the actions of the suicidal and suicide victim. Although it may feel right to say that suicide is not autonomy – that it is the ultimate sign of irrationality – we must also concede that this is because, in reaching that conclusion, we bring to bear our own preconceptions and ideals, which is something that individual autonomy precludes us from doing where acts do not affect us directly. Instead, as several commentators have argued, suicide is the ultimate act of autonomy.[53] It is the final decision.

III. Autonomy and Automatons

In this section, I return to the topic I introduced in Chapter 6, in the context of accuracy clauses, to consider the treatment of reader autonomy within SRT. For, looking at reader-oriented clauses, more generally, with paternalism and autonomy in mind, reveals a distinct pattern. Although ostensibly seeking to protect reader interests, they seem instead to be attempting to constrain them. Consider this clause from the Austrian Presserat's Ehrenkodex:

> Adequate coverage shall be given to any important court decision or finding of another public authority regarding a subject on which the newspaper or magazine has reported or to any essential new findings concerning said subject that have emerged in some other way.[54]

---

[53] See, eg, TL Beauchamp, 'The Right to Die as the Triumph of Autonomy' (2006) 31 *Journal of Medicine and Philosophy* 643; ME Button, 'Suicide and Social Justice: Toward a Political Approach to Suicide' (2016) 69(2) *Political Research Quarterly* 270; M Norden, '*Whose Life Is It Anyway?* A Study in Respect for Autonomy' (1995) 21 *Journal of Medical Ethics* 179; R Marra and M Orrú, 'Social Images of Suicide' (1991) 42(2) *The British Journal of Sociology* 273.

[54] Cl 2.6, (n 8).

Or this one, used by Norway's Pressens Faglige Utvalg:

> It is the task of the press to protect individuals and groups against injustices or neglect, committed by public authorities and institutions, private enterprises, or others.[55]

Elsewhere, the Austrian code, in a clause labelled 'special editorial areas', says:

> 9.1. Travelogues and reports of a touristic nature shall include, in suitable form, information about the social and political background and conditions prevailing in the country or region in question (such as serious human rights violations).
>
> 9.2. Environmental, transport and energy policy matters shall, amongst other things, be given adequate consideration in the paper's motor section.

Slovakia has a similar clause: 'The journalist shall not directly or indirectly support the violation of human rights, violence, or harm to the environment.'[56] Germany has this one: 'Reports on medical matters should not be of an unnecessarily sensationalist nature since they might lead to unfounded hopes or fears on the part of some readers.'[57] Ireland: 'Readers are entitled to have news and comment presented with respect for the privacy and sensibilities of individuals.'[58] Meanwhile, Switzerland's code contains something like a plurality obligation: directive 2.2 says 'Multiple viewpoints contribute to freedom of information. It is most necessary when the media outlet is in a monopoly position.'[59]

These provisions idealise the reader. How else are we to explain the Austrian obligation to provide important court decisions, or the Slovakian view that newspapers must respect the environment, or even the Irish belief that readers do not want gratuitous privacy-invading expression? This is not driven by consumerism, for the market caters well for those that want this sort of material. There is not some consumer shortfall to be addressed – although commentators will often say that this is so. What we see, instead, is the SRT ideal that newspaper content is driven by civic need, not personal want. That readers want easy reading, celebrity gossip or reactionary diatribes seems plain enough from the market share enjoyed by titles like the *Daily Mail*, *The Sun*, and the *Daily Telegraph* in the UK or, in Europe, Germany's *Bild-Zeitung* and *Die Welt*, Sweden's *Svenska Dagbladet* and *Expressen*, or the Netherlands's *De Telegraaf*. These reader-oriented code provisions do not reflect this reality, though. Instead, they are fairly transparent in their bid to improve both the quality of press speech and, consequently, the quality of readership.

Such clauses echo the dominant themes in the SRT literature. The Hutchins Commission, for example, placed the onus as much on readers as it did the press itself. It spoke of 'the accountable press and the responsible community.'[60]

---

[55] Cl 1.5, (n 12).
[56] Pt III, cl 6, (n 5).
[57] Cl 14, (n 10).
[58] Principle 5.2, (n 11).
[59] (N 14).
[60] See, eg, The Commission on Freedom of the Press, *A Free and Responsible Press* (Chicago, University of Chicago Press, 1947), 125–128.

The reader, it said, had the obligation to be a 'responsible critic, gadfly, and source of incentive.'[61] William Hocking put it this way: 'Within the community at large, also, there must be a profounder sense of responsibility for one's own thinking and for the level of emotional life, in recreation and the use of leisure.'[62] We see it also in the current literature, for when the commentary says that 'an ethical media that informs a democratic citizenry is paramount',[63] it makes assumptions about both the press and the audience. Even the term 'audience' is used as a proxy for a specific type of audience: the educated audience is the beneficiary of SRT;[64] the uneducated or uncritical audience is the problem.[65] In this way, consumer expectations that distract from the collectivist goals of SRT need solving. Yet, although the Hutchins Commission recognises, clearly enough, the dilemma this causes (the press, it says, is 'caught between its desire to please and extend its audience and its desire to give a picture of events and people as they really are'),[66] it offers no solutions, but simply shrugs the shoulders and moves on.

This sort of thinking is enjoying something of a renaissance presently in the moral panic surrounding 'filter bubbles' and 'echo chambers.'[67] It was Cass Sunstein who first drew attention to the phenomena, as early as 2001, when he expressed concern that the public debate was characterised by a division that was – and seemingly still is – insurmountable because each side listens, and responds to, only those views which coincide with their own.[68] This concern has gained traction because of the internet's distinctive features, in which consumers can now either actively filter out contrary viewpoints, through their preferences, or else find that their favourite search engines are masking particular results, etc, that they think would be uninteresting to the user, based on previous viewing habits.

Commentators readily conclude that this is disastrous for democratic participation and social progress, albeit for reasons that seem dubious at best. For what *is* the difference between the internet's fine-tuning of our online experiences and the decisions we make for ourselves, in the real world, concerning our location, our livelihood, our friends, our neighbours, our newspapers, our favourite

---

[61] Ibid, 127.

[62] WE Hocking, *Freedom of the Press: A Framework of Principle* (Chicago, University of Chicago Press, 1947), 206.

[63] T Dwyer, *Legal & Ethical Issues in the Media* (Basingstoke, Palgrave Macmillan, 2012), 1.

[64] See, eg, F Williams, *Dangerous Estate* (Cambridge, Patrick Stevens Ltd, 1957), 233–234; K Martin, *The Press the Public Wants* (London, the Hogarth Press, 1947), 125–139.

[65] See discussion in T O'Malley and C Soley, *Regulating the Press* (London, Pluto Press, 2000), 60–61.

[66] The Commission on Freedom of the Press, (n 60), 57.

[67] See, eg, CR Sunstein, *#Republic: Divided Democracy in the Age of Social Media* (Princeton, Princeton University Press, 2018); J Bartlett, *The People vs Tech: How the Internet is Killing Democracy* (London, Ebury Press, 2018); T Baldwin, *Ctrl Alt Delete* (London, Hurst & Co, 2018); S Umoja Noble, *Algorithms of Oppression*, (New York, NYU Press, 2018); D Sumpter, *Outnumbered* (London, Bloomsbury Sigma, 2018); E Pariser, *The Filter Bubble* (London, Penguin Books, 2011); N Carr, *The Shallows* (London, Atlantic Books, 2011); J Clark and T Van Slyke, *Beyond the Echo Chamber* (New York, The New Press, 2010); K Hall Jamieson and JN Cappella, *Echo Chamber* (Oxford, OUP, 2010).

[68] CR Sunstein, *Echo Chambers: Bush v Gore Impeachment, and Beyond* (Princeton, Princeton University Press, 2001).

authors, our favourite music, our pastimes? Commentators complain that echo chambers are insidious because it limits our exposure to contrary ideas and the lived experiences of others, especially minorities, but this seems to be an inevitable feature of life, in which, unless lifestyle choices dictate otherwise, many people live parochially – going to the same places, taking the same commute, meeting the same friends, encountering the same ideas, and surrounding themselves with the familiar and the easy-going. For many people, the path of least resistance – including in their intellectual pursuits – is the key to the good life. By doing so, they surround themselves with either like-minded or otherwise a tolerable level of difference. And was it not ever thus? Why should the online world be any different?

What stands out from this reasoning – which is symptomatic of SRT generally – is the unrealised tension that this creates for individual autonomy. For example, Theodore Peterson, in describing the central tenets of SRT says that it reduces the reader to something like an untrustworthy automaton: it 'does not deny the rationality of man ... but it does seem to deny that man is innately motivated to search for truth and accept it as his guide.'[69] Consequently, he says, under SRT, 'man is viewed not so much irrational as lethargic. He is capable of using his reason, but he is loath to do so': readers are an 'easy prey for demagogues, advertising pitchmen and others who would manipulate [them] for their selfish ends.'[70] This leads him to the conclusion that: '[humankind's] mental faculties have become stultified and are in danger of atrophy ... If man is to remain free ... the more alert elements of the community must goad him into the exercise of his reason. Without such goading, man is not likely to be moved to seek truth.'[71] Autonomy fares poorly in this conception of humankind. This is not autonomy as Mill and Kant saw it, as the inner domain of deciding for oneself, but something that is directed, even determined, by external influences. In this way, qualities like independence, originality, and individuality become meaningless, or otherwise somewhat chimeric.

Yet adherents do not see this problem. Onora O'Neill's and Judith Lichtenberg's treatment of readers is paradigmatic. As we saw in previous chapters, both argue for a differential interpretation of press freedom compared to individual freedom. O'Neill's claim, which, as we saw in Chapter 3, was endorsed by Lord Justice Leveson,[72] is the same as Lichtenberg's:[73] the press freedom concept cannot benefit from John Stuart Mill's argument, in *On Liberty*,[74] that freedom of expression

---

[69] T Peterson 'The Social Responsibility Theory of the Press' in FS Siebert, T Peterson, and W Schramm (eds), *Four Theories of the Press* (Chicago, University of Illinois Press, 1956), 100.

[70] Ibid.

[71] Ibid.

[72] Lord Justice Leveson, *An Inquiry into the Culture, Practices and Ethics of the Press: Report* (HC 780, 2012), 62, [3.3].

[73] J Lichtenberg, 'Foundations and limits of freedom of the press' in J Lichtenberg (ed), *Democracy and the Mass Media*, (Cambridge, Cambridge University Press, 1990), 112–114.

[74] JS Mill, *On Liberty*, in *Collected Works of John Stuart Mill*, vol XVIII, JM Robson (ed), (first published 1859) (Toronto, University of Toronto Press, 1977), 213.

'serves a central function in promoting individual autonomy and self-fulfilment' because the press is not a 'self' in the relevant sense.[75] From this position, as we have seen, O'Neill argues for greater 'accessibility and assessability' in newspaper content, whilst Lichtenberg argues for greater plurality, because, she says, 'a multiplicity of voices is central to achieving individual autonomy and not only to the more obviously social goods, democracy and truth.'[76]

Lichtenberg's and O'Neill's views are compelling, if we confine them purely to epistemology. In saying that the perfection of self-development depends upon the sort of critical faculties that enables agents to test the veracity of claims before acting upon them, both must be right. In this, plurality, self-development, and autonomy must be closely linked, as Lichtenberg says,[77] especially if we wish to realise von Humboldt's claim that 'the end of man ... is the highest and most harmonious development of his powers to a complete and consistent whole.'[78] Thus, it is understandable that she would conclude: 'there must be a multiplicity of voices if free speech is to advance the causes of democracy and truth.'[79] Similarly, O'Neill's rejection of spontaneous or even deliberate choosing as manifestations of autonomy[80] is intuitive, and her conclusion that autonomous decision-making is contingent: that, the decision to act upon advice depends upon the instinct to verify. Without that instinct, we shall not know good from bad advice. Acting autonomously, then, relies on the capacity to know *why* that advice is valuable, otherwise we are reduced to emulation or simulation. Thus, in the context of informed consent, she says 'when we draw on friendly – or on expert – help we ultimately have to *judge for ourselves where to place our trust*. To do this we need to find trustworthy information. This can be dauntingly hard in a world of one-way communication.'[81]

Problems occur, though, when these arguments leave the realm of epistemology, as a moral concern, and inveigle their way into the teleological conception of press freedom, as a justification for interference with agency. O'Neill does this when she references Bernard Williams's claim, as she does on several occasions,[82] that, in institutions dedicated to truth-discovery, 'speech is not at all unregulated.'[83] Consequently, she says, anything which holds, what she calls, 'informational content' may be subjected to greater scrutiny.[84] This is dangerous territory. Three problems are especially striking: first, the argument can be used

---

[75] Leveson Report, (n 72), 62, [3.3].

[76] Lichtenberg, (n 73), 112–113.

[77] Ibid.

[78] Ibid, 112.

[79] Ibid, 114.

[80] O O'Neill, *A Question of Trust* (Cambridge, Cambridge University Press, 2002), 86.

[81] Ibid, 87.

[82] O O'Neill, 'The Rights of Journalists and the Needs of Audiences' in J Lewis and P Crick (eds), *Media Law & Ethics in the 21st Century* (Basingstoke, Palgrave Macmillan, 2014), 38; 'Ethics for Communication?', (n 3), 172; "It's the newspapers I can't stand" (2005) 2 *Philosophy at Cambridge* 7, 7.

[83] B Williams, *Truth and Truthfulness* (Princeton, Princeton University Press, 2002), 217.

[84] O'Neill, 'Ethics for Communication?', (n 3), 171.

malevolently against the autonomous agent; secondly, self-development would be seriously harmed if O'Neill's vision, especially, were realised; and, thirdly, there is an unrecognised redundancy in O'Neill's claim.

Taking each in turn, if the test of autonomous decision-making is not simply the exhibition of agency, but the quality of it, then it is possible to deny a decision was made autonomously if its grounds were flawed. O'Neill seems to hold this view. She says:

> A New York student of mine once stripped and streaked across Broadway with a group of male contemporaries, and so convinced herself that she was *autonomous*. She had at least shown that she could act in defiance of convention, and probably of her parents, but hardly of her male contemporaries. Her eccentric choice was at least harmless, but in other cases *spontaneous choosing* can be harmful or disastrous. Other people identify individual autonomy not with spontaneous but with *deliberate choosing*. But deliberate choosing doesn't guarantee much either.[85]

Similarly, Lichtenberg says 'autonomy is not a matter of believing what you feel like believing ...' and neither is self-development, since both can only come from 'subjecting one's ideas, which come largely from others, to certain tests',[86] and so concludes 'autonomy and self-development in an intellectual vacuum are impossible.'[87] This invites the conclusion that external interferences with agency are justified when this 'multiplicity of voices' do not inform the agent's actions because that decision is not the product of *authentic* autonomy.

It implies that such interference is justified to achieve not only structural guarantees to aid epistemic advance, but substantive ones. To explain, let us imagine there is such a thing as the 'right' information and, further, that there is such a thing as the 'right' outcome, which results from this information's use. A structural guarantee ensures individuals receive the 'right' information, but accepts that people can still ignore, misunderstand, and disagree with it, so as to act contrary to it and thus reach the 'wrong' outcome. A substantive guarantee, meanwhile, seeks to ensure individuals reach the 'right' outcome. Since it is in the nature of autonomy that these ethical questions – about what are 'right' and 'wrong' sorts of information or outcome – are for them, and them alone, to decide, the notion of autonomy does not fare well in either system. It is particularly disadvantaged in the latter.

This leads to the second problem: that these obligations, if performed, harm self-development. Think of the balance of labour involved in the communicative process, if O'Neill's claims about 'accessibility' and 'assessability' are implemented. If, as she says, newspapers are expected to do 'more' to achieve optimal assessability,[88] then readers are expected to do less. They become passive receptors,

[85] *A Question of Trust*, (n 80), 86.
[86] Lichtenberg, (n 73), 114.
[87] Ibid.
[88] Ibid, 177.

not active interrogators. In this way, the critical faculties become enfeebled, for the attitude prevails that somebody, somewhere protects them from receiving untruth; that everything newspapers say must be truth for they are 'not allowed' (whatever that means) to do otherwise. Thirdly, we see the redundancy in O'Neill's claims: if she is right that the 'need' to test the validity of advice through independent, reliable information converts to an imposable obligation on the press to provide 'trustworthy' information, then the 'need' for advice diminishes to a vanishing point. Why bother consulting the fallible 'expert' when the 'infallible' font of knowledge is available?

These images of autonomy, as contingent upon the quality of decision-making, conflict with liberal principle in deeply problematic ways. Most obviously, they are paternalistic. Equally, when they call on Mill in support, they misrepresent his position, and, especially, the connection between truth-discovery and freedom of expression that he describes. For Mill's argument, in *On Liberty*, is not that truth *will* be discovered[89] – that is Milton's position in *Areopagitica*[90] – nor that individuals can be forced either to realise truth, or, even, to realise their truth-discovery potential.[91] Instead, his position is, simply put, that government has no right to determine what is truth nor what is the right way to live, unless the harm principle is satisfied. It is, then, a hypothetical imperative: if we want to realise the best conditions for realising these ends (truth-discovery and the good life), then a culture of tolerating divergent viewpoints and of encouraging disagreement is critical. It is, then, an argument about control – and commentators spectacularly miss this point when they purport to rely upon him to promote paternalistic schemes.

This does not mean that 'wrongheadedness' is instrumentally valuable, nor that it should enjoy absolute protection. Clearly, when it unduly threatens the rights of others, we have an ostensible justification to interfere. Otherwise, though, we must accept that 'faulty' decision-making – self-delusion and other forms of bad conclusions – must be permitted; these are legitimate outcomes of autonomous decision-making. All this is evident in Mill's conception of autonomy:

> the only freedom which deserves the name, is that of pursuing our own good in our own way, so long as we do not attempt to deprive others of theirs ... Each is the proper guardian of his own health, whether bodily, or mental or spiritual.[92]

He also says that a person's 'own good, either physical or moral, is not a sufficient warrant'[93] to impose constraints. It does not matter that these interventions might make her 'happier' or 'better' or even because 'in the opinion of others, to do so would be wise, or even right.'[94] Describing this principle in more detail,

---

[89] Mill, (n 74), 238.
[90] J Milton, *Areopagitica* (first published 1644) (London, JM Dent & Sons Ltd, 1941).
[91] Mill, (n 74), 223–224.
[92] Ibid, 226.
[93] Ibid, 223.
[94] Ibid, 224.

he said that it 'requires liberty of tastes and pursuits; of framing the plan of our life to suit our own character; of doing as we like, subject to such consequences as may follow: without impediment from our fellow-creatures,... even though they should think our conduct foolish, perverse, or wrong.'[95] Of course, Mill here is discussing interferences with the actor directly, and not third-party interventions, as when a regulator moderates press behaviour in the reader's name. But the principle is the same. This is true even if the reader is not exercising optimal levels of healthy scepticism when she makes her choice. It is true even if she makes her choice deliberately or spontaneously. She can choose to believe what she reads, and adopt the mantra as her own, or use the information to change or else reinforce her position. Or she can choose not to believe it. Regardless, the decision to rely on the information is hers, and hers alone. No one forces her to do so. No one can prevent her from doing so.

Here, I think, we see why Mill was so keen to deny the authority to prevent someone doing what they wish to do, or think what they wish to think, for autonomy *must be* the act of thinking for oneself, regardless of the conclusions that one reaches. This does not affect Mill's endorsement of von Humboldt's claims about the ends of humankind. Maximal self-development is our most important goal. Yet the use of autonomy to achieve this end is itself a form of hypothetical imperative: to achieve our best form, we must use our initiative: the initiative to develop the critical functions, to seek out information, and to make reasoned decisions. All of that is undermined by the idea that the individual can *demand* information, that they are *entitled* to have information presented to them in an easily digestible form. This is not self-development but dependence.

The paternalism animating SRT's reductive treatment of autonomy takes several forms. It arises, for instance, in the claim that external intervention is justified because the agent's capacity to realise the scale of press unreliability is impaired: that, in the words of the Hutchins Commission: 'They [the audience] have not yet understood how far the performance of the press falls short of the requirements of a free society in the world today.'[96] It also arises in the view that, in public and private decision-making, not every conceivable view should be heard, but, as Alexander Meiklejohn put it, only that which is 'worth saying shall be said.'[97] This finds expression in the Hutchins Commission's conclusion that 'it is the whole point of a free press that ideas deserving a public hearing shall get a public hearing.'[98] This, though, tells us something important about the meaning of 'plurality' and 'multiplicity of voices' in the SRT scheme. When O'Neill argues against the 'power of dominant ideology' and the need for a 'deep commitment to

---

[95] Ibid.
[96] The Commission on Freedom of the Press, (n 60), 97.
[97] A Meiklejohn, *Political Freedom: The Constitutional Powers of the People* (First Published 1948) (New York, Oxford University Press, 1965), 26.
[98] The Commission on Freedom of the Press, (n 60), 119.

respecting and hearing other voices',[99] she is not defending disreputable ideas or even unpopular, disliked ideas per se. We see this clearly in her earlier work:

> ... communications and expressions which denigrate or mock or bully others, or more generally fail to respect them, may make it harder or impossible for some to think for themselves ... Communications and expressions which foment divisions between persons and groups may make it harder to follow the maxim of enlarged thought. Hence some forms of censorship and restriction of private uses of reason may be acceptable (indeed required) when (but only when) they are needed to foster or sustain capacities for communication with the world at large.[100]

Instead, she is demanding greater priority for progressive, liberal ideals, which is why she chooses feminism as her exemplar.[101] Yet here is the liberal paradox in action, for we shall not realise the benefit of these progressive ideals – of true equality, tolerance, and enlightenment – if they are foisted upon society, for that will only breed resentment, ignorance, and intolerance.

We also see this paternalism in Kingsley Martin's view that regulation of press speech is required to address the declining societal interest in serious political discourse:

> comparatively few people have a passion for truth ... or care about public events [unless it affects them personally] ... the public hands out fortunes, not to those who present the truest possible picture of public events, but to the showman who can provide the most entertaining kaleidoscope.[102]

Martin's views were written, it seems, independently of the Hutchins Commission's work, but he was clearly thinking similarly. Indeed, Martin is the ideal commentator by which to judge the thoughts of proto-social responsibility theorists of that time for, as Malcolm Muggeridge would later say of him, 'in his heyday [he] was the Left incarnate ...'[103]

His view speaks to the atrophied state of the citizen's public-minded thinking that Peterson describes. Even if we accept that he is right, is the cure really to *indulge* this necrotic state by feeding citizens only what they *need*? How will that nourish and grow the analytical functions necessary for healthy scepticism? What troubles me most about SRT, as I have said elsewhere, is the image it conjures up: of 'the press carrying the public in a sedan chair on the long road to utopia.'[104] People, in their public activities, will make bad decisions, as they do in their private lives. For the British, this possibility became real when the public voted for Brexit: a decision whose cataclysmic consequences may not be felt by the baby-boomer generation that voted, in overwhelming numbers, for

---

[99] O'Neill, 'Practices of Toleration' in Lichtenberg (ed), *Democracy and the Mass Media*, (n 73), 173.

[100] O'Neill, 'Public Use of Reason' (1986) 14(4) *Political Theory* 523, 547.

[101] O'Neill, 'Practices of Toleration', (n 99), 173.

[102] Martin, (n 64), 66.

[103] M Muggeridge, 'Standard-bearer of the Left', *The Observer*, 31 March 1968.

[104] P Wragg, 'The Limits of Press Accountability' in RL Weaver, A Koltay, MD Cole and SI Friedland (eds), *Free Speech and Media Law in the 21st Century* (Carolina Academic Press, 2019), 81.

it; it may be felt most by those who will be left to bear those consequences: the children of today and tomorrow. This impending tragedy is unlike that which befell the US when it made Donald Trump president, for at least that farce has an end date. It may take several generations for the effects of Brexit to be undone, if they can be undone at all. Nevertheless, this reminds us – because, apparently, we need reminding – that social progress is not constant and uniform. It is an uncertain and fragile thing.

This is the only consequence of recognising autonomy that we can be sure of: freedom means the freedom to make poor and uninformed choices, and the cost is having to live with those bad decisions: to either succumb to them, or learn from them. This is the true relationship between autonomy and self-development, not the artificial one that Lichtenberg sees. They are not equivalent. Autonomy may lead to self-development, but self-development does not lead to autonomy. Autonomy is absolute, self-development is qualified. Autonomy is a *right*. Self-development is a *choice*. The autonomous being can choose to be ignorant. As Mill says, the autonomous being can live *as she likes* – subject only to the harm principle. Although Mill believed that the best form of life was one of maximum self-development, he meant this as nothing more than an ethical claim. But his view on autonomy was a legal claim. No judge ever saw this more clearly than Oliver Wendell Holmes Jr. The Constitution, he said 'is an experiment, as all life is an experiment. Every year if not every day we have to wager our salvation upon some prophecy based upon imperfect knowledge.'[105]

The investiture of autonomy into every human being is, as he recognised, sacrosanct, not because all will take optimal advantage of their autonomy – far from it – but because there is no alternative. This is why human progress is a matter of faith and hope, not certainty. Consequently, we can say, with Hannah Arendt, that debate, in the scheme of democratic participation, is 'of joining with one's equals in assuming the effort of persuasion and *running the risk of failure*.'[106] This is something that SRT singularly refuses to recognise, for, as Peterson's description suggests, readers are not to be trusted. This forms part of the unspoken but self-evident view that SRT espouses: that people must be exposed only to information of the *right* kind so as to ensure the *right* decisions are made. Partly, this belief reflects the Soviet-inspired undertones of SRT – prior to the events in Budapest of 1956, that is, when the Hungarian Revolution was brutally crushed, and before the true state of Stalinist Russia was known. The most explicit recognition of this influence can be found in Kingsley Martin, in his admiration for the Soviet press and its readership:

> [newspapers deal] almost exclusively with political, economic, and cultural affairs. They are eagerly read by millions who have never learnt to expect the crime, sex, and human-interest stories which entertain the reader of Western newspapers ... No one tempts the reader to buy that which he does not conspicuously need.[107]

---

[105] *Abrams v United States* 250 US 616, 630 (1919).
[106] H Arendt, *Between Past and Future* (first published, 1961) (London, Penguin Books, 2006), 173.
[107] Martin, (n 64), 100.

Furthermore, he says, 'from the journalist's point of view, there must be advantages in writing leading articles in Soviet papers with space to develop an argument and no doubts about what you have to say.'[108] He glosses over the inconvenient truth that any criticism of the Soviet system, or even a failure to publish current policy, is liable to lead to dismissal 'or perhaps ... prison.'[109] Remarkably, his only meaningful criticism of this regime is the misleading impression it creates of foreign affairs: 'The ordinary Russian newspaper, for instance, has no appreciation of the social progress made in foreign countries, or of the genuine friendship for Russia that exists abroad.'[110]

Martin's work also draws attention to what is an otherwise overlooked point: although, in its communist leanings, it distorts the ambitions of SRT, it does not entirely misrepresent them. Martin's admiration of Soviet communism – praise of politics' monopoly on newspaper content, the admiration of the focused reader, the emphasis on 'need' over 'want' – speaks to the central themes of SRT. But the comparison to Soviet-era communism also highlights, in stark terms, the dangers of neglecting autonomy and of prioritising the collective over the individual. As Hannah Arendt would later note, when this happens, as it did in Hitler's Germany and Stalin's Russia, individuality has no meaning and human rights wither away to nothing.[111] Indeed, the horrors of twentieth-century totalitarianism give new meaning to Mill's warning that even when:

> the government is entirely at one with the people, and never thinks of exerting any power of coercion unless in agreement with what it conceives to be their voice ... I deny the right of the people to exercise such coercion, either by themselves or by their government. The power itself is illegitimate.[112]

This is why we should not draw the parameters of press freedom according to what the reader *needs*, for, if we are not to determine 'need' according to the free choices that consumers make in an open market, we must fall back on some idealised view that is vulnerable to political ideology.

IV. Conclusion

It is not that reader-oriented clauses are never justifiable in a scheme of coercive independent press regulation. But they are deeply problematic to justify, especially in the form in which they appear in the UK and European press codes. They pretend to legitimacy by claiming the readers' best interests as their object – which may be to address some perceived information deficit in the formation of the

---

[108] Ibid, 101.
[109] Ibid.
[110] Ibid.
[111] H Arendt, *The Origins of Totalitarianism* (first published, 1951) (London, Penguin Books, 2017), 349–396.
[112] Mill, (n 74), 229.

contract (such as the conflict of interest clauses) or else to limit their exposure to harmful speech. Yet, when analysed through the lens of the accountability model, the ostensible justification evaporates all too often. Even if we accept that the harm these clauses seek to regulate is real, we struggle either to establish sufficient causation between that harm and the newspapers actions (as in the conflict of interest clauses) or else cannot establish wrongdoing on the part of the newspaper (as in the suicide clauses).

Moreover, there is something deeply troubling about the reader-oriented clauses, when examined collectively, and that is the failure to respect autonomy. It manifests in this tension in regulatory design, which we see in the SRT literature, between the consumer protection oriented approach, of speaking *for* the reader, to realise their unfulfilled wants and needs (ie, as O'Neill and Lichtenberg say, to achieve greater plurality of ideas or, as the Hutchins Commission put it, to represent the community at large), and the paternalism of speaking *against* the reader, to dictate their sense of unfulfilled wants and needs. The audience is treated with something like disdain or, otherwise, deep mistrust. It is ironic, then, that underpinning O'Neill's criticisms, in *A Question of Trust*, about the trustworthiness of public institutions and the press, is an unspoken and, surely, inadvertent attack on the trustworthiness of society at large, to use their powers of autonomous decision-making productively. For when, in her earlier work, she said that communicators 'must adopt and reveal a certain view both of their own communicating and *of their audience* ... they must *respect the voices of the audience*'[113] she echoed the sentiments of the Hutchins Commission that 'the press must now take on the community's public objectives as its own objectives.'[114] And yet neither O'Neill nor the Hutchins Commission meant 'audience' or 'community' in a literal sense, as 'readers', for as Nick Davies tells us, the audience voices of, say, the *Daily Mail* are perfectly represented in that newspaper – they are the only voices that matter.[115] Instead, they meant audience and community in an idealised sense, as a group that is both a) not catered for by the newspaper (and so, in a sense, is disenfranchised) and b) (crucially) is virtuous in its views. SRT has no interest in plurality in a prosaic sense of the full spectrum of views, and neither is it advocating the corruption of broad-minded people through exposure to damaging ideas that they would otherwise have avoided. In this way, plurality means a greater voice for liberalism and the liberal voices of minorities. In case it needs saying: this is not a criticism of liberalism – it can be readily admitted that liberalism is vital for successful, harmonious collective living. But that value has to be realised individually, through autonomous decision-making. Clumsily foisting it upon others, through heavy-handed paternalism is not the preservation of liberalism. It is its betrayal.

[113] O'Neill, 'Practices of Toleration', (n 99), 171.
[114] The Commission on Freedom of the Press, (n 60), 126.
[115] N Davies, *Flat Earth News* (London, Chatto & Windus, 2008), 372.

PART 4

Realisation

9

How?

I. Introduction

The discussion so far, especially in Parts 2 and 3, has said much about the flaws in SRT, and little about the comparable flaws we find in libertarianism's attitude toward press regulation. This disparity suggests that, given the choice, libertarianism is the preferred position, or else the least problematic. This final part aims to correct this impression. For in libertarianism, we find great cause for concern. Whatever criticisms can be made of SRT, it is at least laudable for its relentless determination to do *something* about the very real problems that press malfeasance generates. By comparison, libertarianism is derelict. When it is not championing press interests myopically, as if malfeasance is simply spirited horseplay or misplaced exuberance, it dismisses the worse kinds with a shrug of resignation, as if unjustified harm, whilst regrettable, is simply the cost of living in an open society; as if the occasional victim is nothing compared to the greater good press freedom serves. The audacity of this indifference is surpassed only by its insensitivity towards press victims. Libertarians commonly treat them disdainfully, as if their maltreatment is deserved or else not worth the bother.

Consequently, although libertarianism's dominant grip on government policy is understandable – for SRT offers no real alternative, as we have seen – it is regrettable. It cannot address, let alone appreciate, the terrible consequences that decades of unchecked press abuse have caused. That it sometimes supports variations in the self-regulatory regime – what Leveson called 'cosmetic change'[1] – hardly counts. As we saw in Chapter 2, the dominant factions have been at such loggerheads that no alternative to self-regulation has been identified, let alone agreed upon. And yet there is an alternative: the introduction of mandatory regulation, created by means of statute, with coercive powers to enforce its code of conduct by means of sanctions (ideally, compensatory in nature). That statute would also establish the regulator's composition, determine the field of members, its relationship with members, and the standards by which members are judged (or else outline those standards in broad terms, as the Royal Charter on the Self-Regulation of the Press does).[2]

---

[1] Lord Justice Leveson, *An Inquiry into the Culture, Practices and Ethics of the Press: Report* (HC 780, 2012), 1538, [4.34].

[2] At sch 3, cl 8, see discussion below.

For obvious reasons, the right will not accept this alternative and, for less obvious reasons, neither will the left. This impasse, though, conveys the unfortunate impression that self-regulation is the most meritorious solution – and, in a sense, it is, but only because no other solution exists that would satisfy the irreducible minima of demands that both sides to this contest make. Lurking at the heart of this deadlock is a proposition which both sides seem to agree upon: that statutory regulation is unconstitutional. This is not universally accepted, of course, but there is sufficient agreement that even Lord Justice Leveson seemed to think it inviolable (as will be seen). And yet the full extent of this objection is never set out lucidly and comprehensively (as the Leveson report demonstrates); it is only ever hinted at darkly (which, of course, is very convenient for the press). This chapter challenges this view. The objection cannot withstand close scrutiny and it is time it was dismissed. Not only is statutory regulation the *best* means, it is the *only* means that will serve the regulatory goals that Leveson articulated: that of providing redress for the 'real harm' that serious press malfeasance inflicts on 'real people.'[3] The argument has two grounds: first, that the structural flaws of the contractual model of regulation mean that our regulatory goals can never be realised through this system (this argument is set out in section II); secondly, that the press's objections to statutory regulation is unsustainable (section III). Statutory regulation is not only legitimate; it is *necessary*. Finally, in section IV, I defend my claim that the regulator ought to have the power to award compensation.

My interest here is not in setting out the precise terms of this arrangement (as is consistent with the overall objective of concentrating on the philosophical, rather than the practical). It is, instead, on the questions of principle relating to mandatory press regulation. The one practical matter that I will address (since it has philosophical significance), albeit only in this introduction, is the question of *who* shall be regulated. This question has attracted a great deal of academic interest, certainly in the US. From the debate between Sonja West[4] and Eugene Volokh[5] on whether the press clause, in the First Amendment, is an institutional (West) or else a technological guarantee (Volokh) to the more practical question of identifying journalists amongst freelancers, bloggers, and social media users, the literature provides a wide range of opinions.[6] A consistent, but by no means universal, theme in this discussion is the perceived difficulty, if not impossibility, of defining what is

---

[3] Leveson, (n 1), 50, [2.2].

[4] See, eg, S West, 'Press exceptionalism' (2014) 127 *Harvard Law Review* 2434; 'Awakening the press clause' (2011) 58 *UCLA Law Review* 1025.

[5] E Volokh, 'Freedom for the press as an industry, or the press as a technology?' (2012) 160 *University of Pennsylvania Law Review* 459.

[6] Sonja West provides a comprehensive list of this literature in 'Awakening the press clause' (n 4), 1030, n 32. See also, eg, D Lange, 'The Speech and Press Clauses', (1975) 23 *UCLA Law Review* 77; RP Bezanson, 'Whither Freedom of the Press?' (2012) 97 *Iowa Law Review* 1259; I Cram, *Citizen Journalists* (Cheltenham, Edward Elgar, 2015); J Oster, Theory and Doctrine of 'Media Freedom' as a Legal Concept (2013) 5(1) *Journal of Media Law* 57; P Coe, 'Redefining 'Media' using 'Media-as-a-Constitutional-Component' Concept' (2017) 37(1) *Legal Studies* 25.

meant by the term 'press' and thus, in the US context, of saying who benefits from the press clause if that means something different to individual speech under the First Amendment. West summarises the literature well when she says: 'The myriad problems with determining who is or is not the press have been called "definitional monsters", "difficult and vexing", and "painful".'[7]

To my mind, this question does not raise especially difficult problems in principle. For one thing, the idea that there are 'definitional monsters' does not square with the complaint that a newspaper is too expensive to establish, nor AJ Liebling's rebuke that 'freedom of the press is guaranteed only to those who own one.'[8] This obstacle alone crystallises the market, leaving only the task of finding the right verbiage to describe it. And if that task causes difficulties, it is surely only at the margins, for we all know who we mean when we talk of the national and regional press. Furthermore, as noted above, we can find examples of such definitions in practice, eg, in section 41 of the Crime and Courts Act 2013 which defines 'relevant publisher' as a 'person who, in the course of a business (whether or not carried on with a view to profit), publishes news related material (a) which is written by different authors, and (b) which is to any extent subject to editorial control.'[9] Alternatively, we can look to section 1 of the Media Liability Act 1991 in Denmark, which states, simply, that the 'Act shall apply to … domestic periodical publications, including images and other representations that are printed or in any other manner duplicated.' Indeed, when we look at the European experience of press regulation, we find regulators have no difficulties in defining the press. In Sweden, regulation is split between the Press Ombudsman (Allmänhetens Pressombudsman),[10] which hears complaints about the content of articles, and the Journalists' Association's Professional Ethics Committee (Journalist Förbundet). The Allmänhetens Pressombudsman will listen to complaints about any periodical (whether that is a newspaper or magazine) and its associated website.[11] A periodical is defined as a publication with at least four issues per year.[12] Similarly, the Deutscher Presserat hears complaints about any member of the press, which it defines simply as 'print media (newspapers and magazines).'[13] Moreover, in the UK, newspapers are exempt from VAT charges[14] – no definitional problems have arisen from this arrangement and, unsurprisingly, the press has never complained that such might arise.

---

[7] West, 'Awakening the press clause', (n 6), 1029.

[8] AJ Liebling, *The New Yorker*, 14 May 1960.

[9] This is subject to two exceptions: first, those who are named in Sch 15 are excluded from the definition, such as broadcasters like the BBC; secondly, those that are defined as micro-businesses.

[10] Pressens Opinionsnämnd. June 2018. Code of Ethics for Press, Radio and Television in Sweden.

[11] See s 1 of the Charter, (n 10).

[12] Pressens Opinionsnämnd. June 2018. Code of Ethics for Press, Radio and Television in Sweden.

[13] Deutscher Presserat. March 2017. German Press Code – Guidelines for journalistic work as recommended by the German Press Council.

[14] S 30 and Sch 8, Value Added Tax Act 1994.

In this final part, we shall narrow our gaze to focus almost exclusively on the UK position and its singular failure to realise meaningful redress for victims of press malfeasance. This focus is influenced by two curious features of the UK experience: the peculiarity of the press's proclivity for privacy-invading expression (which, of itself, sets it apart from the press in other jurisdictions, especially Scandinavia) and its apparent disregard – some would say outright contempt – toward regulatory rebukes, which is unparalleled in Western democracy (although perhaps only because the French and Americans have no regulatory systems in place). Whereas the Nordic press is typically sheepish, and the Teutonic press, sincere, when admonished, the UK press tends to be vitriolic, and sometimes downright petulant.[15] It cannot be said, and perhaps never could be, that the UK press recognises the authority of a press regulator – any regulator – even when that regulator is comprised of its own, as IPSO is, and the PCC – as well as the Press Council before it – was. Consequently, the UK context represents the ideal crucible in which to test concerns about statutory regulation.

II. Terminal Failings in the Contractual Model

The Press Complaints Commission failed, as a regulator, for several reasons. It did not achieve total industry support (a major publisher, Northern & Shell, departed; others, like the *Financial Times*, never joined), its close proximity with the industry suggested that regulatory capture had occurred (certainly, it could not eradicate the impression of bias); and it had no powers by which to discipline members.[16] Although Leveson's recommendations for press reform clearly recognise these issues,[17] they misdiagnose the root cause, and thus provide an ineffective solution. For he placed too much emphasis upon the installation of meaningful powers and demonstrable independence from industry and too little upon compulsory membership. Without the latter, his reforms, even if implemented exactly, are bound to fail.

Although he said, on several occasions, that, to be effective, 'the new system must include everyone',[18] his recommendations contain no mechanism for achieving this. Thus, the austere language, underscored by the moral opprobrium that press victims and the wider public would not 'understand if the industry did not grasp this opportunity',[19] is undone by the weak-willed concession that 'the goal

---

[15] The perfect example of this is: J Delingpole, 'IPSO: a great new way for bullies to muzzle the press' *The Spectator*, 6 June 2015.

[16] See, eg, J Rowbottom, *Media Law* (Oxford, Hart Publishing, 2018), 279; E Barendt, J Bosland, R Craufurd-Smith and L Hitchens, *Media Law: Text, Cases and Materials* (Harlow, Pearson, 2014), 51; K Hughes, 'Parliament Reports on the Law of Privacy and Injunctions' (2012) 4(1) *Journal of Media Law* 17, 26.

[17] See discussion, Leveson, (n 1), 1544–1561.

[18] Ibid, 1751, [3.1] and 1754, [3.14].

[19] Ibid, 1782, [7.9].

here is *voluntary* independent self-regulation.'[20] This is an odd choice of words. First, it is inconsistent with the preceding passages in the report, which had clearly indicated that effective regulation was the goal. But, secondly, the language, and the implications of that language, conflict with Leveson's key recommendation that anything short of 'universal coverage' signals regulatory failure: 'I do not consider that it is possible for a regime to be considered effective if a major national newspaper group can choose to sit outside it without consequences.'[21]

In a voluntary scheme, though, this possibility is unavoidable. Indeed, none of Leveson's regulatory goals are guaranteed under such a scheme, for the regulated member's decision to abide by regulatory decision-making is always an indulgent submission of the will. The problem lies in the nature of the agreement between the regulator and the regulated. In the typical contractual exchange of goods or services for payment, both parties are incentivised to comply with its terms because both want something. This reciprocity is notably absent in the regulatory context – what does the regulated member receive for their compliance? For example, when we examine the contract that IPSO uses to 'bind' its members, we find that its obligations toward members – essentially, a promise to perform the role of regulator[22] – contains nothing that would incentivise the regulated member to compromise their autonomy.[23] Perhaps it is in recognition of this dubious exchange that the IPSO agreement is executed as a deed rather than a contract (thus avoiding the doctrine of consideration). Consequently, the only thing that ensures compliance is the fear of adverse consequences. But what would those be? Orders for specific performance are unavailable in deeds lacking consideration,[24] and are difficult to obtain where personal services[25] or constant supervision[26] are required. Damages could be claimed, but what would they represent? What would the regulator be compensated for?

Leveson saw something of this problem, but not the full extent. Although he thought contracts problematic as a foundation for regulation,[27] his chief concern was with their duration (he baulked at the industry's suggestion of a five-year term)[28] rather than their nature. He realised the importance of finding incentives for sustained membership, but emerged empty-handed. The best – and, really,

[20] Ibid, 1757, [3.28]. Emphasis added.

[21] Leveson, (n 1), 1584, [2.1].

[22] It speaks of IPSO's 'obligations' to the member: to ensure all members are bound by the same terms, to carry out its functions according to the contract, to act 'fairly and proportionately', to have regard to the member's circumstances when exercising its powers, and to exercise its powers in accordance with its rules (which, amongst other things, prevents IPSO from awarding compensation to press victims).

[23] www.ipso.co.uk/media/1813/ipso-scheme-membership-agreement-2019-v-sep19.pdf.

[24] See, eg, *Re McKay's Settlement* [1939] Ch 329.

[25] See, eg, *De Francesco v Barnum* (1890) 45 Ch D 430.

[26] See, eg, *Co-operative Insurance Society Ltd v Argyll Stores (Holdings) Ltd* [1998] AC 1.

[27] See, eg, Leveson, (n 1), 1620, [2.32] and 1649, [8.3].

[28] Ibid, 1750, [2.3].

the only – 'incentive' he could identify was the prospect of a 'kitemark' scheme,[29] which was something Lara Fielden had suggested in her report.[30] This idea is not entirely devoid of merit. For new market entrants, a kitemark evidencing, so to speak, excellence in journalism, could be a productive means of building a readership.[31] Of course, given the enormous costs of establishing a newspaper, these new entrants are likely to be small, internet-based concerns. This incentive, then, is of limited value to the traditional market; quite possibly, it would interest no 'relevant publisher', ie, those bound by the Royal Charter for the Self-Regulation of the Press, since this definition excludes micro-businesses (those with fewer than 10 employees and with annual turnover not exceeding £2 million) who publish news-related material by means of a multi-author blog or else publish such incidentally to their main activities.[32] As Leveson conceded, it is 'unlikely to have significant impact in persuading publishers who do not otherwise want to join a self-regulatory standards regime to do so.'[33]

Most participants, in the Leveson inquiry, thought little could be done to attract the recalcitrant press to a regulatory scheme, if it were set against it, and so, in the discussion, the term 'incentive' quickly assumed the most forced meaning possible, to capture not so much reasons for embracing Leveson's scheme, but, really, the reasons for fearing the alternative. Thus, discussion turned to whether the press's exemption from VAT could be removed for non-members of a recognised regulator (to which the answer was 'no' – and, anyway, as was pointed out, removal of the exemption would penalise purchasers rather than the newspaper itself, since it would mean consumers paying more for the same thing),[34] or whether non-members could be denied access to industry services, such as Press Association copy or statistics from the Audit Bureau of Circulations and the National Readership Survey,[35] or, most bizarrely of all, whether advertisers might be enlisted to withhold advertising from non-member newspapers, or else require non-members to pay a levy on advertising revenue.[36] Needless to say, all of these suggestions were rejected. What did emerge,[37] and was subsequently enacted (but never in force), was a cost-shifting legislative provision,[38] whose rationale recognised the cost savings inherent in the mandatory arbitration scheme required

---

[29] Leveson, (n 1), 1659, [5.2]–[5.4].

[30] L Fielden, *Regulating the Press* (Oxford, Reuters Institute for the Study of Journalism, 2012), 100–101.

[31] This point was put to Leveson by the Media Regulation Roundtable, https://webarchive.nation-alarchives.gov.uk/20140122192127/http://www.levesoninquiry.org.uk/wp-content/uploads/2012/07/Submission-by-Media-Regulation-Round-Table.pdf, 21, [72]. See Leveson, (n 1), 1659, [5.3].

[32] This definition is to be found at s 41, Crime and Courts Act 2013 and para 8 of Sch 15 of that Act.

[33] Leveson, (n 1), 1659, [5.4].

[34] Leveson, (n 1), 1660, [5.5] – 1662, [5.13].

[35] Ibid, 1662, [5.15] – 1663, [5.20].

[36] Ibid, 1664, [5.21].

[37] Ibid, 1781, [7.3].

[38] S 40, Crime and Courts Act 2013.

by a Leveson-compliant regulator. Thus, anyone deprived of using this scheme should be compensated for the disproportionate cost of pursuing legal action. Consequently, those outside a recognised regulator would have been liable to pay the claimant's legal costs, even if that claim was dismissed, whilst, conversely, members of a recognised regulator would have been compensated for wasted costs, even if they lost the legal action. The World Association of Newspapers and News Publishers strongly criticised this provision, which it called unfairly coercive.[39]

We will explore these concerns about a mandatory scheme shortly. Prior to that, let us consider the capacity of a voluntary scheme to achieve our regulatory aims (of holding the press accountable for wrongdoing). As noted above, Leveson seemed sure that those aims could be achieved if the press joined a regulator, of its own volition, and if that regulator was both demonstrably independent of the press industry and had the power to discipline members through financial sanctions. This situation has been realised, to an extent. Most of the press is part of IPSO, which claims to be independent, and has the power to fine.[40] It has yet to use this power.[41] This failing is a source of frustration for commentators[42] given the terrible malfeasance that continues to plague the industry.[43]

These disciplinary failings, though, are inevitable in a contractual system for the simple reason that the regulator has no leverage. In any contract, the decision to perform one's obligations are a matter of choice. It is an exercise in risk based upon the cost-benefit analysis of compliance compared to non-compliance. If the cost of non-compliance is less than the cost of performance, then breaching the contract becomes the more attractive option. For even when terms are written in the language of the categorical imperative, the decision to abide by them is always a choice, along the lines of a hypothetical imperative (if I wish to comply with the standards code, then I should …). This illustrates another fundamental quality of contracts: they are always terminable – through performance, notice, or breach. It is this essential quality that renders contract entirely futile for our purposes, for we will never have the leverage, by this means, to hold the press accountable in any sort of meaningful, intellectually satisfying, sense.

This inevitability informs IPSO's failure to fine. In the period between its commencement in 2014 and March 2019, it had upheld 1,702 code violation complaints. It is hard to believe that none of these was sufficiently serious

---

[39] WAN-IFRA, *Press Freedom in the United Kingdom*, 15 March 2014.

[40] www.ipso.co.uk/monitoring/standards-investigations/.

[41] IPSO's annual reports of 2015–2018 show that it has not yet even launched what it calls a 'standards investigation' – the process that would lead to the imposition of a fine.

[42] P McGrath, 'Bob the Builder: can IPSO fix it?' *Inforrm*, 8 November 2018; B Cathcart, 'IPSO: The Toothless Puppet Rolls over for its Masters (Again)' *Inforrm*, 26 October 2018, and B Cathcart, 'Sam Allardyce, the Telegraph and another IPSO failure' *Inforrm*, 3 September 2018.

[43] See the allegations made against Andrew Norfolk of *The Times* concerning the accuracy of stories involving Muslims: B Cathcart, 'Scandal at the Times: Another Journalistic Cover-Up', *Inforrm*, 29 June 2019; B Cathcart and P French, *Unmasked: Andrew Norfolk, The Times Newspaper and Anti-Muslim Reporting – A Case to Answer*, (London, Unmasked Books, 2019).

to warrant sanctions, even harder to believe there is not yet proof of systematic failures to comply with the code. Yet IPSO knows, as we do, that penalising members only serves to weaken the edifice. This is not to say that IPSO cannot fine, but that the decision to fine is an exercise in calculated risk. This, of itself, defeats the purpose of providing the regulator with its arsenal. Yet IPSO – perhaps recognising this point – has acted sneakily to raise the standard of violation required to justify sanctions. When IPSO was established, it committed to apply the same standard that Leveson recommended in his report, and which was incorporated into the Royal Charter on Self-Regulation of the Press, ie, that sanctions may be applied where there are serious *or* systematic violations of the code. Without explanation, though, the IPSO regulations, at clause 53, say that sanctions cannot be applied unless there have been serious *and* systematic violations.[44] Consequently, a single breach of a serious nature nor multiple unserious breaches will be sufficient, of themselves, to warrant investigation and, therefore, does not 'deliver', as IPSO said it would, this key provision in Leveson's recommendations.[45]

Since sanctions are intended to change attitudes, the regulated should be sufficiently fearful to correct their behaviour, and so avoid violations. That goal is seriously compromised, though, in the contractual model of regulation. Whilst it is possible that the use of sanctions may produce the desired effect (submission of the will), it seems more likely to do no more than foster animosity and contempt, in which either the disciplined newspaper withdraws from the regime altogether (or else threatens to) and/or the membership, as a whole, rally and threaten to depart, causing the whole edifice to collapse. Thus, we see the extreme poverty of the regulator's bargaining power: the threat of sanctions is a burden, not a benefit. In this environment, the use of fines is less a positive measure for securing regulatory goals, more a negative, destabilising one that undermines them, for any use of these disciplinary powers is bound to leave scars and no little resentment.[46] This sort of antagonism toward regulation occurred in Germany when, as Lara Fielden reported to Leveson, the Bauer Media Group (a major publisher) failed to renew its pledge to comply with the standards code in 2011, after the Deutscher Presserat issued 13 public reprimands against it,[47] and has not done so since.[48]

Consequently, a scheme in which both membership and compliance is voluntary – as the contractual model is – will not suffice. If Leveson's regulatory goals are to be realised – of addressing the 'real harm' that press malfeasance causes 'real people' – then the scheme must be mandatory, and that requires state

[44] See discussion in P Wragg, '*The Times*, IPSO, and the Mystery of the Systematic Breaches Sanction' (2019) 24(3) *Communications Law* 93.

[45] www.news.co.uk/2013/07/independent-press-standards-organisation/.

[46] See, eg, Delingpole, (n 15).

[47] Fielden, (n 30), 42.

[48] This has generated some criticism amongst commentators, see, eg, https://uebermedien.de/17299/bei-diaet-werbung-macht-sich-der-bauer-verlag-einen-schlanken-fuss/.

intervention, by means of statute. Yet, as we shall see, the press, and libertarians generally, claim that this would be unconstitutional. The following section scrutinises the validity of this claim.

III. Statutory Regulation, Press Freedom, and Pareidolia

A. The Threat of Statutory Regulation: A Paradox

Given these obvious flaws in the contractual model, why did Leveson believe that voluntary, not mandatory, regulation was ideal? (He called it the goal).[49] Scrutinising the language Leveson uses in this discussion is revealing, for he panders, noticeably, to the industry view that only a scheme that could command industry confidence would be legitimate.[50] Consequently, although Leveson acknowledges that the government could introduce a mandatory scheme – which he calls the 'backstop regulator'[51] – he is positively remorseful about the prospect:

> It would be a great pity, however, if the intransigence of a few resulted in the *imposition* of a system which everyone in *the industry has said they do not want* and which, in all probability, *very few others would actually want to see in place.*[52]

To this, he adds:

> I *would much prefer* that the focus of all concerned should be on attempting to deliver the effective self-regulation that I have set out. In my judgment, this provides *the least intrusive* method of ensuring some form of adequate independent regulatory oversight of press standards for the future.[53]

If we consider the passages I have emphasised, it is interesting that Leveson should choose to call statutory regulation an 'imposition' of something that not only the industry does not want, but also, although he does not explain why he says this, 'very few others' would either. Further, in light of his concerns about the industry's consistent failure to create an effective scheme of self-regulation, it is also interesting that he should describe this as not only his *preferred* outcome, but also to consider it meritorious because it is 'the least intrusive.' Given what is at stake, his statements are strikingly odd. Perhaps this is simply an exercise in *Realpolitik*, but it sends entirely the wrong signal. What has industry disapproval to do with

---

[49] See Preface.
[50] See, eg, Lord Black's comments: https://webarchive.nationalarchives.gov.uk/20140122203055/ http://www.levesoninquiry.org.uk/wp-content/uploads/2012/07/Transcript-of-Morning-Hearing-9-July-2012.pdf.
[51] Leveson, (n 1), 1782, [7.7] and [7.10].
[52] Ibid, [7.11] (emphasis added).
[53] Ibid, [7.12] (emphasis added).

legitimacy? Of course, industry approval may have practical value in securing compliance more readily, and in that sense, might have political value, but it has no normative value, for industry approval is not a pre-requisite for legitimacy. Similarly, although we might consult with regulated industries to discover means of optimising regulation, we do not require their blessing beforehand to the fact of mandatory regulation. The factory owner polluting the water supply is not excused because he 'needs' to do so, nor because he claims that pollution is a necessary by-product of the public interest in supplying his goods.

Yet Leveson's reticence foreshadowed the government's response to the prospect of statutory regulation. David Cameron, then Prime Minister, clearly thought statutory press regulation unconstitutional. It would be, he said, to 'cross the Rubicon.'[54] Although, as Eric Barendt noted, this is 'normally a metaphor for political (or military) courage, [it was] used by him pejoratively to denote a dreadful step which no liberal politician should ever contemplate.'[55] Libertarians were convinced of this point, of which Lord Black[56] was the most vocal – indeed, he was incredulous – at the prospect of statutory regulation:

> I – there is a fundamental objection that I have and I believe that the bulk of the industry has in allowing the state to write the rules of a regulator that governs editorial content. It's not just writing the rules, but presumably producing the style of the system and the type of the system that will be there to enforce it. It's not a circle, I think, that can be squared. It is a fundamental philosophical objection to the role of the state in the content of newspapers and magazines.[57]

Paul Dacre said something similar: 'I now fear that ANY parliamentary involvement [in press regulation] would be the "thin edge of the wedge" which could result in fuller statutory control of the press' and, thus, only a system of industry-run self-regulation could achieve the 'correct balance between the public's right to know and the need to protect the rights of the public.'[58]

Although Leveson was dismissive of such concerns,[59] he clearly thought there was *something* problematic in mandatory, statutory regulation. For, although he said 'I do not accept that there is any issue of principle preventing, in any circumstance or howsoever framed, the use of legislation in respect of press standards,'[60] he indulged this view by founding his regulatory solution on a scheme of 'statutory underpinning.' That he spent time distinguishing 'statutory underpinning'

---

[54] HC Deb, vol 554, col 449 (29 November 2012).

[55] E Barendt, 'Statutory Underpinning: A Threat to Press Freedom?' (2013) 5(2) *Journal of Media Law* 189.

[56] Lord Black is an executive director of the Telegraph Media Group and was chairman of the shadowy Press Standards Board of Finance (PressBoF), which oversaw the operation of the PCC, before being dissolved in 2016.

[57] Leveson, (n 1), 1675, [7.6].

[58] https://webarchive.nationalarchives.gov.uk/20140122193415/http://www.levesoninquiry.org.uk/wp-content/uploads/2012/06/Submission-by-Paul-Dacre1.pdf.

[59] Leveson, (n 1), 1782, [7.8].

[60] Ibid, 1680, [7.28].

(by which he meant the use of statute to set up certain structural features of the voluntary self-regulatory scheme he recommended)[61] from 'statutory regulation' (by which he meant a state-run or state-backed scheme of mandatory regulation) gave the libertarian neurosis about state control of press regulation a legitimacy that it did not warrant.

In light of this, there is something very strange about Leveson's threat that the industry should obey him or else endure government intervention. If Black, and others, are right that statutory regulation is unconstitutional, then this threat is not only idle, it fools no one. The promise of meaningful reform will always be an empty one, for there is nothing to be done should the press fail to deliver meaningful reform; we shall be hostage to fortune in perpetuity. If though, as the threat implies, statutory regulation *is* constitutional, then why bother with the charade any longer? Seventy years of asking the press to try reforming itself – just one last time[62] – has not worked. As James Curran notes, the second Royal Commission on the Press, of 1962, although critical of the press, concluded that it 'should be given another opportunity itself voluntarily to establish an authoritative General Council', and he traces this theme through subsequent inquiries, concluding with the statement of then Home Secretary, David Waddington, to the House of Commons, in 1990, that 'this is positively the last chance for the industry to establish an effective non-statutory system of regulation.' In 2012, Leveson said 'I cannot, and will not, recommend another last chance saloon for the press',[63] shortly before he did just that.

The paradox of the backstop regulator threat, though, appears to have gone unnoticed. This, of itself, may suggest that both the press and the government realise the 'unconstitutionality' point is bogus but the pretence serves them well by dampening public expectations. This would explain why the English press chose to make changes to its self-regulatory regime that, it claimed, matched 'all the key Leveson recommendations' and marked 'a complete break with the past',[64] whilst maintaining, across its pages, the air of defiance toward the Royal Charter on Self-Regulation of the Press. Both the act of reconstitution and the decision, at least by the majority of the British press, to belong to IPSO smacks of fear: the fear of state reprisals. Certainly, Leveson thought he detected this in Black's testimony: 'I have no doubt that the proposals put before me by Black spring solely from the fear that I might recommend a legislative regulatory solution.'[65] This sort of fear, it seems, motivated the Irish press industry into action when the Irish Government threatened to intervene if it did not. At least, this is what

---

[61] These eventually appeared in the Crime and Court Act 2013.
[62] J Curran and J Seaton, *Power Without Responsibility* 8th edn (Oxford: Routledge, 2018), 470, citing Royal Commission on the Press 161–2 Report (1962) Cmnd 1811, 102.
[63] Leveson, (n 1), 1757, [3.33].
[64] www.news.co.uk/2013/07/independent-press-standards-organisation/.
[65] Leveson, (n 1), 1670, [5.48].

the Irish Press Ombudsman, John Horgan, told Leveson.[66] With the British press, the portrayal of fear is a pretence, surely – as we have seen, it suits it to maintain the present scheme of self-regulation, which gives them control over the terms of compliance.

Consequently, we should recognise the ulterior motive at work in its protests against statutory regulation. For, as Steven Barnett has said, the press's reaction to Leveson was 'carefully orchestrated hysteria.'[67] Likewise, James Curran reminds us that the reason why the PCC failed was due to the press 'deliberately dragg[ing] their feet' – 'they were determined that [reform to self-regulation] would not develop into a homegrown monster, reprimanding them one moment and telling them to apologise the next.'[68] Proper regulation, the press fear, would be bad for business. And, of course, as industries go, the press's situation is unique: the government of the day has an obvious self-interest in keeping the press on its side; the introduction of coercive, independent press regulation jeopardises its prospects of re-election. In this way, uncertainty works in the press's favour, for, as long as people believe that there is *something* in the argument that statutory press regulation is insidious, the press can maintain the pretence of a principled objection by which to hide their actual complaint, which is financial, from public scrutiny. Nevertheless, the very fact of voluntarily belonging to a regulator smacks of fear of *something*. Otherwise, why bother to belong to *any* sort of regulator?[69]

Perhaps there was a moment when the industry was genuinely afraid that Parliament was of a mind to implement statutory regulation *despite* its (supposed) unconstitutionality. Certainly, Leveson did not seem to be bluffing, or if he was, he did it very well. At one point, he said 'ultimately, the one incentive that we have heard about that has been demonstrated to be effective is the realistic threat of press standards legislation if an adequate voluntary body with full coverage is not forthcoming.'[70] He repeats the point later on, in his recommendations: if the industry does not reform itself sufficiently, then 'my view is that there would then be no alternative but to provide in legislation for a backstop regulator to apply and enforce a Code.'[71]

And yet Leveson is not alone in making this threat. Sir David Calcutt said virtually the same thing when he investigated press malfeasance in the late 1980s: if 'the PCC [were] not set up in time, or were there to be a low rate of compliance or large-scale flouting of its adjudications then the government should establish a "statutory tribunal with statutory powers and implementing a statutory code

---

[66] Ibid, 1669, [5.4].

[67] S Barnett, 'Leveson Past, Present and Future: The Politics of Press Regulation' (2013) 84(3) *Political Quarterly* 353, 353.

[68] J Curran and J Seaton, *Power Without Responsibility* 8th edn (Abingdon, Routledge, 2018), 471.

[69] Indeed, three national British titles do not: *The Independent*, *The Guardian*, and the *Financial Times*. No state reaction or other adverse consequences has followed from this.

[70] Ibid.

[71] Ibid, [7.10], 1782.

of conduct.'"[72] And, as we saw in earlier chapters, this was also the Hutchins Commission's view: 'if [the press] does not become [accountable] of its own motion, the power of government will be used, as a last resort, to force it to be so.'[73] Consequently, given how readily others have resorted to this threat, it is hard to accept that Lord Justice Leveson was bluffing, or that Parliament's prospective complicity would have been a rogue act.

Indeed, from a positivist perspective, we can readily dismiss the claim that mandatory regulation is incompatible with Article 10 of the European Convention on Human Rights or, as a group of experts told Leveson, somewhat mysteriously, 'may ... be difficult to justify.'[74] Denmark's press regulatory scheme, which *is* both mandatory and statutory in nature, has caused no constitutional crisis, nor has the ECtHR seen fit to interfere. In fact, Leveson had the proof of this in his hands – Lara Fielden had told him about it in her report[75] – but, for some reason, chose not to use it. Admittedly, the fact that the positive law allows for this does not make it philosophically sound – and so, in the next subsection, I scrutinise the claim of compatibility with press freedom at a normative level.

B. Statute as the Source of Regulatory Power

According to Leveson, the principled objection to a mandatory scheme, established by statute, has four parts. We have touched upon the first already. It relates to effectiveness: that a mandatory scheme would be ineffective because it would be repulsive to the press; only a scheme commanding industry approval would produce 'genuinely willing participants.'[76] Secondly, that mandatory regulation is, or else risks degenerating into, state control of the press. Even if the scheme itself did not unduly threaten press freedom, such legislation would be the 'thin end of the wedge' allowing more censorial measures to be passed more easily in the future. Thirdly, that statute is too cumbersome: 'Any mandatory system would require some form of legislation; it is argued that this would make the resultant system inflexible and unable to move to react to changes in the market or in technology'[77] or, as Black put it, 'keep pace with a fast-moving industry in the way that self-regulation could.'[78] Finally, that mandatory regulation generates irresolvable definitional issues.

---

[72] T O'Malley and C Soley, *Regulating the Press* (London, Pluto Press, 2000), 89.
[73] The Commission on Freedom of the Press, *A Free and Responsible Press* (Chicago, University of Chicago Press, 1947), 80.
[74] Media Regulation Roundtable, (n 31), 17, [58].
Leveson refers to this at, (n 1), 1655, [4.1].
[75] Fielden, (n 30), 20–21.
[76] Leveson, (n 1), 1656, [4.2].
[77] Ibid, 1656, [4.3].
[78] Ibid, 1674, [7.3].

I have already discussed the fourth objection in the introduction to this chapter. The third is easily dismissed, for we can say, with Eric Barendt, that it fundamentally misunderstands the point of statute, which is to establish the structure not the substance of press regulation.[79] Of the two remaining objections, the first lacks normative content. It is not a claim about the compatibility of regulation with press freedom; it simply describes an attitude toward compulsion: that press petulance will scupper it. The second claim is normative, but its contingency diminishes its significance. For the root of this concern lies in the *perception* of what mandatory, statutory regulation represents, and how it could be used. When we look, not only at Leveson, but the established literature, and other inquiries, we see this perception at work. People hear the phrase 'statutory regulation' or 'mandatory regulation' and they impress some dark meaning upon it. In this way, the phrase takes on a meaning that is never acknowledged lucidly, candidly, and comprehensively, but only hinted at darkly. In other words, the common reaction is one of seeing what we want to see, of imposing an order or a meaning upon a form that is not necessarily true. Psychologists call this phenomenon 'pareidolia.' We look at the moon and see a face. We look at shadows cast from some innocuous object and see a monster. It is this phenomenon, of seeing what we want to see or expect to see, which characterises the debate on press freedom and press regulation. Hannah Arendt could have been describing this phenomenon when she said: 'it certainly is a category of the mind to bring order into all sensory data, whatever their nature may be, and thus it makes experience possible.'[80] We think these terms stand for something and, consequently, this something then determines both the limits of state action in relation to that thing and the nature of the guarantees that the thing provides. It strikes me that if we are alive to this phenomenon's presence, in the debate, we can make progress.

During the Leveson inquiry, participants saw in the phrase 'mandatory regulation' their worst fears realised: that 'Parliament is itching to control the press and that this would be an opportunity to do so';[81] that it would 'make it easier to amend an existing Act than to bring in a new one';[82] that it is bound to have a 'chilling effect on free speech or press freedom';[83] and that it portends 'freedom of expression Armageddon.'[84] We see this pareidolia elsewhere. For example, we see it in Parliament's reaction to Leveson in 2012. We see it also in its reaction in 1946, when sections of the Commons feared that the appointment of a Royal Commission into press practices would lead to some legislative solution:

> It was this implied threat of legislation which evoked thunderous denunciation from some of the newspapers ... They can scarcely have thought that a British Labour

---

[79] Barendt, (n 55), 195.
[80] H Arendt, *Between Past and Future* (first published, 1954) (London, Penguin Books, 2006), 143.
[81] Leveson, (n 1), 1780, [6.38].
[82] Ibid, [6.39].
[83] Ibid, 1782, [7.8].
[84] Ibid, 1783, [1.3].

Government in 1946 was in the least likely to imitate the methods of totalitarian countries, to nationalise the press, or to institute a censorship. But in evoking the principle of "the freedom of the press" they were sure of a ready response from Liberal England ... [85]

We see it in the Royal Commission's response: 'we [do not] see a solution in any form of state control of the Press.'[86] We see it also in Black's conclusion that statutory regulation would be 'repugnant to a proper view of the freedom of the press,'[87] and Post-Leveson, the press's response that it would end '300 years of press freedom' and imperil serious investigative journalism.[88] Clearly, there is a perception here of some insidious force lurking in the idea of statutory regulation.

In an important sense, the fear of state control is unjustifiably alarmist. Specifically, the claim that mandatory regulation amounts to 'licensing' is a powerful but manipulative trope to generate unwarranted sympathy for the press, intended to reference not the sort of scheme that applies in the broadcasting context, but that censorious system that prevailed in the UK until 1695. Under this system, the Star Chamber, that most pernicious of judicial bodies, during the reign of the Stuarts, utilised terrifying methods to punish heresy and criticisms of Royal policy, as when the puritan William Prynne was branded on both cheeks with the letters S and L to indicate his crime of seditious libel against the Crown.[89] Mandatory press regulation is no more comparable to the Star Chamber than the Clergy Discipline Commission is to the Spanish Inquisition.

Nevertheless, the source of this pareidolia is not merely paranoia but the teleological conception of press freedom itself. According to this, the regulation of the press's contribution to democratic participation is justified. We can readily find provisions of this sort in the European regulatory codes, albeit these are not enforced coercively. Nevertheless, they exist: Denmark's Pressenævnets instructs publishers not to withhold information of vital public importance;[90] Finland's Julkisen Sanan Neuvosto says that readers have a 'right to know what is happening in society,'[91] as does Belgium's Raad voor de Journalistiek[92] and the Swiss Press Council;[93] Norway's Pressens Faglige Utvalg says it is the press's 'task ... to protect

---

[85] K Martin, *The Press the Public Wants* (London: The Hogarth Press, 1947), 20.

[86] Royal Commission on the Press, 1947–49, *Report* (Cmnd 7700), Ch XI, [683].

[87] Leveson, (n 1), 67, [5.11].

[88] See, eg, 'Press freedom in Britain is under attack – again', *The Spectator*, 31 December 2016; 'Daily Mail Comment: After 300 years, the freedom of Britain's Press is in peril. YOU can save it', *Daily Mail*, 9 January 2017; G Rayner, 'Investigative journalism to be 'stopped dead in tracks' by 'menacing' laws after Leveson Inquiry', *The Independent*, 15 October 2015.

[89] LW Levy, *Emergence of a Free Press*, (Oxford, Oxford University Press, 1985), 132; M Kishlansky, 'A Whipper Whipped: the Sedition of William Prynne', (2013) 56(3) *The Historical Journal* 603.

[90] As noted in the Preface, the preamble to the Danish press code says 'Breach of sound press ethics also includes the withholding of rightful publication of information of essential importance to the public', Pressenævnet. May 2013. The Press Ethical Rules.

[91] Cl 1 of the Finnish code, Julkisen sanan neuvosto. January 2014. Guidelines for Journalists and Annex.

[92] Pt I, cl 1, Raad voor de Journalistiek. December 2016. Code of Practice.

[93] Directive 6.2, Geschäftsstelle Schweizer Presserat. Directives relating to the 'Declaration of the Duties and Rights of the Journalist' [July 2017] & Declaration [June 2008].

individuals and groups against injustices';[94] whilst, the Swedish Allmänhetens Pressombudsman says that 'the role played by the mass media in society and the trust of the public of these media call for accurate and objective news reporting.'[95] Given statements like this, it is understandable that the press should fear regulatory function creep. The commentary feeds this pareidolia through the confused use of ethics (in the SRT model, at least), and in its erroneous insistence upon the existence of a press 'duty' to serve the public good and, likewise, to act 'responsibly' in the use of power. Even libertarianism contributes through its agreement with SRT that the press has a purpose to fulfil. Thus, both sides overburden the phrase press freedom and the parameters of press regulation with this pareidolia. This, in turn, drives the libertarian fear that unwarranted interference with press speech could occur unchecked because we would lack the language to articulate the unconstitutionality of the function creep.

Yet, this fear is misplaced. The accountability model, outlined in Chapters 5 to 8, provides us with this language. By rejecting the teleological account, it demonstrates that the range of permissible regulatory codes is more limited than those caught in the grip of pareidolia fear. Accordingly, it would not be legitimate to operate provisions ostensibly regulating 'truth', 'the public's right to know', or indeed any clauses imposing 'duties' to enable democratic participation, educate the public, or check on power. Such provisions are beyond the scope of legitimate regulation. As Part 3 demonstrates, the regulatory rules are themselves subject to rules of design. All provisions must correspond to the formula of wrongdoing-causation-harm that the liberal tradition recognises. It is only if these governing rules are followed that the provision is compatible with press freedom. Thus, the fear that, say, press criticism of the state could be penalised – now, or in the future – does not arise by virtue of linguistic vulnerability, and cannot, therefore, arise from function creep, because we have the language to designate it an unconstitutional act. The fact that we can both articulate the nature of press freedom and the limits of legitimate regulatory rules of conduct means that we have the critical vocabulary by which to identify mandate breaches by the regulator or government. We can say what is a legitimate use of coercive power and what is not. Consequently, the pareidolia is rendered nugatory.

Accordingly, the state could enact legislation to create a mandatory scheme of coercive independent press regulation without compromising press freedom. Indeed, the Royal Charter on Self-Regulation of the Press is an example of this, albeit that scheme is not compulsory. Nevertheless, it contains an essential framework by which to establish a press freedom compliant code of conduct, at schedule 3, clause 8, which instructs the regulator to devise a code that upholds freedom of speech, the right to privacy, and freedom from undue intrusion, amongst other things.

---

[94] Cl 1.5, Norsk Presseforbund. June 2015. Code of Ethics of the Norwegian Press.
[95] (N 10).

Yet, the press is bound to think this controversial. In Black's testimony to the Leveson inquiry, we see esoterism creep into his description of the task of drafting the code for, according to him, 'only serving editors would have the practical day-to-day understanding of what life was like in newsrooms.'[96] Quite why only serving editors are uniquely qualified is not clear. Leveson rejected that claim, albeit he did not altogether dismiss it. On several occasions, we see him say that a 'strong editorial voice' on standards was 'important',[97] 'invaluable'[98] and 'obviously necessary'.[99] This conclusion is worth scrutinising, for what is the unique contribution that serving editors make? Consider a different regulatory context – say, medicine or law. In those fields, the input of members *is* 'obviously necessary' for we cannot say what amounts to medical or legal malfeasance unless we have knowledge of those professions.[100] This is not true of journalism. It does not involve the same sort of 'special skill' that would necessitate practitioner input. Of course, editors are bound to hold views on what is useful or desirable, but, clearly, that is not the same thing. The reason for this is apparent from previous chapters: that the only code provisions that can be enforced coercively against the press are those that protect *rights*. These, then, are questions of law, not journalism. The regulator is not required to know – to be on the inside of – journalism to determine these standards. Not only are journalists unnecessary in this process, they are irrelevant, and, quite possibly, a hindrance. For what can they say about the realities of newsgathering and the intricacies of reporting technique that is vital to the rights claims at stake?

Of course, none of this removes the need for vigilance in ensuring neither the regulator or the government exceeds their mandate. We must always guard against complacency. The government's self-interest in a subdued press should never been forgotten. Neither should we think that UK Government is somehow immune to corruption, incompetence, or abuse of power. Nor that the independent regulator is beyond such either. This concern, though, is not an unassailable argument against the creation of a coercive, independent press regulator. Far from it. Instead, it is an argument in favour of ensuring the proper safeguards exist to monitor or otherwise address the possibility of regulatory failings. To ensure that the regulator's power is not abused, its actions should be subject to some sort of oversight or transparency – and, of course, the usual means of doing this is judicial review, so that instances of errant regulatory decision-making can be remedied.[101] Ireland's regulatory scheme, for example, contains an additional layer of transparency by operating an appeals process in which first instance decisions by the press ombudsman can be overturned and replaced by decisions of the press

---

[96] Leveson, (n 1), 1624, [3.4].

[97] Ibid, [3.6].

[98] Ibid, 1527, [3.30].

[99] Ibid, 1529, [3.39].

[100] See, eg, *Montgomery v Lanarkshire Health Board* [2015] UKSC 11; *Bolam v Friern Hospital Management Committee* [1957] 1 WLR 582.

[101] The PCC was also subject to judicial review, see *R v PCC ex parte Stewart-Brady* [1997] EMLR 185.

council on appeal.[102] The Royal Charter provides a different, important, safeguard against, especially, systematic failings by the regulator. This arises in the form of the 'recognition body' – a separate entity that is independent of the state, the industry, and the regulator itself – which is tasked with appointing the regulator, in the first place, according to specific criteria set out in the Royal Charter[103] and with conducting reviews of the regulator's performance, at least once every three years after the regulator has been appointed,[104] but also on an 'ad hoc' basis, either because the recognition panel suspects that there has been a serious breach (or breaches) of the recognition criteria or because there is a 'significant public interest' in such a review.[105]

IV. Sanctions

In this final section, I want to say something, briefly, about the ideal range of sanctions that ought to be available to the regulator. In short, I will argue for victim compensation and against the power to order corrections and (so-called) rights to reply.

During the inquiry, a group of experts told Leveson that a mandatory scheme of regulation generated three insurmountable problems. First, that the 'ultimate sanction' for non-compliance 'would have to be "striking off the register", in other words forbidding a media organisation from continuing to publish', which, 'would … have to be backed by legal sanctions: either criminal prosecution or proceedings for injunctive relief (with committal for contempt of court as the ultimate sanction).'[106] Secondly, that there would need to be some scheme of 'prosecution or committal' for those who refuse to participate in the scheme or else '[publish] … whilst not being registered' which 'would be perceived by the media and the public as censorship and would not be credible. It is too high a price to pay for the advantages of comprehensive regulation.'[107] Finally, that 'compulsory regulation would be extremely difficult to enforce in practice' because disgruntled publishers could simply 'avoid regulation by operating offshore.'[108]

Disappointingly, Leveson blithely accepted some of these (including, bizarrely, the last one) and ignored the rest.[109] He wasted the opportunity to subject these objections to proper scrutiny. Had he done so, he could have shown that these concerns were misplaced, and in some places, simply alarmist. Take the idea that

---

[102] Press Council of Ireland. June 2015. Code of Practice.
[103] Sch 3.
[104] These are known as cyclical reviews, under cl 5, sch 2.
[105] Cl 8, sch 2.
[106] Media Regulation Roundtable, (n 31), 18, [59].
[107] Ibid, [60].
[108] Ibid, [61].
[109] See Leveson, (n 1), 1655, [4.1] and 1656, [4.4].

the 'ultimate sanction' for mandatory regulation 'would have to be' ostracization, as if the regulator could banish the recalcitrant newspaper to exile or else remove their 'licence' to publish. Both the notion itself and the use of the categorical imperative to support it is incredible. Indeed, we need only notice the *fact* of the Danish regulatory scheme to realise just how far-fetched the assertion is for, as we have seen, that scheme *is* compulsory and relies on nothing like a power to 'strike off' to support it. Those that refuse to comply with the order to publish adverse adjudications may be fined and that is it.[110] Consequently, the idea that mandatory regulation *must* include the draconian measure to strike off is wild fantasy. Indeed, how would it be achieved? How could the regulator possibly revoke this hypothetical licence to publish? The idea that one could 'forbid' a media organisation from publishing seems not only impossible – what prevents them 'rebranding' and re-emerging in a different form, as when the *News of the World* became the *Sun on Sunday*? Are we saying that only the 'owner' is prevented? Or the editor too? The logistics are phenomenal, and to what end? – but also unnecessary and disproportionate.

Similarly, the idea that the newspaper *must* perform some positive act to become a member (and so could refuse to do so) is also mistaken. For example, if we look to the data protection regime overseen by the Information Commissioner, we do not find that companies can refuse to engage with the scheme or be exempt from the rules simply because they refuse to pay the fee required by the Data Protection (Charges and Information) Regulations 2018. In Denmark, all domestic periodical publications are subject to regulation by the Pressenævnets by virtue of section 1 of the Media Liability Act 1991. Membership is automatic; no registration is required. All publications published in Denmark at least twice-yearly fall under the Pressenævnets's jurisdiction. Section 34 obliges the press to conform with the rules on good press practice (god presseskik). This is mandatory.

Notice, though, the pareidolia at work, again – for the complaint is made that any scheme of enforcement 'would be *perceived ... as censorship* and would not be *credible*. It is *too high a price to pay ...*' Yet, there has been no suggestion, in the preceding discussion, or, indeed, during the Leveson inquiry, that a regulator *should* have the power to censor content and, in fact, the regulator would be unable to do so, for obvious reasons. This, of itself, renders the comparison to the licensing system of the Stuarts redundant, for in that system, copy had to be approved *before* it could be published. But, of course, these commentators do not mean censorship in its technical, proper sense of a scheme by which a person is authorised to scrutinise speech before it is published and excise offensive and harmful passages, as happens, for example, in the film industry (where the British Board of Film Classification can insist scenes are cut or edited before they will grant a certificate). Instead, they mean censorship in its wider, colloquial sense as *any*

---

[110] S 49, Media Liability Act 1991.

interference with speech, such as post-publication fines. It is merely a happy coincidence that the word censorship connotes licensing and so provokes a stronger emotional response.

Finally, the idea that publishers will emigrate to avoid the regime is the most far-fetched of all. It would certainly make for uneasy editorials if, say, the *Daily Mail* were to relocate to Europe or further afield given its protectionist, not to mention nationalist, attitudes. Yet, it also raises an interesting point of principle, for, given that the free speech guarantee is one owed by the state to its people, complaints by foreign entities about interferences with their speech do not have the same purchase.

Nevertheless, these concerns beg the question about the nature and scope of applicable sanctions that the regulator could use. The Royal Charter on Self-Regulation of the Press does not specify what it means by sanctions, it merely says that they should be 'appropriate'.[111] It does, however, authorise, or appear to authorise, the use of fines since, in clause 19A of schedule 3, it says that the Regulator may use the 'receipts from financial sanctions' to fund investigatory and enforcement activities. Yet, if, as was argued in Chapters 6 to 8, the only justifiable code provisions are those that protect rights, then compensation rather than fines is the most appropriate sanction. In either case – compensation or fines – the newspaper incurs a debt, but why is it a debt to society (in the form of the regulator) rather than the wronged individual? Compensating the victim for the wrong they have suffered optimally captures the spirit of Leveson's view that regulation should address the 'real harm' caused to 'real people.'

To put it another way: what is criminal, or potentially criminal, about noncompliance with regulatory obligations? Admittedly, fines are used in other jurisdictions in media law contexts. For example, Denmark imposes criminal liability (upon editors)[112] for defamation[113] and hate speech,[114] amongst other things. This, though, does not settle the normative question. Of course, it could be argued that the 'social debt', justifying the imposition of fines, is the cost of regulation itself – this would be consistent with the wording of clause 19A, albeit clause 6 in the same schedule suggests that the cost should be recovered directly from members. Preferably, the state should fund the scheme; there should be no incentive nor necessity for the regulator to be dependent upon monies raised by fines to fund its activities. Clearly, any incentive to fine risks compromising the integrity of the whole operation.

Of course, the industry will object to a regulatory power to issue compensation. Interestingly, IPSO's membership agreement prevents it from doing so: at clause 5.5, it says 'for the avoidance of doubt the Regulator shall have no power

---

[111] Sch 3, cl 19.
[112] Ss 9–15, Media Liability Act 1991.
[113] See, eg, *Pedersen v Denmark* (2006) 42 EHRR 24.
[114] See, eg, *Roj TV A/S v Denmark* (2018) 67 EHRR SE8 [42].

to require [its members] to make any financial payment under the Regulations to any third party.'[115] The industry is likely to complain that such a power would 'open the floodgates', overwhelming the regulator with claims. Some scepticism is called for, though. First, we are not asking the press to do anything more than the law already requires; the power to avoid paying out compensation resides with the press. All it need do is avoid unjustifiable interference with the rights of others. Secondly, the terms of the Royal Charter establish a high threshold, for it limits the power to issue sanctions to instances of 'serious or systematic breaches of the standards code or governance requirements of the [regulatory] body.' This threshold ensures – or ought to ensure – that sanctions are applied only exceptionally.[116] Moreover, it ensures that frivolous or unmeritorious claims are excluded. Since compensation is not a windfall, the regulator must be satisfied that the effect of the wrongdoing is sufficiently serious to justify the compensatory award. Of course, where the code provisions mirror the positive law, the regulator will have a guide as to the appropriate amount to be awarded. Thirdly, we should recognise the real concern that the 'floodgates' argument speaks to: the improved efficiency of redress that regulation represents. For the press knows, as we do, that it would be more deeply indebted to victims if they were better able to obtain redress for the wrongs that the press does to them. Even so, the press remains in control of its destiny: the way to avoid paying compensation is to respect the rights of others. We should have little sympathy if it chooses to do otherwise.

The power to order corrections or apologies to be published, though, is a source of concern. The Royal Charter provides this power at clause 15 in schedule 3. Whilst apologies and corrections are sometimes valuable substitutes for damages, and have significance as a mitigating factor in the calculation of damages, an order to publish such strikes me as draconian and unprincipled. Interestingly, Tom O'Malley and Clive Soley, who have previously written in favour of tougher press regulation, are against the use of financial sanctions, which, they say, 'put at risk the future publication of a paper', but not orders for corrections or apologies, which they describe as 'by far the best form of sanctions and quite possibly the most effective.'[117] In support of this, they make four statements, each of which seems representative of the literature and thus, detailed analysis of these statements provides a useful way of interrogating the wider view of corrections and apologies.

First, they say that 'these are not onerous sanctions',[118] although they say nothing more to defend this extraordinary statement. Why extraordinary? By forcing newspapers to print corrections and/or apologies, we interfere with their freedom

---

[115] See (n 23).

[116] In his review of its performance to date, Sir Joseph Pilling advised IPSO that 'it would be a serious mistake' to initiate an investigation in anything other than the most 'exceptional' circumstances, Sir J Pilling, *The External IPSO Review*, October 2016, [117].

[117] T O'Malley and C Soley, *Regulating the Press* (London, Pluto Press, 2000), 189.

[118] Ibid.

of expression at a fundamental level by making them say something against their will. When we turn to the common law, we see some recognition of this principle, for example, the rule that specific performance cannot be used to compel personal services: for 'the Courts are bound to be jealous, lest they should turn contracts of service into contracts of slavery.'[119] Admittedly, this is not universally true of the positive law. For example, section 12, Defamation Act 2013 empowers the court to order defendants in a defamation action to publish a summary of the judgment, albeit, even here, there is muted recognition of the point, in its emphasis on the parties reaching prior agreement on the time, manner, place and form of that summary. It is only if the parties cannot agree that the court should determine these matters for them (section 12(4)).

Of course, what O'Malley and Soley mean is that the order to correct and/or apologise is less *financially* onerous to the newspaper, because it does not require the loss of, or additional commitment of, resources to satisfy it. This may be so, but it is incorrect at the level of *principle*, for the intrusion with freedom of speech is such that the newspaper may well prefer to pay a fine (and play the martyr in doing so). This leads to the second statement: 'most newspapers would want to avoid having to publish such corrections regularly and would therefore have an incentive to seek higher standards.'[120] This statement rather contradicts the first, for if the power to order corrections and apologies is not an onerous sanction, then where is the incentive to seek higher standards? O'Malley and Soley might say that it is the anticipated *frequency* of such orders that would make them unappetising – but, even so, that would still amount to a concession that the sanction *is* onerous, if only in specific circumstances.

The third is that 'serious consequences would only arise if an editor chose to defy the court.'[121] This point recognises, albeit not explicitly enough, that the order to correct and/or apologise, is always contingent upon the will, for, ultimately, the court *cannot* compel anyone to do *anything* against their will where it requires a positive act from them. They can fine, imprison, impound and freeze assets, but they cannot force anyone to produce. Finally, they say 'this risk [of serious consequences for non-compliance] already applies in all countries'[122] – as if that somehow proves its legitimacy or compatibility with principle.

V. Conclusion

Commentators are often mistaken about the reason why self-regulation of the press has consistently failed. It is not only because previous regulators (be that the

---

[119] *De Francesco v Barnum*, (n 25), 438.
[120] O'Malley and Soley, 117, 189.
[121] Ibid.
[122] Ibid.

General Council of the Press, the Press Council, the PCC or IPSO) have lacked the power to issue sanctions – for IPSO has these sanctions and *chooses* not to use them. It is that voluntary self-regulation will *always* fail the regulatory goal because the decision to obey regulator commands is *always* a *choice*. It is *always* an indulgent submission of the will. The regulator is not in a superior position of strength compared to the regulated. The regulator is in a vastly *inferior* position. It may have real powers but it cannot use them, for to do so risks irritating the member and jeopardising the very existence of the scheme. For in a voluntary scheme, members are *always* free to leave. That they *indulge* the regulator from time to time with exhibitions of contrition and solemn oaths is merely simulation.

It is only by implementing a mandatory scheme that the chief regulatory goal that Leveson set – of addressing the 'real harm' caused to 'real people' – can be realised. Yet those on the political right, especially, and sometimes on the left, see things in the notion of mandatory regulation that are not there. It is state control, it is censorship, it is the end of press freedom, they say. This pareidolia has petrified the debate for too long. For the faith in market solutions over state interventions will not provide the meaningful regulation we require. Voluntary self-regulation, founded upon contractual agreement, is fatally flawed. The categorical imperative holds no weight in a scheme where compliance only results from indulgent submission of the will. Since contract fails to bind, it is bound to fail.

Yet we betray the very real victims of the press when we ourselves indulge this pareidolia; when we too see monsters lurking in the notion of the mandatory regulation. These monsters are not there. How can I be sure? Because the rules have rules. Regulatory code design is constrained by the accountability model, outlined in Chapter 5, and applied in Chapters 6 to 8. This means that the regulator cannot devise rules that would allow it to regulate the press's contribution to democratic participation, its performance in educating the masses, nor its performance in checking on power. It can only devise rules that correspond to normative rights, especially those relating to victims. Consequently, the function creep that the press fears – the 'thin end of the wedge' – cannot be realised, for the rules provide us with the language by which to identify unjustifiable code provisions, by which to say what is and is not legitimate for the regulator to do.

The regulator needs coercive powers. It needs the power to compel co-operation with its investigations. It needs the power to compel membership of the scheme. It needs the power to issue sanctions. Yet, surely, it is the power to order compensation, rather than fine, that best fits the regulatory aims that Leveson described. Given the type of malfeasance that is regulatable, it is individuals rather than society at large that suffers most, and they ought to receive redress for those wrongs. The power to fine will not achieve that end.

10

Why?

I. Introduction

This final chapter anticipates two major criticisms concerning issues unaddressed in the book, both of which are to be found in the same question: why regulate the press? The first criticism relates to the question: why *regulate* the press? Given the constant refrain that coercive independent press regulation is warranted only where the interference is justifiable as a matter of normative legal theory, am I not, in fact, arguing for a change in the positive law? The second asks why regulate *the press*? An obvious, and recurring, criticism of the Leveson inquiry was that Leveson spent little or no time discussing new forms of journalism, found in online sources, citizen journalism,[1] and the hyper-local press. The final section provides a summary of the book's main arguments.

II. Why *Regulate* the Press?

In Chapter 5, I argued that the hypothetical regulator could institute code provisions more (or less) onerous than the positive law, so long as they remained compatible with normative legal theory. In that chapter, and later in Part 3, the conditions for compatibility were reduced to the formula of wrongdoing-causation-harm. It was further argued that any prospective regulatory code that did not comply with this formula would be unenforceable by coercive means and unsuitable even as a purely ethical or voluntary code provision given the constraints that Kant imposes on ethical lawgiving ('Ethical lawgiving (even if the duties might be external) is that which *can* not [*sic*] be external').[2] Consequently, I noted, as a practical example, that the UK regulatory code could provide complainants with the right to seclusion from intrusion even though that right is unrecognised in the positive law, and that the accuracy clause is regulatable only to the extent it protects reputation.

---

[1] See discussion in I Cram, *Citizen Journalists* (Cheltenham, Edward Elgar, 2015) and P Coe, 'Redefining 'media' using a 'media-as-a-constitutional-component' concept' (2017) 37(1) *Legal Studies* 25.
[2] I Kant, *The Metaphysics of Morals* (first published, 1797), L Denis (ed), M Gregor, trans, revised edn (Cambridge, Cambridge University Press, 2017), [6:221] (emphasis in original).

Critics might say that this is an argument for law reform, not for regulation; that regulation is rendered obsolete in this account. Since privacy, reputation, and rights to a fair trial are all protected by the positive law, press victims can secure their rights, and obtain redress, by recourse to legal action. Any shortfall in legal rights protection is a matter for the common law to address, and if not that, then the legislature.

I will address this criticism in a way that recognises the broader, general concerns that libertarians have with regulation. Characteristically, libertarianism considers the market a more efficient and dynamic means of tackling social problems than state intervention since the latter is unwieldly, bureaucratic, and slow. Of course, this devotion to the power of the market is not simply blind faith, as it sometimes appears to be, in the 'invisible hand' that Adam Smith spoke of.[3] It is, instead, a matter of comparing the market solution with its alternative. For, in its most persuasive form, libertarianism recognises government's incompetence to solve even our most basic social problems by central control, and, thus, we must see that regulatory failure is an equally likely prospect as market failure. As Coase put it: 'Until we realise that we are choosing between social arrangements which are all more or less failures, we are not likely to make much headway.'[4] Consequently, libertarianism encourages a more discerning and sceptical attitude toward the imposition of regulation. The fact of market failure is a necessary but insufficient justification for regulation: regulation must have some quality that makes it *superior* to the status quo; that it would achieve something that market forces alone could not. In other words, we must be clear on why we think regulation will fix the problem.

I shall advance three practical reasons why regulation is preferable nevertheless. The first relates to the nature of the market failure. We should be clear that the market has failed not because the law offers inadequate protection of rights against press wrongdoing (albeit, in the UK, it is only since the advent of meaningful privacy law, following *Campbell v MGN Ltd*,[5] that we have been able to say this), but that access to this market solution is severely curtailed by the financial and emotional costs involved. For we should recognise that those who would say 'there is no need for regulation, the law protects privacy and reputational rights' are indulging in unhelpful blackboard reasoning. To be sure, in the UK, for example, we can point to a broad range of legal measures, but none of that is any comfort to the press victim who simply cannot afford to pursue a legal action. The costs involved are staggering and far outweigh the relatively small size of awards in

---

[3] A Smith, *An Inquiry into the Nature and Causes of the Wealth of Nations*, vols I & II, RH Campbell and AS Skinner (eds), (The Glasgow Edition of the Works and Correspondence of Adam Smith) (Oxford, Oxford University Press, 1976).

[4] RH Coase, *The Firm, the Market and the Law* (Chicago, University of Chicago Press, 1986). See discussion in D Campbell, 'Of Coase and Corn: A (Sort of) Defence of Private Nuisance' (2000) 63(2) *MLR* 197, 198–203.

[5] *Campbell v MGN Ltd* [2004] UKHL 22.

successful claims. Given that the financial consequences of losing are life-changing to all but the privileged few, it is no exaggeration to say that media law is a luxury that very few can afford. In the absence of, say, the introduction of legal aid to cover that cost and eliminate that risk (which is highly unlikely), regulation offers a meaningful solution by providing cheap and fast complaints handling (which, in the previous chapter, I argued should be supplemented by the power to award compensation) and the prospect of providing arbitration to settle disputes outside the court process (which IPSO offers).[6] Yet, the absence of funding is not the only problem. There is also the distinct unevenness in judicial reasoning concerning privacy law, which affects the viability of pursuing legal actions. Consider, for example, cases involving simple 'kiss and tell' stories. Sometimes judges treat these as monstrous invasions of privacy, and compensate the victim accordingly;[7] sometimes judges think them instances of valuable public interest expression.[8] Yet the distinction in fact-patterns between these cases is so slight that the reason for these wildly different outcomes is neither obviously defensible nor easily anticipatable.

The second issue relates to the first, and that is the emotional cost of pursuing litigation. Although all forms of litigation are bound to be emotionally draining, given the adversarial nature of legal disputes, complaints against the press are exceptional in that, both during the process and afterwards, the press can (and does) antagonise the claimant by, say, criticising the decision to pursue litigation. Moreover, those that do pursue complaints risk painting a target on their back. As Leveson said in his report:

> Numerous individuals in public life have complained in evidence to the Inquiry that they have been afraid or unwilling to confront the power of the press ... owing to concerns about personal attack and vilification ... The corpus of evidence relevant to this issue is vast.[9]

Indeed, Leveson devotes an entire section of the report discussing the phenomena of press retribution against those who pursued claims against them.[10] He also relates how, in the phone-hacking litigation, News International pursued a campaign of intimidation against the lawyers representing the victims, to pressure them into withdrawing from the litigation.[11]

If celebrities are vulnerable to this, then ordinary members of the public must be even more so. When we consider that most people have little or no experience of the legal system in practice, and that the closest they come to it is probate and

---

[6] www.ipso.co.uk/arbitration/.

[7] See, eg, *CC v AB* [2006] EWHC 3083 (QB) [36]–[37], [44]; *Mosley v News Group Newspapers Ltd* [2008] EWHC 1777 (QB); *CTB v News Group Newspapers Ltd* [2011] EWHC 1232 (QB) [25]–[26].

[8] See, eg, *Ferdinand v News Group Newspapers Ltd* [2011] EWHC 2454 (QB); *McClaren v News Group Newspapers Ltd* [2012] EWJC 2466; *YXB v TNO* [2015] EWHC 826, [61].

[9] Lord Justice Leveson, *An Inquiry into the Culture, Practices and Ethics of the Press: Report* (HC 780, 2012), 481, [2.39]–[2.40].

[10] Ibid, 704–709.

[11] Ibid, 516–517, [4.35].

the occasional property purchase, then it is understandable why most would find that process daunting. Of course, this is not to say that the anguish felt by those in the public eye is any less real than those who are not. To think that is to engage in the sort of dehumanising of celebrity that the press trades upon to defend its shoddy practices – that strange attitude that because celebrities are rich, or tend to be, they do not feel in the same way we do, which makes them impervious somehow – or, the equally strange view that the cost of celebrity is to become subhuman public property. Nevertheless, since public attention is more familiar to celebrities than non-celebrities, they may have acquired an increased tolerance to the uglier side of it that makes them more resilient. Certainly, for the non-celebrity, finding themselves to be front page news is the sort of overwhelming event for which few other life experiences can prepare one for. Also, celebrities, through their greater resources, are likely to have better access to the sort of support that can help diminish the traumatic effects of unwanted press attention, by means of PR, representation (to field enquiries and form a barrier between hostile press and press victim), counselling, and other forms of support. For the non-celebrity, especially those who live alone and must field the telephone calls and the door-stepping, the experience is both surreal and traumatising.[12]

Regulation alleviates this emotional burden. Partly, it can do so through the faster resolution of complaints, of course. But chiefly it can help by creating a barrier between the victim and her oppressor. As Chapter 7 demonstrated, this can be done during the newsgathering process itself if the regulator operates a scheme whereby the subject of press interest can signal that they wish to be left alone. Also, and in a more meaningful sense, it can be achieved by the regulator's power to initiate and pursue claims of its own volition.[13] This capability presents an opportunity for victims to be shielded from the press's bullying behaviour. One can imagine a scheme in which the knowledge of the initial notification from the victim can be kept hidden from public view such that, externally, it appears that the regulator has initiated the complaint and the victim is merely a respondent to its enquiries. This is not something that can happen in civil actions; only the victim has *locus standi* to pursue actions. Indeed, the court treats non-appearance by the victim as a signal that the claim is not serious, and so will dismiss it on that basis.[14] Admittedly, this cannot eradicate the practice of vindictive retribution, but it does diminish the impetus for that strategy, for it ought to become apparent that attacking the victim only strengthens the regulator's hand to initiate further claims against the publisher. For although the malevolent publisher might think this tactic will prevent the victim from cooperating with the regulator's inquiries, it ought to become apparent that the regulator can find against the publisher even without victim testimony.

---

[12] See further the examples discussed in P Wragg, 'Leveson and Disproportionate Public Interest Reporting' (2013) 5(2) *Journal of Media Law* 241, 247–249.

[13] Royal Charter on Self-Regulation of the Press, Sch 3, Cl 18.

[14] See, eg, *Terry v Persons Unknown* [2010] EWHC 119 (QB), [65]; *YXB v TNO*, n 8, [61, iii, c].

The third reason follows from the second. Regulation provides the sort of transparency about press malfeasance that the legal system cannot. For the self-interest that drives the market's power to tackle problems and, thus, illustrates its strength, is also its chief weakness. The market relies upon individuals to champion their rights and hold harmful wrongdoing to account. The strength of the market rationale is in the sum of its component parts. Accordingly, if every rights-claim against the press was upheld through legal action, then the malfeasant press would face a stark choice: become a force for good or become extinct. Yet, in reality, these component parts are isolated – they are not a homogenous mass, but a series of individuals; other litigants may be unknown to them – and vulnerable to the superior bargaining power of their opponent. Consequently, individual actions are determined not necessarily by the strength of the rights claim but by that individual's resolve and capacity to endure the stultifying effect of the defendant's litigation strategy. Even the most flagrant violations of the law may be concealed from public knowledge by means of early settlement or, worse, by convincing the ill-informed claimant that her case is hopeless. Moreover, this divide and conquer strategy means that even systematic abuses can be dismissed as isolated instances, perpetrated by lone wolves: a strategy that seems to have worked in the case of the phone scandal: the press has convinced the world, it seems, that the practice of illegally obtaining information from mobile phone messaging services was something that only Glenn Mulcaire and Clive Goodman did; a view that has been cemented by the UK Government's decision to quietly drop the second part of the Leveson inquiry, which could have scrutinised this claim rigorously.[15] Thus, the market is a poor method of addressing entrenched malfeasance, for there can be no guarantee that victims have the means to identify each other, share their experiences, and so strengthen their resolve.

Regulation addresses this problem by acting as an important means – in fact, the only means – of holding press power to account. It does not suffer the same weaknesses that a group of individuals does – it cannot be bought off. This accountability function is, as Chapter 5 made clear, an essential function of regulation. If the press serves a valuable function in holding every other source of power to account, it is only right that some institution should exist to monitor the press's use of power. Leveson alludes to this when he says 'who guards the guardians?'[16] – a poor choice of phrase given its implication that regulation exists to protect the press. Of course, what he meant was 'who watches the watchmen?' This is a serious issue because, presently, in the UK, we have no reliable means of determining the extent of press malfeasance. IPSO says that since its inception in August 2014, and up until April 2019, it has received 51,258 complaints, of which 1,717 involved breaches of the code, 723 were found to involve no breach (after investigation), 18,905 were rejected, 4,583 were not pursued, and 25,330 were found to be outside

---

[15] P Walker, 'Leveson inquiry: government confirms second stage axed', *The Guardian*, 1 March 2018.
[16] Leveson, (n 9), 1758, [3.31].

its remit. Although this appears to be a reassuring set of statistics – for it suggests that breaches of the code occur rarely – we cannot trust it, for there is no independent verification of these decisions or the processes for rejecting claims. We have no means of determining how many complaints have been wrongly rejected or misclassified. Also, we do not know how many of the 4,583 complaints that were initiated but not pursued involved breaches of the code, and neither do we know how many further violations of the code have occurred that were not brought to the regulator's attention.

III. Why Regulate *the Press?*

So far, nothing has been said about regulation of non-traditional news outlets: from the online versions of traditional newspapers, to citizen journalist 'blogging', to the hyper-local press, which often appears in online-only form. In this way, the discussion is prone to the same criticism commentators made of Leveson's recommendations: that, by its failure to consider online news sources, it was outdated at the point of publication.[17] Andrew Marr, for example, told Leveson in 2012 that this omission was a mistake because certain bloggers were 'now as influential as any newspaper.'[18] Likewise, Matt Hancock MP, defending his decision, as culture secretary, to abandon Part 2 of the Leveson Inquiry, mentioned the 'seismic changes to the media landscape', in which, he claimed, the existence of newspapers was now seriously threatened by online and other forms of journalism.[19] These other forms include, of course, broadcast journalism – of which I have also said very little. For it could be claimed, rightly, that this form of press is more significant than newspapers.

These claims, about the diminishing significance of newspaper speech compared to other forms, find some support in the limited empirical data available. A survey published by OFCOM in 2018 showed that the broadcast press remains the major source of news for adults in the UK (79 per cent of those surveyed) but the internet is the second-most favoured source (64 per cent).[20] Newspapers were the least consulted source (40 per cent). Radio was in third place (44 per cent). The same survey, though, revealed a generational divide with the internet being the most popular source for 16 to 24-year-olds. A survey by the Pew Research Center, published in August 2017, reveals similar results.[21] Two-thirds of adult

---

[17] See, eg, E Bell, 'The press regulation charter is illiterate about the internet', *The Guardian*, 20 March 2013.

[18] D Sabbagh, 'Lord Justice Leveson discusses role of bloggers', *The Guardian*, 23 May 2012. See also, Marr's submission to the inquiry: https://webarchive.nationalarchives.gov.uk/20140122190526/http://www.levesoninquiry.org.uk/wp-content/uploads/2012/05/Witness-Statement-of-Andrew-Marr.pdf.

[19] (N 15).

[20] www.ofcom.org.uk/__data/assets/pdf_file/0024/116529/news-consumption-2018.pdf.

[21] www.journalism.org/2017/09/07/news-use-across-social-media-platforms-2017/.

Americans said they used social media at least sometimes as a source of news – 20 per cent said they did so often. As may be expected, these figures are on the rise. This, of itself, speaks to a need to investigate, at least, the potential need for regulation of such speech and, in fact, there is a burgeoning literature that does so, albeit not only press-type speech.[22]

Nevertheless, there are several reasons why I have focused upon the printed press to the exclusion of all other forms. The most significant reason is that clarity about the conception of press freedom underpinning the printed form is productive both in the debate about printed press malfeasance and in debates about its online equivalent. That, in order to say something meaningful about the treatment of newer forms of press-type speech, we must first achieve certainty about the older forms. If, as the orthodox view has it, traditional press speech is a special form of speech, then the reasons for that specialness have to be clearly established to know whether that quality (of specialness) is transferable to the online medium, otherwise we cannot say whether online press speech is different to all other forms of speech online. Neither would it be possible to say whether it is separate from traditional press speech. Absent this initial analysis, we are left with a dilemma. For if we apply the orthodox view that traditional press speech has a special rationale that makes it different to not only other forms of speech but also broadcast press speech, then we must ask ourselves whether online press speech is like printed press speech, in which case the opportunity for regulation is limited (at least, according to SR theorists and libertarians) or, alternatively, whether it is akin to broadcast press speech, in which case regulation (for example, the imposition of an obligation of impartiality) is acceptable. Indeed, there is a third possibility, that we conclude online press speech is neither like the traditional press nor broadcast press and so is *sui generis*.

Consequently, it strikes me that this conundrum cannot be resolved without reappraisal of the underlying reasons for our differential treatment of printed and broadcast press. As I said at the outset, this inquiry is long overdue. Frankly, despite the newspaper being around for 400 years,[23] and existing in something like its present form since the turn of the last century, and at the very least, the late 1960s, we have never gotten to grips with the meaning of press freedom, at least not as a matter of normative legal theory. As we saw in Chapter 1, the orthodox view of its status as a champion for and educator of the people is an outmoded view that does not describe the newspaper in its current incarnation, but when it

---

[22] Eg, see A Koltay, *New Media and Freedom of Expression: Rethinking the Constitutional Foundations of the Public Sphere* (Oxford, Hart Publishing, 2019); RL Weaver, *From Gutenberg to the Internet* 2nd edn (Durham, NC, Carolina Academic Press, 2019); D Mac Síthigh, *Medium Law* (Abingdon, Routledge, 2018); P Coe, 'National security and the 'fourth estate' in a brave new social media world' in L Scaife (ed), *Social Networks as the New Frontier of Terrorism* (Abingdon, Routledge, 2017), 165.

[23] The *Relation aller Fürnemmen und gedenckwürdigen Historien* is said to be the oldest European newspaper, published in Strasbourg, in 1604. There was also the *Avisa Relation oder Zeitung* published in Germany in 1609 and the *Courante uyt Italien, Duytslandt, &c* in Amsterdam in 1618. See J Weber, 'Strassburg, 1605; The Origins of the Newspaper in Europe' (2006) 24(3) *German History* 387.

was a vehicle owned and used by, initially, the Liberal party to serve specific political goals (ie, educating the newly extended franchise in the ways of politics) and, later, the Conservative Party. That this romantic view has not only survived but flourished despite the very different patterns of ownership and economic aims of newspapers today is remarkable.

The project to better understand the press freedom concept in its printed form remains a priority, not least for its application to the other traditional forms (television and radio) and newer forms. For it is only through this project, for example, that we can resolve the dispute between left and right over whether the broadcast regulatory model is applicable to the printed press. Those on the left tend to argue that it is, and, further, that the broadcast regulation model is attractive because it achieves the goals of SRT without compromising press freedom.[24] Understandably, post-Leveson, those arguments have re-emerged with added urgency.[25] Those on the right, and those left-leaning thinkers who oppose SRT, argue that broadcast regulation is tolerable only *because* the printed press is free from such constraints, and so can inform and provoke the agenda in a way that the broadcast press cannot. Paul Dacre made this point clearly in his evidence to Leveson:

> Some point to the example of OFCOM ... but broadcasters are state licensed and, in the case of the BBC, state funded. Such state involvement only works in a democracy because it is balanced by the commercial press and the internet, both of which are unlicensed and therefore genuinely free.[26]

In other words, the concern about coercive broadcast regulation being compatible with press freedom is not settled but merely suspended for so long as the press and the internet is free from such. Or, as Lucas Powe Jr put it, describing the aftermath of Watergate: 'Yet if the regulated broadcasters were too timid, at least some newspapers were willing to risk potentially serious consequences to stand up to the government.'[27] It is this 'exquisite complexity'[28] of asymmetrical regulation that ensures the best of all worlds, according to Lee Bollinger a claim that Cass Sunstein calls pragmatically appealing but under-theorised.[29]

The principles outlined in this book have greater application than simply the printed press. The accountability model offers a solution to this problem by showing that regulation of broadcast content on, say, impartiality and other SRT grounds

---

[24] See, eg, E Barendt, *Freedom of Speech* 2nd edn (Oxford, OUP, 2005), 449–450, T Gibbons, *Regulating the Media* 2nd edn (London, Sweet & Maxwell, 1998); CR Sunstein, *Democracy and the Problem of Free Speech* (London, The Free Press, 1995); G Robertson, *People Against the Press* (London, Quartet Books, 1983), 139–158.

[25] See, eg, P Chamberlain, 'Where now? The Leveson Report and what to do with it' [2013] *Communications Law* 21; J Charney, *The Illusion of the Free Press* (Oxford, Hart Publishing, 2018), 142–144.

[26] https://webarchive.nationalarchives.gov.uk/20140122193415/http://www.levesoninquiry.org.uk/wp-content/uploads/2012/06/Submission-by-Paul-Dacre1.pdf.

[27] LA Powe Jr, *The Fourth Estate and the Constitution* (Berkeley, University of California Press, 1991), 295.

[28] LC Bollinger, *Images of a Free Press* (Chicago, University of Chicago Press, 1991), 143.

[29] CR Sunstein, *Democracy and the Problem of Free Speech* (New York, Free Press, 1995), 111–112.

is an unjustified (and unjustifiable) interference with the freedom of the broadcast press. In this way, it can be said that the anomaly is not the fact of the press being outside the scheme of broadcast regulation, but the fact of broadcast regulation itself. Indeed, it is surprising that this claim is not made more often. After all, certainly in the UK and the US, the limitations placed upon the broadcast press are a matter of historical accident rather than principled design. Ronald Coase has written about this before. As he said 'the press, which is so anxious to remain unshackled by government regulation, has never exerted itself to secure a similar freedom for the broadcasting industry.'[30] Although we might think his view of the BBC as a 'government-controlled monopoly of a source of news and information'[31] is far-fetched, he is surely right to criticise the hypocrisy and egotism of the printed press during the BBC's creation: they supported the heavy constraints placed upon it because they did not want the competition, either for advertising revenue or the supply of news, 'and so they did their best to throttle the BBC, at least as a purveyor of news and information.'[32]

The compatibility of broadcast regulation with the right to freedom of expression is yet to be thoroughly scrutinised. Indeed, reading the established literature, it feels that commentators accept the status quo not because it is justified but because it was ever thus. What little criticism there has been of broadcast regulation has tended to be on practical rather than principled grounds. For example, as we saw in Chapter 6, in the late 1980s, the Federal Communications Commission, in the US, abandoned its policy of requiring broadcasters to present controversial issues of public importance impartially, despite the Supreme Court upholding its constitutionality in *Red Lion Broadcasting Co v FCC*,[33] because it lacked the analytical toolkit to determine when it should operate. Admittedly, there are reasons why some level of independent oversight of broadcasting is justified. The most pressing of these has been, historically, the spectrum argument: that a centralised allocation process has been required to avoid multiple stations broadcasting on the same frequency, which would result in garbled communication. Quite why this practical arrangement should extend to broadening the spectrum of viewpoints heard on radio and television has not been established on anything other than the negative grounds that broadcasters do not own the airwaves and, therefore, cannot resist government compulsion to obey the restrictions that it devises. This is more or less the US Supreme Court's view in the *Red Lion* case, which found that it is the 'right of viewers and listeners, not the right of the broadcasters, which is paramount' – a right, it said, which granted them 'suitable access to social, political, aesthetic, moral, and other ideas and experiences.'[34] The persuasiveness of this

---

[30] RH Coase, 'The Market for Goods and the Market for Ideas' in *Essays on Economics and Economists* (Chicago, University of Chicago Press, 1994), 69.
[31] Ibid.
[32] Ibid.
[33] *Red Lion Broadcasting Co v FCC* 395 US 367 (1969).
[34] Ibid, 390.

view, though, is much diminished in the digital age. Citizens may well still own the airwaves, but, increasingly, broadcasters can reach their audience without having to use the public system, relying instead on privately owned technologies, such as the internet.

The accountability model, presented in this book, is similarly useful for the debate on regulating online press-type speech. By dismantling the press exceptionalism argument, the self-imposed constraints, which block both the left and right from taking action, are removed. Consequently, the way is cleared for us to regulate such speech without having to devise special treatment for the online press. Moreover, having settled the underlying matters of principles, we can concentrate on the practical issues that might limit or curb regulatory intervention on technological grounds. Although there is no need to define members according to labels characterising their press status (ie, citizen journalists, online newspapers, political bloggers, etc), we might want to limit regulation to those entities that are worth regulating, ie, due to their frequency, size, turnover, or audience reach. These would be pragmatic economic decisions rather than matters of principle relating to press freedom.

IV. Why Not?

At the core of the press freedom literature is a riddle. It is a riddle that defies explanation. It is a riddle that is both obvious and yet goes unseen – or seems to. If this book does nothing else, I hope it draws attention to this riddle, so that it can be recognised. The riddle is this: the press is obliged to serve certain functions, variously described as educating the masses, enabling democratic participation, and acting as a public watchdog, whilst simultaneously being not obliged to do so. These societal functions are things it must do and yet there is nothing to ensure that these things are done. So why do we persist with the fallacy? Why do we say that the press has a duty or a responsibility to society at large to do these things when that is plainly false?

This riddle would not be so perplexing if the press were held to these obligations by means of coercive independent press regulation. Yet, as we have seen, the absence of such a scheme is not merely inaction on the state's part but, it is said, something more principled: that coercive independent press regulation would be unconstitutional somehow. Accordingly, the mystery intensifies. The press has obligations that it *cannot* be held to by external agency. If this is true, then the categorical imperative becomes meaningless. There are no obligations.

I have sought to highlight and resolve this riddle.

I have shown its origin. In Chapter 1, we saw how the progressive ideals of, especially, the Liberal Party informed the teleological conception of press freedom during what I called the ideological period (1855–1947), which grafted onto the term 'press freedom' obligations of supporting the newly enfranchised voter, to realise his and (eventually) her democratic duties, by means of education and by playing the part of a notional 'fourth estate'. This conception suited the established press because it described their contribution to society during the romantic period (1600s–1855) and provided a useful means of attacking 'new journalism' or 'yellow journalism' as faux journalism since the newer, cheaper, inauthentic forms did not contribute so productively. Nevertheless, even during the ideological period, the teleological conception could not have been imposed, comprehensively, upon a recalcitrant press. Indeed, the only time in history where it could be said the printed press was *bound* to serve the public was when it was owned by the political parties (in both the UK and US), especially, in the UK, the Liberal Party, whose progressive ideas it was that informed the key tenets of the teleological conception: educate, monitor, enable.

I have shown that despite the collapse of that system, these ideas have continued. The enduring, intuitive appeal of the teleological conception, though, is a manifestation of pareidolia in action. We see within the term press freedom these obligations of public service that are not there. This notion of a purposeful press is so deep-rooted in our culture as to be an example of Mill's dead dogma. The reason it is intuitively powerful is that we have allowed ourselves to be indoctrinated to believe it. Yet, through this constant repetition, we have lost touch with the underlying justification that might once have underpinned the idea. History has given way to mythology. To be sure, the press *does* serve the public, it *does* provide an education, and it *does* enable democratic participation, not least in the form of a public watchdog. But we cannot say that it *must*. The categorical imperative is a relic of Victorian modernity for which no justification, as a matter of philosophy or normative legal theory, remains. We saw this clearly in Chapters 3, 4, and 5.

I have shown that this pareidolia is widespread. Yet, its influence is not easily detected, apparently, because those caught in its grip use phrases like 'press freedom', 'press regulation', 'public interest', 'investigative journalism', 'the public right to know', 'accuracy', 'privacy', etc, as if they were axiomatic. This phenomenon applies also to the perception of 'statutory regulation' and 'mandatory regulation', which are also treated as if nothing but the briefest explanation is required. In doing so, though, commentators, consciously or subconsciously, explicitly or implicitly, impress their *own* interpretation of the term upon its use. This causes havoc for the prospects of serious debate. That libertarians and ST theorists can argue so vehemently against each other demonstrates this phenomenon in action, for both sides are seeing something different to the other in those phrases. How else are we to explain the hysterical press reaction that realisation of Leveson's scheme for meaningful press regulation would end 300 years of press freedom[35]

---

[35] See, eg, 'Press freedom in Britain is under attack – again', *The Spectator*, 31 December 2016; 'Daily Mail Comment: After 300 years, the freedom of Britain's Press is in peril. YOU can save it', *Daily Mail*, 9 January 2017; G Rayner, 'Investigative journalism to be 'stopped dead in tracks' by 'menacing' laws after Leveson Inquiry', *The Independent*, 15 October 2015.

and the SR theorists' unequivocal response that this was nonsense?[36] Pareidolia has plagued the debate on press regulation so much that impasses litter the field and yet because commentators are seeing things in the press regulation debate that are not there, the intangibility of these so-called 'impasses' is not recognised. It is time we saw these impasses for what they are: illusory. It is not matters of principle that prevent us realising a scheme of meaningful, coercive, independent press regulation. It is a fear of ghosts and monsters lurking in shadows.

I have also shown the unhelpful confusion between ethics and law that plagues the debate on meaningful press reform. This is not to say that all commentators are responsible, for some clearly recognise the difference. When Claude-Jean Bertrand writes that codes of conduct should include 'aspirational' ethical standards that the press are not expected to achieve, but should aim to[37] or when John Merrill says that journalists ought to take their civic responsibilities seriously,[38] they intend these as guides for the self-reflective journalist that wants to be a force for good. Yet, as Merrill says, 'an uninhibited *choosing to be ethical* is the operative concept.'[39] It is when commentators seek to smuggle the ethical into the law (and vice versa) that problems arise. For whilst ethics can, and do, inform certain laws, in an obvious way, it is not capable of informing all law. The failure to recognise that those injunctions and restrictions which are defensible ethically are not necessarily realisable in law is surely the most frustrating part of the SRT literature. It is, of course, true that the world would be a better place if the press worked tirelessly and solely for the public good, if audiences were more disciplined and conscientious in their (ethical) obligations to society at large, and if malign political ideology was banished, universally, so that no demagoguery could ever take hold. These are important and laudatory ideals. But they tell us nothing about what press freedom means unless they can show how the imposition of these ideals upon an unwilling audience can be realised in conformity with normative legal theory. If we want to defend a scheme of imposed, meaningful press freedom, then much of these laudatory ideals must be abandoned, or otherwise clearly understood for what they are. It is for this reason that I have referred so little to the work of Jürgen Habermas. For when we look to, say, Habermas, we see a complicated system of discourse theory that seeks to eliminate (malign) political ideology from the public sphere and so ensure the best environment for societal progress and the good of humankind. This, then, is a system of critique rooted in philosophy, sociology, linguistics, and psychology that seeks to describe what is best in humankind and their powers of critical analysis. But it is not an account that is rooted in law. Legal theory is

---

[36] See, eg, S Barnett, 'Leveson Past, Present and Future: The Politics of Press Regulation' (2013) 84(3) *Political Quarterly* 353; G Phillipson, 'Leveson, the Public Interest and Press Freedom' (2013) 5(2) *Journal of Media Law* 220; Barendt, (n 24).

[37] See, eg, C Bertrand, *Media Ethics and Accountability Systems* (Somerset, Transaction Publishers, 2000), 46.

[38] JC Merrill, *The Dialectic in Journalism* (Baton Rouge, Louisiana State University Press, 1989), 38.

[39] Ibid.

largely ignored. This is a serious problem when we come to apply these principles so as to address the problematic press practices that we encounter in reality.

Hannah Arendt saw this problem clearly: 'education can play no part in politics, because in politics we always have to deal with those who are already educated.'[40] For 'whoever wants to educate adults really wants to act as their guardian and prevent them from political activity.'[41] As she said: 'since one cannot educate adults, the word "education" has an evil sound in politics; there is a pretense of education, when the real purpose is coercion without the use of force.'[42] The collective good cannot be pursued at the expense of individual autonomy. This is the immutable, irreducible minima of the open society and the secret to the good life. Ignorance nor error can be erased. Neither should we try. Instead, all we can do is manage harm when it arises.

I have shown that the failure to see this clearly sullies the proposal for coercive independent press regulation. Again, we see pareidolia at work. For both the right, and even the left, think that such a scheme would be abused, would interfere with the legitimate work of the press, and would be insidious. Yet this *is* pareidolia, for as I demonstrated in Part 3, as well as in Chapter 9, the *only* sort of coercive independent press regulation that is legitimate is that which follows the accountability model and regulates acts of wrongdoing-causation-harm. Typically, this means the protection of victim's rights. This has no impact on press freedom as a right, for the press has no *right* to engage in wrongdoing-causation-harm. To be sure, if its activities – be that content or conduct – interfere with rights *justifiably*, by disseminating public interest expression, then regulation is not legitimate and the wrongdoing-causation-harm construct is not satisfied. This, in effect, is the accountability model, outlined in Chapter 5 and established across Chapters 6 to 8.

SRT's great failing is to treat readers, and through them, society at large, as victims of a suboptimal press: that readers are manipulated and suffer when the malfeasant press takes advantage of their gullibility; that to enlighten readers about this malfeasance is justifiable as a form of victim redress; that readers only need see how distorted this impression of the world is from the real world to realise their error and so see the manipulation at work. This is a striking misrepresentation of autonomy. The reader that believes what she reads must be taken to have made a *choice* to believe. Consequently, her conclusions about the information she receives is itself a manifestation of her autonomy. She has chosen to read the information. She has chosen to suspend her critical judgement and accept that information, which may be because it accords with her own worldview. Or she has conducted her own independent research, but poorly so as not to discover the truth. Yet, in any event, these decisions, as defective as they may be, are her own responsibility.

---

[40] H Arendt, *Between Past and Future* (first published, 1961) (London, Penguin Books, 2006), 173–174.

[41] Ibid.

[42] Ibid.

This is true even of the reader who we suspect has not reached her decision *rationally*, which is to say that she has preferred feelings, emotions, and beliefs over reason, scepticism, and analysis. It is true of the reader who chooses sensationalism over the dispassionate. In this way, we should see that the idea of reader – or larger society – here as victim is simply unvarnished paternalism. Moreover, it may well be misplaced paternalism. When we think back to what Nick Davies tells us in *Flat Earth News*, can we really say that, for example, *Daily Mail* readers are victims? As he says, *Daily Mail* reporters write for their audience and so we must assume that they derive some pleasure from reading constantly that their way of life is imperilled by immigrants, single mothers, and bleeding-heart liberals; that the sense of misery and embitterment this instils is important or valuable to them otherwise why do they torture themselves? Presumably, they derive *some* comfort, for it confirms their suspicion that life is not as good as it used to be.

The real victims of press malfeasance do not have the same choices that readers and larger society do. Their autonomy is denied to them in the most outrageous ways. The financial power and social influence of newspapers may be diminishing, but its power to harm shows no signs of abating. It devastates the lives of many people. Leveson saw this clearly. He saw the devastation that the malfeasant press had caused to Christopher Jefferies, to the Bowles family, to Claire Ward. These experiences are not outliers. Leveson heard from hundreds of witnesses whose testimony is strikingly similar. Trawling through the complaints databases of IPSO and other European regulators demonstrates that the problem is not confined to a few hundred people, and certainly not to the rich and famous, but to thousands upon thousands, of ordinary people, whose distinct misfortune it is to find themselves under the press's glare. Why do we continue to allow people to suffer needlessly in this way? Why do we stand by and do nothing whilst their lives are seriously disrupted and even destroyed? Because it is the price of living in the open society? Because without the bad we could not have the good? These are empty, bankrupt claims. It is time we recognised them as such. It is time we demanded real, meaningful change. I have shown that press freedom and press malfeasance are not indivisible. They are separate. They are unrelated. And because they are separate and unrelated, what happens to one will not affect the other. I have shown that a scheme of coercive independent press regulation can be instituted by the state to tackle press malfeasance without harming press freedom. More than that, I have shown that such regulation would not even *touch* press freedom. Meaningful press regulatory reform is *not* an attack on press freedom. It is an attack on press malfeasance.

I have shown that the teleological conception of press freedom is a fiction, but the need for effective press regulation is *not*. Accordingly, the question is not: why coercive independent press regulation? It is: why not?

INDEX